A VISION FOR LONDON 1889–1914

. . . WHAT WAS THE VISION BEHIND THE LCC?
. . . AND THE REALITY?

As the world's largest municipal government, the early London County Council was a laboratory for social experimentation. It sought to master the problems of metropolitan amelioration, political economy and public culture.

Pennybacker's social history tests the vision of London Progressivism against its practitioners' accomplishments. She suggests that the historical memory of the hopes vested in the LCC's achievements and the disillusions spawned by failure are both major forces in today's ambivalent response to metropolitan politics in London.

Susan D. Pennybacker is Associate Professor of History at Trinity College in Hartford. She is also President of the Northeast Conference on British Studies and author of several essays on the social history of turn-of-the-century London.

A VISION FOR LONDON 1889–1914

labour, everyday life and the LCC experiment

Susan D. Pennybacker

London and New York

JS
3625
.P46
1995

First published 1995
by Routledge
11 New Fetter Lane, London EC4P 4EE

Simultaneously published in the USA and Canada
by Routledge
29 West 35th Street, New York, NY 10001

© 1995 Susan D. Pennybacker

Typeset in Garamond by
J&L Composition Ltd, Filey, North Yorkshire
Printed and bound in Great Britain by
Biddles Ltd, Guildford and King's Lynn

British Library Cataloguing in Publication Data
Pennybacker, Susan D.
Vision for London, 1889–1914: Labour,
Everyday Life and the LCC Experiment
I. Title
942.108
ISBN 0–415–03588–0

Library of Congress Cataloguing in Publication Data
Pennybacker, Susan D. (Susan Dabney), 1953–
A vision for London, 1889–1914: labour, everyday life and the LCC
experiment / Susan D. Pennybacker.
p. cm.
ISBN 0–415–03588–0
1. London County Council – History. 2. London Metropolitan Area –
Politics and government. 3. London Metropolitan Area – Social
conditions. 4. Socialism – England – London – History. I. Title.
JS3625.P46 1995
306.2'09421'09041 – dc20
94-41561
CIP

ISBN 0–415–03588–0

For Martha and Albert

CONTENTS

CONTENTS

FIGURES

ACKNOWLEDGEMENTS

This project began as an effort to investigate the 'labour question' as it was manifested in London's 'municipal socialism' before the First World War. It grew into a consideration of related dimensions of metropolitan life and political culture. The subsequent abolition of the Greater London Council and other events of our era suddenly cast their shadows over this work and brought the LCC experiment of long ago into touch with a troubled present. As I come to thank those who assisted me, I am mindful of the current plight of this great city and of many of its inhabitants. At the same time, I know that visions are reconfigured and recur.

I am grateful to Gareth Stedman Jones for his encouragement and inspiration over many years. His unfailing commitment to rethinking a wealth of historical and political problems has benefited and challenged those of us who have had the opportunity to work with him and to know him as a scholar and a friend. I likewise thank David F. Crew for his example, for the influence of his skill and intelligence, and for his interest in the early stages of this work.

I take great delight in conveying my gratitude to the (then) young scholars of London history with whom I worked in the 'London Group' on various shared projects: David Feldman, Jennifer Davis, Tom Jeffery, James Gillespie, Sue Laurence, Deborah Weiner and John Marriott.

I thank the following persons for specific suggestions about the text and for many exchanges about aspects of this work and related undertakings: Gloria Clifton, Dina Copelman, John Davis, Edith Jones, John Mason, Mark Miller, Philip and Deborah Nord, Ian Patterson, Henry Pelling, Marcus Rediker, Eve Rosenhaft, Andrew Saint, Terry Segars, Frederic Paul Smoler, Peter Stansky, H. McKim Steele, Jr., Robert Thorne, Christian Topolav, Stephen Utz, Stephen

Valocchi, Chris Waters and Stephen Williams. Others are thanked in the Notes section. I especially appreciate the insights and assistance offered over many years by Denise Riley, Tom Jeffery, Deborah Thom and James A. Miller.

The entire manuscript was read by David Feldman and Geoffrey Crossick, who made invaluable suggestions based upon their intimate knowledge of London. Anonymous readers for Routledge offered guidance that shaped the general direction of the book. Richard Rodger scrutinised the Introduction and lent his vast knowledge of urban history to the project as it unfolded.

I offered versions of this material as seminar papers in many settings, including the following: the American Historical Association, the Social History Seminar at King's College, Cambridge; the Social Policy seminar at the University of Liverpool; the 'Gender and Social Rationalisation' conference held at Berlin in 1989; the Centre for Metropolitan History and the Institute for Historical Research at the University of London; the Centre for Urban History at the University of Leicester; and several History Workshops. I thank all those who offered criticisms and suggestions in these and other sessions.

Parts of this work have appeared in other forms in several edited collections: Peter Bailey (ed.) *The Business of Pleasure: Victorian Music Hall* (1986); Rudy Koshar (ed.), *Splintered Classes: Politics and the Lower Middle Classes in Interwar Europe* (1990); David Feldman and Gareth Stedman Jones (eds), *Metropolis: London Histories and Representations since 1800* (1989); Dagmar Reese, Eve Rosenhaft, Carola Sachse and Tilla Siegel (eds) *Rationale Beziehungen? Geschlechterverhältnisse im Rationalisierungsprozeß* (1993); and *Genèses: Sciences Sociales et Histoire*, (1994). I thank those who acted as editors and translators.

At the outset of this project I received indispensable support and encouragement, in ways certainly known to them, from Maxine Berg, Jane Caplan, Gillian Sutherland, Lynn Hollen Lees, Betty Wood, Dorothy Thompson and Dorothy J. Thompson of Girton College. I thank them for their advocacy.

I thank the Fellows of Girton College, Cambridge, for their generous financial support of this work and the dissertation that preceded it. I also received grants from Newnham College, Cambridge, the Cambridge Historical Society, the National Endowment for the Humanities and the American Council of Learned Societies for which I am grateful. Trinity College in

ACKNOWLEDGEMENTS

Hartford awarded a Junior Faculty Research leave and support for the technical completion of the manuscript.

John Mason has acted as a research assistant in the completion of certain details of the text; his encyclopedic knowledge of London improved this work. Georgene St. Peter and Jonathan Reiner assisted in many tasks in Hartford. I thank the reference staff of Trinity College Library for their help in locating materials.

I thank the indefatigable staff of the Greater London Record Office, and in particular, Miss Joan Coburn, for years of patient consideration and instruction. The late Mr Alan Neate provided help at County Hall in the days when the LCC archives were still submerged in his basement lair. I also thank the staffs of the other collections mentioned in the section entitled 'Sources' and especially those of the Trades Union Congress Library and the Library of Nuffield College, Oxford. The Greater London Photograph Library and the West Sussex Record Office provided prints and materials for which I thank them.

As a stranger in a strange land, who had planned to stay for a year and stayed for nearly a decade, I close with thanks to those who gave of their intellectual and personal resources in abundance, enriching work and life: Rajnayaran Chandavarkar, Biancamaria Fontana, Andrew Freeman, Istvan and Anna Hont, Alison Jeffery, Angela John, Joel and Jane Jaffey, John and Susan Kellett, Hazel Mills, Richard Mitten, Deena Shiff, and David and Margaret Thompson. None of those mentioned above bears responsibility for errors of fact or judgement; this lies solely at my feet.

This work was finally completed in New England. I thank Sandra Andrews of Trinity College for her ingenious, conscientious and untiring work on the typescript. Claire L'Enfant and her staff at Routledge waited far too long for what must at times have seemed an imaginary proposition. I appreciate their care and patience and the advice so readily and intelligently offered by Catherine Turnbull and others. As for those to whom the volume is dedicated, we journey still.

Hartford, Connecticut
August 1994

ABBREVIATIONS

AMU	Amalgamated Musicians Union
'Association'	The London County Council Staff Association
BMA	British Medical Association
BOE	Board of Education, LCC
CAMB	Central Association of Master Builders
CIV	City Imperial Volunteers
COS	Charity Organisation Society
DNB	*Dictionary of National Biography*
ELO	East London Observer
GLC	Greater London Council
GLRO	Greater London Record Office
GPC	General Purposes Committee, LCC
GPO	General Post Office
ILP	Independent Labour Party
LBTC	London Building Trades Committee
LBTF	London Building Trades Federation
LCC	London County Council
LCC, PP	Presented Papers of an LCC Department or Committee
LGB	Local Government Board
LLP	London Labour Party
LMBA	London Master Builders' Association
LPDL	Liberty and Property Defence League
LSE	London School of Economics
LTC	London Trades Council
LUBTC	London United Building Trades Committee
'Major'	LCC Staff Member of the Major Establishment
MBW	Metropolitan Board of Works
MEA	Municipal Employees' Association

ABBREVIATIONS

'Minor'	LCC Staff Member of the Minor Establishment
MOH	Medical Officer of Health
MP	Member of Parliament
NALGO	National Association of Local Government Officers
NAFL	National Association of Free Labour
NUC	National Union of Clerks
NUT	National Union of Teachers
NVA	National Vigilance Association
PC	Public Control, LCC
PH	Public Health, LCC
POS	Parks and Open Spaces, LCC
PP	Parliamentary Papers; LCC Committee, Presented Papers
RIBA	Royal Institute of British Architects
SDF	Social Democratic Federation
SG	London County Council Staff Association *Staff Gazette*
TMHC	Theatres and Music Halls Committee, LCC
TUC	Trades Union Congress
WC	LCC Works Committee
WD	LCC Works Department
WDI	Works Department Inquiry
YMCA	Young Men's Christian Association

INTRODUCTION

If you walk through central London, you will pass the symbols of municipal endeavour that have survived for a century or more. Sprouting iron fish playfully guard the Embankment. The logo 'LCC' still adorns the remains of public baths, clinics and school buildings. At your feet look for the 'MBW' that straddles the pavement atop a railway viaduct and symbolises the old Metropolitan Board of Works, the London County Council's predecessor. Horse troughs filled with flowers still bear witness. If in the 1990s you are visiting London for the first time, the nearest stranger who is of age may well recognise the three letters LCC; if you are a Londoner you may even live in a former LCC flat with just a single sink (in the kitchen); you may have gone to school on an LCC county scholarship.

Labourers, merchants, shopkeepers, nurses and teachers – all who ever were children in London knew the Council. In its archives in Clerkenwell lie the ceremonial notices that mark the opening of a housing estate, a technical school, a playing field, a concert hall or a lodging house. These are the iconography of a lost municipal era. In them, Salisbury speaks; Henrietta Barnett is honoured. A visiting maharajah offers a toast as Anna Pavlova dances for the Conservative London Municipal Society fete. All the empire receives news of the provocative changes afoot in the 'Mother City'. Many hear the opposing municipal cants and read of the celebrations of municipal achievement. In colonised Africa, former servants of the Council attempt to replicate its institutional presence – to bring the forms of betterment and of order to the outer limits of the realm. In many instances, these municipal missionaries articulate Progressivism's vision.

In London itself, a political culture of evangelicism and social

1

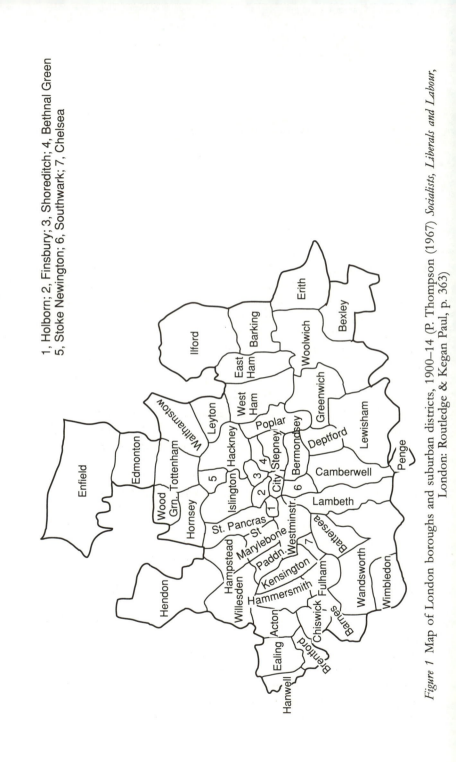

1, Holborn; 2, Finsbury; 3, Shoreditch; 4, Bethnal Green
5, Stoke Newington; 6, Southwark; 7, Chelsea

Figure 1 Map of London boroughs and suburban districts, 1900–14 (P. Thompson (1967) *Socialists, Liberals and Labour*, London: Routledge & Kegan Paul, p. 363)

purity nourished the circles of metropolitan Progressivism at the close of the nineteenth century.[1] Even for those who were not committed religionists, what Martin Wiener has termed 'a secular Evangelicalism' thrived.[2] The Progressives led the London County Council, the world's largest municipal authority of its time, from its founding in 1889 until their defeat in 1907; an unbroken period of Conservative control followed until 1934. The Progressives' ethics and their political strategy prescribed a redemptive role for the government of the imperial capital, a social mission in the secular metropolis. This book assesses the LCC's success in attempting such a mission and in doing so offers a selective portrait of the Council's work, drawn against the background of metropolitan life as it was lived before the Great War.

As the book's title suggests, a vision of a better order for London's inhabitants inspired the early Council leadership. The Nonconformist presence amongst its members was no better epitomised than by LCC councillor John Benn, who in 1892 appealed for civic rejuvenation and righteous retribution:

> Let us peep over this fragment of the old City wall and see how the trustees of the wealth left by our fathers, the old craftsmen of London, are getting on. Ah, the City turtle is on its back, the knees of Gog and Magog are shaking, the Griffin is rocking on his pedestal. Another blast from the slums, and like Jericho, the walls will fall, and a greater, a brighter and a better London will be ours.[3]

Benn saw the financial centre of metropolis and empire crumbling. Already visible through the cracks was the vast wealth that had been willed to Londoners by a centuries-old, noble artisanate. Their legacy could be seized and used. The poor of the East End were the vanguard of the attack. Councillor Benn's zealous invocation of *Ezekiel* belied his evangelicism and the ease and suddenness with which he imagined change occurring. It signalled the Progressives' sense of their own preordination.

John Burns, another visionary, who represented Battersea as the first LCC Labour councillor, was perhaps the most persuasive and popular early rhetorician of Progressivism. He defined the LCC's municipal socialism as 'the effort of the people to do for all what private enterprise does for a few. It is the conscious ordering of the city, through ownership of public services, of its own comfort, happiness and destiny.'[4] He gave voice to the Progressive spirit:

What inspires the devoted bands of councillors whose loving labour for this city is its brightest ornament? . . . slowly, but surely, I can see the face of this grand old London of ours, as the result of our twelve years' work, the realisation of my early dreams and visions, the rearing in happy homes of strong men and fair women, from whose loins will come proud, healthy and strong children.[5]

Burns's eugenicism and his drive for racial fitness is hardly hidden; these were features of the ethos of Progressivism. For the Fabian Sidney Webb, LCC councillor for Deptford, the images of antiquity proved inspiring. He saluted

the growth among its citizens of a greater sense of common life. That 'Municipal Patriotism' which once marked the free cities of Italy, and which is already to be found in our own provincial towns, can, perhaps, best be developed in London by a steady expansion of the sphere of civic as compared with individual action.[6]

Webb championed imperial Rome as a suitable model for the new Council, while Burns titled one of his manifestos 'The London County Council: Towards a Commune', indicating a clear preference for more recent Parisian events.[7] Woolwich trade unionist Ben Tillett, who served as an LCC alderman, spoke in a more dogmatic and militant vein:

What should be seen by all electoral organisations of the working classes is that our problem for the next County Council elections should be absolute municipal collectivism, and at the next general election 'State Collectivism'. The number of relief and charity panaceas for poverty are of no more value than poultices to a wooden leg. What we want is economic revolution and not pious and heroic resolutions.[8]

But the road actually taken by the early LCC is only faintly captured by the declarations of Benn, Burns, Webb and Tillett. While the Council's pre-war experiment was certainly more than 'politics without democracy', it *was* an experiment run by a fraction of the populace elected under a property franchise in which the judgement of a few was exercised in the name of millions of the city's less powerful inhabitants. In a population of over five million (1901), about 600,000 Londoners voted in municipal contests,

100,000 of whom were women.[9] The practitioners of the high politics of the era, Liberals, Unionists and Conservatives, bore the indelible signs of privilege. Fabians, New Liberals, Independent Labour Party and trade union official activists, teachers, social workers and suffragettes also shared a sense of their own entitlement. The expectation of self-fulfilment contributed both to the hopes vested in the Council and to the awkwardness of the professionals' and activists' dealings with the majority of Londoners.

The central subject of this book is the vision of its title, a vision of hope and of compromise. It is about the notion of the future that London Progressivism sought to impart and the ways in which its advocates and those who worked for them attempted to put that vision into practice at the LCC. The three discrete studies that comprise this book's three chapters are meant to illuminate the larger significance of the story. In the United States and on the Continent, notions of municipal socialism and other schemes of metropolitan transformation drew adherents in the days before the First World War.[10] The LCC was observed expectantly and decried as much as it was imitated. After their initial electoral victory of 1889, the London Progressives might have heeded the explicit warning of their narrow win of 1895. When, in 1907, they were finally defeated, the politicians and activists of other great cities either mourned the prophecy unfulfilled or rejoiced in the passing of madness. But the Progressive moment did not entirely fade from view. With stubbornness, in the devolution of London government that has recently occurred under Margaret Thatcher; in the 'privatisation' debates of our present time (the era of the 'death of socialism') and in the debates about the efficacy of state social welfare and government intervention in industrial relations, John Benn's Gog and Magog and the Griffin are still ominously visible. The 'public penury and private ostentation' referred to by Masterman as describing Benn's time once again symbolise London's fortunes.[11]

THE HISTORICAL RECORD

Two decades ago the literary scholar Edward Hynes delivered a simple verdict on the parliamentary party most implicated in London Progressivism, commenting that 'though the Liberals came to power in 1906 with an overwhelming majority and remained in power until the war came, they did not significantly alter the social conditions that they deplored'.[12] What was true of the party at the national level was also true for the municipal grouping that represented many of Liberalism's interests in London. In tracing the history of the initiatives that led to the formation of the LCC in 1888, historians have been mindful both of London's vast size and of its intransigent parochialisms. John Davis concedes that despite all the attempts at unification 'the metropolis remained a foreign concept even to its natives'.[13]

The history of unification and of devolution can be seen as a history of wars of mutually hostile interests. John Benn was not the first to assault the City Corporation. Since the ninth century, its accumulated wealth and power has stymied and obstructed attempts at incremental reform. From 1688 onward, this single square mile's control of the river traffic, its absorption of the coal dues, its exemption from the powers of the Metropolitan police, its livery companies, its guilds and lucrative estates, were formidable barriers to equitable and comprehensive government. How ironic it is that today the Corporation owns the LCC archives in the wake of the demise of the Greater London Council. In 1800, most of London's million inhabitants lived outside of the City's walls, and its concentrated power had still not passed to them. Nor has it today.

The prehistory of the LCC extends back into what Penelope Corfield termed the 'haphazard' history of municipal acquisition.[14] Over 300 local bodies ruled the London parishes during the eighteenth century. Varying wealth brought varying services. Some parishes had zealous and committed authorities that were chosen from amongst a limited electorate. Other impoverished and disinterested parishes lacked rudimentary maintenance. The radicalism of the century's close gave warning of the volatile presence of a largely unenfranchised but activist 'urban working class'. As Corfield notes, never again could urban politics be conducted without reference to its ranks.[15]

Incorporation came to the nation in 1835 but London did not benefit from the new government structures. The Municipal Corporations Act of that year, in tandem with the Great Reform Act of 1832, created municipalities in which as many as a fifth of the population elected its officials. Charges of scandal and corruption were frequent. Commissions of inquiry began to address some aspects of the conditions of urban life. Provincial town councils increasingly encompassed heretofore-excluded sectors of business and the professions. But local government's mandate, even outside London, still remained narrow.[16] As the American historian David Owen observed, in the *absence* of government initiative, leasehold estates, private railway, gas and water companies and speculative builders provided land, supervised planning, provided sanitation, lighting, transport and cheap housing.[17] The tension between what this private infrastructure offered urban dwellers and what was beyond its parameters of profit and philanthropy was a catalyst to the development of local government and did enhance the provincial capacity to tap public monies.[18] The administrative historian who fails to address the larger political stresses upon the warring elites of the nineteenth century fails to explain the very transitions he or she describes.

Gareth Stedman Jones's pioneering and indispensable study, *Outcast London*, identified a mid-century metropolitan crisis that was exacerbated at the century's close. Languages altered; 'chronic poverty was the dominant social question'.[19] London had certainly earned such recognition. Until the establishment of a Commissioner of Sewers in 1847, fully eight different authorities had charge of London's waste. Sir Edwin Chadwick's failures and the triumph of Sir John Simon's centralised authority offered a new model of organisation and relief. But with the cholera epidemic of 1854 the problem of inadequate drainage was manifest.[20] The need for a central authority seemed self-evident. The mid-century had also inspired notions of self-determination amongst London radicals. Out of the Continental events of 1848 arose the example of the *ateliers-nationaux* and attempts at local democracy.[21] In England, both the recognition of European developments and the absence of universal manhood suffrage compounded the fears of overarching authority and enhanced the desire for the preservation of local autonomy. There was the perceived threat of local monies being swallowed up by a body appointed to lavish revenues on social ills as a substitute for more profound economic solutions. A parish's resources might easily be exhausted.

When in 1855 London's Metropolitan Board of Works (MBW) came into being under the aegis of the Metropolis Management Act as an attempt to straddle local and metropolitan concerns, the question of finance remained unsolved. Taxation, the erection of artisan housing and the regulation of public transport throughout the parish districts all gave cause for collaboration and for dissension.[22] As David Reeder explains in his useful conclusion to David Owen's work, large vestries and district bodies that absorbed the old parish structure could obstruct progress by holding out on the MBW.[23] The poor law, London education and the charities remained independent of the MBW. The Board's powers were limited, as was its electorate. Davis notes that fewer than a thousand of the 12,000 houses in Bermondsey fulfilled the twenty-five-pound assessment qualification for enfranchisement in vestry elections; the members of the MBW were in turn appointed by the vestries.[24] Fully 300 bodies now had responsibility for carrying out the precepts of over 250 pieces of urban legislation. If the absence of popular participation hampered the Board's credibility at the ground level, its slavish juridical relationship to a Parliament which had to approve its every move hindered its direction from above.

The Board's 'shopocratic' composition and questionable practices often lent themselves well to caricature.[25] When scandal erupted over the MBW's financial dealings, it became known as the 'Board of Perks' to its detractors. But Stedman Jones calls attention to another important circle of mid-century critics. Figures such as T.H. Green and Alfred Marshall had begun to argue in favour of a 'moralised capitalism'.[26] Just when the first-tier authorities were labouring under the duress of helping to finance major 'improvements' such as slum clearance, the political economists were asserting the need for even greater (and more costly) intervention. A ferocious debate about the nature and extent of state and local government involvement in the economy ensued. In London, clearance efforts led to greater overcrowding in poor districts, and the insidious absence of provision for rehousing created havoc.

Meanwhile, a boom in speculative suburban building resulted from attempts to capitalise on expanding transportation systems. Pressure on the housing market resulted in extended rackrenting in the inner areas, particularly in the East End. By the time of the last great cholera epidemic of the 1860s, the metropolitan crisis had accelerated. The demands for poor law reform and for the abolition of outdoor relief sprang up in the midst of selective philanthropic efforts such as those of the Charity Organisation Society and of Octavia Hill. The division of the poor into deserving and undeserving camps, so avidly championed later by Burns during the Great Dock Strike and under the LCC, was a gesture meant to defy the eroding material structures of London life and to replace them with a moral and often genetic or racialist theory of culpability. The collapse of Thames shipbuilding symbolised the symmetry of economic and social decline.[27]

London government was not unresponsive, but, like the populace it barely represented, it was poor. Its actions often reflected the concerns of its members, as was also the case in the provincial towns and cities. In 1866, the passage of the Metropolitan Poor Law Amendment Act established the Metropolitan Asylums Board and with it the rudiments of a public hospital system (a system now threatened with dismantlement in the 1990s). The creation of a Metropolitan Common Poor Fund was the first gesture toward serious equalisation of finance through transfers of monies from wealthy to poorer areas.[28] This step pressured leaseholders (those who owned shops and residential properties), and the costs of the necessary compensation required for massive street improvement programmes strained the MBW's resources beyond the limit. The implication of the 1875 Artisans and Labourers Dwelling Act were similar. The centre could not hold against the clamouring ratepayers' associations, especially when the members of the public boards were appointed, not elected. As Davis observes, neither the resolution of first- and second-tier rivalries nor the financial integration of the local and metropolitan authorities was achieved in the days of the MBW.[29]

By the 1880s, the decade of royal commissions on housing and on London traffic, a nascent party system was growing more widespread. The radical club movement and the organisations spearheaded by reformers J.B. Firth and John Lloyd (the original architects of London government reform) were giving way to the more official Liberal and Radical Associations.[30] The 'many and mostly ephemeral' ratepayers' associations would soon be largely appropriated by the Conservative party machine, though for a time London government would belong to Liberalism. Still, the local held great currency; as Ken Young jibed, 'Metropolitan London' appealed 'as a radical slogan' only after 1880.[31]

The passage of the 1884 Reform Act hastened the emergence of the LCC. London's electorate increased by 30 per cent; the number of London MPs outside the City rose from eighteen to fifty-seven. In 1885, Chamberlain's Radical Programme called for the municipalities across the land to carry out sanitary reform and to control and improve parks, streets and artisan dwellings. This spirit thrived in some London circles where the Liberal Party formations had adopted the Birmingham caucus system. The Liberal imperialist Lord Rosebery became the LCC's first Chairman. Though Rosebery would subsequently declare socialism to be 'the end of all things', he did represent a significant faction of the party's elite on Council. From the outset this Liberal inclusiveness was typical of the movement that evolved into Progressivism.[32] The unemployment riots of 1886–87 were reminders of the capacity for mobilisation that even the least powerful of London's citizens possessed. The disorders discredited the growing demand for police powers to be ceded to the local authorities. Some of those startled by the riots now envisaged Crown control of the police. (The spectre of 'the Commune', a prominent feature of conservative rhetoric, would later inspire those who opposed municipal control of the police to deride the LCC's County Hall as the '*hôtel de ville*'.)[33]

THE LCC'S CREATION

With the passage of the Local Government Act of 1888, the metropolis came under the jurisdiction of a single county authority. Six years after the promulgation of the Municipal Corporations Act, the imperial capital had finally acquired the powers already ceded to other English counties. The duties of the MBW and of the justices were absorbed by the new LCC. But the second-tier District and Vestry Boards were left untouched and so was the City Corporation (as Benn asserted in the speech cited on p. 3). Neither policing nor the control of education or public utilities accrued to the LCC. Unlike those of any other county in the realm, the LCC's decisions were still entirely subject to parliamentary approval.[34]

The first LCC election of 1889 drew greater public attention than had any previous municipal contest in London, though the prudent historian does not claim a profound popular interest in the Council's electoral fortunes *per se*. The Progressives somewhat unexpectedly captured seventy-three of 118 seats, seventy-one of which went to Liberals. John Burns and Sidney Webb were both seated in 1889, and a small Labour bench crystallised in the elections of 1892. The Progressive Party in London bore the imprint of its prominent wirepullers and of their parliamentary ties. Benn, Costelloe, Dickinson and MacKinnon Wood were amongst the key players.[35] John Davis persuasively discarded the claim that theirs was an external takeover of the LCC: 'London "New Liberalism" was not . . . handed down by salon theorists or intellectual journalists, but pushed up from the constituency parties.'[36]

In *Socialists, Liberals and Labour*, Paul Thompson asserted that London Liberalism was the beneficiary of early LCC Progressive organisation and of the activities that preceded it. Thompson's account longingly anticipated the emergence of Labour, bemoaning the anomie and sectionalism of London, its lack of industry and its failure to conform to the pattern of the provincial Labour strongholds. But he correctly assessed the chief role played by local Liberal activists in the period.[37] Labour supporters were the Liberals' weaker allies in Progressivism. In the earliest contests the temperance advocates and Nonconformist zealots far outweighed those espousing 'labour politics'. This is hardly surprising, given the composition of the electorate and the political history of second-tier mobilisation.

The LCC was directly elected, making it the first public body, apart from the London School Board, to be so constituted. The Council was composed of members elected from constituencies that neatly observed the boundaries of the parliamentary constituencies for London, each district simply electing two LCC councillors for three-year terms in addition to a single MP at general elections. Women who were heads of households had the right to vote, and they made up between a fifth and a sixth of the county electorate.[38] Main drainage, fire prevention, the maintenance of the parks and open spaces, the Thames bridges and tunnels, the improvement of streets, the enforcement of building regulations, the erection of artisan dwellings, the regulation and eventual ownership of the tramways, and the overseeing of municipal finance all fell to the LCC. Amongst the Council's most notable endeavours were the Holborn to Strand Improvement and the opening of Kingsway in 1905, the building of the vast Boundary Street housing estate in east London, the steady acquisition of the trams between 1891 and 1896, the construction of the Blackwall Tunnel, which allowed underground passage from one side of the river to the other, and the brief operation of a passenger steamboat service.[39]

It is said that the LCC's greatest achievement, and one to which much of this study is devoted, was the elaboration of an innovative labour policy. It continued the practices of paying fair wages that had been inaugurated by the London School Board following a campaign by the London Society of Compositors.[40] It pursued a policy of 'direct labour', labour performed without the intervention of a private contractor, which led to the opening of the LCC Works Department, the largest single public works department in the world in its time. By 1904, the LCC staff had grown from just over 3000 employees to 12,000; the acquisition of the School Board for London added 35,000 employees by the end of 1904. Before the First World War, the Council boasted of being London's largest employer.[41]

Clerks, typists, messengers, housekeepers, rent collectors and schoolteachers were amongst the Council's employees. The Engineer's and Architect's departments and the Solicitor's and Chemical and Gas Testing Departments performed the duties indicated by their titles. The Public Control (and, later, Public Health) Department had the responsibilities for what is now termed social policy. (This area is explored in Chapter 3 of this work.) Council properties were overseen by an Estates and Valuation Department; its veterinary inspectorate regulated the slaughterhouses. The Parks Service and Housing Department had staffs of managers, porters, laundresses and bedmakers, constables and attendants. The Fire Brigade, whose history has been told by Terry Segars, employed officers, firemen, coachmen and pilots. The vast Tramways Department, enlarged by each company takeover, included an inspectorate and hundreds of tram drivers. From Banstead in Surrey to Claybury in Essex, from Colney Hatch in New Southgate to Hanwell, the Council managed asylums that employed night and day attendants, bakers, shoemakers, tailors, cowmen and cooks. A force of general manual workers grew into a separate grade of employees from those in the 'blackcoated' jobs. These were the servants, as they were called, of London's municipal authority.[42] Their counterparts grew in number in the smaller cities and towns, where many tasks similar to those of the LCC were performed on a smaller scale.

All of this cost a great deal, and the administrative history of the early LCC, only touched upon in the present volume, is in the first instance a history of assessment and rating. Recalling his work, Harry Haward, the Council's first Comptroller, neatly summarised what has since become a subject of less succinct historical commentary:

> The amount of the County Rate in the pound was the touchstone of party politics . . . Taking first the rate for all purposes other than education, a rising tide of expenditures characterised the eighteen years of Progressive rule. This was accompanied by dwindling Exchequer contributions, and there was much talk about getting new sources of revenue which came to nothing, and efforts to get, by betterment charge or otherwise, some contribution from the ground landlords of London. Party recriminations on the subject were frequent and I had to prepare statements to explain every increase of the rate.[43]

There were gross increases of 160 per cent in the rates levied by all sectors of local government during the Progressive period.[44] The average county rate in the pound was a measure of the discrepancy between the LCC's income and its costs, as divided in turn by the amount of the county's rateable value. Rateable value was determined by assessments made at the vestry (and, later, the borough) level of the putative 'fair rent' charged for a dwelling, less repairs and insurance costs.[45] As historian Avner Offer concluded in *Property and Politics*, his splendid inquiry into the workings and implications of London's property markets: 'How to adjust the sacrifices to the benefits: that was the fundamental dilemma of urban finances.'[46] This was the most immediate practical problem faced by the LCC, a problem that encompassed and shaped many areas of policy. As a solution to the inequalities of the rating system many radicals and liberals advocated the taxation of 'the unearned increment'; that is, the isolation of profit in the form of rent, and the exacting of charges on that profit. This solution bore the marks of the passion for Henry George's theories, shared by many radicals, including the Fabians.[47] Offer concluded that the preoccupation, indeed fixation, with rent as the foremost taxable form of wealth obstructed the struggle for the equalisation of local taxation across unevenly endowed districts of the city.[48]

Inevitably, under the established system, residents of poor boroughs paid more proportionately than did the rich. According to Offer, Disraeli had advocated a system of 'grants-in-aid' which Liberals and radicals alike viewed as highly 'statist' and therefore repugnant.[49] Although these Exchequer grants ultimately became the basic means of closing the gaps between what a local authority could afford and the needs of its constituents, this was not before the Progressive LCC had paid a bitter price for its ineptitude in matters of political economy. Offer found the sacrifice of progressivist forces especially ironic in light of the fractured nature of London *rentier* capital. He believed that urban owners might have been lured into the camp of the reformers if their own incomes had not been constantly under attack. But as property values collapsed and much of the 'soft money' left London for the suburbs, there was a decline in rateable value and a depreciation of sources of municipal revenue. The municipal debt exceeded what could be had from the rates, which were, of course, rising accordingly.[50]

There was not an easy fit between LCC electoral developments and spiralling rates. Initially, Londoners did not take out the frustrations over their wallets in the ballot box by voting against Progressivism.[51] After a dip in power in 1895, the Progressives recouped some of their losses in 1898, an election in which the opposing Moderates (the Conservatives, who wryly renamed themselves Municipal Reformers after 1906) lost 11 seats. In an act of vengeance, the Metropolitan Boroughs were created by the Conservative Salisbury government in 1899 in part to undercut the authority of the LCC. The new boroughs absorbed the lesser parochial bodies, completing the process of 'delocalising' government that had started in 1837. Davis reminds us that this did not necessarily alter the identities of Londoners, whose first loyalty even to this day may well be to a local area, an area smaller in size than a borough but without its own representative voice.[52]

After another Progressive victory in 1901, activities at the parliamentary level heated up. The London School Board was abolished in 1902 and was taken over by the LCC in 1904. Some viewed this as a retrogressive assault on local democracy. In the wake of the transfer of the School Board, the parliamentary inquiries on municipal trading and on physical deterioration issued their findings in 1903 and 1904 respectively. They confronted the prominent issues of national efficiency and racial improvement that were highlighted in the controversies surrounding the Boer War.[53] Though the LCC was part of the machinery designated to lift up the nation in the face of the material deprivation revealed by these inquiries, the Progressives were not mandated to continue as agents of greater change. They suffered ignominious defeat in the 1907 election, an election that Lord Briggs has termed 'probably the most stirring election which has ever taken place in the history of British local government'.[54] It was an enormous setback for organised Liberalism at the municipal level in London. Not until 1934, with Herbert Morrison's London Labour Party victory, did the reigning municipal programme express 'socialist intention', and this occurred at an entirely different political moment. Individual Progressives continued to hold office into the inter-war period, but the energy of the early days arguably passed to the London Labour Party.[55]

In 1907, the year of the contest that ushered in 27 unbroken years of Conservative control of the LCC, interest rates were up, few houses were being sold, and many in the electorate could feel the force of a 40 per cent decline in the property market.[56] The mobilised rightist opposition in the campaign, preserved for posterity by the frequent reprinting of its anti-socialist political cartoons, felt the jolt of ground rents that were breaking up. The right regarded Progressive collectivism as a fiscal nightmare and as ideological anathema.[57] There has been a good deal of speculation about voting patterns in this contest. The first part of this book is devoted to the 'lower middle class' Londoner whose rates had skyrocketed and who was said to be pivotal to the Progressive defeat in 1907.

London's working class was also feeling the brunt of economic changes; rents rose as landlords passed on the rate increases, though rents were already a full 70 per cent higher than in Birmingham. The inner-London population had finally ceased its centuries-old growth, leaving those in residence unsupported by newcomers who might have taken up the slack as the rates soared.[58] But not all of the survivors of the era were left empty-handed. Progressivism was outlived by its municipal staff, who remained in office as life appointees. These LCC employees included some of those whom Offer described as 'actively canvassed by the advocates and practitioners of "municipal socialism", the administrators, councillors, contractors and professionals who manage society's collective capital at the local and national level'.[59] The municipal bureaucracy was left with the task of administering those policies that prevailed and of serving the Municipal Reformers' version of municipal life, which did not always differ in its imprint from that of the Progressives. Will Sanders, Burns's

Labour colleague from Battersea, described the legacy that had become a mainstay of the rhetoric of all of the parties:

> It is not far from the truth for all that, when it is said that the Council found London a chaos and has given it form and shape. It has not only administered, but it has created an idea – the idea of a new, brighter, healthier and more beautiful London.

Of the coming 1902 election, he added:

> If failure comes to us in March next, the last living centre of Democratic faith in London will be lost, and there will be nothing left to relieve the monotony of squalid apathy and deadening reaction which seems to have claimed the Empire for its own.[60]

Neither Progressive programme nor Conservative practice bore out his predictions, but his fervent message conveyed the gospel of many Progressives of his day.

The LCC staff who remained behind when the Progressive train finally did derail had to continue to forge links, in spite of Progressive defeat, with millions of Londoners whom they were paid to serve. Londoners formed more than a quarter of the English and Welsh populations in the early 1880s.[61] By 1884, a fifth of all the adults in England and Wales resided there. London's population was three times that of New York or Berlin and surpassed the entire Irish population. The overwhelming pressure of these numbers alone warranted a body empowered to act swiftly and decisively. The necessity of parliamentary approval of LCC policy heightened the weight of the national upon the local while simultaneously extending the tedium of legislative processes. Hynes's remark upon the inefficacy of Liberalism's achievement in terms of social reform is a charge that extends down to the parliamentary Liberal Party's junior partners in London. At the end of the tumultuous era of Progressivism, from the first victory in the elections of 1889 to the defeat of 1907, the LCC record of achievement when compared with its aspirations is decidedly mixed and predictably remained so under the Conservatives until August 1914. Never did the vast private utility companies yield control of gas, water or electricity to the LCC. Never were the London docks municipalised.[62]

Historians who salute the 'LCC achievement' call attention to the onset of municipal housing, the takeover of the School Board for London by the LCC under the provisions of the 1902 Education Act, and the municipalisation of the tramways. But they cannot boast the acquisition of police control, the control of markets, or even the expansion of public sector housing to more than 15 per cent of the London market before the war. 'Labour policy' – the adoption of 'fair wages' provisions that were in turn adopted by the Commons in 1892, and the attempts at 'direct labour' and public works efforts – was meant as a first example of how local government incursion into the economy might create avenues of just and secure employment. But the forging of a radical labour policy did not necessarily provide an electoral advantage. Other elements of the Progressive programme brought losses. The control of London education was so controversial that it may ultimately have cost the Progressives many decisive votes in 1907; the religious interests that had always warred over English education and those who wished to preserve a democratic and independent London School Board fell foul of the Progressives on the Education Act. Nonconformity could no longer bolster Progressivism with unanimity. And in the balance lay the fate of the provisions of the Act taking hold in London. Many attempts at deep structural reform were confounded by the problem of the absence of the redistribution of capital by the early LCC. Liberal commitment to the free market remained tenacious. J.A. Hobson's theory that progressive national taxation would stimulate home demand sufficiently to offset a building slump and a fall in property values proved incorrect.[63] The labour markets in both manual and blackcoated labour tightened concomitantly and irreversibly.

These failings were signs of global and national vulnerabilities, and the LCC, however unwittingly, found itself at an epicentre of these stresses. Even the members of the Council, and not least the illustrious first Chairman, Lord Rosebery, personified such conflicts. They could hardly shirk the national or global implications of their municipal commitments; few linen-drapers and buttermakers these. The Liberal intelligentsia, the heads of the Tory Party, the Labour leadership and the Fabian high command all found their way to Spring Gardens sooner or later and widened the LCC's political horizons. Though the Webbs were nearly finished with their LCC work by 1904, 15 years had passed since their first concerted intervention. Other councillors became

Cabinet members; the early LCC's implication in national politics was as irreducible as was Parliament's desire to constrict its legislative prerogatives.[64]

Despite being tied hook, line and sinker to Westminster at the top, the LCC still had the unenviable task of administering London at the ground level. Hobsbawm described this as a period in which London was 'administratively sub-divided to the point of chaos', with the LCC 'at war' with the second-tier borough authorities and often at issue with Parliament, itself largely Unionist-controlled before the War.[65] When the Liberals took control of national government in 1906, they did not assist the LCC. It may have come as little surprise to Liberals operating in the Commons when, in 1907, their principal allies at the metropolitan level went down to defeat – a defeat that may not have been entirely unwelcomed by those possessing national ambitions.

The paradox of Liberal rule at the national level and Progressive defeat on the LCC was, in part, a rhetorical paradox. Progressivism called for reform in the face of the infeasibility of public ownership. Ironically, London's protracted infrastructural crisis tended to push the posture of 'reform' well along toward one of 'municipalisation'. As Tillett's phrasing above suggests, this latter formulation could then for some Progressive followers become an argument for 'collectivism' or even 'nationalisation'. The fascination with the early LCC experiment, therefore, does not derive from the Council's very nominal success rate any more than the initial popularity of Progressivism depended upon concrete achievement. Its rhetoric pushed it forward; its deeds were problematic and secondary in significance, especially insofar as its public reputation was concerned.

The Metropolitan Board of Works had been abolished in the midst of scandal and corruption, despite the erection of the Thames Embankment, the building of a main drainage system and the laying out of many new streets involving the demolition of over seven thousand unsanitary dwellings. At the very least, the early LCC could claim major improvements such as the Holborn to Strand Improvement, the Boundary Street estate and the engineering feat of the Blackwall Tunnel. But achievement *per se* was not its dynamo. As John Davis claimed, Progressivism's 'controversy was the basis of its popularity'.[66] Unrequited expectation fed the fervour of its most vocal supporters while proximity to power, not the possession of it, rallied its troops, such as they were. The deferment of what could not be contemplated at the national level seemed to prop up hopes at the local level. The People's Budget, the National Insurance Act and the Lloyd George reforms came after the Progressive experiment had run its course.[67] These never satisfied most of the material needs of Londoners. Perhaps it is simply the belated realisation that the LCC attempted more, not less, than would be tried by a halting Liberal government that has allowed it legendary status. But in the terms of this book, the greatest achievement of the Progressive period was the way in which the early LCC tested the outside parameters of what can be categorised as 'social-democratic' and 'municipal socialist' reform in its infancy, in prototype. This testing continued in certain forms right through the seven years of Conservative rule before the Great War.

IMPERIAL METROPOLIS

The LCC's ingenuous attempt to transform metropolitan life has taken on far greater potency in hindsight than its ideological critics of the pre-war period could have imagined possible, even though London's global position anticipated this power. London and the LCC sat at the centre of an empire experiencing a crisis in confidence during the Progressive years. Economic histories do not offer a consensus on the exact nature and extent of decline in the imperial economy before the War or on the issue of how it was perceived by contemporaries. If the impending compromises of empire were not fully predicted, there were indicators that gave pause. The movement for 'national efficiency', for the 'endowment of motherhood' and for the increased militarisation of aspects of daily life, and the very well known anxieties that accompanied the Boer War, are now understood as signs of deficiency. This sense of self-doubt was articulated amongst both government and business elites.[68]

The LCC became a vehicle for some of the attempts to rectify the state of affairs. The attempts had fiscal, political and social proportions. There was hope that local solutions might stave off the need for government intervention and preserve a free market, while the regulation and supervision of working-class life might serve to instil morality, self-improvement and hygiene. The historiographical landscape is thick with illustrations of these impulses.[69] But how did these schemes actually work on an everyday basis if they worked at all? Answering this question is a separate project from identifying national mood. Hynes's observation serves as a useful reminder of the simple fact that the actual living conditions of, in this instance, London's poor did not appreciably improve despite vision and effort. When the LCC was established, fewer than half of London's households had running water in a city with eight private water companies. Most people lived two or more persons to a room; many, six to a room. Anthony Wohl pointed to the *decline* in the number of smallpox vaccinations administered in London between the early 1880s and late 1890s despite a constant and fierce level of need.[70] There are numerous indicators of continuing deprivation. Infant mortality rose while real wages declined.

Given this crisis in the urban infrastructure and the larger strains upon the British economy, the members of the LCC workforce were likely to think that their efforts would shore up empire, make Britain stronger and make its people (meaning its white domestic subjects) freer. These goals were easily articulated within the social-reformist vernacular of the time and they were perfectly compatible with 'municipal socialism'. The intimate connection with empire was assumed even when its validity was sometimes debated. Some LCC clerks entered service already contemplating the transfer of their experiments to urban colonial contexts in Africa. Some who appear in the following pages, such as Lionel Curtis, left the LCC staff to serve in the Boer War. Curtis stayed on in Johannesburg and became a leading architect of British South African labour policy and of apartheid.[71] The manual grades employees applied for jobs with the LCC after years in imperial military and maritime service. Many had travelled the world and sought preferential Council employment as a reward for patriotic sacrifices.[72] The large number of municipal employees of military background accounts in part for the considerable LCC staff participation in the war effort of 1914–18. Veterans were the first to be called up. These men had witnessed empire at first hand and, like most Londoners, would have favoured its sustenance as commensurate with the reform of the mighty imperial capital.

The streets of London could not have failed to provide imperial reminders. Many of the world's peoples congregated there in larger numbers than ever before, and their numbers added to the earlier immigrant populations, notably the Irish; the great migration of central and east Europeans to England and beyond, associated with the last days of the Russian Empire, was now evident. Slavery had been abolished in the British Empire less than sixty years previously and domestic slavery less than a century previously. In scattered districts lived people of African and West Indian extraction who were the slaves' descendants, many of them English-born, 'free-born'.[73] Other Londoners were members of the elite of the colonial territories, in transit or in expatriate residence for life. The white London intelligentsia, and especially the radicals, rubbed shoulders with men and women of colour in political as well as domestic circumstances. (Just as they consorted with trade unionists by day, they enjoyed the comforts provided by domestic servants at night.) Exiled Indians living in the capital publicly promoted the cause of home rule in the years before the Great War.[74] The first Pan-African Conference met in Westminster Hall in 1900 and was attended by African-Americans, including W.E.B. DuBois, as well as by West Indians and Africans. Jane Cobden-Unwin, who had mounted a successful bid for election to the LCC in 1889 as a Progressive (see Figure 2), only to be unseated for being a woman, attended the 1900 conference and served on the short-lived Pan African executive with the black Progressive party politicians John Archer and Henry Sylvester Williams.[75] Archer was the Mayor of Battersea, and Williams served on the Marylebone Borough Council.

There was no absence of irony in these circumstances. Poverty abounded outside the doors of this meeting, a meeting that sought to expose the evils of imperial exploitation. While three decades earlier Dickens and Carlyle had defended Governor Eyre in his trial for the murder of hundreds of black labourers in Jamaica, they and others had also described in considerable detail the dire poverty of the imperial capital and of the northern and Midlands factory districts.[76] In fact, the condition of the domestic working class had ostensibly fuelled Carlyle's sympathy for the reinstitution of slavery; were not the wage slaves of his own flesh and blood meant to be better off than freed savages? Anglo-Jewry, who felt themselves besieged by the darker and impoverished eastern European and Russian Jews, sometimes questioned their brethren's rights to residence and to habitation. Would their troubles not weigh unfairly upon those who had already success-fully struggled to better themselves in gentile society? Such contra-dictions reflected not only the preoccupations of social and racial

ACROSTIC

Dedicated to Miss Jane Cobden

THE LADY MEMBER—NEW COUNTY COUNCIL,

BOW & BROMLEY.

Men of Bow and Bromley let us all rejoice,
In Securing this Election to the Lady of our choice;
Surely the glad tidings did our Womens hearts delight,
Such modern "Joans of Arc" we know, are ready for the fight.

Justice first to all, will be her watchword, and her plan,
And then JANE COBDEN will, with LADY SANDHURST,
lead the van;
New Reforms will be their cry and OUR MEMBER'S words before
Encourage us to KNOW HER as the CHAMPION of the Poor.

Converting alleys. courts and hovels, into dwellings fit to live,
Open spaces for our Children, are among the Gifts to give.
By our County Council too, Ground Landlords TAXED must be,
Do away with Sweating dens, and set our White Slaves Free;
Employers for a FAIR DAYS WORK, A FAIR DAYS WAGE must pay,
Nor stop at this until FREE TRADE for ever holds the sway.

S. COOPER,
Marsh Gate Lane,
Stratford.

Figure 2 'Acrostic' dedicated to Miss Jane Cobden (West Sussex Record Office, Cobden MS 1103, p. 5)

22

hierarchy, but the press of humanity on an entirely inadequate urban infrastructure.[77]

Infant mortality did not experience a significant reduction in London until after 1900 and, even then Wohl reported that life expectancy was low: 20,000 children under the age of one still died every year and the borough with the highest infant death rate, Shoreditch, still had rates twice those of Hampstead, the healthiest borough. (Benn rebuked 'happy Hampstead'.)[78] The contest between the needs of the poor at home and the financial burdens of empire contributed to the palpable pessimism and anxiety noted amongst some sectors of London's elites. The Mafeking celebrations could not assuage the fears of overextension, of underpreparedness, and eventually of socialism. It was as if the 'inside knowledge' of just how serious the crisis in empire and infrastructure was, made those in possession of power secretly attuned to the righteousness of the call for social reconstruction, though they surely feared its costs.

The radical critics of Progressivism shared other first premises with them. No municipal aspiration, however selfless in its articulation, could be entirely separated from a will to efficiency, to racial uplift and to competitive zeal, or from the desire to 'catch up' and to achieve order at home while maintaining hegemony abroad. Free-traders and those arguing for imperial preference defended their respective creeds with these goals in mind. Fabian and other socialists shared these ideals; those who dissented were a minority. In the capital, advocates of the rights of women, votes for women and the causes of labour and of the trade unions employed rhetorics of 'Englishness' and committed themselves to the cause of bettering those whom they saw as their racial and social inferiors. Far from being marginal or incidental aspects of 'municipal socialism' or of the feminisms of the period, these were central purposes and principles.[79] The case of the LCC helps to reveal these attributes of both rhetoric and practice, not for the purpose of establishing the outlines of a sensibility that is largely already known if not always readily acknowledged, but in order to understand the role of that sensibility in shaping a political experience of which it was an endemic, inexpendable part.

The indeterminacy of life for the poor and London's internal structural deterioration were juxtaposed with the wealth and power of the City and many areas of the West End. The contours of the London economy were shaped in the most general sense by those of the domestic British economy as a whole, despite London's peculiarities. C.H. Lee delineated some of that economy's broader features: a low standard of living, a low average income, labour-intensive modes of production, a trade depression for which the working classes paid dearly, the continued dominance of landed wealth and of capital exports in the years before the War, and, finally, the persistent 'international outlook' of the City.[80] These general features appear with more specificity if one considers the position of the wealthy in the metropolis: 45.6 per cent of all 'assessed wealth' was consumed there: 'Much of the unequally distributed wealth of the country was spent in the metropolitan heart of society.'[81]

The broad dimensions of wealth and poverty at mid-century, as depicted by Gareth Stedman Jones, continued until the War. But a dynamic change in the form of the expansion of the service sectors, which generated fully one-fifth of all new jobs in the London and southeastern economy, constituted the bedrock economic structure that frames the discussion of the London lower middle class in Chapter 1. The growth in consumption was mirrored in the expansion of the luxury markets of the West End in order to accommodate the more frugal and cautious purchaser of consumer durables at the century's close. But this did not signal the eradication of casual labour. In fact, London's rates of casuality (and the resultant contribution to the contemporary debates on unemployment) remained higher than in many other regions of the country at over 8 per cent of all labourers.[82] And three-quarters of the London population remained 'working class', a fact that ought to place debates about the nature of the remaining quarter of the city's inhabitants in perspective. In 1889, 30.7 per cent of Londoners were 'living in poverty' in Booth's terms, while just over half enjoyed 'relative comfort and security'.[83]

Guy Routh's income data, perhaps the most refined available (given that reliable incomes data emerge with the expansion of taxes upon income, postdating the War), set the average pre-war professional salary at over three hundred pounds a year.[84] Those in the so-called 'skilled sector' in the country as a whole earned on average a third of that and the 'unskilled' a full 50 per cent less than their more fortunate co-workers.[85] The pyramid structure of incomes was skewed in London by the concentrations of wealth, the absence of heavy industry and the burgeoning service sectors.

Even in 1913, the top tenth of the English population in terms of yearly income wielded control of fully half of the national income, and more than half of British investments of capital were now made overseas. These facts greatly influenced the larger context in which London's wealth and poverty in both the nineteenth and early twentieth centuries must be regarded.[86] A cursory glance suggests that the fivefold increase in government spending over the century still did not touch the power relations of capital.[87] Of equal importance to the argument made here is the political fact that it was not meant to do so.

The political climate in which LCC Progressivism grew was one dictated by these economic relationships in at least one very functional and immediate respect: the persistence of an amended property franchise. Only approximately 600,000 electors participated in LCC contests; as stated, a sixth of those who were eligible to do so were women. Not only do these figures cast doubt upon the assumption that women *qua* women had proportionately little say in London politics, but they diminish in the same breath the claim that the LCC represented a profoundly new and wholly participatory form of urban government.[88] One of the most parochial assumptions of a large historical literature is that an incrementally greater democracy constituted a pronounced and equally demonstrable shift in the fairness of the political and social system. This shift is further portrayed as having negated certain types of inequity and somehow as having instantly established clear proxies for each social class in the form of mixed or class-specific electoral districts. John Davis's very recent work on the problem of the householder and the electorate in poorer districts in London after the 1867 Act, casts even further doubt on the accepted understanding of class and the franchise. The 'random' nature of enfranchisement surely affected LCC contests.[89] 'Hard Labour' and 'hard Tory' strongholds emerge from the pages of London histories as if elections clearly signified 'class' sentiment; conventional wisdom asserts the presence of a tenacious Conservatism in the East End. Labour pockets, such as Battersea as it became, grew strategically, as their spokesmen (Crooks, Burns, Tillett and even Sidney Webb) put Labour on the map at the local and then the parliamentary level.

John Burns's defection to Liberalism notwithstanding, the LCC did convey many Labour as well as Liberal councillors to parliamentary prominence. But no historian has yet studied the electoral movements of the Progressive groupings at the borough level sufficiently to outline their respective political histories in detail.

In Paul Thompson's work on London, and in many subsequent studies, the party (and proto-party) activity, the weighing of Liberal, Labour and Tory presences on the Council, and the measuring of the impact of these on national government have instead constituted an intense focus of scholarly interest.[90] Patricia Hollis has recently documented the initial failed attempt of women to take their elected seats on the Council and the subsequent passage of the Sex Disqualification Act, which finally allowed generations of women to serve as councillors; they did so in increasing numbers after the First World War.[91] An assumed party-political history and the rise to fame of notable councillors appears as a backdrop and is often entirely uninterrogated in social historical accounts; the franchise is regarded as having been sufficiently broad to warrant large generalisations.[92]

In the interpretation that follows, however, the matter of the franchise and of its implications is not similarly resolved. This is not an electoral study but it does begin with the premise that a figure of 48 per cent of males eligible to vote in large, urban working class areas, as adduced by Duncan Tanner for the immediate pre-war period, does not stand as a safe, makeshift proxy for the unenfranchised women or their families, or for the likely majority of men in these areas, who still could not vote.[93] Rule by the majority had no precedent in British history or in any colonial history; this practice had been resorted to by a few of Britain's greatest enemies and by some very lesser powers, and usually at the exclusion of white women or persons of colour. So it is not surprising that historical accounts do not ask this of the municipal sector before the First World War. Still, it must be stated and underscored that only in limited, exemplary terms was the LCC an organ of popular democracy; it simply was not a body mandated under universal suffrage of the 'manhood' type or of any other.

Not all of London's inhabitants had no legal recourse other than to accept the Council as the central governing body of London but, at the same time, most could still not vote for their councillors (or, at the very least, did not vote for their councillors). These are starting points of this particular study of the LCC. This remains so in the moments in which this book concludes with a comment on the influence of the last period of limited unenfranchisement upon subsequent collective political memory. Before 1918, a vision articulated 'for all' could only be affirmed or rejected electorally by some. The 1907 Tory trouncing of the Progressives witnessed a popular vote of over 55 per cent of registered electors, categorically the largest percentage poll in London's municipal history.[94] But the excitement was viewed from an artificial and enforced distance by millions who regularly encountered the LCC face to face in their everyday lives. Any regret that they felt was unassuaged by the prior exercise of choice; they remained unprotected by the power of political scrutiny. While the authority of Labour, Liberal, Unionist or Conservative councillor was an important political fact as regards the life of the Council, it was still unimportant and even unknown to many on the street.

These starting assumptions also address the conventional political history of the period. Loath to allow the Council to pursue many of its goals prior to 1907, the Liberals at a national level ultimately and legitimately claimed some of its projects. There were radical cries urging the restructuring of the London economy through the mechanism of the LCC; these went largely unheeded despite Liberalism's national pretension. Surely this fact is not unconnected to the absence of universal suffrage. The problem of the electoral advantage of radical reform and of its costs was at the centre of Progressivism's dilemma. There were, arguably, diminishing electoral returns on schemes that increased the rate bills and chiefly benefited many who could not vote. This problem preceded another, one that is a truism of municipal politics: the rates are in and of themselves rarely the determinant issue for the elector. Implicit in the 'problem of the rates' is what the rates are to pay for. In this period, there was no tacit agreement about what constituted appropriate municipal expenditure. Much of the bickering about the Progressives reflected that unsolved political issue, which remains unsolved today in its broader manifestations at the level of national government.

A final issue thrown up by a varied historical literature is that of 'class' as a guide to electoral behaviour before the War (and after it).[95] Workers in London did not vote *en masse* in a homogeneous fashion. The elusive 'lower middle class', who form the subject of much of this book, did not vote with unanimity either. Persistent class-based voting patterns are not affirmed by early LCC history. The great 'universal' experience of municipal government was not that of municipal electoral politics *per se*, which was still primarily in the hands of an interested elite, but of municipal provision. The use of the term 'provision' both connotes 'social policy' and suggests a goal of socialism. The Progressives' detractors used the term 'municipal socialist' more frequently than the Council's leadership did. Instead, the councillors themselves for the most part spurned it as hyperbole. Even before the Bolshevik triumph, the label 'socialist' had taken on a sinister cast that warned the Progressives away from its use. Yet the 'hook' of much of Progressive rhetoric was precisely its capacity to impart a picture of a future that would involve a fairer distribution of the wealth hoarded by London's upper strata. The pragmatic dimensions of the strategy to do so were manifested in demands for municipalisation and for the public possession of essential utilities, hence 'gas and water socialism'. These were notions with clear ends, palatable even to some Conservatives.

But there were withering, limiting questions: was the LCC to become a major employer of labour, a major builder of houses and of public works, a major player on the labour market? Skyrocketing residential and commercial land values, rackrenting, compounding and jerrybuilding would be vulnerable to abrupt shifts in London's political economy. Little of Marxist orthodoxy was needed to frighten the opposition. Fabian utilitarianism prevailed: merit and order would be furthered by planning and expertise. Well-meant reassurances still implied ruin to those who had prospered quietly in the absence of serious municipal or national government regulation. Critics of the Progressive LCC regarded its goals as dangerously similar to those of the left-wing parties on the Continent. The experiments of the *conseil municipal* in Paris, and those of many German towns as recently explored by Brian Ladd, had their counterpart in the experimentation at the LCC.[96] As the ideological warfare increased, the spectre of a socialist future became a force in propaganda, often entirely disembodied from the actual record of Progressive practice.

ASSESSMENT

Charles Masterman and others gleefully blamed suburban philistinism for the Progressive electoral loss of 1907, despite abundant evidence of a more nuanced electoral picture.[97] The 1907 contest can be seen as one in which the Progressives' failure to hold and to garner more working class voters was more crucial to their loss than a diminution in 'lower middle class' or 'middle class' support. New voters who were voting for the first time flocked to the Conservative fold, but the purported backlash of the 'lower middle class' was more of a boon to sociological journalism than a reflection of cold fact.[98]

A literary folklore of the 'lower middle class' took many forms ranging from the Grossmiths' *Diary of a Nobody* to Forster's portrayal of the ponderous Leonard Bast.[99] There was no shortage of subjects to draw upon, as places in London's service sector outpaced the sectors of working class employment. But the market was top-heavy and male clerks facing downward mobility were susceptible to political pressure. Many lower middle class men, except the ill-fated lodger, had been enfranchised under the 1884 Reform Act and were ready targets of the party propagandists. The lives of women clerks differed in fundamental ways, not least of all in political terms: almost entirely without the vote, they too found themselves in a swollen labour market. Their services were not always needed and were rarely purchased at a price of their choosing. Subsequent academic inquiry into the lower middle class, notably C. Wright Mills's *White Collar*, a study of the United States, and David Lockwood's *The Blackcoated Worker*, examined the relationships between political behaviour and the social-structural location of white collar workers. If less evocative than Masterman, these works pursued some shared concerns. But unlike Masterman's, Lockwood's verdict on the question emphasised the heterogeneity of the subjects and the crucial centrality of the workplace.[100] This emphasis laid bare the residual question of how a diverse lower middle class stratum, one that so eluded ready generalisations, might have been responsible *en masse* for the electoral defeat of Progressivism.

As fate would have it, the principal recruits to the early LCC bureaucracy were themselves 'lower middle class'; this fact, coupled with the disputed electoral role of Londoners like themselves, provides the inspiration for Chapter 1 of this book. The LCC Clerk's Department, at the hub of the vast departmental and committee structures, is the setting for a case-study of a prestigious sector of white collar employment. The Department of the Clerk was the LCC's head office. This chapter repeats the paradigmatic questions about the relationships between place of work and social and political attitudes that are asked by the sociologists. Central to this exploration is the role played by 'gender relations' (certainly not a term of the 1890s!) in the life strategies adopted by men and women staff.

The second chapter explores the problem of labour in a different sector of London's population: the building industry. The establishment and subsequent abolition of the LCC Works Department allows a vantage point upon the conditions of work in this critical London industry. Building labour was often casual labour and the 'skilled' sectors of the industry clung tenaciously to their proprietorial claims to areas of work at the sites.[101] This study reveals the diversity of an important sector of London's working class and investigates the contention caused by the LCC intervention into the industry. The LCC was the largest public employer to implement fair wage clauses, norms which were shortly taken up by the Commons as a feature of government employment.[102]

Chapter 3 emphasises the problems fostered by direct contact with the LCC on the part of Londoners, especially in areas of social and cultural policy. It examines the proximity to the Council of London's working class inhabitants rather than assuming their distance from the agencies of local government. For very nearly two decades, social-historical investigation of London's Edwardian and twentieth-century working class has steered away from the 'radical working man's heritage' toward an inward proletarian culture and the terrain of social policy endeavour. These policies were devised by philanthropic and state institutions and often involved women as planners, executors and recipients. 'Class struggle London', the London of aggressive Labour strongholds, of new unionism and the unemployed marches, of Eleanor Marx and of Tom Mann, has grown dimmer. Even the idea of culture perceived as a weapon against entrenched bourgeois or aristocratic interests, of leisure forms such as the music hall as satire on bourgeois forms, lost much of its venom as the record of working class conservatism became a subject of greater interest, unmistakably chosen in an effort to explain the British political realities of the 1980s and 1990s.[103]

This book does not seek to revive an undifferentiated 'radical London working class'. But in Chapter 3, it does offer an exploratory survey of selected areas of social and cultural policy in which contact between municipal agents and London's inhabitants proved problematic. Here, to be sure, is a more activist portrait of the working neighbourhoods than one that emphasises a relatively anaesthetised working class fervently celebrating imperial victories and the Jubilee. This chapter uses the very rich LCC archival sources to provide a glimpse of the enormity of municipal presence juxtaposed with the persistence of the *absence* of fundamental relief from want. The great ambivalence inherent in this portrait is its lasting impression.[104]

The wary reader may wonder whether it is possible to discuss LCC social or cultural policy apart from the activities of central government: it is *not* possible in a fully comprehensive sense. Central–local relations do form a backdrop to Chapter 3. In the wider literature, Bentley Gilbert for example, praised the Liberal reforms of the period while bemoaning the blockage of certain features of policy in London, especially changes in London education under the LCC that were slow in coming.[105] Other historians have lauded the Council efforts as precursors of what was to come, as pioneering footsteps on the road to the welfare state. Here it is asked how certain policies seemed to work in practice. How did Londoners, as depicted in the LCC source materials, seem to be affected by specific policies? How were both needs and remedies referred to in the rhetorics of London politics? In this sense the book as a whole seeks through its three discrete inquiries to comment on several large issues with some national implications. The London 'lower middle class', of which LCC white-collar workers in large numbers were a part, along with those who laboured in the building industry, constituted two sectors of the London population without which the Council could not function and without which London's economy would have lost its distinctive character at the end of the century. This project began with an investigation of these two forms of London labour and then spread into the world of social aspiration, and into the languages of how life might be led, of how industry might be rearranged.[106] Finally, the project was extended to survey (in instances selected from a vast and rich set of municipal archival sources) the modes of social and cultural provision which seemed to characterise the practices of the LCC before the First World War. In the spirit of sustained inquiry, this volume closes with a short section entitled 'Sources' in the hope that other researchers will take this work in the many directions in which this book does not venture. Here is a signpost for those who will continue those exercises in recovery.

The 'welfare state' has a retrospective history, one that begins to take shape in the reforms of the early 1900s fought for by Churchill, Beveridge and Lloyd George. While it is often acknowledged that the 1911 National Insurance Act, to cite one case, did not protect most workers and did not apply to most women workers at all, this and other similar legislation can also be described as rudimentary first steps on the long path toward 'what was needed'.[107] In this large, state-dominated discourse, the nuances of local municipal endeavour are too easily forgotten. An entire cohort of London's inhabitants did not even live to see the questionable process of 'welfare state-building' come to fruition. Their exposure to it was circumscribed by harsh limits of time and space. To capture them in their moment is partly to add perspective to the wider framework and to suggest that the LCC was not simply anticipatory. As the Progressives confronted the resistance of capital and the increasing frustration of the minority of the population who voted or paid tax, a set of terms of public debate and dialogue captured these antagonisms and outlasted the early LCC as terms of public rhetoric. In the subsequent decades the elevation of the burdensome dilemmas of argument and efficacy to the heights of national government did not entirely alter the problems of persuasion or the memory of disenchantment.

1

THE WAYS OF LIFE, ASPIRATIONS AND POLITICAL CULTURE OF MEN AND WOMEN 'BLACKCOATED WORKERS'

As the streets that lead from the Strand to the Embankment are very narrow, it is better not to walk down them arm-in-arm. If you persist, lawyers' clerks will have to make flying leaps into the mud; young lady typists will have to fidget behind you. In the streets of London where beauty goes unregarded, eccentricity must pay the penalty, and it is better not to be very tall, to wear a long blue cloak or to beat the air with your left hand.[1]

Virginia Woolf's admonishment to the unsuspecting visitor could hardly have seemed misplaced. The conformity and homogeneity of the London 'lower middle class' was a subject of contemporary commentary, both literary and sociological. 'Blackcoated' men and women workers crowded central London at the end of the century and every tenth employed man on the street was a clerk.[2] The financial and commercial capital of empire, the counting house and insurance broker of the world's money markets, seat of railways and shipping concerns, the sporting ground of merchant princes and *rentier* rakes, London had spawned a vast labour market in blackcoats, which included thousands of clerks who worked for the LCC.

Within this market, the LCC became a bastion of respectable lower middle class employment. Its service to the metropolis was seen as socially useful, its workforce as the 'aristocracy of municipal service' in nation and empire (see Figure 3). And yet LCC employees also inevitably included a diversity of type. Men and women of its white collar staff argued about votes for women in

33

Figure 3 LCC staff dinner, 1903 (Greater London Photograph Library, GLRO)

the 1890s just as they would argue about arms to Spain in 1936. Some rose in the workforce while some never achieved substantial mobility. Most came from the provincial backgrounds of the majority of their fellow Londoners and many were the first in their families to come to the metropolis and certainly the first to stay. Some were fervent Christians, some had lapsed from church and chapel. Some of them read Spencer or Havelock Ellis while many read Kipling and Dickens. Women typists at the LCC favoured Macaulay, Carlyle, Huxley and Gilbert and Sullivan.[3] An LCC clerk wrote forthrightly in September of 1900:

> Whether to my credit or against it, I have no sort of ambition to become a target for Boer bullets on South African hills; but I fancy I would readily give an arm for the power to write as clearly, as charmingly, as truly and as cheerfully as Robert Louis Stevenson.[4]

Many LCC staff would have preferred to live in central London but most lived outside of the inner districts. Most of them made a decision for or against marriage in one fashion or another as well as decisions about childbearing. Each was preoccupied with the problems of wages and salaries and the limits imposed by them. Hopes of prosperity and of political voice overtook the spectres of impecunious obscurity for those who came to work for the LCC. In the 1890s they must have thought that they had a lot to look forward to by living in the capital; the threat of international war was as yet unknown to them. It was worth walking carefully down the streets that led from the Strand to the Embankment.

LCC CLERKS: THE ORGANISATION AND CHARACTER OF MEN'S WORK

Eric Noel Makeham was not entirely typical of recruits to the Department of the Clerk of the Council in the years between 1889 and the outbreak of the War. But if his radical politics were shared by only some of his colleagues, his life circumstances, and those of his death, were common ones. Makeham was born in 1886, and, like most early recruits to LCC men's clerical employment, had completed grammar school. Unlike many, he was a Londoner and attended Battersea Grammar as the recipient of an intermediate county scholarship. After passing the Council's open competitive examination, Makeham entered LCC service as a fourth-class clerk in 1905 at 19 years of age. Many of his colleagues had worked in commercial firms or other branches of central or local government before coming to the LCC.

Makeham served in several branches of Council departmental work: the Library and Records section, the Fire Brigade Committee and the Theatres and Music Halls Committee. Clerks to committees recorded the minutes of the meetings, drafted correspondence, undertook social research, and generally assisted the councillors who sat on the committees. This work was at the centre of the formulation and practical application of LCC policy. In 1909, Makeham was classified as a second-class clerk under a restructured classification system. This reorganisation became the principal spur to blackcoated staff unionisation at the LCC. But a measure of mobility upwards was still allowed within this stratum of the hierarchy.

Makeham was 'keenly interested in religious, social and literary questions . . . a prominent figure in the debates of the Spring Gardens Club', the staff debating society. In 1909 he delivered a paper to the Club called 'How Shall We Save the Family?' in which he called for the establishment of socialism. In a second paper, he called for 'the promotion of international socialism' as part of the 'best means in our power of fighting and finally destroying the red demon of militarism'.[5] Makeham joined the Fabian Society in 1908, and remained a five-shilling subscriber until 1913. His neighbour in Upper Tooting, George H. Robinson, originally another of the fourth-class clerks in the department, also joined the Fabians in 1909, though he was purged a year later for inactivity (Makeham may well have recruited his less enthusiastic colleague). Just before the First World War Makeham joined the radical National Union of Clerks (NUC) at the same moment that many LCC clerks did so. As was true of thousands of his fellow Council workers, Makeham's career was cut short by the War. Excelling as an instructor in the forces, he died in a prisoner-of-war hospital in 1917, having attained the rank of lieutenant. Upon his death, aged 31, his family issued a limited edition of his verse and prose.[6]

Makeham's radicalism was unusual in its intensity, but the LCC was unique in its approach to recruits regardless of their political origins. As the Clerk of the Council put it in 1900:

> The municipal officer's education is not complete when he has left school or college, and as some of the profoundest

economical and social questions are being worked out in the problems which every day arrest the attention of municipal government, it is evident that officers, to be abreast of the work required of them, must be students as well as officers. A clerk is a better clerk if he copies a report not only correctly and neatly but with a full knowledge of the subject matter.[7]

A spirit of civic rejuvenation was evident in the rhetoric and practices of the recruitment process. Gone were the corruption and nepotism characteristic of appointments under the Metropolitan Board of Works (MBW) and other local bodies. Progressive leader John Benn led the Council in forbidding personal canvassing of members by employees.[8] So vehement was the drive against perks that critics of the Council even called for the disenfranchisement of municipal employees during the ensuing years, maintaining that they acted as a 'special interest' group in support of Progressivism.[9]

The charge of political sympathy certainly had substance as a description of the attitudes of some members of staff. A leading LCC architect of the pre-war period, Owen Fleming, was a member of a circle that belonged to the Art Workers Guild. Some of the Architect's staff lived in the LCC housing estates that they had designed. In 1900 Fleming spoke about the building of the great Boundary Street Estate in the East End, saluting his colleagues while adding:

> The efforts of the architects, were, moreover, ably seconded by the great body of skilled artificers who have striven to make this estate a model of good workmanship. Personally I feel a special sense of comradeship with the men who have actually worked on these buildings . . . If any members of this Institute [his audience] are ever tempted to visit Boundary Street, and find the workmanship worthy of admiration, will they think of the silent unnamed workers, by whose patient labour this great structure has been built up?[10]

While sympathy prevailed, a Fabian-style meritocracy was established at County Hall. The Council devised and refined an elaborate hierarchy of promotional ladders for blackcoated employees in the decades after 1889. The desire for promotion coupled with a socially conscious commitment to the job defined the disposition of the cultivated white collar staff worker. A new social camaraderie after hours impressed those who remembered the sombre days of the MBW, when 'It was not felt that the whole body was actuated by the single-minded zeal for the amelioration of London's social conditions which renders the work of the Council so interesting and inspiring . . . there was not as much *esprit de corps* in 1870 as there is now out of office hours amongst the staff.'[11]

Consequent upon the victory of the Progressives, the new County authority's work expanded at a rapid rate. Committee meetings tripled in number within the first nine months. Twice the number of letters arrived. All this new work required more 'officers of a lower grade' capable of carrying out 'additional, superior' work. Their promotions would depend upon their ability to handle these new tasks. Expansion did not mean 'deskilling'; rather, at first, *more* was required of clerical workers.[12] The first public tramways, the Fire Brigade and the massive School Board for London were acquired by the LCC. County Hall off Trafalgar Square could no longer house the central office staff, who spread out amongst many adjacent buildings. The Clerk noted, 'I have great complaints from my department of there being no boy who can be sent by the clerks to carry books, papers and messages from place to place.'[13] The Council labour force grew in number from 3368 to 11,190 between 1889 and 1905 alone.[14]

Amongst the various administrative bodies at the centre of the Council bureaucracy was the Clerk's own department, the secretariat of the Council as a whole, whose head was the LCC's chief administrative officer. This was Makeham's department and he was one of just over a hundred men of the Department's classified staff: 'for this work, general knowledge, a special knowledge of local government, logical method, power of composition and a firm but tactful manner are essential'.[15] Like other departments, the Department of the Clerk absorbed new tasks and witnessed the emergence of the central problem of Council labour policy in the white collar sector: the proliferation of 'routine and mechanical work' of a clerical nature. In the last years of the century business was still conducted by handwritten documents dipped in violet ink and pressed into a jelly tray. The tray was then melted over a fire; such was the state of technology until the transition to typewriting which began in the Council's first years.[16]

The LCC simply had not made adequate provision for the expansion of this kind of work. The Council's dilemma is best understood as part of a wider history of the recruitment practices of the old MBW and of the recruitment of fourth-class clerks under the new LCC. Gloria Clifton has shown that MBW recruits also came to the LCC from clerical posts in the private sector, from the civil service or from a branch of local government.[17] Only a few MBW staff retained by the LCC Clerk's Department had a superior education. Harry Sargent, for example, who as senior assistant earned the second largest salary paid by the department in 1914, had come to the MBW from a position as a clerk to the MBW's law stationer. He was the son of a Stoke Newington hairdresser. More unusual was the case of Thomas Bell, who eventually worked as a clerk to Lord Rosebery, the first Council chairman. Bell had attended Cheltenham and Oxford and had worked as a classics master before coming to the Board. Yet despite the need for 'routine' workers, the LCC actually raised the standards required for both the 'established' and 'unestablished' staff who were 'over-qualified' for the posts that began to become available. Given that most recruits to the clerical divisions before the War came from grammar school backgrounds, as Makeham had, they possessed credentials that might have secured them long-term jobs in the Civil Service, a fact of no little importance as staff grievances mounted. Comparisons with the Civil Service were not only markers of administrative design; as Civil Service employees organised themselves, County Hall workers also began to stir.

Both the Civil Service and the LCC required candidates for advertised clerkships to sit examinations under a scheme administered through City of London College. Sample papers were sold to the public so that prospective candidates could prepare them in advance. Candidates for the fourth class were required to be 18 to 23 years of age and British-born.[18] (This provision took on special significance as a criterion of employment and it was enforced even after 1945. When West Indian nurses arrived in London after the Second World War, they found no posts available at the LCC.) The new examinations in public service were controversial. Did special preparatory courses and narrow cramming now offer a greater chance of success than more conventional educational credentials could offer?[19] The Civil Service Commission of 1889 noted the problem of its own new examination requiring 'a high degree of polish upon a rather low though useful order of accomplishment'.[20] The records of LCC staff members killed in the War reveal that most had attended grammar schools well beyond the leaving age. Most had worked in a private sector clerking job before coming to the Council. But in several cases, like

Makeham's, a candidate was hired directly from school on the basis of his examination results. If past commercial employment may have proved useful in sitting and passing the examination, a candidate's results alone formed the single criterion for appointment. In 1892, the Clerk complained that all of his new recruits were 'young lads' and that he needed some who possessed business experience, yet both the preparation required for examinations and the age restrictions imposed upon applicants allowed the less experienced to soar ahead.[21]

These recruitment norms raise doubts about the homogeneity of the 'lower middle class'. While the provisions of the 1870 Education Act helped to prepare many men for the fight to obtain a clerical job of lesser standing, it did not mandate the more sophisticated instruction adequate to enable a candidate to excel in an examination which included English composition essays like the following, of a type that frequently appeared on the LCC Clerk's exams:

(A choice of one:)
1. Is war ever justifiable?
2. The effect of science on literature.
3. Methods for dealing with the unemployed.[22]

Another set of questions read:

1. 'The evil that men do lives after them, the good is oft interred with their bones.'
2. Is compulsory military service desirable?
3. Imperialism.[23]

In 1902, examinees were asked explicitly to 'discuss the questions at issue in the controversy concerning collectivism (or municipalisation) as applied to Local Authorities'.[24]

It was small wonder that those who were appointed to the clerical and administrative branches of the LCC tended to identify with the Council's purpose, as they saw it. They were self-selected, not simply randomly selected by the Council. One employee recalled, 'I well remember in my own case the well-nigh crusader's zeal with which I threw myself into the work of preparation for the Council's examination, so anxious was I to obtain employment under a body destined, as I thought, to do so much to regenerate this metropolis.'[25] Not only did the recruits themselves often invest a few years of their lives in preparation for the examinations, the Council paid a relatively high price for their labour. The growing need to perform routinised clerical work exposed the ironies of the system. The expansion of boy labour, the introduction of women's work and the hiring of temporary assistants were all attempts to remedy these problems.

Those who were fortunate enough to be hired into the 'classified staff' were arranged within a hierarchy which approximated that of the Civil Service. There were four classes through which a man might progress over twenty years. He earned eighty pounds a year at the outset, and, if promoted, could retire from a position paying £300 a year. The policy was to recognise 'exceptional ability' through 'rapid promotion'. There was automatic promotion from the fourth to the second class; promotion into the first class was by attrition and selection only.[26]

Despite the edge that LCC clerks had amongst salaried workers earning less than £160 a year, their earning potential remained below that of banking and insurance clerks and those in industry, commerce and the railways, who tended to earn less than LCC staff at the start of their careers but to rise more swiftly to higher salaries.[27] On the other side of a divide, the average earnings of dock clerks stood at £62 a year, well below the earnings of the average male clerk on the labour market, who secured £143–221 a year.[28] The average LCC salary in 1910 was £200 per year. Thus the men of the Council's clerical staff, considered collectively, were better off than many skilled workers and most clerks on the labour market, and significantly better off than other vestry and local government employees.[29] And the very fact that regular earnings were a certainty prevented all LCC white collar employees (save the temporary assistants) from suffering gross economic insecurity.[30]

THE 'NEW WOMEN' OF THE LCC

The strains on the Council workload could not be sufficiently absorbed even with the new forms of labour of the 1890s. In 1906, one year before the Progressives were to leave office, a 'Minor Establishment' of male employees was created in an effort to end the practice of employing temporary labour. This new section was made up of lads of 15 to 17 years of age (some drawn from amongst the temporaries) who had either completed elementary school or held certain institutional certificates. They were divided into two sections and earned between fifteen and sixty shillings a week.[31] But a more experienced and older group

41

was actually recruited after the results of the first examination under the proposed scheme were known, suggesting that the Elementary Education Act had not assisted them adequately. The prospective applicants were tested in handwriting, orthography, English composition, arithmetic, geography and general knowledge and were also offered options including languages, experimental science or drawing.[32] Though there was some hope that the 'Minor' in service would swiftly climb the departmental ladders (some Minors did become Majors), the general trends in reorganisation of the service before the War failed to sustain the original conventional levels of salary and distinction and instead relegated many tasks to these new, lower-paid strata of the Minor Establishment, expanding these workers' duties rather than diminishing their usefulness.[33] This new structure continued to cause deep resentment amongst organised staff in the 1920s and 1930s.[34]

Along with exploiting the labour of younger men who would never rise as their predecessors had, the LCC began to employ two other new classes of labour: boy labourers and women clerical workers. Hired to do 'fair copying', 'intelligent lads of from fourteen to sixteen years of age' were discharged at a week's notice or at age 23 if they failed an examination.[35] Several LCC officials were active in the boy labour reform movement, including Alfred Spencer, Chief Officer of the Public Control Department, and they inspired a concern for their own young employees' futures. London's boy labour problem was severe and the LCC was increasingly involved in the policy issues surrounding it. Of over 24,000 boys leaving higher elementary schools in 1901, 40 per cent became errand boys. Under the Shop Hours Act, boys employed in shops could work a seventy-hour week. In response, the LCC eventually sought to offer examination places to its boy employees.[36] But this attempt failed. Boys found it difficult to compete in the examinations because their work prevented them from having enough time to study. Special classes held between 1906 and 1914 only managed to 'make good deficiencies in elementary education'. Passage upward was blocked for this sector of Council labour comprising the younger counterparts of the Minor Establishment. Internal upward mobility was now a severely limited possibility except when artificially induced from above by Council.[37]

As sentiment in favour of abolishing the entire grade of boy clerks grew, the Council discovered that it could use the cheap labour of women in place of boys. In 1898, nine years before women were given the right to sit upon county and borough councils, the LCC established an experimental typewriting and copying department.[38] Typists were hired on the basis of their performance on typing tests, but the first group of applicants included a woman who both failed her test and was unfortunately deemed 'bright, but loquacious and assertive' in her interview – a double jeopardy. A 'businesslike manner' was considered as essential as good typing skills.[39] Though a number of commercial programmes offered classes suitable for typists' training, the clerical labour market for women was hierarchical and highly stratified just as it was for men.[40] Differences amongst women were furthered by the organisation of the market. Training was available at the City of London College, Pitman's School and various polytechnics. Business classes for girls at Regent Street Polytechnic were always filled. The LCC could easily choose its women typists from amongst the 'fairly educated'. And indeed the Glaswegian who would act as the first supervisor of typists, aged 26, lived in Battersea and was 'able to speak a bit of French and German'.[41]

From the first moment it was apparent that the women hired had not replaced men *per se*, but instead comprised a new, cheaper form of labour in the clerical divisions; their work was of a different character.[42] When the National Union of Clerks (NUC) wrote to protest against low pay for women, it had to phrase its demand in terms of the pay of a 'comparable' man's job – that of the commencing junior clerk. The Progressives split on a motion to consider this demand and it failed.[43] But the NUC never abandoned its struggle for what as early as 1890 was termed 'equal pay for [the] same work', inaugurating a Women's League in 1911 led by Mary MacArthur, Gertrude Tuckwell, NUC head Herbert Elvin and Ethical Society stalwart G. O'Dell. One version of the defence of equal pay, offered by NUC leader Dolly Lansbury, interpreted the 'right of woman on the labour market as the right to earn a living however she chooses'. If men were so concerned about the decline of a so-called family wage, said Lansbury, they could support the endowment of motherhood and child supplements. Women's right to 'live independently' was also at stake.[44] These demands were phrased in one of several rhetorical modes that increasingly engaged women at the LCC.

The women's department proved an overwhelming financial success and became permanently established.[45] The department survived for many years and the wages and eventually the salaries offered to women typists at the LCC were more attractive than those that were offered to most London commercial typists.[46] Yet the prospect of greater economic independence for women employees was elusive. The very intimate terms of these young women's existence were challenged by the imposition of a marriage bar that required women employees who married to resign. All Council women employees were subjected to this intrusion upon the realms of their private and legal conduct. Only the school-teachers were exempt from its mandate. The LCC enforced this bar in accordance with a norm already established in many areas of government service. If the LCC assumed that the bar would help to keep salaries down, at the same time it bemoaned the loss of good typists. Fewer than a third of those hired in 1898–99 remained until 1914,[47] though some left the LCC service for a better position rather than for a husband.[48]

The marriage bar is the classic example of what would now be termed a 'gendered labour policy', one which sought to create distinct identities based on juridical and statutory standards imposed upon the personal lives of employees. Needlewomen, checkers on the tramways and inspectors carrying out, for example, the provisions of the Midwives Act were all asked to resign upon marriage. For those whose actual jobs specifically focused on policy geared to the 'special needs' or condition of women in London, like the Midwives inspectors, the deep ironies of policy are apparent. If they suddenly entered a marital union, they were considered unfit to inspect midwives attending other women. Unable to hold onto several 'conflicting' identities, as so deemed by the general spirit of policy, these inspectors, and others like them who filled posts within the bureaucracy that required the greatest education, posed transparent contradictions. Furthermore, LCC electoral propaganda extolled the special role and special work of women staff. In 1913, when women doctors petitioned for exemption from the marriage bar, supported by their male colleagues, they were refused, and their resignations were requested by the Council.[49] The further insistence that men should not perceive this issue as their own was signalled by the Deputy Chairman's statement that sympathetic agitation only showed the 'condition of confusion into which things would get if individual officers or groups of officers were at liberty through the machinery of petition to favour the Council with their uninvited opinions on matters which do not regularly affect them'.[50]

Even abandoned women were not exempt from the workings of the marriage bar, except at the discretion of a committee. In a celebrated case involving the imposition of the bar upon LCC charwomen in 1914, internal memos reveal that Laurence Gomme, the Clerk, felt that while divorce or separation afforded legitimate grounds for exemption from the marriage bar, desertion needed to be proven over time.[51] He felt that two years ought to pass before an abandoned woman could be hired. Gomme disingenuously added that with regard to women living apart from their husbands, he 'did not think any concessions should be made, as inquiries into the domestic affairs of families would be involved'. The LCC ultimately ruled that such a requirement remain a discretionary matter. Gomme was obsessed with the notion of singleness and separateness as a status entirely derivative of the legal married state; if a woman was unattached, having been married, even if she were a charwoman, she might 'bluff' the LCC. Cohabitation outside marriage must certainly have taken place amongst women employees who had male companions.[52] Yet Gomme was equally unwilling to investigate staff lives too deeply; he wished neither to allow the case of a woman to be proven, nor disproven. This issue prompted Tory councillor Susan Lawrence to cross over to the Labour bench. Henceforth, she involved herself deeply in radical causes in London and forged a close collaborative relationship with the trade union leader Mary MacArthur.

The 'lady typists', then, were women employees of a new type; policy establishing new forms of work, new terms of employment and new restrictions upon their life-styles went with the newly established opportunities for respectable employment offered by the LCC. But to stop with such a summary is to do an injustice to subsequent history. In 1935, when the marriage bar was still in place, women staff members were nearly evenly divided on the question of its retention. Male staff members of that generation supported the bar almost two to one. Its restrictiveness should never be confused with the fact of its popularity, before or after the First World War. Meta Zimmeck reports similar divisions amongst civil servants.[53] The women of the staff did not necessarily share the attitudes of the fictional, discursive 'new woman' of Lucy Bland's insightful description.[54] They did contribute to the idealised portrait of her; they were supposed to be 'new women'. Yet 'new women', like the lower middle class from which they purportedly sprang, often lived their most credible lives as cultural fictions.

THE BLACKCOATED MARKET IN LABOUR

An inventive genius would be useless in the City. For the City produces nothing and creates nothing. It is the great go-between of the world . . . anyone who contemplates the City as a profession . . . will not have to face the competition of the flower of his contemporaries, who will be scrambling for briefs, teaching unruly forms in public schools, or rusting in the deadening atmosphere of Government offices. . . . From this comfortable fact he may draw consolation if he does not carry much top hamper in the way of intellect . . . if he is to prosper in the City, according to the City's notion of prosperity; that is to say, to put the matter at a modest valuation, if his income is to express itself in four figures.[55]

Herein lie the commonplace assumptions of those observing the market in men's white collar and professional labour in turn-of-the-century London. Native intelligence and intellectual aspiration were not rewarded in many of the most lucrative jobs, especially in finance. In fact, one's persona as cultivated in the social milieu surrounding work was of greater value in the City.[56] A modicum of education was always required for white collar jobs; there were too few jobs for those who had come simply from the Board schools. Many who had been trained in better grammar schools or commercial schools filled posts in the expanding lower-echelon positions in clerical labour as they did at the LCC. The professions were still largely reserved for public school graduates. Thus, 'the first London Board School boys who entered the higher civil service, the Church or public school teaching, were still worth recording by name'.[57] As the radical NUC organisers Dorothy and Ernest Thurtle put it, 'The myth is that competency, nay all the commercial lore of the LCC evening school, is not of itself sufficient to obtain for the clerk a good living, much less carry him to those dizzy heights conceived by his vaulting ambition.'[58]

The greatest demarcations of the market lay between the various routes by which one acquired professional rank or managed to be hired by a firm or by government. The parameters of the clerical and professional labour market in which LCC employment began to occupy an established niche were set according to the specific types of work on offer, while income levels derived principally from the set terms of work pertaining in a given occupational subgroup. Specific promotion schemes, chances for mobility, pay

46

structure and economic security defined a man's position, especially if he advanced above the most modest levels of clerical employment. At the age of 15 or 16, he could leave school with the justified hope of being hired to do London office work at a salary of £70–80 a year. The income tax line of £160 a year was established in 1895, and contemporary commentary assumed that in order to be placed in the social category of the lower middle class, a man needed to command an income of £150–200 a year.[59] As stated, this sector included 'routine clerks', elementary schoolteachers and lower-ranking civil servants. Charles Booth recorded the income of the 'great mass of artisans' at thirty to sixty shillings a week while the great mass of clerks occupied a similar place in the hierarchy of incomes at £75–150 a year.[60]

By 1891, 12 per cent of the working population (as a census category) were teachers, nurses, shop assistants, clerks or Civil Service employees; this figure rose to 14.1 per cent by 1911. These workers competed on a labour market described by David Lockwood as one in which 'every literate person became a potential clerk'.[61] Blackcoated workers were concentrated in London, where they tended to reside in the outer suburbs less by choice than because of rising rents in the desirable central areas.[62] 'Desirable' had come to mean areas in which life-styles were more comfortable than they had been in the first half of the nineteenth century: 'the middle class standard of living, understood as a concept embracing the norm of ostentatious display, broadened considerably in the fifties and sixties'.[63] This affected those at the bottom of these groups as well. Between 1860 and 1910, some central areas witnessed rent rises of 150 per cent.[64] These new and exorbitant rents greeted the influx of middle class families from the country in which the breadwinner was employed in a non-professional occupation.[65] Since West End rents required that a man have at his disposal a salary of at least £300, even the best lower professional white collar jobs (which started at, for example, £200 a year and rose by only £20 annually) were too low to meet the demand. There could be no thought of moving into town for at least five years. An advocate for the impecunious clerk pleaded the case for lower-cost housing: 'Our clerks are the humble instruments by which vast fortunes have been and are being amassed. They deserve well at the hands of our capitalists. Some effort should be made to deliver them from the fangs of the most voracious blood-suckers of this great parasitic city.'[66]

In summary, the greatest proliferation of jobs was at the bottom end of the income range; a man's education was generally inadequate to prepare him for the competition at the top end of the range of jobs. The sought-after standard of living was for most young men unreachable; they were forced to live in lesser circumstances than those which they had dreamed of. They faced restricted mobility on a labour market that allowed only a small number of young men from conventional working class backgrounds to rise within it before the First World War. A 'Shipper' wrote to the *Office Journal* in 1909 of receiving 640 applications for a single advertised post; only seven of these were from persons whom he considered 'qualified'.[67] This is the context in which the LCC became a premier employer of men's white collar labour in London. As Geoffrey Crossick observed of the sector from which LCC recruitment occurred, 'British society, having created this aspirant lower middle class, was incapable of guaranteeing it stability of status or offering the real chance of continued mobility.' Though a single homogeneous lower middle class never existed, the ethos of advancement, in all its vicissitudes, remained a universal aspect of what was otherwise a fragmented set of experiences.[68]

Why did a young man not choose to struggle in one of the higher-status professions rather than set his sights on a local government job? Some had simply failed to gain admittance to a more preferable office of central government. The chief barrier for almost all of those from working class backgrounds was the absence of sufficient education. A contemporary survey of members of Lincoln's Inn for the periods 1894–1903 and 1912–18 revealed that only 1.8 per cent of those between the ages of 25 and 31 were the sons of skilled waged workers; two-fifths of those between the ages of 45 and 48 came from this background. Thus, few upward paths existed before the War.[69] Those earning over £200 a year in the legal professions, the army, engineering or the military and private medical services for the most part had public school educations. These men could afford to live in London at first, especially if they did not marry until later in life (or married a monied woman: 'Better a fortune in a wife than with a wife'). As J. Edgar Foster put it, 'Virtue is good but a house in Belgravia is better.' They could, as a *Cornhill* writer observed, 'gravitate toward the country as they [grew] older'.[70] At the end of the century many in the City felt threatened by the commerce of the West End; they feared invasion. As if to bolster its sense of impenetrability, it was still said that 'The City has its prizes, but those who run for them do not all start from scratch.'[71]

The home Civil Service provided the career option most like that of the LCC upper echelons. Public school backgrounds predominated. Those who at the age of 20 or 22 had acquired a general 'liberal education' still had to pass a rigorous examination in the post-1870 Service, for which a high degree of polish was required. There was no hope of becoming one's own employer in this line of work; vanished was the model of the nineteenth century clerk who would one day run the firm. At the same time, no longer could it be said that the servants of the government simply spent their days playing 'like the Trafalgar Square fountains, from 12 to 4 o'clock'.[72] Instead, hard work and relatively low pay were compensated for by secure pensions, hopes within a promotional structure, and the public servant's dubious legacy: 'the epitaph that he has tried to do his duty to his country'.[73] If the claim of superior moral virtue suggested by this reflection is difficult to prove, there was no lack of promising credentials. A 1903 survey of posts awarded in the Civil Service upper divisions offers a glimpse at the backgrounds of the examinees. The top man of the form came to the Colonial Office from Eton and Oxford, where he had attained a first-class degree and was a Fellow of All Souls. The man at the bottom of the form became an Assistant Surveyor in the GPO, had attended Aldenham School and received a second in Classics from Clare College, Cambridge.

Contemporaries viewed their peers in the Civil Service as having compromised in life. But for those who were well educated and without the means to enter the professions, which required greater initial capital outlay, the Service still had its appeal. The postponement of marriage offered the possibility of rising from £150 or £200 to even £1000 in a lifetime and enjoying a reasonable middle class existence. But internal promotion required skills unobtainable through academic training:

> The man of the world who is accustomed to mix with his fellows and can meet influential politicians or wealthy City men on equal terms is a far more useful public servant than the shy student whose horizon is limited by the four walls of his office and is far more likely to be selected for important appointments, administrative or otherwise.[74]

An ornate structure of concerns ordered the various factions of London's professional and semi-professional worlds. Money garnered from marriage and family and the prizes obtainable through education and breeding were obvious advantages, even as *not* having these in the right configuration posed an insuperable barrier for the majority of blackcoated workers in the capital. But character and morals also entered in. A personal inclination to function by the rules of one milieu as opposed to another and the motivation 'to serve' one master or another did not fail to influence the futures of bright and not-as-bright young men of the 1890s and the early 1900s. Though the salaries of the permanent secretaries in the Treasury or the Colonial Office were half of those of 'an ordinary Railway Manager',[75] the security and proximity to political life accompanying state service were for some their own inducements.

Appearances aside, the classic study of salaried clerical employees (as distinct from groups within the clerical market in labour who were waged) demonstrated that by 1911 the tier of local government in London offered the best average salaries for those below the £160 income tax line. This made the LCC and some of the second-tier local authorities more attractive in these terms than any other employer in the kingdom (save the educational authorities) for men employed at salaries between £120 and £140 per year. This survey considered the incomes of five million white collar employees, of whom all but 800,000 earned salaries below the £160 line. Even the Civil Service did not offer the same average income within its lower strata.

The *Clerk*, the newspaper of the NUC, bemoaned 'the meanness, the drudgery, the abominable pay, and the stupid classification system of the Post Office'.[76] Fewer than 1 per cent of London local government clerks earned below £120 a year, which was a better rate of 'collective pay' than that of any male subgroup within the occupations classified as 'intermediate' between professional groups above the £160 line and 'manual workers'. For women (excepting teachers in the Scottish boroughs), London local government also offered the highest average wage under the £160 line, at £86 a year.[77] This illustrates the further complexity of this labour market. There were overwhelmingly fewer positions available to women. But for men whose education did not allow them to compete effectively for a place in the higher division of the Civil Service, the LCC lower ranks seemed to offer the very best starting positions and the greatest hopes for advancement. Even if the Progressive project did not inspire, an applicant for work at the LCC would have found his potential salary attractive. Even as late as 1912, the *Clerk* asserted in a largely unfounded jibe that 'the well-paid jobs at Dock Office and Spring Gardens are reserved for the gilded youths with influence behind them'.[78] The selectivity of the LCC was rigid enough to suggest nepotism.

EXPECTATIONS AND IDENTITIES AT THE LCC

By 1900 the 'secretarial department of the Council' had grown from forty to 400 members, almost all of whom were men. The Clerk's staff occupied the political centre of London's government: all LCC work was handled through the committee structure and a committee might hear its members' candid views more often than the Council as a whole did. In these forums Progressive councillors such as Burns and Webb excelled and made their reputations. The male clerks of the end of the century copied by hand much of the business of their committees, and each classified assistant developed expertise in a particular area of policy. As the Clerk himself put it: 'the work done in the department is . . . connected with every service administered by the Council . . . for this work general knowledge, a special knowledge of local government, logical method, power of composition and a firm but tactful manner are essential'.[79] From recording meetings of the committees on Theatres and Music Halls, the Housing of the Working Classes and Public Control, to licensing motor vehicles and carrying out the provisions of the Cinematography Act, the members of this department possessed a grand overview of municipal endeavour. White collar staff worked for each department of the LCC, some handling only internal administrative matters, such as those who worked for the Comptroller. Others were involved in highly interventionist work, including the staff of the ill-fated Works Department and of the Architect's Department.

One could shift between departments and thereby develop a facility in several areas. Most non-manual staff worked a forty-two and a half hour week, a shorter work week than pertained in the private sector. There were substantial sick pay and overtime benefits for permanent LCC employees long before unionisation, though the perennial complaint about clerical overtime work quickly arose. The staff superannuation scheme was unique for the period in that it covered a wide range of grades of employment. Nevertheless – and this was an important element of the risk calculation that characterised a decision to apply for LCC work –

the scheme was widely felt by the staff to be inadequate; this grievance could serve as grounds for taking a Civil Service job. Though the scheme was modified several times, it remained based upon a calculation of earnings over the whole of an employee's working life rather than upon the earnings of the last five years of service. Someone entering service toward the end of a career might receive a higher pension than a colleague who had served twenty dutiful years. The struggle for the scheme's creation was quickly extended into the struggle to make it more equitable.

It is not difficult to surmise that the immediate concerns of LCC white collar clerical labour – both men and women employees – revolved around the predictable issues of occupational mobility, pay and salary and security of tenure. The elaborate hierarchical bureaucratic system readily adopted by the new LCC served to divide and isolate discrete groups of white collar employees by the distinctions of age, sex and seniority and was supported by an examination system that simultaneously sought to recruit both a relatively small group of talented and well-educated officials and a larger group of routine workers. The Minor, unestablished staff were not downwardly mobile or 'proletarianised' within the system; they were, instead, new additions to a workforce whose expansion signalled both the geometric growth in imperial and commercial London in the period and the concomitant growth in government services. But their life histories, at least insofar as we can know them from their involvement over decades at the LCC, contribute to a wider understanding of the underlying mechanics of decision-making amongst certain larger groups of Londoners before the First World War. The conventional history of the lower middle class has tended to lump a variety of experiences and identities together. Here instead is a look at the specific parameters within which LCC white collar workers could move; particular attention is paid to the system of what can be termed 'gender relations' which influenced many of their decisions about life and work, if not in the same ways for each of them. This system was at the centre of their political economy. Ironically, the 'deferred gratification' of social existence was itself the *sine qua non* of the LCC staff's working institutional existence.

MEN'S LIFE CIRCUMSTANCES AND LIFE STORIES

The records left by the families of male members of the Clerk's Department indicate, as we have seen, that they largely had grammar school, not public school, backgrounds. Almost all had worked elsewhere before coming to the Council, and clearly viewed a job at the LCC as a step up. Many had come from state service of one sort or another – in local government at the vestry or borough level as inspectors or school attendance officers, or in business offices or on the railways as clerks, or as teachers in secondary school; they came from employment overseas as lower-ranked clerks in the merchant firms of the empire or as members of colonial bodies such as the Indian police. Once hired, many went to university as part-time students. When war broke out, they interrupted their studies in law, economics, engineering or actuarial science. Inevitably, many came from the provinces to seek a better life in the capital.[80]

They were avid participants in local sports clubs, institutions such as the chapels, the Church Army or the Jewish Lads' Brigades, St. John's Ambulance, Sunday schools and the YMCA. Hobbies such as gardening, reading, photography, music and cycling were widespread. The politics of personal and intellectual betterment permeate the wartime honour rolls; unfulfilled goals and suspended lives appear boldface on the pages and memberships in the territorials abound. To what degree do honour roll entries also reflect the ways in which their families reconstructed the lives of the dead? The ubiquity of a conscious self-selection of employment is suggested by these accounts. Moral concerns are evident in the histories of those who sought work at the LCC. But this evidence, taken together with a description of the attractions of Council employment, still does not reveal the deeper character of individual sentiment. Regrettably, only a few detailed life stories remain.

William Kent was born in 1884 in Upper Kennington, and as a young man came to work as a clerk in the LCC Education Officer's Department. In the 1930s, he wrote a memoir of his early life, *Testament of a Victorian Youth*, which he described as a 'sample of young Non-conformity'. His father, a devout chapel-goer, considered Shaw blasphemous. As a boy, Kent was forbidden from going to the theatre. After leaving school, he worked in a warehouse, became involved in the religious Wheatsheaf Institute and 'had not improprieties or infidelities'.[81] A mixture of muscular and social Christianity inspired an ascetic existence during these years: Bible reading, billiards, the Young Men's Institute Library and its gymnasium were his passions. At Wheatsheaf, he attended lectures on

Jews and Unitarians, Evolution, the Nationalisation of the Railways, the Housing of the Working Classes, and 'Should Christians Smoke?'. (Kent fancied that 'the War must have taken some juice out of this controversy'.) He wrote of the Institute years: 'It is hardly necessary to say that the most important subjects for young men, love, courtship and marriage were never tackled.' Of masturbation, 'so ignorant was I that I had no idea of the biological significance of my impulses, no understanding of the naturalness and innocence of my physical urge'. He was 'wed to the pious prophylactic that anti-prudery was synonymous with obscenity'.[82]

In his first foray into metropolitan employment of a better sort, Kent worked as a boy clerk in the Civil Service. Robert Blatchford's Clarion movement was a subject of debate amongst his colleagues, and the temperance movement sought to organise them against drinking, gambling and 'impurity'. Just as the LCC Christian Union would succeed in recruiting only the very devout, so the Junior Civil Service Christian Union had few takers. Kent explained: 'I suppose the explanation is that Modernism tends to be a branch of the Church of Laodicea.' In his later period of working for the Civil Service, he finally read Huxley, and, feeling faithless, started subscribing to the *Clarion*. He snared a job in the LCC Education offices, starting at thirty shillings a week. He recalled that absences from work were always questioned; that even when employees were in the lavatory, the doors were kept open. The staff were watched over during lunch. In 1905, he transferred to another section and found himself working alongside mostly married colleagues who valued overtime, chiding, 'Don't work too hard chaps, make a bit of OT.' He found their language 'unchaste'. His friend (ironically named) Webb read books like *Human Personality and Its Survival of Bodily Death*. Another 'drank as freely and as much as Dick Swivveler'.[83] A needy colleague pawned his umbrellas at lunch for food and drink, a practice that Forster would have revelled in.

Kent began to buy books in Paternoster Row with his pay packet, he too forgoing lunches. In 1907, the year of the Progressives' defeat and Kent's first attendance at a Shaw play, *The Devil's Disciple*, he was made a permanent employee in the LCC Solicitor's Department. The actual work made him doubt his earlier convictions: 'I must say I did not find Christian evidence at all compatible with the laws of evidence that I had to learn, and my daily avocation conspired with my leisure pursuits to push religious orthodoxy out of my being.'[84] He spent more time at the theatre, sampled the 'diluted faith' of the Brixton Independent Church, and joined a literary course in Arnold and Shakespeare at Kennington Road Evening School. Here, he and other young men of like mind formed a literary club in order to undertake mutual endeavours, collaborative publications and joint reading. They met at Isaac's Fish Restaurant in Brixton and counted amongst their members devotees of Blake, Edward Carpenter and Byron, as well as a 'onetime Balham socialist'.

They read Ibsen together, published five issues of the *Moocher* (until January 1914), heard a phrenologist speak, went on rambles and attended the theatre. Kent was involved in the Adult School Movement and finally in the pacifist movement during the War. Spiritualism, the War itself, as well as his socialism and its increasing incompatibility with the Christianity of his parents, led Kent away from religious belief. He recalled the assumptions of his committed years:

> Of sex, a matter more important than religion, I knew hardly anything. Physically, I was quite normal but sex was represented as some kind of fetid sewer that you must not want to explore . . . I had an idea that at the altar (I had never heard of marriages at registry offices) . . . the priest performed some kind of miracle, similar to transubstantiation, whereby children came.[85]

Kent's conversion to atheism, and his embarrassment over his mistaken notions of human sexuality, were clearest to him after the War. The experience of working for the LCC, however, had opened up many gates for him. After he was thrown in amongst a diverse group of colleagues, the forces of nineteenth century Nonconformity in Kent grappled with his notion of 'modernism' and with anti-prudery. The charge of 'prudery' would come to burden his Progressive employers.

At the centre of the life strategies that Kent and many others ultimately embarked upon was the transition not only from a state of purity to a state of awareness, but, for many, from the single to the married state, the homoeroticism of early manhood forgone or transformed. As we have seen, the London professions from which a young man might choose presented various calculuses of marital possibility. To marry too early was fatal, to fail to marry denied a man access to inherited money if his betrothed was rich.

More commonly, it delayed his access to the considerable benefits that accrued from having a wife to assume charge of the social reproduction necessary for his maintenance and well-being.

In the most prevalent contemporary view, the sober and boring London suburbanite, if not a convert to Kent's youthful muscular Christianity, was at least resigned to the 'armed neutrality' of marriage and the leisure patterns of the outlying districts removed from the West End.[86] Here one found

> oyster bars, Methodist chapels, free public libraries, small shops, ha'penny newspapers, cheap music-halls, police and county courts, billiard-matches, minor race-meetings, third class railway carriages, public museums, public baths, indifferent academies for young ladies: whatever, in short, strikes the superior mind as deficient in completeness, excellence and distinction, may with absolute safety be called suburban.[87]

Yet the purity of suburbia vested certain powers in the literary lower middle class, powers which prompted both derision and expectation. Holbrook Jackson termed its members the 'guardians of British respectability', echoing Arnold.[88] In describing the lower middle class budget of £150 to £200 a year, *The Cornhill Magazine* explained in 1901 'that the subject is one of the highest importance to the nation as well as to the individual, will be at once apparent when we remember . . . that the lower middle class of which we write is the backbone of the Commonwealth'.[89]

Alongside these portraits of an essential, if submissive, group of 'nobodies' arose a literary image of the 'Bohemian' lower middle class, reminiscent of the older, errant Kent. This minority inherited the traditions of the Georgian rakes. They discussed socialism in bars where Johnson had once imbibed, bore a faint resemblance to the mid-century swells, and practised the 'new hedonism', as Grant Allen christened it. Eschewing Calvinism, they were said to live by the credo 'be happy and you will be virtuous'.[90] Allen explained:

> A 'woman's-right woman' gave me . . . a watchword which would form a perfect motto for a hedonist society. It was this – 'self-development is better than self-sacrifice.' . . . Self-development is our aim for all; an aim which will make all stronger and saner and wiser and better. It will make each in the end more helpful to humanity. To be sound in mind and

limb; to be healthy of body and mind; to be educated, to be emancipated, to be free, to be beautiful . . . [91]

Few living Bohemians embodied all these ideals. Yet traces of the Bohemian tendency were visible in the consciously undomesticated, even anti-suburban life-style of certain types of London clerk – both men and women. Despair could engulf those who tried to moralise the clerk. His condition was explicable only in terms of material deprivation: 'The cumulative increase of the landlady's dirt is the only thing which equals the cumulative increase of her extortionate charges . . . From the miseries of the cheap lodging-house he flies to the doubtful distractions of the public-house, the cheap play-house or the night club.'[92]

Arthur Sherwell wrote about Soho as 'honey-combed with clubs, wine-rooms, restaurants and saloons', and he decried Bohemia.[93] While the Soho lingerer was for Sherwell less detestable than the 'vicious spirit of the idle and well-dressed lounger in Piccadilly', the unnatural environment of the West End was demoralising and hardly less deserving of reproach than the notorious East. The sincerity of the provincial, the natural purity of the rural, was corrupted by city life. Sherwell bemoaned the 'utter artificiality which colours so deeply the entire life of West London, and the anarchic state of social life in the district generally'.[94] Coffee houses shrouded gambling dens, clubs had secret, private entrances, streets were crowded with prostitutes. Licentiousness and loneliness abounded. Yet the West End offered its consolations, most sought after by the lower middle class deviant in possession of 'what is at bottom a mad and irresistible craving for excitement, stimulated by the excitements and vicious luxury of the West End life: a serious and wilful revolt against the monotony of commonplace ideals and the uninspired drudgery of everyday life'.[95]

For the poet and writer Arthur Ransome, Bohemia was merely a 'stage in a man's life . . . he may stay a little time, and then go back whence he came, to start again in another direction as a civil servant, or a respectable man of business; only a few settle down in the tavern, forever postponing their departure'.[96] But, while in Bohemia's possession, its disciples were dominated by the will to forsake their provincial backgrounds and their doting families. Ransome describes the mass of Bohemians not as hard-drinking artistes so much as people who engaged in a regular but, in reality, not very ostentatious night life. Even the conspicuous were not all that they seemed to be. One character in the drinking hall of the Provence in Leicester Square often caught the writer's eye; his long beard and gregarious conversation were inimitable. Ransome finally bid him share a drink: 'He came, and it turned out that he worked in a bank from ten to four every day and played the wild Bohemian every night. His beard was a disguise.'[97]

In this version of Bohemia, women were patronised but not absent. Journals in the Beardsley mode such as the *Yellow Book*, the *Savoy*, the *Pageant*, the *Butterfly* and the *Dial* were 'discussed by all the crowd of young women who, by dressing in green gowns without collars, wearing embroidered yokes, scorning the *Daily Mail*, and following the fortunes of the studios, keep in the forefront of artistic and literary progress'.[98] The reader of *Jacob's Room* will recognise the scene. This mystical world of Bohemia was itself a fantasy of those who courted it; thus Ransome admitted that it fostered a less exotic existence even in its midst, in which the 'nobodies' of the insalubrious lower middle class were noticeable. Of the Café de l'Europe, a drinking hall with a band, Ransome acknowledged:

> This place, like all the other cafes, is not exclusively Bohemian; we are only there on sufferance, in isolated parties, and it is a curious contrast to look away to the clerks, demimondaines, and men about town, sitting at the other tables; faces that have left their illusions with their youth, faces with protruding lips and receding chins, weak foolish faces with watery eyes, office boys trying to be men, and worn-out men trying to be boys, and women ridiculously dressed and painted.[99]

Thus Bohemia co-existed with suburbia, artists with clerks, Soho with the City. The LCC *Staff Gazette* reviewed Ransome's book, saluting the author's remonstrance that Bohemia was 'not a place, it is an attitude of the mind'.[100] Wherever one looked for description, a common language loomed. How can these two contradictory images, the one sober, the other dissipated, the one passionless, the other romantic, the one suburban, the other footloose, be explained? The mixed imagery obligingly supports the case for a variegated 'lower middle class'. Certainly the diversity and the heterogeneity of those who may even have identified themselves as such wrought havoc on the utility of the category as sociology. A single individual inhabited multiple, fluctuating social identities, or tried to do so – a project brilliantly suggested by Denise Riley's *Am I That Name?*.[101] Still, this very contradictory discursive presence of the 'lower middle class' gave it a kind of 'real' existence and reflected the palpable tensions of the metropolitan environment.

THE PROBLEM OF LIFE CHANCES

Charles Masterman wrote of the suburban as conjuring up 'a vision of life in which the trivial and heroic things were alike exhibited, but in which there is no adequate test or judgement, which are the heroic, which are the trivial'.[102] But for those men who aspired to heights of comfort and style, in a time when incomes at or above the £150 line were levelling and prices were rising, it was necessary to be open to ambiguity. Thus, 'the functional need for thrift was powerfully counteracted by the high cost of gentility'.[103] Many displayed behaviour patterns at variance with one another in different periods of the life cycle. And not all of life's advantages were calculable. At the heart of what created the *idea* of the lower middle class – more than a recognition of men of inadequate income and half-realised aspirations for material and cultural betterment – were courtship, marriage and the ultimate recognition of women as participants in a man's life strategies. These formed the core of 'lower middle class' ritual and fantasy.

Apart from the LCC, women's occupations in the white collar sector of turn-of-the-century London were several. Many typists, schoolteachers, sanitary inspectors, telephonists, governesses and nurses were more educated than their job titles suggested.[104] The limited number of women's jobs obviously constrained women's mobility and earning capacities. Most women still married and, as many of the available, 'respectable' jobs on offer were restricted to the unmarried, there was a buyer's market in women's labour. At the start of the 1890s, the Remington typewriter began to be used at the Foreign Office under Salisbury. Another appeared at Hatfield House and sixty others at the London and Northwest Railway Company. By then a leading white collar women's employer in London was the Prudential, which hired over 200 young women between the ages of 17 and 25, offering a 300 volume library and various diversions, such as musical concerts for the pleasure of the new members of its workforce, who were predominantly the daughters of professional men.[105]

But these women were the most privileged of a sector of

employees who were not only very poorly paid, but for whom the conditions of work, the hours and the hopes for advancement were absent or thin at best. And women, like men but more so, were largely unorganised, despite the notable exceptions of the Board school teachers (themselves LCC employees after 1904 and members of the early NUT), some civil servants, and members of exclusively women's organisations whose largest impact was as propagandists. The London Association of Shorthand Writers and Typists was formed in 1912 though there is no evidence of its work amongst LCC women staff.[106] Dorothy Lansbury Thurtle, who along with her husband Ernest led the NUC before the War, wrote in 'Comradeship for clerks' of 'The Girl on Her Own' who worked out of financial necessity, observing economies in daily life 'such that men never adopt . . . It serves to bolster up the superstition that women can live more cheaply than men.' They wrote of the 'Pin Money Girl' who had additional resources and of the 'Destined to Marry' who undercut men's wages by agreeing to work for less than men did. The Thurtles beckoned suffragist women, 'feminists' like themselves as they put it, to see that votes alone, without support for the union, would not bring better wages and conditions.[107] However popular their perceptions of women on the market may have been, the cry for union support found relatively few women adherents.

Marriage, it would seem, posed a more viable alternative for many. Witness this description of the lives of women teachers:

> The worst of life, and, I fancy, the lives of most women teachers is its intense isolation . . . here I am in this great city and I don't know a soul but the other teachers living in lodgings like myself and of whom I am heartily sick after nine months of the year's daily and close intercourse. I don't know a man up here, and I long – it is most unenlightened and retrograde isn't it? – for the society of a sensible man . . . the lives we lead are utterly unnatural and unhealthy.[108]

The 'wifely' figure in the orthodox lower middle class portrait was the suburban woman waiting anxiously for her husband to return from his daily foray into London. She hoped that he had purchased food in the cheaper inner-London markets, always stretching an inadequate income in order to keep up social appearances. But perhaps she too had once been a Bohemian. Perhaps those who in many other ways were like her, the celebrated 'independent women', never married.[109] 'Lower middle class women' were not a distinct group any more than were their male counterparts. Instead, complex patterns of association and work, of habit, commitment and identity, characterised their lives.

The differences amongst women were rivalled by those between men and women, and by the ambiguities of life for the given individual, tested by outward economic insecurity and unpredictability. Ethereal figures of fantasy in Bohemia, women could equally be understood as encumbering men. Manliness took forms other than those exhibited on the battlefield or on the playing field:

> If good liquor, talk and smoke are to be enjoyed to the utmost, why then get you half a dozen honest fellows about you, with no particular qualification, and have your evening out. Go to a tavern or a coffee house where you will be left to yourselves. Be free from womenfolk with their pestilential seriousness or more aggravating flippancy. Get you and your company into a cosy room, with a bright fire and a closed door, where you may be free men before the universe.[110]

In the fanciful world of Bohemia, men were curious about women and about sexuality. But the realities of contagious diseases, of the requirements of childrearing and of the need for a well-managed domestic routine, if not the joys of courtship and romance, could ultimately lead even a Bohemian to marry.[111] The forestalling of marriage, as suggested by the preliminary work of the Bankses, was superseded after the mid-century by the practice of abstention or other forms of birth control in the 'middle class' marriage: 'thus, from attempting to persuade the working classes to cure their poverty by self-restraint, the members of the middle classes found themselves applying the theme of control to their own way of life'.[112]

This 'way of life' was not Bohemia; in fact Bohemia was defined largely as an unmarried state: 'The door into the Registrar's Office is the door out of Bohemia . . . Bohemia is not the place for bringing up a family.'[113] The fraudulent Bohemian youth metamorphosed into the earnest suburban husband by his late twenties. Of course Bohemians were only one fragment of the mass of people being depicted as lower middle class on the eve of the War. Socialists and vegetarians, feminists and suffragettes, clerical trade union organisers, spiritualists, homosexuals, cyclists, ramblers and pacifists – these and dozens of overlapping and discrete categories of person existed within lower middle class life. Even the rebellion against the tyranny of respectability and of parochial family repressiveness had its origin not simply within the margins, but within the mainstream; commuting suburbanites could wear, or had worn, several hats.

Once the decision to marry was made, each London neighbourhood presented its distinctive financial demands upon the bachelor or the married couple. The advice literature of the period conveys a sense of shrewd calculation in its discussions of how to live on £200 a year or £1200 a year or how to manage a budget so as to ensure a rental payment in town instead of in the suburbs. This cult of domesticity, of material possessions and of marital harmony, was manifest in ordered rituals: to err could mean a lifetime of misery. As we have seen, a man choosing to compete for a place at the LCC was obviously unlikely to possess inherited wealth. He could bolster his increments by part-time study and the hope of a major promotion or a transfer to the Civil or Colonial Service. But for most LCC clerks, marriage had to occur at the moment when a man was finally earning an adequate income. He had to have the means to keep a wife and carefully planned children. The staff jester derided the attempt to find another solution:

> 'Twas love that stole the pilgrim's staff
> And stayed our comrade's feet –
> Each lunchtime finds him munching half
> A biscuit in the street,
> His only dream to win a maid
> (Whose father's in the timber trade.)[114]

The presence of this calculus suggests that the very precise and individual circumstances of a man's employment separated him from others in seemingly comparable career trajectories and definitively distinguished him from his women colleagues (always single at the LCC) and from those women whom he met away from work. Without this recognition of the frantic considerations of a London existence, and of the crucial role that considerations of gender played within it, the life of the LCC employee remains an enigma. There is little insight conveyed by the generic category 'LCC clerk' and none by the invocation of an undifferentiated 'lower middle class'. Simply describing subgroups which were actually conflicting, or even addressing 'differences between men and women', does not suggest the various identities adopted by men and women over the course of their lifetimes, or over the course of the working day. Nor does it do justice to the significance of individual development, as William Kent's unabashed writings confirm. Such new departures in self-perception would come to constitute a kind of 'internal challenge' to LCC municipal socialism, which sought conformity in bureaucracy and limits to individual mobility and self-expression.

WOMEN AND THE SOCIAL NEXUS

The NUC's newspaper the *Clerk* published 'Girls Who Are in Demand' in 1890:

> The girls that are wanted are girls with hearts,
> They are wanted for mothers and wives.
> Wanted to cradle in loving arms,
> the strongest and frailest lives.
> The clever, the witty, the brilliant girls
> There are few who can understand;
> But oh! for the wise, loving home girls,
> There's a constant steady demand.

The prospect of meeting a man whose needs were expressed in these terms suited many women in clerical positions. For others, like some women clerks at the LCC, the desire to stay on at work after marriage simply had to be suppressed. The bureaucratic dictates of the LCC, and the degree to which Council statutes buoyed the hopes of their men colleagues, and even of men whom they met away from work, conspired to dash that aspiration.

Frances Wood noted that in London in this period there was a larger proportion of unmarried men and women aged between 15 and 25 than in the previous years of the century. But conventional wisdom still had it, as Clara Collett put it, that 'the average woman marries; it is the exceptionally intellectual or the exceptionally feeble-minded who do not'.[115] Collett also ventured, in the same breath, that wifely 'economic independence' was not 'an ideal, but a reality', and so it must have been for LCC teachers.[116] Sidney Webb, the great architect of many of the norms of LCC employment and his co-author, Beatrice Webb, wrote of 'routine mental work': 'But the men's work is their life-career; the women's a mere prelude to matrimony, and often only a source of pocket-money.'

In this discursive context, the new woman, rightly termed by Lucy Bland a 'journalistic construction', needs to be understood in several guises, all of which were visible at the LCC.[117] The woman expecting and planning marriage could have a short, respectable career of a new type more readily than she could become the more elusive woman of a new type. A brief, rather than protracted, courtship could then be followed by marriage to an 'equal' and could result in a smaller, well-planned family, allowing both partners more income and the capacity to pay a higher rent and to purchase more of life's affordable accoutrements. Mutual self-improvement might follow, though the man would remain the sole earner and his career would require a careful strategy, as we have seen. A second type of 'new woman', the 'moral, spiritual' woman who, Judith Walkowitz suggests, made 'no positive assertion of female sexuality', might pursue a lifelong career quite sheltered in private life from 'carnal, animalistic man'.[118]

One can regard the resolutely single career women of the LCC in these terms, though women at the LCC experienced greater inter-action at work with male colleagues than did 'independent women' committed to a separate women's community whose workplaces were also women's domains. There were also 'new women' who wished for greater interaction with men on more equal terms, for whom marriage was not a final goal, and who hoped that political and aesthetic concerns might triumph. Most women of the LCC staff found themselves, temporarily at least, with access to a milieu in which these ideas had currency. Their activities and the language of their joint discussions with men colleagues exude this predis-position. To consider the implications of everyday life and con-versation at work, it is necessary to abandon a rudimentary notion of social class as defined at the workplace and to acknowledge that its simplicity ignores the multiple experiences of both men and women. In this rethinking, the larger categories of 'men' and 'women' can themselves lose some of their significance. The concerns of the 'married', 'permanently single' and particularly of those seeking companionship momentarily served as the delimit-ing, redefined markers of social existence. A barrister's life project and expectations differed fundamentally in their social possibilities from those of an LCC clerk.

The concepts of 'patriarchy' and of 'gendered work' are also not specific or accurate enough to address the nature of women's LCC employment. Marriage was a fundamental block to hiring and a reason to leave the workforce. LCC typists' jobs and the para-professional and professional jobs that opened up in greater numbers at the LCC in later years were all highly respectable posts within the wider women's labour market. But even at the LCC, many women were employed in positions that did not test the skills that they already possessed when they entered the work-force. Girton girls became secondary school teachers. In this way the imagery of 'the new woman' acted as a veil covering the practice of paying women less than men and of continuing to exclude them from many types of work classified as unsuitable. It equally served as a rhetorical prop to encourage refined women of education to contribute to public service in capacities for which they were told that they were especially suitable or especially caring. Thus Millicent Garret Fawcett yanked Philippa Fawcett out of Cambridge, dissuaded her from undertaking postgraduate work and eventually influenced her to take up employment at the LCC, despite her daughter's brilliant performance in mathematics as an undergraduate. Fawcett became one of the foremost women activists of the staff, but her initial commitment did not result from her innate expertise in municipal management, but from her mother's domineering intervention in order to fulfil feminist and political prescriptions. For the radical intelligentsia, the LCC briefly served as a sinecure.[119]

Those women amongst LCC staff like Miss Fawcett, who did not marry right away, like some of their male colleagues, were touched by the deep anxiety induced by a superior education and shared cultural and political aspirations beyond their monetary reach. Clara Collett described the white collar woman worker who possessed only one dress appropriate for concerts.[120] The appear-ance of self-confidence on a meagre income, the yearning for social contact and for cultural uplift, was akin to the false beards of the men of Bohemia: women could reveal themselves only for a single night. The struggle to live in a better way had its political mani-festations. Suffrage can be seen as one; white collar union organis-ing as another. The will to end poverty was a third; the attraction to Progressivism and socialism, a fourth. Other avenues presented themselves. But these particular forms of activism were very often chosen.

POLITICAL AND SOCIAL PREOCCUPATIONS

The investigation of 'progressive' ideas and programmes dominated the small gatherings and quiet arguments among the visible, politically committed LCC staff before the War. Little organised conservatism was in evidence, while vocal leftward radicals formed a distinct minority. Few of their number spoke of themselves explicitly as socialists. Yet a spirit of associationism spread during and after the War amongst LCC and other white collar workers across London. Goals and programmes mentioned by a minority before the War gained credibility amongst a majority and became part of a common language spoken by inter-war period white collar activists. The 'lower middle class' appeared even less homogeneous in the 1920s and 1930s, when there were 'more of them' and their political fragmentation was even more explicit. Those amongst them who identified with radicalism were indebted to the pioneers of the 1890s and the early 1900s.[121]

The overriding concern of the typical LCC clerk in terms of his worklife socialising was not politics *per se*; it was instead the availability of women whom he might meet through Council activities. Politics was often depicted as a prattish distraction or a luxury for the well-heeled, as in Ransome's Hampstead: 'for Hampstead has always her causes, forsaken one by one'.[122] The paucity of women on the staff and their relative poverty encouraged men to invite women from outside the Council to staff events:[123] 'It is somewhat amusing to notice the great interest one takes in a hitherto unknown colleague when one suddenly discovers he has a very pretty sister or two.'[124] At staff engagement parties, the prospective spouse was adorned with gifts of domestic items such as 'a handsome brass standard lamp, of a corinthian column pattern, with embroidered silk shade'.[125] But once married, the man became an object of derision as his wife spent his income for him. Those who were unmarried, ostensibly chaste and left behind, lamented the loss of their colleague to domestic drudgery. Hence the exit from Bohemia as satire:

> Each morn out Joseph quite elate
> Will don his office coat,
> And tell each carping celibate
> His latest anecdote;
> How baby's cold is rather worse –
> How yesterday it bit its nurse.

Although myself a single chap
('By choice' I hate to say)
I learn a thing or two on pap
Or teething every day . . .
There was a time when sporting things
Supplied our daily talk.
But now we range from rubber rings
To 'When should infants walk?'[126]

The dynamic of waiting, of deferring marriage until one had a viable income and of pursuing a particular life-style just beyond reach informed much of the literary record left by LCC clerks before the War. The discrepancy between what a man could actually afford and the prestige of LCC employment increasingly provided grounds for outcry and bitterness amongst the staff. The elaborate pursuit of a confident self-identity was reflected in the fastidiousness of self-expression:

An official who does not belong to the professional part of the staff is at a loss for a concise and at the same time definitive description of his status in the business world. (He discards the term 'civil servant' explaining, I am not enamoured of the term 'servant' which is perhaps the common domestic variety.) 'London County Council official' would be concise and definite . . . but then some people have a strong objection to the term 'official', and prefer the old-fashioned 'clerk'.[127]

Life at work was socially segregated. Not only were the women typists regrettably housed in separate quarters but there was only minimal contact between white collar Central Office staff and LCC manual grades employees. Most of a man's day was spent scurrying after officials, or sitting at a desk alongside his peers; hierarchy was ever-present. There was a proliferation of distinctions at the bottom of the ladder as more Minor Establishment and eventually 'general grade' employees arrived. But the proletarian members of staff were invisible. Their territory lay beyond the homes of the central bureaucracy in the neighbourhoods and outlying districts of London. The Londoners who were the recipients of LCC social policy appeared over and over in the pages that the clerks copied by hand and later by machine. But they were physically absent at the head offices, save the charwomen, the messenger boys or the fleet-footed, out-of-sight delivery men. When the clerical staff

67

assisted in municipal inspections of theatres or of housing estates, these ordinary inhabitants surfaced, and surely the blackcoated staff could then see themselves as men in uniform, raised for a moment above the mass of the people. The etiquette of 'officialdom' was, on such visits, readily observed. Organised social and recreational activities, as much as the debating societies and associational activities of early blackcoated union drives, were conducted entirely separated from the world of the manual grades employees, such as the asylum workers or firemen. Their labour activity took place in other realms.

Despite the inflated status of LCC work, the demands of daily life in London remained. The junior clerk worried about his financial position made so conspicuously visible by the expensive and enticing city around him. The decline of real wages before the War and the erosion of chances for advancement within the Council bureaucracy reduced him. There was also the initial risk a man faced even should he advance: the top Minor Establishment position paid more than the entry-level job at the bottom of the second class of the Majors.[128] Given the increasing numbers of Minor Establishment men on the staff, a great number of LCC clerks shared the concerns of the average London commercial clerk. Cheap food near work was scarce; there was 'nothing between an elevated coffee shop and the expensive salon'.[129] There was no affordable housing available in central areas near the Council; surviving staff addresses indicate that the better-paid had suburban residences. Yet Saturday hours at work prevented 'much in the way of rural rambling . . . except in the longest days of summer'.[130] Ransome lamented, 'London is full of people who keep the country in their hearts.'[131] As in many aspects of life, consolation appeared close at hand only to elude even the most earnest. The irony of enduring rural place names inspired one staff pundit:

The Alluring East (End)

When office work and office worries harass you
And you feel you need repose and change of scene
You needn't let the lack of cash embarrass you
Just take a little trip to Bethnal Green.

Or if Dame Nature's wilder beauties beckon you
And call to the wild spirit hid beneath

Your always calm exterior, I reckon you
Might just as well go on to Cambridge Heath

In case for joys more pastoral you sigh a bit
And long for that deep peace which Nature yields
To those who truly love her, go and lie a bit
And rusticate in lovely London Fields.

When dales and lofty hills insistent call for you
To leave behind the turmoil of the towns
An untold wealth of beauty waits – 'tis all for you,
Go climb the virgin slopes of Hackney Downs.[132]

Hackney local history suggests a provocative reading of an otherwise mildly amusing effort. Both London Fields and the Downs were well-known haunts of prostitutes and their clients.[133] At first glance the adulation of the rural can be read simply as the desire to be out of London. But behind it could lie a more complicated complaint which neither inner nor outer London satisfied. Owen Fleming, the progressive architect, spoke for many:

A far too large proportion of our . . . income that should be devoted to the education of our children and other good purposes, is now spent in exorbitant rents for inferior accommodation and in railway season tickets to say nothing of the time we have to waste daily in travelling in unpunctual railway carriages, in order that our families may breathe a purer air than that of smoke-laden London.[134]

Single clerks lived as lodgers in the suburbs or in town. The frustrating search for suitable lodgings, exacerbated by the presence of an overly intrusive landlady, prompted some to stretch their resources in order to rent a self-contained flat.[135] The demands of frugal budgeting, the irritating burden of being educated 'beyond one's means', elicited a sense of resignation:

This . . . is intended to appeal to such men as second class clerks in the chrysalis stage or a Minor man in all stages or to any class of official who has the added expenditure of matrimony . . . It must be remembered that gaudy waistcoats, extravagant footwear, multi-coloured silk socks, Harris Tweed or Jaeger garments . . . in fact anything out of the ordinary (and therefore expensive if it is at all good) is not for the man whose station in life forces him to place twelve pounds a year as his dressing allowance.[136]

It is tempting to treat these banalities, the surface matter of existence, as superfluous to politicisation or as impediments to radicalisation – as timeless false consciousness. But the fury engendered by the impossibility of satisfying material needs had its concomitant in the desire for spiritual and intellectual fulfilment, cheaper come by than a tailor-made suit. The cumulative lack of recognition of what each white collar LCC employee conceivably saw as his own unique talent and self-sacrificing zeal for redemption seemed manifest in low salaries. These imposed constraints upon the gifted, who ought, they thought, to be supported in pursuing a creative life-style. The less high-minded of them at least thought that if they were giving their working lives to London, then they deserved a good time in their hours off.

Neighbourhood clubs and old school clubs provided some recreative enjoyment. But at work, societies also flourished. Clubs for music, swimming, photography, cycling, horticulture, drama, chess, shooting, singing and physical training grew up. The Christian Union offered weekly sermons and supported its own missionary. A typical meeting was the Union's ninth annual, held in January 1900: 'First came a reference to the War in South Africa and the success to British arms for which we all were looking confidently in that quarter, notwithstanding the recent serious reverses, then a comparison with the defeat of the Israelites at Ai.'[137]

Some staff members fought in the Boer War, and many were active in the Territorials.[138] Those who served in South Africa sent reports back, and were warmly supported by many colleagues for their spirit, as one put it, 'whatever one thinks of the war'.[139] The *Staff Gazette* covered the War and its participants closely. Lionel Curtis, destined for a place in the new South African government, was a *Roundtable* contributor. The imperial concerns of many ambitious staff are exemplified by Curtis's very successful career for which the LCC Clerk's Department and Curtis's East End involvements prior to his LCC service had provided a useful background.[140] When, in 1901, Curtis was chosen to organise the new municipality of Johannesburg, a colleague recalled living with him for several years in model dwellings in Stepney. He became the colonial labour policymaker and apartheid advocate.

Athletic matches pitted LCC teams formed in each Council department against other London clubs and teams. Departmental dinners, whist drives, charity visits to London schoolchildren, the organisation of a 'Poor Children's Breakfast and Dinner Fund', outings and dances brought colleagues and their guests together after work. The Sports Annual of 1900 was the occasion for a gathering of thousands of staff and their families, who were addressed by a senior officer: 'All true lovers of manly sports and all who wish to see the national character exalted and not debased, must have echoed the grave and earnest sentences in which he denounced the practice of gambling in connection with athletics.' This puritanism was standard fare. Temperance was exalted on such occasions; the 'new man' in the service was doted upon by his superiors. An old-timer remarked: 'the chiefs take a keen interest in the sports and pastimes and general welfare of their staff'.[141] Occasionally women participated in sports as part of all-women teams; predictably, manual workers were separated from the white collar staff.[142] But the boundaries of these forms of 'municipal puritanism' were fluid and could be overstepped. Women typists avidly discussed issues of the day amongst themselves and in print. The Spring Gardens Club brought men and women staff members together in formal sessions. The National Union of Clerks recruited staff radicals; the Fabians organised reading groups. The LCC Staff Association, predecessor to the white collar staff union, counted its membership in the thousands by the outbreak of the War.

The typists' discussion centred upon the social and domestic standing of working women who held positions like their own. They discussed the purported decline of housework skills, often cited as a consequence of the entry of women into new sectors of the labour force. Their anxiety about their relations with men was apparent: 'It is the pretty or the well-dressed woman who gains admiration from men and partners at a dance, the merely domesticated girl is shunned; one who goes to the dance with the reputation of a "bluestocking" probably leaves it with that of a "wallflower".' This typist was pledged to what she understood as the ideals of Ruskin's *Sesame and Lilies*. She believed that through the 'evolution of Humanity' men might come to appreciate women's useful as well as ornamental qualities. At present, women could neither earn a living nor 'praise and admiration' from 'mere churning and washing'.[143]

Yet she evaded the full weight of Ruskin's argument. He had actually bemoaned the fate of 'girls who have never been taught to do a single useful thing', their 'womanhood made vain, and the glory of their pure consciences warped into fruitless agony concerning questions which the laws of common serviceable life would either have solved for them in an instant, or kept out of their way'. He distinguished between men and women: 'the man's power is active, progressive, defensive. He is eminently the doer, the creator, the defender . . . the woman's power is for rule not for battle, – and her intellect is not for invention or creation, but for sweet ordering, arrangement and decision'. Ruskin stressed the importance of a woman's 'household office', of 'the economy of the kitchen'. Significantly, he urged women to assist the poor in employing such skills.[144] This was reminiscent of the rhetoric of 'municipal housekeeping' that coloured municipal electoral manifestos in London throughout the period. Revealingly, the typist's rendition of Ruskin appropriated his insistence on the value of domestic skills even for the educated woman, while ignoring his argument *against* a working life outside the home.

A second typist had no fear of the 'professional woman' not being able to make a transition back to the home upon marriage. (Collett would have differed: 'Those who only take up employment as a stopgap until marriage never become really efficient, and when later on they find that there is no prospect of release, they become positively inefficient.')[145] Perhaps this was a key to the appropriation of Ruskin as well: 'The power of concentration once acquired can be easily distributed. Is a pudding one-half as troublesome to manipulate as, say, a specification?' This writer-typist advocated the 'industrial system of cooperative and subdivided labour', arguing that without this 'many a woman is little more than an overworked mechanical cooking, washing and sewing machine, with never a moment for mental cultivation, without which no woman can be a guide to her children or a comrade to her husband'.[146] In keeping with the notion that women ultimately were bound for a companionate marriage, she pleaded that women ought not to undercut men's wages, while suggesting that she might have agreed with those who opposed women taking up white collar jobs for less pay than that which men received.[147] Agitation around this issue was common. Though her argument could be read several ways, in the light of her overall case, it is clear that this woman, just as her colleague did, perceived women's role in the white collar labour market as supplementary to that of men and as a step to be taken before marriage.

Yet a third typist tried to promote the ideal of a woman of many talents possessing both domestic and social skills. She felt her colleagues had ignored 'the numerous class of educated working young women who must perforce acquaint themselves with the gentle art of housekeeping, darning and even cooking, preserving and nursing, and who nonetheless are able to cycle, sew and dress suitable to all occasions'. It was not only the 'brainless' who were devoted to 'self-adornment . . . the really best-educated will be able amongst other things to dress and to cook'.[148] The several identities of working women at the LCC sparked debate. Both men and women employees reacted to women coming to work for the Council in terms of the implications of their present positions for the future of marriage and the family. These 'new women' were not committed to careers over marriage, perhaps in part because the Council offered so little in comparison. But they did display anxiety at the prospect of being devalued as objects of sexual interest on the part of men because of their jobs or because of the various connotations of availability and asexuality that surrounded the notion of the 'working woman'. They wrote of meeting a man, making a marriage and even of leaving the workforce as their ultimate aspirations.

Within such a framework, women made adjustments for the advantages offered by education; mental training could be used to improve a marriage partnership and a future home environment. Women working in these lower capacities for the LCC argued that if they needed to work in order to survive financially, they were also subject to the demands placed upon them by the men whom they were meeting. They wanted to appear attractive. They wanted to acquire the skills with which to manage a home. They did not wish to acquire commercial skills and general education at the expense of the development of attributes that would help to sustain their sexual appeal. Though the women typists supported the right of women's entry into white collar jobs, even suggesting that domestic duties might be performed more quickly through the use of time-saving methods, they did not object to the notion that domestic labour was the province of women alone. Women on the staff who expressed themselves on these issues commonly advocated political rights for women and defended their right to work, albeit in a circumscribed way, without ever broaching the question of the reordering of the sexual division of labour in the home. A rhetoric of sameness, in relation to men, was absent, as the 'comparable work' position of the NUC attested. When an NUC officer proclaimed the need for the clerk to 'be considered and treated as a *man*' (his emphasis), he quickly added hilariously, 'These remarks, of course, also apply to the female clerk as a woman.'[149]

But no single radical rhetoric was heard; no single recognisable orthodoxy was audible in the debates of the staff. Eric Makeham delivered a paper to the Spring Gardens Club entitled 'The Family'. He affirmed his support for the continuance of the family as the central affective and living unit of capitalism and of the future 'post-capitalist' society. While he supported the right of women to work under their current economic circumstances, he did so on the basis of a theory of 'emiseration'; at present, he believed, women were *forced* to enter the workforce. A better society of the future would eliminate that necessity and would allow women to return to the home.[150] This was certainly not an unutterable position for a committed socialist. The assumptions that all women were prospective wives and that marriage always meant the prospect of a man alone supporting a family, albeit with the eventual assistance of the State, was common in turn-of-the-century radical discourse. Men trade unionists often defended their wage demands as the means by which their wives could stop working outside the home. Few socialists or women activists stood outside this discourse. Clearly, women's work, most prevalent in the working classes, was a necessary and, from many socialist points of view, temporary evil. The 'new women' employees at the LCC integrated these views of the working woman with other 'feminist' notions of women's rights. The discrepancies amongst attitudes did not alter a commitment to this version of feminism.[151]

The unfolding process of discussion in the Spring Gardens Club offers a view of what the politicised wing of the staff thought about major social and economic questions of the day and suggests ways in which the Council's own political circumstances influenced such discussions. One of its most active participants defined the Club's purpose in 1910 as the pursuit of 'impartial deliberation on public questions' to the furtherance of 'longer, wider and more charitable views on the great problems of life and duty', and saluted the Club's members for the 'mental and moral advantages which their free discussion has gained for them'. Referring to the staff's Fabian-inspired study sessions on the new poor law, he urged 'the necessity for a keener interest on the part of all in social questions'.[152]

In 1905, the Club debated 'free trade versus protection'. In defending protection, one speaker referred to a bygone 'hatred of the Corn Laws'. He opposed what he termed a 'Nietzschean creed', arguing instead for social reform to assist the victims of 'natural selection'. The accumulation of national wealth was less important than a rigorous examination of the means by which wealth was distributed. The working class as a whole ought to be protected by the State from the exigencies of an uncontrolled market society just as lunatics were. Yet those Club members who opposed protection from a leftward view heckled the first speaker as a 'Balfourite-cum-socialist'. Why would protection benefit 'any but the landowners and the smugglers? They grind the faces of the poor and stifle the growth of a nation.'[153]

The years leading up to the repeal of the Corn Laws had witnessed the hardships caused by protectionism: 'Our exports declined, wages declined, while discontent, riots and the Chartist movement bore evidence to the sufferings of the poor, and in 1842 no less than one in eleven were on the rates.' The fate of the poor was not separated from the fate of the empire in this argument. Colonial preference and 'retaliation schemes, both elements of protectionist projects, might risk the empire'. The NUC opposed tariff reform as liable to provoke a tariff war that would crush the German worker, who was at this moment still an object of international proletarian solidarity. NUC members' opinions were not, however, recorded in the LCC debate; a verbatim record of full-floor discussions does not survive.[154] Poverty and the condition of the working class, the national economy and its potential for change, Britain's global standing and the credibility of nineteenth century political thought (and in particular its prescriptive role for the State and for social ownership) were the preoccupations of Club members before the War. Progressivism, municipal socialism and the role of the LCC in London figured in their conversations. Many members supported limited forms of municipalisation and they voiced a range of attitudes toward municipal ownership. There was clearly a mixed internal reaction to the Progressives' goals and legacy.

A member of the Clerk's Department, for example, spoke after the Moderate Party victory in 1908 on the question 'Is Socialism

Inevitable?' He distinguished between the roles of the State and the individual and compared the writings of Plato and Spencer. In discussing municipalisation, he sought to separate the realms of public action and individual will: 'Socialism was gaining ground everyday in things material, but . . . in things spiritual and mental we were becoming more individualistic.'[155] There was no prescriptive municipal socialist orthodoxy, and Club discussions could take unpredictable turns. This speaker resolved his dilemma by enumerating the separable component parts of 'socialism': 'All who agree to the advantages of County Council powers, of factory legislation, local self-government, free education, free libraries, government limitation of contract between master and man, and government control of industries, have distinctly socialist sympathies.' But 'free love' and 'atheism' had no place. Socialism could solve the 'industrial problem'. Unlike tariff reform, which sought to take advantage of another country for Britain's sake, socialism would 'permanently' increase the 'work of the world'. A 'crowded and enthusiastic' meeting supported the following motion, which, in a commonly held and very basic platform, conveyed the sense that local experimentation had national implications:

> That this meeting, recognising the beneficial effects which have been produced in this country by socialistic measures, expresses the opinion that a more advanced state of Socialism is both desirable and inevitable as its application offers the only permanent solution to the many economical difficulties which exist.[156]

Thus industry and economy were fair realms for this version of socialism; the cultural, affective and religious spheres lay behind a separate door. This is a significant division. 'Socialism' implied both sexual liberty and opposition to Christianity. Here the attempt was to cleanse it of these connotations and to appropriate it rhetorically as a representation of the economically rational society of the future. The conflict between the 'moral' and the 'economic' remains implicit here and was starkly apparent in the dilemmas of the LCC that are explored below. The Council pursued the 'economic' tasks of reordering the London environment through the manipulation of the relations of the LCC and the private sector and through the achievement of greater municipal ownership. In the eyes of some of its critics, these goals were too often conflated with a moral imperative, a joyless quest for regeneration and spiritual renewal repugnant to free-thought advocates of any politics. In this instance, the Spring Gardens Club speaker, and presumably the meeting, sought an accommodation with 'socialism' by divesting it of its anti-individualist cum libertarian and anti-religious elements. This suggests a plausible link with everyday London politics.

Though occasional club meetings were devoted to literary or travel subjects ('Alfred, Lord Tennyson', 'Gilbert and Sullivan', 'The Nineteenth Century in Literature and Art' or 'A Tour of Canada'), the leading social questions of the day remained the Club's lifeblood. Inevitably, there were many sessions devoted to the woman question and the family. Though a majority present at such meetings supported the demand for 'votes to women', some felt that only married women were uniquely qualified to vote, 'especially from their greater interest in the welfare of the country produced by marriage and the bringing up of children'. Similarly, LCC politicians boasted of women's 'municipal housekeeping skills' in seeking to attract voters who believed that women acquired special talents through marriage or possessed them by nature. Progressives and Conservatives shared this rhetoric.[157] The debaters acknowledged that if votes were first granted only to married women, these wives might simply be swayed by their husbands while the poor would be excluded from the simple extension of existing rights to all. Their grievances would remain unresolved. Most LCC electoral appeals assumed a ready fit amongst class, gender and voting patterns, a fit for which the evidence is slim. The club debate spoke to that literature. It was stated that, in fairness, all women should not get the vote unless all men got the vote, yet the speaker did not call for universal suffrage; if it were enacted, the majority of voters would be women, and 'government by women' was 'too great a risk for such an empire as Great Britain to face'. Further, the extension of votes to women implied women's right to occupy seats in the Commons and other state offices when childrearing ought clearly to be their central preoccupation.[158] Significantly, by the time of this debate, there were women holding LCC seats as a result of the 1907 elections and the passage of the Sex Disqualification Act.[159]

In another replication of London electoral rhetoric, a speaker on 'Women's Place in Municipal Life' pleaded for the careful election of women to suitable government posts concerned with the 'domestic life or public housekeeping of the nation':

Many of the members of local bodies were of the small shopkeeper type, of small leisure and less ability, where there were large numbers of ladies of education and refinement and with abundant leisure, who were at present engaged in philanthropic and social work, and who would be most admirably fitted to look after the ratepayers' municipal housekeeping . . . It was . . . only right that woman should have a deciding voice in that which so intimately concerned her sex, and although there were certain broad lines of demarcation, there were well-recognised fields of labour where men might assist but could never eclipse or surpass women. One of these fields was the care of women and children, both socially and morally.[160]

'Women' were not the actual subject of this or other pleas, any more than 'men' as a fully inclusive category were the actual representatives on local bodies or the purveyors of policies best suited to their 'sex'. The categories of 'men' and 'women' instead meant women and men of a certain background, of certain leisure and income and of a certain sensibility. Disguised as a generality, these class-bound categories of person represented discrete subgroups of people that the term 'class' would have connoted in the period. Just as there was no guarantee that women would vote for women or that workers voted for trade unionists or the educated simply for the educated, there was no demonstrable proof offered of men's or women's exclusive suitability for municipal work or of their predisposition toward generosity and acquired expertise in undertaking it. These were discursive notions.

The condition of working people was a frequent topic of club discussion. The scientist nature of LCC policy work necessarily influenced these conversations. A detailed record of London's social conditions could be found on staff members' desks each morning. Makeham's paper on the question 'How shall we save the family?', for example, offered a strongly Fabian argument and situated 'the family' in proletarian surroundings. Better wages for men, better housing for the poor, better wages for women (along with restrictions upon women performing jobs requiring heavy labour), the removal of the 'fear of starvation' and the 'endowment of motherhood' – all would improve the quality of the family and the race. The eugenicist biases and the programmatic pursuit of paid motherhood were mainstays of Fabian rhetoric.[161]

Makeham explained the employment of married women as a

negative result of poverty and of the organisation of economic life then current. The impossibility of women surviving without a man's economic support equally contributed to the deterioration of the family. Women were forced into loveless marriages. The 'endowment of motherhood' was construed as a demand for economic stability in the childbearing and childrearing years; it assumed both women's primary function as mothers and the State's responsibility for financing a natalist project. Makeham's socialism consisted in large part in his contention that only the abolition of class privilege could ensure the establishment of such a policy. Given the ready acceptance by his colleagues of the need to save the family, and their greater ambivalence about socialism's unique capacity to accomplish this, it is not surprising that Makeham's motion was altered on the floor of the meeting. The motion originally read, 'that family life can only be saved from destruction and put into a healthy condition by the establishment of socialism', but was amended and passed as simply 'family life can be saved from destruction and put into a wholesome condition by the establishment of improved methods of education'. The discrepancy between Makeham's version and the consensus version is a fair indicator of the distance between the views of a majority of staff and those of the staff radicals.[162]

Curiosity about the lives of working people and a search for a cure for poverty preoccupied many activists on the staff. This overriding concern with poverty also lay at the heart of Progressivism and was visible in the individual efforts of staff members like Maggie Tubbs, who joined the Fabian Women's Group in the 1910s and remained a radical activist until the 1930s, participating in the Peacemakers' Pilgrimage, inter-war period staff union agitation and in efforts such as support for the Help China Fund.[163] In 1912, Tubbs spoke on the question 'Does Poverty Improve the Mind?' Predictably, given her Fabian membership, she concluded that 'poverty exercises an injurious and stultifying influence upon the mind, and that how to abolish it ought to be one of the most pressing questions of the age'. She offered a typology of attitudes to poverty – the romantic, the strenuous and the sentimental – while criticising the notion of virtuous poverty. She called attention to the problem of a popular hostility to charity: 'Giving was as likely to cause hatred as gratitude. Working men were beginning to question the justice of the whole social system.' Such hostility was more present in London than was any widespread critique of the workings of society. Tubbs remonstrated that slum living fostered unsavoury qualities: 'the poor were rich in patience and fortitude, but deficient in sternness and enterprise . . . one could not have a bath with one's family grouped around one'. The poor were unchaste, lacking in 'bodily pride and dignity' and mentally faulty.[164] The Fabian Society's records list Tubbs as living first in north London and then at Kew. She worked in the Clerk's Department, and held Fabian membership in 1909 and 1910 and again from 1934 to 1947. In 1911, Tubbs spoke on Shaw's 'Moral and Civic Ideals', and her paper was reportedly the best ever offered to the club. She linked Shaw's writings with the call for women's suffrage.

This type of Fabian influence was so prevalent both in Council and amongst white collar activists that historians have often overplayed its singularity. The membership files of the Fabian Society indicate that teachers formed a major occupational subgroup amongst the Fabian Society in London as a whole before 1914. Of these, many were undoubtedly LCC board teachers. Even apart from Sidney Webb, Fabians such as R.C.K. Ensor, Charles Ammon, Somerville Hastings, Stewart Headlam, George Lansbury, Herbert Morrison, William Pincombe (secretary of the London Teachers' Association) and John Scurr served on the LCC.[165] The Poor Law Commission Reading Group organised amongst County Hall staff is but one example of Fabian practice.

The Fabian Women's Group, formed in 1911, undertook many projects that anticipated a municipal arena of activity.[166] Maggie Tubbs's socialism was fully compatible with her employment at the LCC. The Council's social policy was implemented by an intellectually stimulated and literate staff whose understandings of poverty were constructed along eugenicist lines. More in vogue than the philanthropic prescriptives of late-Victorian London were the socialist doctrines that emanated from a sense of innate moral superiority over those in less fortunate positions. Makeham, Tubbs and their socialist colleagues articulated a refined political vision that assigned a decisive role to people exactly like themselves in any forthcoming social transformation. The LCC was a laboratory for the experiment of attempting to begin to live out that vision.

THE £200 BARRIER AND THE PRE-WAR MOBILISATION

A vocal minority of staff participated in the Spring Gardens Club debates. But union activity, or what is better termed 'associational activity', through the formation of the LCC Staff Association and the growth of the NUC (whose branch was smaller than that of the Staff Association), involved the vast majority of central office employees by 1914. The Conservative administration that came to power in 1907 diligently continued the labour rationalisation processes initiated by the Progressives. Municipal Reform, as the Conservatives were now known, voted against instituting a minimum adult wage, which the Progressives would have supported. Several London boroughs had enacted such a measure. But a policy based upon the customary practices of trade unions and employer associations was shrewdly characterised in LCC debate as disarming the guarantee of a minimum wage. Councillors Frank Smith and R.C.K. Ensor attempted to put forward proposals about pay and conditions that were part of the NUC programme. These were rejected by Council in 1910.[167] Municipal Reform skilfully used Progressive insistence on trade union convention to inhibit the protection of non-union workers and of those whose pay was far more likely to be stipulated by an employer association than by a union. Amongst the vulnerable were not just the many unprotected sectors within the manual grades of Council employment: clerks still had no union representation, and NUC demands were not accepted as customary within the wider clerical labour market and thereby were rendered largely propagandistic in value.

As a further refinement of policy, the new administration erected the '£200 barrier', as it became known, a bar to upward mobility above the salary of £200 a year. These hurdles imitated the Civil Service bars which existed both at £200 and at £70 a year.[168] One of the motivations for the higher barrier was the contention that responsibility amongst this group of employees was difficult to judge, an affront to the clerk's notion of his own self-worth. Until this moment, a clerk had enjoyed a secure and promising position in relative terms and not simply through earning a relatively better salary, as we have seen. Though it might have taken him twenty years to do so, a clerk at the LCC had enjoyed a good chance of attaining £245 to £300 a year.[169] Longevity in employment had been the key to success; if a clerk stayed with the LCC over the long haul, he would make good financially.[170] Now this pattern would never be replicated in the experience of new generations of clerks.

After this profound restructuring of the classification system, promotion remained partly in order to allow the Council to continue to appeal to applicants of quality. But it was henceforth based only upon a real expansion of the required work of the departments. The tighter promotion system and the use of men from the Minor Establishment to perform routine work placed a greater premium upon education for those accepted into the classified staff. No high-salaried employee would be wasted upon inconsequential tasks of a rudimentary nature. This system conformed to the patterns of limited upward mobility outside the public sector. Even in the railway companies, those from university and public school backgrounds were now increasingly filling the higher grades.[171] This is the technical working out of the anxiety of status so often glibly ascribed to middle and lower middle class Londoners. Here it becomes clearer in a particular case that hopes *were* dashed, that promises *were* reneged upon. The materialism of the dilemma is clearer. Probation would now be enforced with greater stringency until the end of the first year of employment. Exceptional merit might continue to warrant special treatment, but an actual barrier to any routine promotion above the level of £200 was now in effect. One staff member described being on the low side of the barrier as 'waiting for dead men's shoes'.[172]

In summary, individual merit was now the only criterion for what had been a matter-of-course series of promotions, despite last-minute attempts by the Progressives Will Sanders and Stewart Headlam to postpone a final decision on the changes.[173] These provisions were extended to women typists such that advancement to the top of the second class would now occur only rarely.[174] Minor Establishment men also were placed under these provisions in 1910–11, as the typists had been. Much more pressure to perform well was added; this alone would 'justify the advance'.[175] The individual performance now brought benefits once accruing to a group of employees as a whole. While the immediate implications of this new direction hit only the LCC blackcoated staff, the struggle to oppose the new £200 barrier had widespread influence upon the more general mobilisation of white collar labour throughout London and the provincial cities. It divided the staff from the Council; it reinforced the suspicion of the municipality as employer. It called into question the notion of the progressive nature of public sector policies in a political climate in which much of the electorate had already registered its disappointment with the LCC by 1907. Paradoxically, the members of staff who most resembled those who were supposed to have dumped the Progressives at the polls were precisely those who were now under attack from the LCC Conservatives' labour policy.

A mass meeting at Birkbeck College in December 1908, on the heels of the announcement of the '£200 barrier' decision, drew over 600 employees from all grades, who complained that their terms of employment had now decisively diminished.[176] Though there was evidence for the press's conclusion that the staff favoured the Progressives, the meeting carefully declared its non-partisanship, fearing a threat to its cause if it declared a party preference.[177] For the first time since the 1890s, the Council agreed to see an employee deputation, but the visit was to no avail. The LCC Staff Association was born of this dispute, boasting a membership of 1100 in 1911 and of 2000 in 1919, a considerably larger body than, for example, the London Fabian Society.[178] The Association's early leaders were pressured by the Council to resign and some did so. Its founder, George Grigs, a first-class officer in the Education Department, was threatened with dismissal.

One participant recalled that the Council regarded these first fledgling organisational activities as if they had been gatherings of 'nihilists meeting in a Moscow cellar during the czarist regime'.[179] The Association finally won the right to meet in Council premises in 1910.[180] The 1910 representatives to its executive from the Clerk's Department were each from a different grade, and women staff of the department had their own representative. In the first year of the general leadership committee, a typist received the highest number of votes.[181] Association membership was opened up to the unestablished staff. The Association formed an affiliation to NALGO (the National Association of Local Government Officers). A cell of the National Union of Clerks (NUC) operated both within the Association and independently.

There was a concerted effort on the part of the Association to recruit 'fourth-class' officers, those who were at the end of the chain of clerks who could advance and whose hopes of doing so were objectively largely unfounded. But one of their number later admitted that many of them still 'had the sneaking feeling that they were all so able that no £200 barrier could keep them for long out of the first class in the dim and distant future when they would run up against it'.[182] The Minor Establishment, on the other hand, who were those arguably with most to gain from organisation and most open to understanding the benefits of collective action, were excluded from membership in the Association at its founding. This invidious policy epitomises the status-conscious spirit of organisation before the War and belies both its purposes and its commitments to its ostensible bedrock constituency.

The attempt in 1910 to argue the case for 'trade union' wages for clerks, using the pay demands drawn up by the NUC, did bear witness to the growth of an organisation whose efforts were aimed specifically at the Minor Establishment. NUC organiser Dolly Lansbury Thurtle was the daughter of George Lansbury, one of three councillors on the LCC Labour bench, which was formed in 1910; its other members were Frank Smith and R.C.K. Ensor. Even the Progressives, who were once again defeated in the 1910 elections, called for a trade union wage policy for employees at the LCC.[183] Supporters of the demand did not mince their words: 'It is simply scandalous that a clerk, with a sound general education, and a good knowledge of shorthand and typewriting, should be offered a sweating wage by the chief authority of the most important city in the world.'[184]

By 1912 the Association itself was prepared to take direct action on its own agenda and presented a memorial signed by more than 2000 officers from the permanent staff calling for a review of the £200 barrier decision. That same year, men from the Minor Establishment petitioned the Council for exemption from the 1911 National Insurance Act and asked that their relationship to the LCC superannuation fund be reconsidered. This was an effort to acquire greater pension rights, and it formed the inaugural campaign of the NUC at County Hall. The NUC demanded the elimination of barriers between the Minor and the second-class clerical positions, a pay rise, accelerated promotions, merit pay, a smaller pension payment and extended holidays. Any form of pension was rare in blackcoated employment at this time and the burden it imposed on low-paid staff undercut their long-range interests.

The crux of the dynamic of staff grievances as they would be expressed over the next two decades emerged in these disputes: the Minor men contended that their work was often of a similar nature to that performed by second-class clerks. Through collective action they demanded individual rights to upward mobility.

They wanted access to an improved position to the same degree that those above them possessed it. The fate of the individual was to be secured through the demands levelled by him and his colleagues as a collectivity. But the necessary outcome, should victory be achieved, would be to propel each man out of a state of greater dependence on collective action.[185] The NUC branch fighting this campaign was led by L.A. Goldwater of the Public Health Department branch at Savoy Hill. In 1913 it boasted 300 members, who were mostly Minor Establishment men.

The Council's response to the Minors' demands clarified and embodied the classic pattern of LCC white collar employment. It signalled the onset of a restriction of the possibility of betterment, which was the chief catalyst to the fury expressed by white collar workers in many professions, especially after the War. It helped to forge new self-conceptions and, importantly, new understandings and interpretations of the nature of state and local government employment. Though the barrier between Minor and Major sections would be formally removed, no advancement for merit was established in a division thought to have no 'scope for merit'. The Council granted a pay rise and, in a symbolic gesture, began to reserve 10 per cent of vacancies in the second class for Minor candidates, on the grounds that infrequent examinations and age barriers acted as arbitrary blocks to the acceptance of Minors into the upper grades.[186]

The nuanced divisions so characteristic of the LCC staff as an occupational subgroup were strengthened. While the Association rejoiced at 'victory', the Minors understood the greater realities of a relatively meaningless concession. The separation of Minors from the classified staff was complete. The two divisions were self-contained, and mobility from one to the other was not only structurally limited but financially compromising as well; few would attempt the transition, a fact that lent hollowness to the Council's offer and accentuated the increasing contentions amongst staff:

> The fact that a Minor sitting for the examination as a result of the Committee's recent concession would, if successful, be put back to £80 a year and in many cases, suffer a loss of income for a period of 12–15 years, not only nullifies the benefit of the concession asked for . . . but shows that the Minor men who did not avail themselves of the opportunity are not lacking in wisdom.[187]

Not surprisingly, antagonism between the NUC and the Association grew. Although the Association finally changed its membership rules in order to accommodate the Minor man, the NUC was for a time able to pull more than its own weight. It sponsored a lecture series and held 'Bohemian' concerts, while successfully defending an employee who had claimed unfair dismissal, and it undertook a successful struggle against a £100 barrier in the Tramways Department.[188] By 1912, over 100 men were 'marking time' at the £200 level. Despite further pressure brought to bear upon the Council by both the Staff Association and its affiliate, NALGO, in the wake of the 1913 election the LCC failed to reconstitute a more open advancement system. NALGO's historian noted that 'NALGO's leaders repeatedly and emphatically disavowed every suggestion that [it] was or might become a trade union'.[189] A few second-class officers received a series of fifteen-pound annual increments, but their promotions simply created what was termed 'a £245 backwater' beyond the £200 barrier. There were no new provisions for incoming applicants or for those recruited after 1909.[190]

The Staff Association faced the challenge of whether to affiliate to NALGO, a staid and moderate professional body, or to the NUC, whose radical reputation was anathema to large sections of the staff. The NUC propagandised clerks as a mass, calling them 'wage earners the same as manual workers'.[191] This doctrine elided the distinctions amongst white collar workers, which were often of a political nature, and transcended the simpler classifications afforded them by virtue of departmental or grade status within the LCC. But in reality, a wide gulf separated supporters of Goldwater's 'trade union' from the more respectable and heterogeneous Association. As one Association supporter wrote of the NUC:

> It would indeed be deplorable if the zeal of the officers of a union which, if wisely directed, has a career of great utility before it, were to be the means of betraying that organisation into a kind of 'internecine class war' against another grade of officers (the Major Staff), whose relation to their colleagues of the minor establishment may easily be misapprehended by a stranger, and who, in point of fact, have more and greater interests in common with the 'minor' than the latter have with most of the clientele of the NUC.[192]

Here the play on words is instructive: the term 'class war' has entered political discourse, yet it is diluted to signify seemingly needless hostility between grades. The notion of a community of interests, admittedly imperceptible to the outsider, is asserted. The claims of the 'left' are presented as divisive and false.

Yet the NUC actually urged clerks to join both the Association and the NUC. Its supporters maintained that the creation of a national municipal clerks' guild would best protect the interest of Minor men under attack:

Under the modern wage system the *employers* have acquired the sole control of the production of labour, and we see everywhere today under the guise of educational progress a consistent policy of flooding every branch of industry with a surplus of labour, with a consequent weakening of its bargaining power. The recent innovation of the Minor Establishment affords a concrete example of the helplessness of unorganised labour under such conditions.[193]

Absent is any wistful rhetorical appeal to the public-spirited employer. This staff member contends that employment in the Minor Establishment now paid less than it had paid previously for the same work.

Without a national union, any offer made had to be accepted. Only a committed minority of London white collar employees before the War believed in the notion of a white collar union. The NUC tried to speak for all clerks, advocating 'irrespective of age, sex or nationality, a permanent improvement in the conditions of their employment'.[194] The NUC collaborated with Continental white collar organisations just as the LCC Staff Association did. As early as 1890, NUC representatives attended the Third International Congress of Shorthand Writers at Munich. But the radicals did not always maintain a breadth of vision on matters such as women's labour; the NUC was under great pressure from its constituency on such issues.[195] Even women activists, in keeping with the debates recorded above, could speak in favour of higher wages for men as an ultimate solution to women's undercutting. Higher wages could mean that men would be able, as one woman put it, 'to keep their wives and daughters at home'.[196] The NUC sought to appeal to clerks such as those at the LCC, calling for a wage that 'will enable them [clerks] to live as educated citizens . . . sound minds, healthy bodies; hours for the development of faculties and their individuality'.[197] Still hovering at around 250 members in early 1914, the NUC representatives from the County Hall branch attended conferences entitled 'War, Trade Unionism and Political Action' and 'The Higher Education of Working People'.[198] The LCC branch sent NUC contingents to suffrage demonstrations organised by the Women's Social and Political Union and the Women's Freedom League, and an NUC-led contingent of women clerks was organised by an LCC typist.[199] The contradictions between their positions on suffrage and women's work were hardly resolved.

One month before the outbreak of war, the LCC branch raised its subscription fees, a decision of no importance given the number of staff standing unknowingly at death's door. But in this last peacetime decision, these early radicals lost the ballot to remain the voice of the Minor men; the Staff Association achieved an inconsequential victory. Those who stuck with the NUC prepared themselves, not for war, but to embark upon the course of bona fide trade unionism.[200] The war years imposed that goal upon an otherwise reluctant majority, though a 'trade union consciousness' had never fully taken hold even when the GLC was dissolved during the early 1980s. Instead, factionalisms, a panoply of ideas, programmes and organisations dominated. Neither a class, nor a caste, nor a status group emerged. Rather, political groupings arranged themselves within a discourse in which the lore of the 1890s and the early 1900s still hung in the air and continued to influence the everyday political culture of work at County Hall.

CONCLUSION: THE POLITICAL CLAIM RETHOUGHT

After condemning his subjects for looking to John Burns (this, two years before the 1907 Progressive defeat), T.W.H. Crosland's diatribe on suburbia reaches its apotheosis in his commentary on Wells:

The instances of rank suburbanism contained in 'A Modern Utopia' are well-nigh infinite. Everything is arranged to work out in precisely the way the London County Council could wish it to work out. I append a day-dream for donkeys of which the LCC will approve as an ass approves thistles. Great multitudes of people will pass softly to and fro in this central space – beautiful girls and youths going to the University classes that are held in the stately palaces about us, grave, capable men and women going to their businesses, children meandering along to their schools, holiday-makers, lovers, getting out upon a hundred quests.[201]

With implacable hostility, Crosland represented lower middle class Londoners as politically destructive because of their earnest gullibility. Yet in the same moment, Charles Masterman speculated that 'the work of the world' actually depended upon recruiting 'suburban and professional people' to the ranks of public service.[202]

Observers found the social habits of the lower middle class as varied as their occupations. The conviction of one commentator was unwittingly challenged by another's equally fervent and opposite description. The historians of the lower middle class have perpetuated these ambiguities: Hobsbawm borrowed the term *nouvelle couche sociale* to signify lower middle class Fabian activism, while R.Q. Gray wrote of the 'morality of villadom' and of the 'acceptance of hegemonic values . . . deeper and harder, to shake than that of parts of the working class'.[203]

Given this literary precedent, few who watched the LCC elections would have been surprised to glean from the press or from Masterman a notion of who was responsible for the defeat of London Progressivism in 1907 and why:

No one fears the Middle Classes, the suburbans; and perhaps for that reason, no one respects them . . . Strong in numbers, and in possession of a vigorous and even tyrannical convention of manners, they lack organisation, energy and ideas . . . So in an unexpected whirlwind of ferocity, a Progressive Party, hitherto unconquerable, finds itself almost annihilated; the general effect is that of being suddenly butted by a sheep.[204]

When the Progressives were defeated in 1907, even the NUC accused their 'middle class' colleagues of faint-hearted conservatism.[205] The press claimed that the Progressives were calling for 'the capital of the British empire' to be 'converted into a fully-developed commune . . . to translate the communist vision into administrative action'. The creation of a 'local socialist republic' was threatened, and those who had said no have become legendary.[206] Though the electoral data are inconclusive, suggesting a more complex set of circumstances, the 1907 defeat of London

Progressivism in a middle class and lower middle class backlash has become a historical commonplace.[207] Masterman perhaps bears first responsibility for cultivating this explanation as a literary myth. He described the Progressives' opponents in *The Condition of England*: 'they rise suddenly, impervious to argument, unreasoning and resolute'.[208] Ascetic, priggish Nonconformists had been overwhelmed by the suburban onslaught against sham social progress and high taxation, against the proletariat and its Fabianesque mentors and against Liberalism. The explanation of what was classified as lower middle class electoral behaviour in 1907 was journalistically linked to the intrinsic qualities of the lower middle class generally: small-mindedness, a lack of heroism, inwardness, class hostility and anti-urbanness.

Yet the history of the LCC clerks, both men and women, challenges Masterman's portrait of an immutable lower middle class consciousness. Their stories were like those of others in the metropolis whose experiences at the turn of the century were varied, intrepid and questioning. A sure sense of diversity, of debate, and of an awkward, stumbling experiment with collective forms of expression emerged. And the volatility of the mobilisations from 1909 to 1914, in which thousands of LCC employees participated, can be juxtaposed with the assertions of passivity, individual aggrandisement, pettiness and deferred gratification that were also present. The ambiguities, anxieties and frustrations that inspired the Staff Association, a society which serves well as a representative model of pre-war white collar 'unionisation', are apparent. Born of athleticism, militarism and of a rejection of the more radical NUC, the Association failed to serve the lowest order of men clerks in the division that would become the 'general grade' during the inter-war period. This division ultimately overwhelmed those above it by sheer numbers and became the principal tier of entry into LCC employment.[209]

Priggishness, snobbery and a frantic desire to reassert lost prestige led in part to the coming together of the staff under the new Municipal Reform administration in defiance of the £200 barrier. One negotiator perceived a staff grievance as the fact that 'The Council secure men who have been through the public schools and then do not keep faith with them.'[210] The early work of Cannan and Bowley demonstrated that LCC staff members were the best-paid clerks in local government in the realm, and, not surprisingly, the Association that was their pride was termed a 'glorified savings bank' by its more militant-minded critics. Herbert Morrison would refer to it in the 1930s as 'nothing but a ruddy goose club'.[211] Alec Spoor, NALGO's historian, reflected, 'anything savouring of trade unionism is nausea to the local government officer and his Association'.[212] NALGO restricted itself to the upper reaches of potential recruits and was not wholeheartedly convinced of the urgency of even the limited grievances of the LCC Staff Association. The radicals chided: 'The NALGO is all right for friendly whist drives and cricket matches, but if the municipal clerk wants his conditions improved, let him look to the NUC.'[213]

The privileges enjoyed by staff and denied most Londoners in clerical employment were not exclusively manifested in LCC clerks' complicity in 'bourgeois values' or their ambitiousness. The degree of critical activism and the engagement of social questions grew in spite of privilege or perhaps because the literate fluency in politics afforded by jobs at the LCC fostered an inquisitive sensibility. Questions about the relations between men and women, about marriage and about life-styles, took centre stage in a setting in which both activists and their more conformist colleagues reflected upon London, nation and empire. The record of what remains for us to know of their self-expressions indicates that these issues were primary, formative and irreducible in their force. The irony with which political matters were treated was a testament to their irritating pervasiveness. A *Staff Gazette* reader who called himself 'Neither' lambasted even that staid journal for offering 'an *apologia* for socialism'. These aphorisms followed:

> While an Individualist has usually got all he wants (? Ed.) a Socialist wants all he can get.

> Socialism is a plan to obviate the necessity of saying 'thank-you'.

> The strongest obstacle to equality for all is the existence of two sexes.

> A Socialist does at least know what he wants, and that is everything.[214]

These phrases remind the reader of the potency of anti-socialist ridicule as much as of the presence of a minority of 'fellow travellers' at the LCC. The contemplation of equal rights for women was easily abandoned. But at work, women colleagues, however 'unequal', did not disappear. For some women (those hired as typists, in particular) and for some men (those keen to marry), LCC employment provided not only a niche in the labour market, but a prospective spouse on the marriage market. Perhaps the marriage bar assisted women in securing a mate; it certainly also deterred them from planning careers which, as Jane Lewis suggests in reference to bars in other jobs, would hardly have been as economically viable as marriage.[215] The category of the 'new woman' remains elusive in discussing women at the LCC. To whom ought it apply? Women who chose to marry were staff activists. Single women, resembling both Hobsbawm's 'emancipated' women and Martha Vicinus's 'independent women', sought LCC employment, stayed in it, used it as a battleground for causes but certainly did not shun collaboration with men amongst their colleagues.[216] They were not the nurses, teachers and settlement workers who lived and worked in exclusive communities of women, though certainly some of them may have chosen a split existence; they may have lived privately in ways very much at odds with their workaday world.

For some men on the staff, postponement of marriage, the search for a suitable income and for suitable housing, and the sudden collapse of the junior clerk's chances for upward mobility were major preoccupations.[217] Their market position deteriorated between 1890 and 1914 in the face of rapid pre-war inflation, Council opposition to staff collectivism and the rising costs of living in London in the style to which they aspired. For some of them, remaining single and living in 'Bohemia' reduced the bills, and allowed for freer leisure. Perhaps it was possible to meet women in clubs or music halls without forming long-term attachments, as Jacob Flanders did. What is certain is that the staff reflected the conflicts between hedonism and asceticism that characterised London as a whole. This conflict haunted LCC cultural policy and surfaced frequently in the controversies surrounding music hall policy.[218]

The LCC was constructed as a Fabian meritocracy in which clerks were required to accept their redemptive mission without a fight. The Progressives had succeeded in instilling certain changes in the conditions of employment for white collar workers during their period of power. They struck out against nepotism with the establishment of standardised pay scales and a rationalised bureaucracy. But the cost of their expansive and interventionist policies was the blow dealt to blackcoated staff in 1909. The Progressives had been the first to hire women, to expand juvenile employment and to point the way toward a lower-paid tier of workers who could perform routine work. The activists saw the links between Progressive and Conservative policy. No bureaucracy operating under the fiscal constraints of the LCC could afford to continue to treat its house servants well. In 1910, John Burns, who had joined the Liberal Party, was not even amongst prospective MPs (as polled by the NUC) who were willing to support the inclusion of clerks in the fair wage clauses of public contracts – nor was Charles Masterman. Hilaire Belloc, interestingly, declared in favour.

The LCC boasted of being London's largest single employer in 1914 and certainly did command a larger workforce than did any single department of the Civil Service or any single industrial concern. When the typing section and the Minor Establishment opened up, thousands of hopefuls studied late into the night after work at lesser jobs in order to pass the LCC examinations. Yet even in success, they effectively forfeited the opportunity of greater advancement. The selflessness of long hours of overtime, the attention given to the pressing needs of other Londoners (whom they could easily come to identify as their social inferiors), the self-restraint so characteristic of the clerk who wanted to get promoted, were all galvanised by the LCC bureaucracy. Having nursed a civic-minded, rather idealistic group of young men and women in the 1890s, the LCC compromised its credibility as a model employer because it sacrificed those most loyal to it in the face of fiscal and political pressure.

This was not a process of 'proletarianisation' or of 'downgrading'. Nor was it a process of 'substitution' in which a 'gendered policy' literally meant that women replaced men. Women tended to undercut each other rather than affecting men's position in a precise way.[219] Instead, work was reassigned; it was rendered more easily done by less-educated recruits, though there had never been an easy fit between education and position at the LCC. The absence of the potential to move forward, especially given the assumptions enshrined in the LCC's propaganda, contributed to staff activism but not in the way that the Council had intended. Rather than the gifted individual of any grade seeing himself or herself as the central focus of Council labour policy, gender and age divisions separated groups of clerks. Each newly recruited wave became divided from those hired in the previous wave. Many members of the staff simply remained conventionally non-political, uninspired by Progressivism or simply struck by its hypocrisy. For them, social clubs, outings, reading, walking and, above all, romance were the stuff of life, at least until 1914.

The outbreak of war resolved one phase of the debate on the merits of militarism and of empire that had ranged from Makeham's condemnation of 'hysterical sentimentalism as to the glory of Empire'[220] to the NUC discussion on 'Colour' on the eve of the war, a meeting to which guests of colour were invited in order to participate in dialogue. It is useful to pose this small and clearly inconsequential discussion of 'race' against the record of exchanges with German clerical workers mentioned above. In 1910, the NUC had confidently prognosticated, 'These international visits have now come to stay, and it is hoped that they will play their part in not only drawing Anglo-Saxon and Teuton together, but in cementing peace between the nations of the world.'[221] Given the predominant commitment to an elevated notion of north European racial and national identity, the War would strengthen both the ties of the staff to empire and the credibility of socialist and radical critiques of domestic policy. The discourse of municipalism, which elevated the LCC as a vanguard body, was superseded by a nationally centred discourse as the War proceeded. Strands of thinking like those present in the pre-war NUC rhetoric, which held that socialism was as 'native' to England as 'Trade Unionism', 'Cooperation' and 'Factory Legislation', enjoyed greater currency after the War.[222]

Makeham and many of his fellow radicals never came home to participate in these conversations. Lionel Curtis, their former colleague in the Clerk's Department, was in many ways representative of the aspirations of those who survived from their generation of staff. In 1900 he had written back to County Hall from South Africa, 'But with ordinary Tommies, an officer who might study and understand his men . . . could do something to develop their intelligence, and communicate what are supposed to be the ideas of an English gentleman.'[223] After that first war, Curtis stayed on as Town Clerk of Johannesburg, as the architect of the importation of Chinese labour and ultimately as the theorist of segregation conceived as a means to secure white rule. He later became an authority on 'innate racial behaviour patterns' and a leading member of Lord Milner's Liberal imperialist circle, returning to Oxford in 1912.[224] Curtis's career was exceptional but his political choices were not. If few of the pre-war staff were readers of the *Roundtable*, many would have shared Curtis's views on imperial reform.

The 'alternative hero', anti-militarist Makeham, served valiantly in the trenches. There is little in his or many others' pre-war radical rhetoric that justifies surprise at his willingness to support the War, a willingness plainly displayed by the staff as a whole. Both the NUC and the Spring Gardens Club were dormant during the War and irrelevant to everyday matters.[225] On the other hand, those many staff who had served with the Territorials or the Volunteer 'F Corps' of the Civil Service Rifles under LCC sponsorship were poised for wartime service. Hundreds had taken advantage of free rail tickets to ride out to the Council rifle range at Staines for practice sessions and camaraderie in peacetime. Now they would test their skills in France and the Low Countries.

2

'THE INDUSTRIAL REORGANISATION OF SOCIETY': THE LCC WORKS DEPARTMENT, A MUNICIPAL SOCIALIST EXPERIMENT[1]

In 1902, the Reverend H.G.D. Latham eavesdropped in a London working men's club (for *The Cornhill Magazine*) and recorded the following conversation, occasioned by the memory of 'toffs' who had been routinely attacked in a court nearby the club's premises:

'and half an hour after he'd come out half-naked and robbed of every penny-piece! You don't see that now.' 'No, the County Council's changed all that' – 'The County Council? Bah!' retorts somebody else, and in a moment the fat is in the fire. One side maintains with zeal that the council is the working man's best friend, a model employer, and the best representative of progress in London. Trams, model dwellings, the Works Department, and several quite inaccurate statistics are fleeing at other speakers' heads. John Burns is prominently to the front . . . then the other side gets a word in edgeways. 'The County Council? Look what they've done down Clare Market way! Pulled down half the houses, turned the people out of the other half as insanitary, and then let tenants into 'em and sent all the respectable people to go and crowd into Holborn as best they can. When they get up their new buildings will they let 'em to you or me? Not much. Look what they charge down in Shoreditch. They'll let us go to Tottenham, that's what they'll do.'[2]

This conversation conveys the dilemma that rapidly gripped the Progressive LCC as it sought to impose its order on the London economy. Expectations ran high and were rarely met; the Council's critics absorbed some of its most coveted supporters, including articulate working men and trade unionists. In the foregoing instance observed by Latham, the Council is charged with implementing an inadequate and hypocritical housing policy. Inner-London housing estates remain prohibitively expensive according to these men; only estates distant from the centre, like one in Tottenham possibly alluded to here, are assigned to workers like themselves. This was a typical complaint of the Progressive era and its implications form much of the subject of the chapters that follow below.

The preceding chapter described how the blackcoated staff wrestled with the Progressive LCC's vision. In this chapter, the problems that the LCC encountered in trying to galvanise other layers of London's population emerge, a theme pursued again in Chapter 3. The Works Department referred to casually (and positively) above by the working men is its central subject. Though the Department became the world's largest public works project of its era, its demise would have been easy to predict: so much scandalous propaganda was unleashed upon it that anyone on the street could probably have seen that its days were numbered. But this account seeks to illuminate the rhetorical process of the Department's undoing for very particular reasons. The arguments for and against the Department reflected the first concerns about 'socialism' as an institutional political project to appear since the time of the Owenite communities. It had been decades since property was held in common for the useful production of services to a community of producers and consumers who were constituted (somewhat) democratically and who were in a position to exercise even indirect control over their conditions and terms of labour. In the pre-1917 world, such experiments did not occur every day. Even the local struggles for municipal control of resources, which began in the 1830s and resulted in the 'gas and water' socialism of the Chamberlain period, did not involve the use of mass proletarian labour, did not engage the trade unions to such a degree and often did not challenge powerful, vested interests with a plea for transforming a local economy as in the case of the LCC. The challenge was levelled in the largest metropolitan economy in Europe of its time. The trade union struggles that accompanied the battle of the Works Department were not simply a reflection of the dynamics of the building industry as a whole in London, or nationally. The Works Department contest was larger than the struggles that Richard Price identified as 'pressure from the men to exert a control over the work'.[3] At stake here were the ideas of a public sector for labour explicated in very large terms for the first time. No grander sustained and formalised undertaking had ever been attempted by a government authority in the domestic or imperial economy.

In light of the specific historical moment, what is especially important about the rhetoric examined below is the insistence that individual worth is lost in a process of collectivisation involving a government bureaucracy. Why did this thought occur then? Presumably, economies of scale had been effected in the private sector without a similar, concomitant loss. Even if we take everything said in a public inquiry advisedly, recognising that people often do not say what they mean, the ideas are so endemic and effortlessly articulated in the Works Department inquiry that they have an air of indelible authenticity. Long before the vanguard party, there is a fear of not being able to earn a shilling up front, ethically, through hard work. There is a loathing of 'false profit', of losses that are not really fiscal losses. There is a fear of collaboration between the corporate entities of the union and the municipality. And there is the very deep class suspicion that leads capital always to assume that labour wishes to work less, that workmen can only produce quality work for monetary incentive or for short-term political gain. There is an arrogant assumption that the masses cannot comprehend a civic aesthetic; civic virtue to them is unknown. The charge of 'economism' is made here perhaps before Lenin formulated it, and in this instance it is made by the opponents of organised labour. It is not surprising that these views should have had currency amongst London master builders or Conservative politicians, but it is useful to see them in high relief in the Works Department controversy.

A clear suggestion of historical timing also appears in the case: many views expressed by critics of the LCC flow from a critique of 'socialism' that is already firmly in place by 1896, well before collective property forms have become an international reality. This critique damned an unwitting Progressivism, a priori. It was not necessary for the Progressives to have achieved a consensus around John Burns's admittedly Darwinian notions of exemplary labour. It was not necessary for the unions to have all the Progressive councillors in their hip pockets. Since the deck was already stacked, the irreconcilable contradictions of the movement thrived on ambiguity. In Chapter 3, when this account turns to examine the ways in which Progressivism manifested itself in social policy endeavours, and in the realm of metropolitan culture, other very deep contradictions and ambiguities appear. The moral inter-rogation of socialism which informed that rectitude that ultimately resided with the honest businessman rather than with the corrupt public servant, continued. The 'moral puritanism' of the Prog-ressives, their self-righteous crusade to uplift and to regenerate despite an ever-decreasing bank balance, only further inspired the pundits who were having a field day with the Works Department.

RHETORICAL PRECEDENTS AND 'DIRECT LABOUR'

The prehistory of the 'municipal socialism' of the 1890s stretches back across a broad landscape of London radicalism. The following pages suggest that within this radicalism's various rhetorics, includ-ing the rhetoric of 'municipal socialism', what can be termed 'the labour question' was assigned a crucial role, either as a source of strength for dogma and programme, or as a source of division in building a consensus around the need for a transformative process of change in social and productive relations in London. The very recent past, the 1860s or perhaps the 1870s, had, for example, witnessed the publication of 'A Non-elector's Reform Bill compris-ing new institutions which will enable everyman to have a house, his own private property free from Rent, Rate or Tax, also to earn and enjoy £400 every year without asking employment from or being dependent on the interest or will of his fellow man'.

The author, B. Slater of Blackfriars Road, London, proposed public stores in each electoral district for the sale of goods at their 'real value', the collective ownership of land and factories by the workers and the public ownership of 'railways, canals, bridges, roads, docks, wharves, warehouses, markets, waterworks, tele-graph works, mail and postal services and cemeteries'. To these he added a provision for the unemployed: the construction of 'new works of public utility, which shall fully employ all persons who may not find employment in the present "crammed up channels" of trade and commerce, during the time absolutely necessary to reform society'.[4]

In his plea for the public ownership of utilities and for public works, Slater exemplified one strand of thought by which we come to 'municipal socialist' rhetoric at the turn of the century. He called attention to the incapacity of the metropolitan economy to absorb all those who are employable and presupposed the duty of government to address their situation. Slater can be read juxtaposed with the initiatives emanating from the movements for town planning, which did not necessarily share a strong vision of public ownership.[5] The struggles at the local level to install former Chartists as municipal leaders in the 1840s were followed by movements such as Joseph Chamberlain's municipal reform campaigns in Birmingham, and these form yet another strand of thought and practice. But Slater's radical republican statement is distinct in its linking of the problem of public ownership with that of unemployment. Herein lay the challenge to his socialist successors: how to contend for municipal power while at the same time using the municipal arena as a jumping-off point for the aspirations of labour; how to link the 'labour question' with the 'municipal question'? This was a clear departure from the charitable paternalism of the poor law. For Slater, the reform of society entailed a permanent end to unemployment. Public ownership would ultimately ensure that. His insistence on the private ownership of individual houses is noteworthy. Twentieth century council housing would have seemed unpalatable to him. Yet the image of London transformed by public ownership stayed with radicals and socialists, who accepted the existence or necessity of local government. Their attempts to recruit the support of London workers bore fruit. An important reason for their success was the vision of municipal socialism glimpsed in the practices of the LCC Works Department.

The movement for the reform of local government was led in the 1880s by the London Municipal Reform League.[6] Working men's clubs, the backbone of metropolitan trade unionism in this decade, petitioned the League in support of local government reform, thereby irrevocably linking the capital's fledgling labour organisation to municipalism. The LCC was created under the aegis of the 1888 Local Government Act in the period in which a campaign around the restructuring and expansion of government employment increasingly preoccupied the national labour and trade union movement, further linking trade unionism with the municipal sector. In 1881, a 'Conference of delegates from working men's clubs, and political and other associations', chaired by J.B. Firth, accordingly adopted the following resolution:

That this meeting of Delegates of Working Men's Clubs of London, representing many thousands of artisans, is of the opinion that the present condition of London Government is utterly unworthy of the Capital, and ought to be forthwith replaced by representative municipal institutions. This meeting, believing that the London Municipal Reform League is so constituted as to materially advance these ends, is of the further opinion that it deserves the support of the Working Men of London.[7]

Meanwhile, the campaign for higher standards in government employment was reflected in an 1883 TUC call for the eight-hour day in government departments, and in a subsequent TUC investigation in 1885 which revealed just how much overtime workers on such contracts were expected to perform so as to limit the effects of the existing nine hours' practice.[8] The 1889 Annual Report of the Amalgamated Society of Carpenters and Joiners recorded an additional and related complaint:

The subject of public contracts requires our constant attention because of the practice which largely prevails in accepting tenders from the employers who persistently refuse to pay the recognised rate of wages in their respective districts, thereby effectively preventing any trade unionist from deriving the slightest benefit from the employment which such work should afford them.[9]

The Society advocated municipal activism for its members in order to fight for more representation of trade union candidates on local bodies, a strategy that London unionists would successfully adopt at the LCC. While writing her history of cooperation, Beatrice Webb attended an 1890 conference of Glasgow cooperators and reported that one delegate addressed the issue of public contracts with a sense of foreboding, suggesting that some organised workers had come to regard any government employment with suspicion. He asserted that 'the workers employed by the State and Municipalities were less well cared for than by Private Employers, and moreover when the whole body of the people were employers, they would oppress the workers of the special trades they dealt with . . . each section of the working class would be oppressed by all other sections'.[10] Though many sectors of trade unionism sought standard wage rates in government employment, this comment demonstrates the early existence of a fear of losing control of the trades in the face of bureaucracy and political democracy.

Significantly, the employers in London's building industry had no quarrel with the contemporary description of wage rates being paid for public contracts. The *Building News* of July 1890 stated that 'the lowest rate of wages is that in the schedule of Government departments, and as these are tendered upon at a discount of ten per cent and upwards, it may be inferred that the labour supplied at such prices cannot be of the highest quality'. But the employers also believed that many men were willing to perform government work at a lower wage if 'relative' permanence of employment were possible.[11]

In exploring the problem of how to make a more profitable use of labour in the building industry, avoiding the pitfalls of government contracts for both employer and worker, one employer advocate suggested the use of economies of scale:

> In a large work various labour-saving expedients may be adopted, which in a smaller one would be unreasonable. In such as these the advantages of competition lie with those contractors who are constantly engaged upon great works, with the requisite plant for the purpose.[12]

Here was the presumption of efficiency with which the LCC would undertake the largest public works department of the century. These two assumptions of the employers, the first that a larger building works would garner greater profits if certain controls were imposed, and the second that labour employed by a public body was consistently 'underpaid', were both important to the increasing sophistication of the trade union position. The challenge was to effect both a strategy for the erection of government works and a strategy for the guarantee of trade union wage rates. The Carpenters and Joiners, for example, pointed out that it was hard to unionise the building trades because of the scattered work locations of the industry and that a larger works, therefore, offered a certain attraction.[13]

If the industry's employers preferred to establish larger works and even presupposed the coexistence of public and private contracting in building, the trade unions began to speak of 'direct labour', the direct employment of workers without the intervention of an outside contractor, as it was defined in contemporary language. In their agitation for labour representation on public bodies, linked to the continuing struggle for a wider men's franchise, the demand for 'fair wage clauses' occupied a central programmatic place. Their opponents quickly took up the challenge.

JOHN BURNS

John Burns, not only LCC councillor for Battersea but also socialist leader of the 'Great Dock Strike' of 1889, was the central figure in the direct labour controversy as it emerged in London in the 1890s. Burns stood firmly for the use of direct labour by the LCC in his electoral platforms of 1889 and 1892 and was responsible for offering the first Council motions for its enactment.[14] His strategy represented a fusing of the tactical militancy of the dock strike with the underlying parliamentary and legislative goals of a broadly conceived municipal socialism. Membership in the LCC was a cornerstone of Burns's strategy, a complement to his work in Battersea and a prelude to his adventures as a Liberal in the Commons.[15] His biographer, Kenneth Brown, attributes Burns's ideas in part to the mentor of his youth, Victor Delayhe, whose first principle was the belief that 'political power is vital in order to secure the economic reforms desired by the workers; consequently, the political and social questions are inextricably linked'.[16]

Burns's work on the LCC can be seen as an extension of his commitment to 'new unionism', an observation which casts doubt on the 'revolutionary' character of the meteoric new union drives amongst some of London's least privileged workers. The beliefs of 'new unionism' offered negative vindication of Burns's growing insistence that local government routes to power created a greater foothold for his supporters than did strikes that achieved mostly short-term organisational gains.[17] Burns's socialism depended upon his being able to show its utility in the form of immediate projects. And, rather than simply relying on municipal reform as a means to establish local power, Burns saw municipal reform as the first step in the establishment of a socialist political economy at the national level. Thus in March 1889, on the occasion of the opening of the new ferry at Woolwich, he stated: 'When socialists as a body have secured for the people of these islands, some instalment, however trifling, of the material improvement about which they talk so much and to attain which they do so little, Socialism will be a power.'[18]

The establishment of direct labour schemes and the enactment of fair wage clauses by public bodies would demonstrate that the intervention of the State on behalf of the trade unions might accomplish more than trade unionism alone could accomplish. Burns commented on forty-five of the sixty resolutions passed by the 1890 Liverpool TUC as being 'nothing more or less than direct appeals to the state and municipalities of this country to do for the workman what Trade Unionism "Old" and "New" has proved itself incapable of doing'. He reportedly described these as 'resolutions . . . asking for state or municipal interference on behalf of the weak against the strong'.[19]

In December 1892, Burns contributed a piece on the relationships between direct labour, public works and the question of the unemployed to the *Nineteenth Century*; it later appeared as a Fabian Society tract. Here he presented a more detailed outline of the future role of this form of labour in the 'industrial reorganisation of society'. He included a brief history of public works efforts, pointing to the example set by the Battersea vestry in its employment practices. These he felt protected older workers from the severe competition for jobs on the open market, forcing the employer, through the rates, to pay his 'share of the public duty towards the veterans of industry'. He referred to the LCC Works Department as 'the first scientific step yet taken for the unemployed question', a step that he hoped would lead to the creation of a 'Central Labour Bureau' which could keep regular records of the numbers of unemployed workmen and separate the 'labouring sheep . . . from the loafing goats'.[20] But these elementary schemes were not enough according to Burns. He even termed them 'permanently useless until the influx from the country is stopped, and machinery is made the servant and not, as now, the master of men'. He necessarily supported the municipalisation of agriculture not 'by the unskilled, unemployed plus an in-and-out army of loafers, casuals and wastrels, but by the best of labour attracted by those better conditions which would accompany such an undertaking started by people with brains along lines followed by the LCC in doing its own work'.[21]

While his desire to end unemployment and at the same time to assist only the better-trained and better-educated workmen may seem contradictory, in fact Burns's overarching theory reconciled both notions. Public works on the roads, in the parks and elsewhere could be arranged in order to cope with the worst crises.

The 'loafers' would be weeded out in a selection process that was anticipated by the 1889 dock strike, which had, after all, sought to eliminate the loafer from the docks.[22] The more respectable groups within London's working classes would immediately receive more permanent, secure jobs. The elimination of over-time, the use of the shift system and decasualisation through a careful public regulation of workers in, for example, the painting trades would play an exemplary role in the attainment of the most comprehensive changes foreseen by Burns. These steps depended upon the municipalisation of industry and would lead to the eventual 'nationalisation of the monopolies'.[23]

As Burns would explain on the occasion of the opening of Battersea Vestry Works Department in 1898: 'The system of direct employment is of immense value to the workman. For him, it does away with the present system of intermittent labour and hunger today, and bursting tomorrow. Properly managed direct employment earns regularity of work for the best workmen.'[24] Bureaucracy would accompany the institutionalisation of the direct labour programme. The call for the categorisation of labour and a concomitant system of 'just rewards' was a typical feature of popular socialist rhetoric and, in this instance, was articulated by the best-known socialist orator of his day, who would be remem-bered as the most powerful speaker of his time on the LCC. Comptroller Haward recalled Burns as the councillor 'whose oratory on certain broad questions affecting the amenities of London directly influenced more votes in the Council than that of any other member'.[25]

FABIANS AND THE INDEPENDENT LABOUR PARTY

The Fabian Society consistently supported campaigns for fair wages and raised the call for direct labour. Many of the Fabian tracts emphasised these issues and they appeared in a series of questionnaires that the Society asked the public to send to incum-bent and prospective LCC councillors. The candidates' replies were the basis upon which the society proposed to offer electoral support. A central role in Fabian theory was assigned to municipal employment. The state sector of employment was the exemplary arena, the model to be emulated, as Burns had described it.[26] Beatrice Webb wrote of the socialist future as she envisioned it:

'All I assert is that starting from state ownership, and reasoning from what we already know of the cooperative employment of labour in the municipalities and in cooperative concerns, the worker would receive the competitive worth of his labour.'[27] But Webb was disappointed that trade unionists often did not seem to recognise the potential of this form of employment, and wrote of an 1890 meeting in Toynbee Hall in which they expressed a preference for working for private firms: 'The fact that [local government] corporations pay no better wages than private firms and sometimes not as good makes them [trade unionists] cry out; what good their extending their action?' Here there is a hint of the concerns that would preoccupy some labour critics who questioned the new emphasis on the public sector; rather than seeing the State or the municipality as a panacea, they would deplore the contingent nature of wage negotiations. The wage rate was the crucial determinant of their political stance, and the Works Department would serve as a test case of their reservations about relinquishing certain prerogatives. Webb also addressed a related ground for labour discord when she noted that socialists seemed 'repelled' that workers needed the protection of their unions.[28]

The ILP was a small faction within London socialism, though it assisted the Fabians and the trade unions in the building of the Labour party and, on questions of direct labour, shared much of the Fabian perspective. The ILP clearly supported municipalisation efforts, as shown in this reply of the ILP City Branch to the critics of municipalisation: 'opposed to this anti-social view we have the growing sense of citizenship which would use the collective power of the community to organise on its own behalf the monopolies its existence creates. Between these views there cannot be any reconciliation.'[29] The notions of communal democracy and economic cooperation are linked. This connection was at the heart of the LCC effort: a newly formed, popularly elected body could, in theory, supersede the sort of limited control that Parliament exercised in economic affairs. A late nineteenth century London socialist was not eager to sever the tie between economic and political decision-making. Neither enfranchisement nor economic self-management had been tested. Here lay an unrivalled opportunity. As late as 1912, the ILP's annual report emphasised its activities within local bodies, and its programme included calls for the general extension of municipal enterprise, a minimum wage for municipal employees, fair wage clauses and direct employment.[30]

Even after the Fabians had largely abandoned the LCC as an activist arena, both because of the 1907 Conservative victory and because of their parliamentary focus, an ILP conference delegate still contended that his party 'would accomplish far more socialism on local bodies than in Parliament'.[31] Another echoed Burns's pragmatism: 'if there was any force in the repeated statement made that today socialism consists not so much in the reiteration of principle, as the active applications of principles, then on our local governing bodies we have every opportunity of proving this'.[32] Though the ILP was relatively weak in London, George Lansbury, a member of its Executive, sat on the LCC. His presence, as well as the presence of many elected trade unionists without Fabian ties, signalled the diversity amongst the supporters of municipal socialism. There was danger in an untested consensus; potentially conflicting interpretations of doctrine and action could not always peacefully coexist.

TRADE UNION CONCEPTIONS

'The Government must not be allowed to remain indifferent, the jobber and the sweater must be exterminated, and fair contracts and fair wages must reign supreme.' So read the Carpenters and Joiners Annual Report of 1890, citing the records of the London United Building Trades Committee.[33] The trade unions were organised in the fledgling TUC and, as represented most significantly in London through the official organisations of building trades workers, became ardent advocates of the pursuit of municipal office and of fair wage clauses and direct labour. Although these efforts coincided with the growth of municipal socialist discourse and derived strength from its popularity, they must be seen as a discrete and separate development within the institutions of the labour movement. Their distinct origins would allow trade unionists to conceive of themselves as independent of Progressivism in London, if and when the LCC failed to accommodate them. The rhetorical appropriation of an earlier trade union sentiment by LCC Progressivism, and its integration in some instances into a language of municipal socialism, should not be understood as the abandonment of an independent vision of municipal promise by London labour.

In 1888, the year of the first LCC election, the Carpenters and Joiners attempted to force the office of the First Commissioner of

Her Majesty's Works to end sweating and to institute fair wages clauses in all Government contracts. Agitation and support from Sir Charles Russell and John Lubbock, amongst others, resulted in limited success: the government agreed to put an end to the sweating of its employees, but claimed it could not enforce the payment of fair wages.[34] The Carpenters and Joiners thereafter began to push their membership to become more strongly involved in municipal affairs,

> helping so far as they can to swell the number of those towns which have elected to their school boards and other corporate bodies, working class representatives pledged to see that every contractor who undertakes to execute public work shall guarantee that he pays to his employees the acknowledged standard wages of the district.[35]

By 1889, the actions taken by the LCC on fair wages began to influence positions taken by the TUC. The TUC Annual Conference noted that its opposition to assigning over or underletting was part of a 'general movement . . . being made to secure its [the LCC's fair wages policy] general application'.[36] A more aggressive 1890 conference demanded trade union wage rates and that 'power should at once be granted to each municipality or county council to establish workshops and factories under municipal control'.[37] The 1892 proposals were bolder still, again attacking government subcontracting and calling for the use of the Employers' Liability Act of 1880 on behalf of government workers. The TUC Parliamentary Committee was instructed to fight for resolutions which would give government contracts only to those paying trade union wages, and this demand was linked to demands for the eight-hour day and the forty-eight-hour week. There was a call for the creation of a Labour Exchange on the model of the Parisian Bourse de Travail.[38] The labour reporter for the Board of Trade shrewdly noted that increased municipal action on the part of trade unions posed the question of whether municipal bodies would ultimately prove as efficient as private enterprise.[39]

The case of the Carpenters and Joiners illustrates the development of trade union municipal views in the 1890s. After calling for representation on municipal bodies in 1889, several branches of the union passed motions in solidarity with Burns's fair-wage motion of 1891, approved by the LCC. A movement for cooperative workshops then spread through the union in 1892, originating in the Poplar branch. The Camberwell branch, for example, wanted four depots of a cooperative building department established in their district to be administered by elected officers. The branch manifesto added:

> We feel that its establishment by us as trade unionists needs no advocacy. In the preface of the rules of our society (written years ago) it is anticipated. The whole tendency of our times declares its future existence inevitable. Many trades are on the point of adopting it, some have already done so. But chiefly it is the central generalisation of the ethics of industrial science; the facts of the last half-century demonstrating beyond dispute that while machinery (which displaces labour) and the industries, which the respective trades subserve, are outside the control of the workers, little or no permanent good can be secured.[40]

Here the understanding of municipal enterprise, conceived at the borough level, is related to a notion of trade union control and of trade union representation in administrative decision-making. This outcome is portrayed as the inevitable result of an empirical and ethical appraisal of the economy. The statement reveals a tension within the forces that supported forms of municipal socialism; nowhere would the Progressives speak of workers' control, only of better conditions in which municipalised industry might employ trade unionists.

In an elaboration of this vision, the union saw its cooperative workshops as competing with private contractors and believed that the quality of its members' own work would be higher and that its costs would result in a savings for the ratepayer. From the trade union position, this was unquestionable; their men would work harder if they were their own masters:

> Now, having proved to the ratepayers and people at large that we are quite as well able to build as the so-termed master-builders, when contracts are issued for municipal buildings, corporation and school building works, etc., we should be able to enter into competition with the master builders, and we do not for the minute think that they would have the slightest chance against us.[41]

In 1893, some branches began to keep track of which government agencies were paying trade union wages, and by May 1894 the Bermondsey branch, following the lead of the Bricklayers' Society, whose member H.R. Taylor had been appointed an LCC alderman four years earlier, pointed to the 'necessity of [our] trade being represented on the LCC by at least one member of the London District'. They asked the Executive Committee to 'take the opinion of the branches within the twelve-mile radius for that purpose'.[42]

Other unions representing workers outside of the building trades, notably the London Society of Compositors, consistently demanded that the public authorities for whom they worked pay trade union wages. The London Society of Compositors succeeded in this demand *vis-à-vis* the School Board for London,[43] a demand that was fully integrated into trade union programmes at the national and local levels by 1894. It was clearly articulated in the larger campaigns for municipalisation in which the municipal arena was given central place in trade union strategy. Trade unionists were 'seeking pledges from candidates' for the LCC from the first Council election of 1889.[44]

Within this context, the building trades' agitation was particularly visible at the LCC. When these trades federated in the wake of the carpenters' strike of 1891, their lobbying efforts grew more influential. Their commitment to the municipal sphere of action was evident. When the London Building Trades Federation held its second annual demonstration in Hyde Park on 29 June 1894, 50,000 people gathered to hear a resolution offered by E.C. Gibbs of the House Decorators and Painters, which unanimously approved:

> That this mass meeting of building trades workers considers the time has arrived for the return of members of the building trades on all local and municipal bodies within the London district to press forward the enforcement of the provisions of the agreement of June, 1892, by the insertion of trade union clauses in all contracts; and further, we pledge ourselves to use every legitimate means at our disposal for the direct employment of labour under trade union conditions, by all local and municipal bodies.[45]

THE ESTABLISHMENT OF THE LCC WORKS DEPARTMENT

The London Building Trades Committee (LBTC) was formed in 1888 partly in order to lobby the government for more pay on government contract work. After initial success in petitioning the London School Board, the LBTC worked with the London Society of Compositors in the LCC election campaign of 1889, on behalf of candidates who supported fair wage clauses and direct labour proposals.[46] The trades amalgamated further into the London Building Trades Federation (LBTF), winning important concessions from employers during 1891–92, which resulted in collectively negotiated wage and hour scales for the London district. Thus the LBTC quickly became a major force in the story of the LCC Works Department. The Central Association of Master Builders acted as the contractors' bargaining representative in these negotiations and, in turn, acted on its own behalf in lobbying the LCC.

It had already become established practice for the LCC to hire its own workers directly and without a contractor for certain works carried out in the parks and open spaces – for works on Hampstead Heath, Wandsworth Common and Wapping Recreation Ground, for example.[47] In 1890 delegations from the LBTC protested against the practices of contractors, charging them with 'driving their workmen to scamp their work' and 'employing inferior workmen at low wages, and complaining of common and unscrupulous contracting'. In what would become the generic language of the trade unions throughout the Works Department battles, the LBTC representatives asked that the LCC use only London firms, refuse to hire labour brought in from outside of London and commit itself to establishing direct labour projects.[48]

Further pressure was brought to bear upon the Council in 1891 over the conditions endured by the LCC's clothing trades workers. The debates about direct labour had thus far referred only to work performed by men; now women outworkers and factory workers engaged upon LCC work were mentioned. An inquiry recommended that steps be taken to regulate such labour. The LCC would now post wage rates, visit the factories and open the firms' books to inspection.[49] In debate on these proposals, some councillors indicated that they found the intervention of the LCC into relations between tailors and their employees insupportable. Wage minimums, as Aeneas Smith argued, would result in the position of English workmen's wages being 'reduced to those which foreign paupers were prepared to accept'.[50] The LCC was pressured by all sides on issues relating to labour policy. Even the Social Democratic Federation (SDF) attempted to intervene on behalf of the unemployed. When Rosebery, then Chairman, refused to admit an SDF dockworker to speak about the unemployed in the Council chamber, the man stormed in wearing a red Phrygian hat and was promptly arrested.

Though Burns was initially accused of being a mere 'trade union mouthpiece' when he urged the LCC to compel its contractors to pay trade union wages, his motion to do so was eventually passed.[51] Many government departments had not yet adopted the practice of posting a wage schedule for their outside labour. This was a Progressive victory, though Sir Thomas Farrar amended Burns's motion, ensuring that the Council would not, as Burns had desired, restrict its recruitment to London firms. In the light of negotiations between employers' organisations and the building trades unions in the London area, the Council's actions guaranteed that standard agreements on wages and hours would be upheld in this important sector of public employment. Six employers, members of the London Master Builders' Association (LMBA), and six unions, members of the LBTC, negotiated these wage rates following the 1891 carpenters' dispute in London. This development, fused with the movement amongst the Council's fledgling manual workers for unionisation, as documented by historian Stephen Williams, rendered the LCC a hotbed of trade union agitation and signalled a new type of discourse around the obligations of ostensibly progressive public bodies toward all forms of labour that fell within the purview of their policy and action.[52]

Even to this day, in order to drive into London from many parts of Kent and points further south, one must pass through the Blackwall Tunnel. Its curious mock-gothic facade seems out of place in the midst of never-ending queues of traffic seeking either shelter from the present hardships of east London or passage from suburbia into town. The tunnel became in part a monument to those who died constructing it, and the construction of new approaches to it was the occasion for the establishment of the Works Department of the LCC. There was a pressing need to rehouse persons displaced by this massive building works in 1891, and Burns and John Benn were successful in their bid to have a group of artisans' dwellings constructed by the LCC's own workmen. The *Building News* was 'certain . . . that the "labour" party of the Council [had] cried out for the "municipal workshop" since the formation of the Council'.[53] The high tenders placed by contractors who bid on the Tunnel project in response to the new trade union wage clauses reassured those who argued that it ought to be built with direct labour.[54]

The Engineer and the Architect were less than enthusiastic about the new department's prospects. Both doubted whether the Council could carry out the works more cheaply than a private contractor could, an important reservation in the light of later events. The staffing problems were immense. Officials would be vulnerable to bribes common in the building industry, especially given Progressive opposition to existing salary levels for Council officials. The Architect, Thomas Blashill, predicted many problems in hiring building workers:

> No contractor could make a job pay who did not take on and dismiss at a few hours notice. If any man who was dismissed should be at liberty to canvass the Members of the Council and to appeal to a Committee, the matter would become too troublesome and difficult for ordinary management, . . . and the cost must be largely increased. The only question would be whether this extra cost would be recouped by extra work.[55]

The engineer, Alexander Binnie, echoed the moral concerns of Blashill: the workmen's incentives would diminish, not multiply, in his view: 'men working for a public body are more apt to be lazy and careless than when acting immediately under the eye and supervision of a private employer'.[56] He contended that firms such as Pearsons, the contractors who had originally worked on the Blackwall Tunnel for the Council, had a vast knowledge and experience in the industry gained in part from executing massive works overseas in Mexico and in Egypt; how could the Council be as adept at paying men well and at keeping costs down? (In fact, the firm was not paying trade union wages and became the object of a workmen's petition campaign shortly thereafter.)[57]

But the LCC had finally committed itself to building a department to be administered by a Works Committee of councillors and a manager, Thomas Holloway. Burns wrote of this success as 'the biggest thing done for Collectivism and into which I have put as much time, energy and ability for four years as for any piece of work I have yet undertaken' – no small claim.[58] He had been closely assisted by Will Steadman and by Taylor of the Bricklayers. They had been opposed by Edward White, a builder on the Council. Their victory inaugurated a new era in metropolitan industrial relations. With the new factor of a massive local government building interest, sustained not simply by workers paid handsomely by private firms but, instead, by labour hired directly by the Council, the relations between government, employers and workers were perceived in a different way by some of the public than they had been before. The Works Department was now seen as a test case of municipal socialism or, as some would have it, as a new adjudicator of the 'labour question' in London.

THE EMPLOYERS' VIEWS

Building contractors were intimately involved in municipal politics, even if many of them were to form a very strong lobby against experiments such as the Works Department. Their views were no more monolithic than those of their adversaries. They were not unconditionally opposed to guaranteeing certain kinds of reforms in the industry or to the codification of what they saw as customary practices. In fact, the onset of municipal experimentation may have inspired some employers to political action on a variety of fronts.

When the first LCC was elected in 1889, the industry was prominently represented amongst the councillors. Amongst the victors at the polls were two architects, two civil engineers, four builders, a stained-glass manufacturer, a timber merchant, a saw-mill proprietor and a paper-hanging manufacturer.[59] Within two years of their election, the representatives of the industry were given the opportunity for public reflection when the Royal Commission on Labour was convened in 1892. Several controversial issues surfaced in these hearings: the right of contractors to employ non-unionists; the right of employers to keep blacklists and to circulate them; the Employers Liability Act of 1880 and the short payment period allowed employers under it; the right to subcontract; and the general decline of speedily accomplished work of high quality performed by tradesmen in the industry.[60] The discussion of this last issue assumed that wages had risen and that hours of labour had declined in the previous twenty or thirty years. Three and four hundred bricks were laid in a nine-hour day, while it was claimed that, in the past, a bricklayer had laid a thousand bricks in a ten-hour day.[61]

But the employers' journal, the *Building News*, generally supported the payment of fair wages, defined as 'wages paid to competent hands', and admitted that 'contractors know too well that the actual quality of labour is seldom detected and it is upon faith that many enter into competition'. It supported 'fixed conditions of contract', which were seen as the ultimate purpose of fair wage clauses: 'The effect will be to encourage a uniform rate of wages in the building trade, and as far as public works go, to prevent the too-frequent and disastrous results of undercutting.'[62] Thus, fair wage clauses were viewed by some employers as useful in helping to establish greater harmony in relations between the state, employers and men. This was not a defence of *trade union wages* for all. The crux of the argument was that while all workers did not have a right to a trade union wage, a fair day's work performed by a reliable workman deserved a fair day's pay. (Socialists Burns and Tom Mann had both referred to the best workman benefiting from the greater regulation of labour and, in so doing, had invoked the conventional distinction between deserving and undeserving.) The employers' argument did not necessarily cater to workmen of 'advanced skill' but rather to dependability and competence in any part of a labour process in which a given worker found himself.[63]

The leading employers' association in the industry, the Central Association of Master Builders (CAMB), a virulently anti-union body, still maintained that 'it was always in the interest of employers to keep good workmen as regularly employed as possible'. They were against both jerrybuilding and scamping, arguing for proper supervision on the building sites. Yet they argued, as many employers would do in the coming years, that trade union wages and the LCC were 'bringing master builders to a stop'.[64] The contradictions between interest groups amongst the employers were evident. The largest contractors, who figure prominently in the story of the Works Department, always sought compromises that were anathema to the jerrybuilder. In a predominantly non-unionised workforce, trade union advocates and representatives negotiated for a minority of more secure workers.

THE CONSERVATIVES, MUNICIPALISATION AND 'DIRECT LABOUR'

In 1894, the Liberty and Property Defence League (LPDL), London's militant ratepayer organisation, declared that the Irish Question had been transformed in significance with Parnell's death: 'the Labour Question is now given a first place on all authorised programmes'.[65] In justifying its new focus and the reconstruction of a 'London Ratepayers' Defence League' to fight battles over the LCC, the League explained that support for the 'natural right to freedom so insisted upon by the working man of the Chartist period' was revitalised. Opposition to 'personal liberty' was rife. This theory of natural rights in the LPDL's view fuelled present-day trade unionism: 'the majority of the in-roads are now made by the same trades-unionism that had its origin in that movement'.[66]

In this way, a critique of municipal socialism began to take shape in the metropolis that was informed by a shared rendition of nineteenth century history. For some, its origin lay in the adherence to *laissez-faire* principles. Even within a Tory paternalist tradition, a workman's individual rights could be perceived to transcend his corporate rights as articulated by a trade society. Thus, on the occasion of a visit from their colleagues on the Parisian *conseil municipal*, the LPDL spoke of the LCC as if it were linked explicitly to what was seen as 'municipal socialism': the LCC 'by accomplished facts and projected programmes has firmly established "municipal socialism" as one of the errors of the immediate future'.[67]

The usurpation of natural rights on the part of the trade unions had its counterpart in the abridgement of the natural functioning of commercial endeavours. This argument assumed the unprofitable nature of publicly owned industry. The LCC was perceived by its critics as a purveyor of unsound business, as unnatural in its drive for interference and regulation. When the Council commenced discussion of proposals for the use of direct labour, the *Spectator* commented:

> It would compel the Council to establish an industrial army of its own, would create a great desire in the Administrative Committee for needless grandeur in all the works attempted, and would compel them to keep their forces employed, even when there was no work urgently required to be done.[68]

The classic ingredients of many future arguments against socialism are present here: antagonism toward a workforce commanded by the State; support for the individual discretion of the single employer; the insistence that bureaucracy legitimate itself; the concept of waste, as directly linked to the absence of material incentive. Put one way, it portrays socialism as a system in which morality and politics hold sway over economic realities.

The author was quick to explain that while it was wrong to prohibit acts of collaboration amongst workmen (he could support the repeal of the Combination Laws in retrospect), wages still had to be 'haggled out' in the marketplace. Instead of the LCC establishing its own self-sufficient system of guaranteed wages and guaranteed work, workmen ought to preserve competition so as to prevent the artificial stimulation of wages and the concomitant forcing up of, for example, house prices. While the LCC did not have to worry about financial losses necessitating the immediate closure of its works, those in the private sector did. The absence of a brake on spending thus ultimately resulted in a very different outcome from that anticipated by the LCC when it enacted fair wage clauses. Total wages in the building industry would rise, but unemployment would increase as the amount invested in building remained static. Thus, the very constituency ostensibly aided by labour and socialist interests would suffer most. Again, the most basic argument with socialism is evident: it is portrayed as incapable of fighting poverty because of its insatiable need to satisfy special interests, interests whose participation in the system of work and wages was vital to its maintenance.[69]

Finally, the LCC's critics saw direct labour and fair wage clauses as posing threats to the organised power of municipal employees who would arbitrarily benefit from LCC schemes: 'The Council will make itself liable, if its hands form organised unions amongst themselves, to demands for wages limited only by the impatience of the ratepayers, who attend to such matters very little.'[70] Of the Progressive LCC majority it was pointedly asked, 'Surely they are not trying to bind the huge union vote permanently to their party?'[71] The spectre of a politics of class, governed by a spoils system, was invoked by the LCC's conservative critics. A free market in labour ought, it seemed to them, to allow for free electoral choice. Socialism at the municipal level threatened democracy with antipathetic interest groups.

THE LIBERALS

W.H. Massingham's *Star*, a mouthpiece of Progressivism, also expressed concern with the relations between those in elected office and the members of the building industry who would be directly involved in LCC contracts. But, instead of fearing the manipulation of the Council by the unions, the *Star* viewed the employers' side with suspicion, admonishing: 'The Council should be independent of any class which in its corporate capacity it would have to employ. We do not want upon it any of the sort of men who could be so much as suspected of having a personal interest in the selection of firms or the placing of contracts.'[72] It gave its support to the London Compositors' demand for an end to the practice of sweating by firms contracting with the municipalities: 'Public authorities should set a good example to private employers, instead of setting an example all the other way, as municipal authorities, and still more, Government departments, too often do at present.'[73]

Official Liberals often only committed themselves to a limited programme of municipalisation, thereby influencing the splits within London Progressivism that helped shorten its life. Emil Garcke, founder of the Industrial Freedom League, spoke before the National Liberal Club in 1900, arguing that the production of capital goods by private owners ought not to be disrupted by the State: 'not trading and commercial operations of the community, but the collective measures which make for the health, education, recreation, protection and furtherance of other similar interests of its individuals' were the proper tasks of municipal enterprise.[74] Like the Conservatives, Liberals of this persuasion saw neither rate reductions nor lower prices for goods produced by public industries on the horizon, and instead feared political nepotism.

Perhaps because the expanded franchise was still such a novelty, Garcke and others who supported his style of argument could only associate municipal socialism with a new style of political favouritism, merely the most basic form of political loyalty to constituency characteristic of an expanding democracy: 'the danger attending the employment by municipalities of a large number of men [is that they] will be able to use their votes for the purpose of enforcing their demands for shorter hours, higher pay and generally better conditions'. The coincidence of the members of a municipal workforce voting for the first time under a municipal socialist regime prompted Garcke to point to the fact that the Town Clerk of Birmingham had suggested that 'municipal employees should be disqualified as voters'.[75]

Garcke was willing to allow for the ownership of 'non-profit industry' on the part of a municipality and in so doing answered the conservative argument that public ownership could never be profitable; he assumed that profit was not the proper motive in the first place. On the other hand, he shared the conservative belief in a 'neutral' local state, itself swayed by the interests neither of employers nor employees. Thus, he did not lend his support to 'direct labour' and, unlike supporters of trade unions, did not see political independence on the part of public employees' unions as legitimate. A similar and widespread view of policies as transcending naked interest was a familiar rationale for opposing the extension of the franchise.[76]

While Liberal Progressives and the Labour interest went much further in advocating direct labour and public works projects, they too limited their conception according to the precepts of certain moral and economic views. The London Reform Union, for example, which acted as the official organisation of the Progressive Party in the LCC and borough elections, extended the notion of 'public services' as supported by mainstream Liberals (that is, services necessary for a ratepaying public) to include public works and direct labour projects that they hoped would provide antidotes to London's unemployment.[77] But, in so doing, they invoked the customary distinction between the 'deserving' and the 'undeserving' poor; only the first category of person should benefit from public works. Economic dislocation and the current absence of municipal enterprise were responsible for only some types of unemployment. In this vision of a municipal future, those who of their own doing (or moral undoing) found themselves unemployed would not be reintegrated into the labour force under the aegis of local government.

The Works Department was not to survive; a notorious scandal erupted in 1896 which began rather routinely and quietly. It was certainly not obvious that a chance finding on the part of the Comptroller's office would result in over five hundred pages of public testimony taken in two separate inquiries, the firing of several LCC staff members and a generalised political debate involving representatives of London's business elite as well as the metropolitan labour leadership. Sir Arthur Arnold, then Chairman of the Council, wrote that 'he could not remember in his experience of local government – more or less extended over forty years – an inquiry which excited a larger degree of public attention'.[78] The dispute that occurred is of the greatest significance as a signpost in the decline of the viability of municipal socialist conceptions of political economy. The balancing act between government, the contractors and the building trades, sought so desperately by Burns and many other Progressives, proved a sham not because of financial insolvency but because of the moral and political conflicts inevitably arising from an attempt to reconcile bureaucratic organisation and public service with the need to compete effectively on a labour market in London's key industry. An examination of the detailed history of the department and of the scandal which was its ruin exposes the hopeful expectations of the early days as both naive and provocative. But, even more importantly, it becomes evident that the very ethical framework in which a 'public sector' was justified had itself become an issue for all sides. This elevates the story of the Works Department to a place in our understanding of how the expressions about a 'socialist state', so familiar at the end of the twentieth century, originated in the experience of an experiment of the 1890s.

THE DEPARTMENT'S STRUCTURE AND THE NOTION OF EXEMPLARY WORKMANSHIP

Bartram's Wharf, between Waterloo and Westminster Bridges, was the site chosen for the new department, where a group of workshops were built to store building materials and to house the tradesmen whose labour sustained building efforts out across many miles of the metropolis. This site is star-crossed: on it now sits the carcass of County Hall, lone reminder of the LCC and its successor, the GLC. Ironically, the fiscal complaints that besieged the GLC's radical leader Ken Livingstone in the early 1980s were only too familiar to supporters of the Works Department. All of its earliest jobs were completed in excess of their estimates, the very first being a fire station at New Cross.[79] There were two principal types of departmental tasks: jobbing works, carried out under the Architect and the Engineer (and including the hoarding and shoring work of any Council department); and estimated works – housing, schools, and other structures of public use. As the Comptroller would later point out, the Council could not actually 'contract with itself' in the customary meaning of the term.[80]

Nevertheless, the LCC departments offered estimates for each project, and a system of 'debits' and 'credits' was devised, however artificial. Private contractors also bid on each job, and they often differed considerably in their offers and budgets. The Council's commitment to 'correct' inaccurate estimates had little precedent within the private sector and such a notion fitted awkwardly with the contractors' own considerations in which the profit motive lurked alongside the skill of anticipating the bare costs of a job.[81] But, the most serious financial discrepancies that arose were those between the LCC's own estimates and the financial needs encountered in actually carrying out a job, a discrepancy borne by the private firm alone in a privately contracted job. These tended to originate in some aspect of the problem of labour. In order to interpret the meaning of these difficulties for the wider problem of the failure to build confidence in a direct labour experiment, it is useful to know how the department functioned on an everyday basis.

A central white collar staff of a few dozen ran the department between 1892 and 1909, the year of its closure under the new Conservative majority. These employees formed the only permanent core of the department. Workmen, timekeepers and foremen were taken on only as they were needed for a particular job.[82] The top members of the staff were ranked according to the classification system described in Chapter 1 and were presided over by the Manager of Works, who earned £1500 during 1898–99, a considerable sum of money. Building and engineering assistants, an accountant and his assistants, surveyors and their assistants who drew weekly wages, drawing room and general office workers, all comprised the construction and accounting sections of the department. A yard staff and several permanent foremen occupied the workshops.

Much of the clerical work of the department required that those carrying it out possess prior experience in the building industry.[83] The National Union of Clerks (NUC) complained about the low pay of departmental employees. And indeed, departmental records list few wage rises for clerical assistants at the time of the NUC agitation of 1899.[84] These employees shared in other aspects of LCC staff life. The records of football and cricket matches indicate that departmental employees played on teams together. The department held smokers and was 'proud of its success in efforts to feed the poorest of children in six board schools in Lambeth'.[85] The Works white collar staff clearly associated with their counterparts at County Hall rather than with tradesmen and manual workers in the department's employ, replicating the overall segregated patterns of staff sociability. The department's workmen, on the other hand, had the whole county of London to conquer; wherever building and engineering works were under construction, the rank and file of the department could be found.[86]

Foremen were instructed to hire men from the neighbourhoods nearby the works so long as they were 'equal in all respects to other men engaged in a similar class of work'. 'Incompetent men' were not to be kept on merely because of their living nearby, and labourers were not recruited at the building sites alone.[87] Workmen could apply for jobs as individuals using, for example, the signature of a former local government employer. The sons of Council workmen and foremen were given prior claim to jobs, though foremen could not hire their own sons to work directly under them. After 1896, in keeping with the prevailing practices of the LBTF, the LCC employed a fixed quota of 'improvers': that is, apprentices without indenture, aged 15–21.[88] During the course of a given year, between the first year of the department until its last, as many as 3300 men on average were employed in the Works Department in a given week. This figure reached its peak in 1905, after the scandal of which this chapter is the subject, when 4051 were employed in a single week.[89] In the last two years of the department's existence, figures declined.

Those hired were not chosen entirely randomly, a fact that became politically significant. The policy of hiring improvers was enacted in the context of an ongoing discussion throughout the building industry on the decline of apprenticeship, purportedly an integral part of an overall decline in workmanship. Owen Fleming, the activist member of the LCC Architect's Department, spoke on the question in an open forum, stating that London youths commonly acted as errand boys on worksites throughout the industry, picking up trades as they went along.[90] The average bricklayer started out as an odd boy and a labourer in the suburbs and eventually attempted to 'move up' from speculative building jobs by presenting himself as a qualified bricklayer in central London. A master builder, in attendance at Fleming's lecture, commented that the average 30- or 40-year-old joiner still had to have his work laid out for him and that the central reason for decline was the workman's inability to come up with the premium required to pay for an apprentice. Workmen simply could not afford to teach youths the trades. The LCC Architect, Blashill, also present, added that he preferred to take on men from outside London (contrary to official policy), contending that London boys had 'too many opportunities to earn a few shillings a week as an office boy to induce the youth to work in a trade, or his father to put him to it'.[91]

The LCC played a further role in cultivating a certain type of

London building labour even apart from its Works Department practices. Until 1903, the Technical Education Department bore increasing responsibility for establishing programmes designed to improve the quality of workmanship in the London trades. The Council considered, for example, requiring plumbers to register, since of 134,000 men in the industry, under 300 men in a given trade could be found in training classes. By 1902, the Board offered training in five institutions: Camberwell School of Arts and Crafts, the Carriage Builders' School of Regent Street Polytechnic, the Central School of Arts and Crafts, Shoreditch Technical Institute and Westminster Technical Institute.

Although the principal of Battersea Polytechnic maintained in 1893 that many young men resented the drudgery of elementary classes and wanted only advanced work – they 'came in not to be masons or joiners but to be clerks of works' – it is apparent that by the century's close, training centres largely run by the LCC influenced the complexion of the trades themselves.[92] In 1902, the London Trades Council, authoritative voice of the most privileged and organised sectors of the London workforce, reported that 2000 men already working in the trades were attending the Board's classes: 'Special attention is given at the Trades Training School to the mechanical and at the Central School of Arts and Crafts, to the artistic side of the Building Crafts.' Lady Monkswell, whose husband served as an LCC councillor, founded the Shoreditch Institute where hundreds studied woodwork, building construction, engineering and attended a women's course in domestic economy.[93] The Council's desire to establish training procedures and to keep a portion of the hiring 'in the family', and its insistence upon competence regardless of a workman's residence near the worksite, promoted a notion of exemplary workmanship that had currency in wider debate in London: Fleming used it, skilled workers spoke of it, architects, Fabians and Progressives such as Burns adhered to it. The Council and the department remained faithful to this notion in its practices far more than it confronted the general problems of the unemployed in London.

WAGES AND CONDITIONS OF WORK

From the first days of the Works Department, the building unions petitioned the Works Committee, which oversaw the department, and the Committee consulted with them and with employers' associations. The LCC did not pursue an independent or neutral course. It explicitly agreed to pay the rates and uphold the hours set by the unions following a conference held after the 1891 Carpenters and Joiners' strike in London. This resolve was extended in 1897 to give additional recognition to negotiated scales, which contained the minimum rates and maximum hours 'recognised by associations of employers and trade unions and in practice obtained in London'.[94] Hourly rates were in effect in a majority of trades. Some of the engineering and electrical trades were included with the building trades in the LCC schedule. There were also rates for independent machinists and stable and river workers. Hourly rates, customary in the building trades, were paid to workers, who could be dismissed at any time; the week's notice was not won until 1962.[95] LCC navvies and labourers averaged more than 24s a week in 1898 for fifty-two weeks' work and averaged 29s a week for all but the twelve weeks of winter. They worked fifty hours a week at seven pence an hour. London wages were higher than elsewhere, but trade unionists perceived their purchasing power to be lower than in the provincial towns. As the Carpenters and Joiners added in 1891, in the towns outside the metropolis, 'the surroundings were more conducive to health and comfort'.[96]

The LCC wage schedule was indicative of the strength of the unions *vis-à-vis* the Council and was clearly of political origin; it was not a sign of the progress of unionisation in the industry as a whole in London except in the case of workers in certain trades to whom it was now customary to pay such wages when these workers were employed by the largest private employers, who also adhered to the schedule. The casual nature of the industry was not altered by LCC practices, but workers may well have been engaged more frequently or for longer periods of time by the Council than they were in the private sector.[97] This was in part due to the scale of the Council's undertakings.

But 'direct labour' should not be confused with permanent employment even for privileged, unionised workers. The only absolute certainty attached to it was the guarantee of a high wage. Plumbers working for the LCC in 1898 were paid eleven pence an hour; not until 1914 did London and Liverpool ship joiners, for example, earn a shilling an hour, the top wage in the industry. Charles Booth interviewed a London plumber in 1896 who worked a fifty-six and a half hour week (when he worked) and earned nine pence an hour. He regularly pawned his tools and did wallpapering when he could not find plumbing work. His wife made garments for sale, and their four shillings a week rent in a 'lower middle class neighbourhood' in London (that legendary locale) sustained a life-style which did not include the theatre or any outside entertainment; the man felt embarrassed, he said, to enter a public building.[98] The Works Department's employees' higher wages and possibly greater security may have provided them with a momentary rise in living standards. There were guaranteed holidays set each year by the Works Manager, and workmen's compensation was available under both the Employers' Liability Act of 1880 and the later Act of 1897.[99] Certainly, the pervasive presence of the trade unions at the worksites, in great disproportion to their visibility in the industry as a whole, fostered an exceptional political atmosphere for workers on LCC jobs.

Rigid practices pertained on the sites. From the moment that a man reported to the timekeeper for work, he was responsible for making sure that firewood was not stolen, for keeping a diary of major events on the site, for recording accidents, filing daily report sheets and ordering necessary materials from the wharf and elsewhere.[100] He supervised the movements of workers from one job to another and calculated costs according to expense; some trade societies allowed members to claim travelling and outdoor expenses while others did not. The official role of the foreman was clearly defined as that of a loyal manager for the LCC and as supervisor of the workers below him, yet his behaviour did not always conform to this prescription.

DISPUTES AND PROBLEMS AT THE WORKSITES: PRELUDE TO SCANDAL

From the day of its establishment, the Works Department was watched closely by earnest public observers. Each possible abridgement of employer or union practice, each departure from political rectitude was a subject of reaction. This reaction often reached a wider audience through an attentive press. In addition to wage and jurisdictional disputes, the Works Committee of LCC councillors had to deal with a host of outside bodies which expected certain concessions. In these matters, both the decisions of the LCC and the state of industrial relations in the London building trades as a whole were interconnected, as illustrated by the presence of LCC Alderman Taylor and a member of the Bricklayers Society, who sat on the original 1892 industry negotiation team as a representative of labour. This team got the standards negotiated in the wake of the 1891–92 strike and lockout.

The problem of non-union men

The 1891 lockout in London did not establish agreement upon the rules governing the presence of non-union workmen on the sites, though after the first negotiated wage and hour schedules, greater gains could obviously accrue for those minority of workers who were unionised, as indicated by the industry's historian, Richard Price.[101] These negotiations were the last in which non-union workers had any representation, though the employers continued to resist the growing power of union labour on the sites. The employers' opposition was fuelled by a desire to increase payment by piecework (on the whole a move resisted by the unions) and by the desire to maintain the practice of subcontracting. As the *Building News and Engineering Journal* asserted:

> Those who resist piecework for every class of work are generally the drones, while those who seek to obtain a larger share of the work in their own hands are the men who make our future builders and contractors . . . It is a ridiculous fallacy to contend for equal wages in the building trades. The attempt to reduce wages to a uniform standard is about as absurd as to propose that all men should be reduced to an equality in other things.[102]

Again, the rhetoric of exemplary labour is invoked. The notion that equality of work would mean a reduction in value or quality and the analogy drawn to the broader issue of civil equality imply sympathy with a strand of meritocratic thinking characteristic of utilitarianism and Fabianism alike. That this should come from an employers' journal is evidence of its widespread discursive popularity as an argument against trade unionism in many forms and ultimately against what were understood to be the egalitarian precepts of 'doctrinaire' socialism (socialism's own problematic notions of equality notwithstanding). This rhetoric suggests one of the important conflicts associated with the Works Department. Indeed, controversy over the presence of non-union and union labour on the LCC worksites raged from 1893 until 1896. Foremen and timekeepers were accused of asking workers to show their union tickets on the sites, a practice which the Council did not condone, maintaining that workmen had the right to work. A workman's union status was not a valid criterion for employment. On the other hand, the LCC was under pressure, for example, from the Plumbers Company, to hire only registered plumbers, and the unions constantly petitioned the Council on behalf of their members, trying to push beyond the already established commitment to union pay scales.[103] Unions demanded that their representatives have the right to visit the sites. Despite pressure from labour activist Will Thorne and from the municipal workers to accede to his demand, the Council ruled that only its own employees could check union tickets at meal times; no strangers could come onto the sites. In this way, the vital link to the unions that could exist on an everyday basis was partially severed. The prohibition of official visits insured that there would be less harassment of non-union workmen. Yet sentiment amongst the Works Department labour force was very strongly pro-union. In 1894, there was a militant struggle against the continued employment of a class of deal-porter foremen. Thousands of London workmen held a mass meeting to protest against non-union labour in the industry as a whole and against the employment of non-unionists at the LCC in particular. Three thousand LCC employees threatened to strike. The press predicted that the Works Committee would cave into pressure as a result of its concern over the 'Lambeth vote', and, in fact, a foreman in question did join a union; his decision averted the strike.[104]

This incident was the occasion for the intervention of the National Association of Free Labour (NAFL), which was involved in a growing alliance with the CAMB throughout the period. The NAFL, which had developed successful strike-breaking organisations outside London, sent a deputation to the Works Committee which alleged that the LCC was capitulating to the unions. The deputation brought along seven workers who had sought employment at LCC works. Each said that he had been denied work because he was a non-unionist. The NAFL explained: 'At the present time an overwhelming majority of the workmen employed by the Council are members of trade unions . . . those non-union men who are in the service of the Council owe their position to the influence of members specially exerted on their behalf.'[105] Burns and Will Crooks, trade unionist and councillor for Woolwich, were present at the Committee hearing and did not respond to the charges.

At an open meeting of the NAFL, the LCC was condemned for its 'tyrannical and arbitrary conduct in refusing to employ non-unionist free labour men'. The LCC discovered a case of one of its contractors refusing a union man work but also found that many of its own foremen were not union members. The NAFL had charged that only one in seven workmen on LCC sites were non-unionists, yet Council foremen submitted figures showing that of over five hundred currently in its employ, a third were non-unionists. Burns called the NAFL's contentions 'bogus' and 'flimsy', adding that 80 or 90 per cent of the bricklaying trade, for example, was unionised, and these were 'certainly the best of the men' (perhaps his labouring goats). Yes, the Labour members of Council *were* inclined to want to employ union men only.[106]

During 1895, employer fears of unauthorised strikes in the industry grew. The CAMB began to post notices at all their sites stating that there would be no victimisation of non-union labour; the LCC declined to do so on their own works. During 1895, the CAMB encouraged free labour organisation and an NAFL register containing 20,000 names of non-unionists was made available to contractors.[107] Under the Trades Union Act, independent societies of carpenters and joiners, bricklayers and others escaped membership in the LBTF and could have appeared on such a list. Finally, in June 1896, after a one-day strike against non-unionists on a Council site at Kingsland Fire Station, in which two councillors were charged by the Works Committee with coercion, the LCC voted to post notices at all its worksites stating that no man in the Council service was to be harassed by reason of being either a unionist or a non-unionist.[108]

Provocative foremen and jurisdictional disputes

LCC foremen adopted several styles of operation at the building sites. Some were members of various building trades unions; others belonged to foremen's organisations.[109] Some saw themselves as their societies' watchdogs, while others were in danger of provoking protest from the men working under them because they were non-union. Building employers in the private sector often preferred a foreman who had worked his way up in the ranks; a 'bullying' foreman did not win compliance from his men. Bribes and drinks were offered to foremen by other workers and corruption took many forms. As one employer reported: 'there are foremen who let apartments and take good care of those who lodge with them, whether they are good workmen or not, and of course the master is the sufferer'.[110] This employer pointed out that it was better to pay a foreman well and hold him to his job than to pay him too little and have him ruin the work.

Many of the issues under general scrutiny in the industry arose on the LCC sites. In 1893, a dispute at Claybury Asylum resulted in the banning of any foreman's relatives from employment at the central works. A timekeeper and his labourer were accused of falsifying pay packet accounts and conspiring to defraud the Council. If such cases occurred infrequently, cases of workmen bickering with foremen in the course of disputes were common, and the foremen were involved in the few strikes of the early 1890s.[111] In 1895, a group of bricklayers struck at the Cable Street Dwellings over being discharged for drunkenness and slack work. The men claimed the foremen had actually fired their co-workers for being 'grey-haired', thereby violating customary procedure in the industry. An inquiry determined that old age had not been the cause of the dismissals, but the case illustrates the simple fact that even if LCC foremen were perhaps more sympathetic to trade unionism than were other foremen in the private sector, their jobs did not differ significantly nor did the ways in which the rank and file perceived them.[112] Foremen were inevitably in the line of fire.

'Bad workmanship', so often invoked in debates about the department and the building industry as a whole, was seen by a union leader as connected to what he termed the 'subdivision and overlapping' of the trades. The employers likewise perceived a connection between quality of work and the uncertain division of labour that often prompted disputes between trades. Prior to 1895, the employers attempted to gain full decision-making power in demarcation disputes, a right that the unions refused to concede.[113] The Works Department witnessed its share of contests that the Committee and Council were seldom disposed to settle without advice and, by 1896, loath to adjudicate at all. The issue of piecework arose. The LCC was required by union regulations to institute piecework for certain trades, despite its prohibition in others. Sometimes, hourly workers and pieceworkers on LCC worksites, found themselves side by side, which caused tensions.[114] Other disputes were peculiar to the fact that the work in question was being performed for the Council, revealing the moral and political imperatives felt by various and sometimes antagonistic sections of the trade union movement.

In 1893, Sidney Webb became involved in such a conflict between a branch of the Plasterers and the London and Counties House Painters and Decorators Trade Society. The plasterers wrote to him: 'it seems in our absence we are forgot and left in the street hoping this receives due consideration'. Their rivals wrote:

> it is principle that is at stake and if the LCC does their Business in the way they have done it there, the sooner we Federated put a stop to it the better as a painter of over 30 years in London I have always maintained that we have no use with a trowel in our hands I hope we shall be able to put a stop to this sort of Business wishing you every success I remain yours in unity.

Webb wrote to the Works Committee:

> Here are two more letters about the case . . . in which painters were alleged [*sic*] to do plasterers' work and were discharged for refusing . . . when the painters refused to do the plastering, a bricklayer, and not a plasterer was sent to do it and he was seen laying Portland Cement hearths which I am told is plasterers' work. Would you mind asking for enquiry to be made into this? It is only by making a fuss about every alleged infringement that we can drive it into the minds of our foremen that we mean Trade Union rules to be observed. Might I suggest that it might be desirable for an express rule to be made and published to all our foremen that no man is to be called upon to do any work belonging to a trade union not his own.[115]

And, even if trade union rules were stipulated, the question of which union's rules were to be in effect still arose.[116] Other disputes were settled only following inquiries involving both the employers of the CAMB and the unions of the LBTF. A celebrated case involved plumbers at the Boundary Street estate who refused to submit to a decision made by anybody other than the Works Committee; they would not participate in a conference with other employers or with the rival fitters' union. Meanwhile, work desperately needed doing on the estate, so much so that Councillors Tillett and Freak of the Public Health and Housing Committee threatened to call in an outside contractor, an irony symbolic of the entire problematic: hellbent on serving the public, the LCC found itself denying vital services in an effort to soothe irreconcilable union differences. It had to threaten, in this instance, to hire non-union labour. The plumbers' intransigence foreshadowed the actions of other trades. In 1895, the bricklayers' union rejected the notion of Conciliation Boards. The period before scandal broke at the LCC was one of general mounting tension in the industry.[117] The Council's hesitancy to adjudicate disputes without the advice of leading firms or the opinion of the CAMB was a manifestation of one of its basic contradictions: its political responsibilities to the unions as a whole made choosing amongst unions invidious. The Committee took testimony passively, relying on the accuracy of foremen or supervisory personnel such as the Architect.

At the same moment that London building employers were seeking rights to settle disputes unilaterally, the Council was pursuing a 'round table' mode of conciliation in which the LCC convened interest groups rather than acting decisively. Few decisions were taken on the sites themselves and, indeed, few strikes occurred. Ultimately, however, the central task of completing the works in the service of London presented itself. This led Ben Tillett, a strong Labour member, to threaten the use of non-union labour. Once in power, a putative labour interest was revealed as a complex set of mutually exclusive goals. In fact, the notion of a monolithic 'labour interest' was to prove a fiction, a piece of rhetoric useless in other than episodic electoral terms. But this was not yet apparent.

External demands

Certainly the trade unions formed the most unconcealed everyday pressure upon the Works Committee and the department which it oversaw. The unions did not simply wish to defend their wage agreements vigilantly and to ensure that they were followed to the letter. They also petitioned in cases of workers' compensation and in the cases involving conditions at the worksites. Will Thorne himself took up the cause of a crane driver, three of whose fingers were amputated as a result of an accident that occurred at the Holloway Sewer project. Because the site of conflict was London, where the national leaders of the 'new unions' resided, each case like this became politicised in an extraordinary way.[118] This form of pressure only added to the existing tensions between the Council and its own long-term employees in other departments, both in the manual grade and among blackcoated staff. The LCC Employees' Labour Union met at Battersea Park gates in 1894 to address Council manual workers' grievances. John Jallop, general secretary, spoke typically: 'the Progressive members of the Council boasted of the generous ways in which they treated their employees, but the majority of the men thought that they were better off under the Metropolitan Board of Works'. Even the Works Department was useless. It was too expensive and the 'work was not done as well as by a contractor'. Burns was condemned for having one foot in the 'Liberal Party' and one in the 'Labour Party'. He was quickly defended by other workers present, but the jibes were nevertheless audible.[119] The solicitation of individual councillors was often a source of friction. A worker's complaint against the Council was taken to an outside, 'umbrella' labour group which, in turn, received private encouragement from an LCC councillor before it ever came before the Works Committee.[120] A workman approached the committee somewhat disingenuously: 'I have every confidence in the justice of the Committee and their desire to emancipate labour, and as you have heard only one side, I trust to your sense of fairness and love of fair play to hear the other side.'[121] He would not have ventured this defence if he had been addressing a private contractor.

The LCC 'first principles' were redefined by each petitioner, reinterpreted by each supplicant. Ratepayers wandered London observing the Council's works and looking for signs of inefficiency. A letter arrived concerning the Embankment improvements: 'there appears no lack of Steam Rollers but only one at work and that made very slow progress but there [were] a great many men standing about the others quite unemployed'.[122] A proprietary sense of collective management and an insistence on 'getting one's money's worth' epitomised the mass psychology that the Progressive experiment depended on. But the way it worked best was in the negative: waste rather than plenty attracted attention and stimulated debate and criticism. The more democratic the participation of at least a portion of the population, the more suspicion was bred, especially as the more affluent Londoners were those who had been most likely to cast their votes.

The state of unemployment in London provided a basis for other kinds of demands levelled at the Works Department. Labour and charitable organisations believed that it was a primary responsibility of the Council to offer jobs to unemployed workmen in their own districts. Controversy inevitably ensued. When a member of the Wesleyan East End Mission wrote to the Works Committee about the Cable Street Dwellings site, stating that there were a number of unemployed in the district, the spokesman added, 'but up to now they have been passed by, and strangers from other parts of London are at work. They feel hurt about it, and I think naturally so.'[123] He added that he would only recommend efficient workmen for hire. Private firms did not receive such missives. Even London's lower-tier authorities began to forward such requests on to the Council. The Fulham Union wrote of painters amongst its constituents who were in 'a state of destitution through being unable to obtain employment'. Some had applied for work on a Council painting job at Hammersmith Bridge and had been refused work. The Union wanted jobs like these to be reserved exclusively for men from Hammersmith and Fulham.[124] The North Lambeth Liberal and Radical Club asked for work on Waterloo Bridge: 'as there is plenty of surplus labour to be utilised . . . [they advised] not to delay the execution of public works in an important thoroughfare when a few more men would greatly expedite the work and would cost no more to the LCC or the ratepayers'.[125]

The LCC failed to honour some requests and sought to prevent charges of nepotism by even refusing councillors on occasion. The Committee also refused to meet the demands of groups who sought to contravene the existing system of labour recruitment. When the St Martin-in-the-Fields and Strand Board of Works Joint Labour Exchange asked to be notified of existing Council jobs, the committee flatly replied 'that workmen are taken on by the fore-men of the various works in accordance with the custom of the building trade'.[126] The department and the committee also avoided links with any other government or voluntary societies through which men might indirectly approach them; their loyalty to the trade unions in this way diminished their public profile on the issue of unemployment. These decisions were not administrative so much as political. Under the watchful eyes of ratepayers, of groups of workmen seeking employment and being denied it, and of a host of societies seeking consolation, including the labour bodies, the department was burdened with increasing criticism.

In the mid-1890s the collaboration between the building industry employers in the CAMB, the free labour advocates and groups
such as the Liberty and Property Defence League threatened the
Works Department. A virulent exchange in Council at the very end
of 1894, between Burns and a private contractor from Reed, Blight
and Co., foreshadowed the embittered debate of the coming years.
While Burns acknowledged that the costs of the department's
works had in many cases exceeded their estimates, he maintained
that departmental projects were of a superior quality as compared
to those carried out by private contractors. Incensed, the contractor's man pointed out that his firm had constructed the Private
Lunatic Asylum at Claybury, Dynamo House and the Electric Light
building and such public projects as the original foundations for
Yabsley Street buildings, Poplar. Demanding an investigation, the
firm offered to donate fifty pounds to any hospital chosen by the
Council, if its efforts could be shown to have been inadequate.
Debate was approaching a boiling point.[127]

Two months before the 1895 LCC election, the *East London
Observer* charged, 'The present majority desires to bring about for
London workmen a millennial state of living at the cost of the
ratepayers, while the Moderates, opposing the socialistic tendency,
believe that each man, even a working man, must create his own
millennium'.[128] The ideological temperature of the campaigns had
risen. Will Steadman, Labour candidate in Stepney, who was to play
a major role in the Works Department scandal inquiry, was
described approvingly, while the SDF was derided: 'he does not
indulge in wild Socialism and stupid Communism; he says plainly
that he is a working man and hopes to help in the cause of labour
and trades unionism'.[129] The election witnessed 'a remarkable
accession of strength to the Moderate Party'. *The Times* chastised
the Progressives for being content with the old Gladstonian cry of
'progress not politics' while the Conservatives had clearly organised themselves for the first time along tight party-political lines.[130]

The Works Department figured prominently in Conservative
electoral propaganda.[131] Reaction at the Liberal Club, where 'a
crowd of several thousand persons' watched the results, indicated
that the LCC's relationship to the building industry as a whole had
been at stake. One member 'referred to the results of the contests
as a strengthening of the hands of the sweater, the builder, and the
ground landlord'.[132] All the Labour and socialist candidates were
defeated, receiving very little support where they chose to run

(Chelsea, Whitechapel and Limehouse), with the exception of Deptford. Burns called the defeat 'a great democratic disaster . . . [caused by] ignorance and apathy'.[133] The peculiarities of Progressive losses in heavily working class areas tended to result in a dismissal of the idea that the Progressive LCC still stood squarely for what London's working class presumably wanted, the selectively restrictive franchise notwithstanding.

The *Parisian* dramatically noted that 'London, and, curiously enough, East-end London, the London of endemic and permanent pauperism, refuses to enter on the path of municipal Socialism. This is the end of a grand dream for certain enthusiasts. It is also a serious warning for the Liberal Party.'[134] The unwillingness of the Rosebery government to come forth strongly in support of the unification of London government was a particularly severe handicap for Progressivism. Unification and the municipalisation of London's water were two key Progressive demands in this campaign, and neither had government support. These projects were too dangerous for an already unstable regime to endorse.

The language of the campaign did little to assuage anxiety about the Works Department or to reassure Progressives that unity in defence of the department was in the Party's best interest. *The Times* carried an inflammatory letter from the General Secretary of the NAFL suggesting that canvassing in working class areas by his workers had convinced voters of the evil of the Works Department and that a majority of the electorate preferred to be outside the union movement in any case. The NAFL campaigned in areas of Conservative success: Battersea, St George's in the East, Mile End, Finsbury and Stepney. Indeed, as stated the London Reform Union had given the further extension of direct labour, not just at the LCC but in government departments, a central place in its electoral programme. A bequest from Passmore Edwards allowed the LRU to circulate three million leaflets during the election campaign.[135]

Some East End candidates included the demand for the LCC to undertake its own tailoring and bootmaking in direct response to the interests of the trades in the area, citing the Works Department as a precedent for such new projects. Even some Conservative candidates, such as H.H. Marks in St. George's in the East, were willing to come out for direct labour and trade union wages 'wherever practicable'.[136] The use of Progressive rhetoric by Conservative candidates suggests a weak case for any claim that all the electorate opposed 'direct labour'. But the victory of Marks over Martineau in the district does indicate that the distinctiveness of Progressivism had been compromised. There is little reason to doubt that the department was now known across London in a way that few government departments ever had been, especially in sectors of London's population where contact with any local government officials had been rare. Poised on the edge, wistfully incapable of transforming this interest into constructive support, the department now faced a period of reinterpretation, redirection and ultimate demise.

The dilemma of the Works Department reflected the discourse in the 1890s on the problem of the role of labour in municipal socialism and in other forms of municipal collectivism. The London trade union movement, small as it was, sought to make inroads into areas of government employment during the early 1890s. This was true in the white collar sector of employment at the LCC and even more so in the case of building labour. Short-term promises were made to the labour movement by figures such as Burns, yet a wider and more complex project than a direct labour department was envisaged by him. He assumed that a municipally controlled department would create jobs at trade union rates of pay and simultaneously result in the cultivation of a higher standard of workmanship than the private sector was able to achieve. But the success of this effort was dependent on the private contractors being squeezed out of the municipal sector of building and upon the cooperation of the existing labour unions whose members, after all, formed Burns's constituency. The unions, however, were first and foremost committed to the goals they had set *vis-à-vis* their employers in the emerging system of collective bargaining in the industry in London. They sought to act out their demands in the arena of the LCC in order to reinforce an adherence to trade union wages and hours while the employers, for their part, were quick to take up a new offensive as their will to oppose the department grew stronger. In June 1895, the tottering Rosebery government fell; the Liberals suffered a monumental defeat at the polls in the 1896 general election on the back of an exceedingly narrow victory for Progressivism the previous spring.

SCANDAL

In March 1896, the Comptroller, Harry Haward, dutifully informed Council officials that he had uncovered a bogus list of materials transfers from a Works Department project at Colney Hatch to Bexleyheath and the Lewisham sewer. These had been signed away at Colney but were never signed for at the other end, while at Bexley no work was under way at all. An inquiry into this rather routine discrepancy was arranged; the Progressive Henry Ward, who was chairman of the Works Committee, and the Moderate Edmund White (a builder) both sat on the inquiry subcommittee.[137] Initially, no party-political issues arose. The intention of those involved in this intrigue had been to 'transfer a portion of the "loss" or "profit" from one job to another but . . . not [to] alter the total results'. The subcommittee was to establish both the identity of the culprits and, more importantly, to uncover their motives, especially as no personal monetary profit could have accrued from the falsification of records.[138]

Thomas Holloway, the Works Manager, at first produced tickets for a small portion of the missing materials. He reported that his clerk of works and immediate subaltern, Dyson, had confessed to cajoling a foreman into signing transfers 'in order to get these credits into the books before the end of the financial year', an act in keeping with Holloway's own advice to his men. He acknowledged having suggested that if materials went unused, they might be deducted at form cost, a higher price than the department's list price.[139]

The wider investigation, however, uncovered a staggering £2000 worth of bogus credits. The department had been under orders from Dyson not to exceed a limit of £19,500 for the Colney job. After Dyson's handiwork was finished, the cost on paper was reduced from over £22,000 to just over £20,000. Dyson acknowledged that public disclosure at the end of the financial year had been a prime concern.[140] Dyson was asked if he found the various means of fiddling with the books unfair or dishonest. He replied, 'Well, we don't look at it that way . . . We had a lot of blame about difficult jobs. If we showed a big profit we got in a row – or if we showed a loss. The system of publishing the prime cost is fatal to the department.'[141] A general atmosphere of recrimination apparently existed between the respective staffs of departments. If Works showed a large profit, the other departments were made to account for an overly cautious and high estimate.

Dyson did not believe that his actions were unethical: 'It was to the advantage of the department . . . [he] knew what business was . . . chicanery in trade is not lying. To get the best terms is what has to be done.'[142] When his staff were interviewed, one man feigned ignorance; another invoked the disadvantageous position of the department in relation to private contractors as a justification for his actions. This defence suggested that the defendants did perform a crucial moral and political test of their 'crime'. Whatever liberties had been taken, the ratepayers' money had not been wasted, only shifted from one piece of paper to another, rather symbolically: 'while the ratepayers were receiving no harm, I was benefiting my manager and strengthening his position.'[143]

TENSIONS ENSUE

Holloway, Dyson and some of the staff were fired, but several large questions had emerged which would not disappear. The very notion of 'profit' and of 'loss' in a publicly owned works department seemed dubious upon contemplation. The words were used with reference to an intangible excess that might have existed *if* the Council had let a private contractor carry out a given job. Or would it have existed? Were contractors, as Dyson intimated, unwilling to tender at a rate as low as that suggested by the Architect's and Engineer's estimates? Were these estimates often purposely low in order to give the new department a lot of good work or out of a cynical desire to see the department fail? Were the actions of the staff merely *pro forma* practices in the building industry or the inevitable result of the licence that accompanied 'socialist' experiments – projects that did not allow an individual entrepreneur the incentive to make his own clear and very tangible profit?

Answers to these questions would be sought in a highly charged setting. In June 1896, the Works Committee had finally agreed to post the signs at worksites forbidding discrimination against non-unionists. During that same month, a strike of LCC plasterers, in solidarity with a general strike in the London building trades, forced the Committee to sublet the work that strikers had been engaged upon. Burns, who was on the committee, was under considerable pressure. The Operative Plasterers wrote to him in protest at the LCC's failure to reply to their previous epistle: 'For if the LCC are holding a brief for the Central Association of Master Builders, it is as well they should tell us.'[144] Burns evidently intervened strongly on the union's behalf.[145] Yet a constant undercurrent of criticism now plagued the everyday life of the department. Its failing results, defined now as real costs as compared with estimated costs, were attributed by Edmund White to 'the idleness of the workmen employed'.[146] Councillors and builders alike assumed that Works Department building trades employees lacked incentive to work rapidly and skilfully, partly because their political mentors were thought to have encouraged them to view Council employment as a sinecure and as less demanding than their past work for private contractors. A vote to award the department any additional funds was lost 'to loud Moderate cheers'.[147]

In related moves, the Council swung back and forth between concessions to unions and concessions to employers during the period prior to this first inquiry into the department's functioning. The Institute of Builders pressed for the affirmation of the principle of outside arbitration in disputes and the LCC began to comply with the request. Other union demands were upheld, including the protection of the twenty-five-mile limit and the restriction of overtime. Behind closed doors, in the Progressive inner sanctum, the Moderates' desire to thwart the department was acknowledged openly. There was fear that Moderate Works Committee members would succeed in creating 'a disturbance amongst the Council's workmen'.[148]

INITIAL FINDINGS

The first inquiry's explosive findings hit the LCC like a thunderbolt. Burns suggested that the Moderates' obsession with the Works Department was meant 'to divert from the actions with regard to the water supply and tramways while Lord Dunraven stated that the wrongdoings had been committed out of a desire to bolster up some particular economic theories of a party for political motives'.[149] Dunraven (W.T. Wyndham-Quin), hardly in unfamiliar territory, had chaired the House of Lords Commission on Sweating in the late 1880s.[150] In the ensuing debate, 'the Moderates gave their opponents the severest thrashing they had ever received'. The *East London Observer* deemed the remarks of Burns, Benn and Ward: 'from a practical point . . . ridiculous'.[151] The defensive acrobatics of the department's supporters were often transparent. Burns indulged in reductionism, arguing that such malpractices always occurred in the private sector. At least in this instance, they had been committed 'for the benefit of the people and the saving of their money'.[152] The *Star* did not defend the department as an expression of socialism but as 'the most useful expression of London's municipal energy . . . business not politics is what

London wants'. It called for firings, treating the affair as an ordinary business scandal. Accused of politicising the proceedings, Councillors Beachcroft and Hughes reminded the paper that the Moderates did not always oppose direct labour in principle.[153]

But, certainly, many in their camp were emphatically opposed. The *Master Builders' Association Journal* gloated:

> they have turned out to be absolutely unsatisfactory builders. The Socialistic effort has failed, for it has been nothing but jobbery. . . so much for the integrity of those entrusted with a share of the control . . . the state of socialism is such that those who work the hardest in a Socialistic community are just doing extra work for the 'love of a thing', for the harder they work the easier others labour.[154]

Here, shiftless direct labour employees are portrayed as having provided a rationale for the machinations of the simultaneously idealistic and panic-stricken office staff.

Lord Onslow, who would be remembered for posterity as 'in all respects a good representative of the country gentleman', pushed for the creation of an 'investigatory commission'.[155] He questioned the Council's existence in melodramatic language. He suggested that as contractors now paid fair wages, the department had no legitimacy: 'Mr. Benn's mare's nest had turned out to be a series of melancholy malpractices to cover the failure of a political party.' He was now anxious to hear the 'whole history and all the facts of this gigantic effort in the direction of socialistic municipalisation'. Even W.C. Steadman felt compelled to confess that the department 'caused more anxiety to the Labour bench than any other department in the Council', seemingly an indisputable fact.[156]

London was enraptured by the debates: 'the public gallery was again packed in every part. Scores anxious to witness the proceedings of "London's Parliament" were unable, even after long waiting, to secure a seat.'[157] There seemed little choice but to inquire into all things more deeply, and the LCC voted to appoint the commission proposed by Onslow. Beneath this motion were the gnawing practicalities of getting on with the building work of the Council either through an attempted *rapprochement* with the more respectable contractors or by renewed vigilance in the administration of the Works Department, if it survived. There was reason for caution in predicting the result, a fact exemplified by a letter written to Burns nine days before the first testimony was taken. It apparently refers to a controversial polemic written by Burns in defence of the department:

Dear Burns,

I am sorry you are not on the Committee of the London Reform Union which prepared the pamphlet . . . But you are misinformed, there was never any suggestion that the Works Department should confine itself to any particular work. And when the proof was submitted to me, I knocked out a reference to its comparative ill-successes in building, as to leave only 'rough outdoor painting' as the work in which it cannot compete with the contractor. It was thought unwise to claim that the Works department can do everything at once. I agree with that view.

Sidney Webb[158]

The Progressives lacked a unified and coherent approach, which was not surprising given their internal diversity.

THE INQUIRY

The Commission began meeting on 16 December 1896. Its members included Sir Arthur Arnold, the Council Chairman, who also acted as chair of the proceedings. Arnold had begun his career as a land agent and surveyor. He directed the construction of the Thames Embankment at the mid-century and wrote a book on this project, as well as several sensational novels. His *History of the Cotton Famine* was inspired by his stint as Inspector of Public Works in the 1860s. He was involved in land law reform and the early struggle for the enfranchisement of women, and, in sharp contrast to Onslow, chaired the Free Land League in the 1880s, a group favouring land nationalisation. As MP for Salford, Arnold had greatly influenced the particulars of the 1884 Reform Bill.[159] He was also a committed Liberal imperialist.

W.J. Collins, Progressive member for St Pancras West and vice-chairman of the Council, also served. The Moderate R.M. Beachcroft, a solicitor,[160] as well as three other members from each party completed the inquiry board. Amongst these were W. Davies (Progressive, Battersea), J.S. Fletcher (Moderate, Hampstead)[161] and A. Torrance (Progressive, Islington East).[162] C.J. Stewart, Clerk, was present at the hearings, and the LCC co-opted

E.A. Gruning of the RIBA and Edwin Waterhouse of Price, Waterhouse, to act as assessors. Waterhouse recalled giving three full months to the inquiry.[163] Only a brief synopsis of the more than five hundred pages of testimony is possible here. The most significant dialogue is, however, occasionally cited verbatim. Similar themes did appear over and over in testimony and exchanges, and were predictably varied in emphasis according to the perspective of the questioner as well as the technical, bureaucratic or political role or roles that a given witness had played in the everyday life of the department.

Alexander R. Binnie, the Council Engineer and an early witness,[164] explained the discrepancy between 'cost' and estimate as attributable to the price of labour on the Council's works. He revealed that the first direct labour project had actually been undertaken because contractors had refused to bid on it at all, fearing the cost of LCC labour clauses. In addition, the process of accepting bids was itself artificial; since his original estimates were always published in the LCC Minutes, contractors were tipped off to them. Contractors who did bid always included 'provision money' that made their bids higher in the short run.[165] And their fears of labour costs remained, though abolition of the department would not alter these costs. Instead, Binnie focused on motivational and supervisory issues: 'The men employed by a public body will, I think, in the long run do the work better than they would for a contractor . . . but . . . They do not do the same amount; they do not exert themselves to the same extent.'[166] Behind this leisurely approach lurked the problem of an inadequate authority structure. LCC foremen did not have the right to fire men on the spot as they would have in the private sector. Even if the very best men in the industry were willing to work for the department, only a better supervisory system could capitalise upon their talents.[167] Ironically, Binnie faulted the Works Department for not offering more permanent work, for hiring men only for the given job. The strict adherence to trade union rules and wages allowed few penalties for lax work or rewards for more rapidly accomplished work. Unlike the norm in the private sector, no threats of firings could stimulate a piecework system (given that a worker's job, rather than the pay levels at which he worked, were linked to output). The rewards *could* spawn more rapid work patterns; men could not be let go for failing to finish a given amount of work in a day.

Binnie favoured engineering works as direct labour projects, sewerage construction or 'one in a generation' endeavours such as the Blackwall Tunnel, especially as dishonest contractors could take greater advantage of underground work, which was hardest to supervise. His experiences in India, where the government hired labour directly, so to speak, had persuaded him of the limited case in its favour whether or not a 'profit' was made.[168] He felt that architectural works, which had incurred the greatest 'losses', should periodically be given out to contractors without 'undignified' and 'invidious' competition from the Council. More commercial spirit and professionalism were needed on the Works Committee. After all, if losses did result, it was the ratepayers who paid; a private contractor saw his *personal* profits diminish. He might work more aggressively but would be 'acting on different principles . . . Of course you know that the best contractor (I will be quite bold and straight) from the first time that he takes his contract until he finishes the work is continually trying to make money in every possible direction.'[169] Binnie felt that at least the trade unionists had helped in disciplining the workmen on the sites![170]

The theoretical contours of the inquiry are captured by this earliest testimony. The language of competition, of industrial spirit, the belief in the individual motivations of workmen and employers in the private sector permeated the proceedings. While this was a critique of 'socialism' that took a classic form, the acceptance of limited public works was not incompatible with it. At issue was the psychology of the marketplace; could that be supplanted by an alternative moral and motivational framework? Even those who remained least sceptical knew that the price for the experiment thus far had proved to be very high.

Thomas Blashill, the Architect, was asked by Beachcroft whether he could support the work of the department 'merely for the sake of employing labour'. Blashill, who, like Binnie, favoured a pluralist model in which some direct labour works and some contracted works were undertaken, ingenuously replied: 'I am only thinking of labour which has to be employed anyhow, and as to the mode of employment which would have to be done by a municipal authority or anyone else. The employment of labour for the good of the community in that sense is beyond what I have considered.'[171]

When Haward, the Council Comptroller, came to the stand, the committee attempted to expose the absurdity of notions of 'profits' and 'losses' as applied to public enterprises. Haward was obviously indirectly implicated here; his auditing methods had failed to uncover error until it became glaringly obvious. He tried to stress the absence of real 'pecuniary loss'. But on the other hand, of course, there had been no 'gain', though the books now showed the department almost £900 in the black. Sir Godfrey Lushington[172] pushed Haward:

'If we congratulated ourselves then upon a profit of more than £889, we were doomed beforehand, were we not, in the course of time when the accounts of the works before un-completed came in to find . . . a loss of . . . precisely the same sum?'

'Yes, you would find a corresponding debit to that credit.'

'Is it not clear, then, that the Works Committee were themselves at that time under an hallucination as to the effect of their own profit and loss account?'

'I should hardly like to say they were under an hallucination.'

'Well, misconception, we will put it?'

'Well, I would rather not say . . .'

'Would you object to answer this question: Do you think it high time that so fallacious a title as profit and loss account should now be abolished?'

'I think we might probably devise some better title. It is rather a difficult matter to exactly express in a short way what the account purports to be.'[173]

The element of Haward's testimony that proved the most unsettl-ing politically was his admission that the LCC, as a public body, at least theoretically possessed unlimited revenues with which to pay its bills. To most politicians in a pre-Keynesian world, this was heresy. Now the debate extended a step deeper. Capital restrictions on the department, which might have engendered greater integrity in the estimate system, were declared illegal early on. Haward pointed out that the Works commitments were not contracts made 'at a given sum'. Profit in the business sense never really accrued. Surpluses and 'deficiencies' were not reaped or owed. What remained understated was the fact that a vote to extend an excess of money was needed; the fundamentally political feature of the transaction, relatively autonomous of 'pure' financial concerns, was protruding.

A single lower-ranking employee was interviewed: Jacobs, a foreman. He contradicted Blashill and Binnie by maintaining that he had full control over his men and that he freely dismissed them for unsatisfactory behaviour or substandard work. He personally hired the men and often took on those whom he had known for years, and these workers followed him from job to job. He had not adhered strictly to the practice of taking men on from the immediate neighbourhoods unless they were good workmen. He was presently running a job in the Boundary Street area, where he came from, and in this single instance he had known and hired men from the area. Though wage rates at the LCC were not, he felt, higher than those paid on other jobs, piecework and scamping were still prevalent in the private sector; the best and cheapest work would be done by the Works Department. Jacobs was amongst the department's unqualified supporters: 'workmen seem to have a better spirit to work with the Council. They seem to do their work better than what they do for a contractor.' Jacobs resolutely refused, under duress, to tie this sense of greater morale to the security of wage paid by the LCC.[174] Again the cultural and political meaning of public employment, as yet unstigmatised by the latter-day associations with a 'welfare state' or Stalinist bureaucracy, is palpable. Let it be noted as well that Jacobs's job, as distinct from those of most others testifying, depended on the outcome of the inquiry.

From another vantage point, that of the Chairman of the Committee, Henry Ward, the inquiry commission was asked to consider the quality of work rather than the money 'saved'. The Committee was relinquishing arguments of fiscal success: 'Certainly with the Works Committee, the idea of profit-making should become, to my mind, at any rate, quite secondary to the quality.'[175] Ward shamelessly stated that he would find no fault with the LCC should it become the largest employer in London, prompting Councillor Fletcher to ask whether he was not seeking to 'deprive honest builders and engineers of a part of their business – men whose rates are expended in producing the very profit which we have been striving to obtain?'[176] Capturing the dilemma of Progressive labour policy generally, Ward glibly declared that the LCC had no duty to protect contractors and that if direct labour was viewed as 'a little doubtful among the ratepayers of London', he nevertheless felt that it was a policy that was 'in harmony with the trend of present opinion. One sees everybody moving in the same direction.'[177]

While some evidence submitted to the Commission supported

Ward's last contention, a high proportion of the data collected from local authorities and railway companies severely qualified his assertion. Some of these bodies did engage workers directly for some tasks, but there had been less than a wholehearted move in that direction on the part of many of these authorities when compared to the very grand efforts of the LCC. The ultimate check on the department, Ward explained, was the Council's right to abolish it; he tempted fate in order to support his otherwise cheery observation that at least the department, unlike firms it contracted with, could not go bankrupt. A pluralist model would force the hands of the contractors; certain jobs ought to be farmed out. Already the department was forcing lower bids by its very existence. The firms knew that if they bid too high the Works Department was there in the shadows, ready to undertake the work itself if it came to that.

As if to vent the fury of the opposing camp, the Commission next called Edward White, Works Committee vice-chairman and a London builder. He began his counterattack by asserting that workers in the private sector enjoyed the same conditions of work and wages as Council employees did. But his testimony painted a very different picture of the private sector in other respects. He admitted that there was a ring of contractors in the industry as there was in other trades. Indeed, contractors had upped bids enormously lest they risk incurring unforeseen expenses deriving from the enforcement of LCC codes. The policy of the 'open book' and the levying of fines by the Council were insults and deterrents to tendering by 'respectable' firms.[178] In the private sector certain union rules could be avoided; but the Council honoured complaints brought against contractors by the workmen, and this caused fear.[179]

White wanted the Works Committee abolished, if not the entire department. It could not function as a builder should; its site visits were 'subversive of discipline'. Firings on the sites were not always vindicated by the committee in the way that any builder would support his foremen. As for Jacobs, his jobs had all been done at a loss, despite his bravado on the stand. Of course one way for any foreman to maintain discipline was to be lax with the men. During a strike at Cable Street over non-unionists on the site the foreman had allowed non-unionists to be driven away; White would have fired any foreman who was so vulnerable to pressure from his men.[180] Finally, White also favoured engineering works as within

146

the purview of the Council. Built largely by unskilled labourers, these works were easiest to supervise. Here he unwittingly provided one of the best defences of direct labour in purely monetary terms. He said that if large works were given over to private contractors, the LCC would lose the part of the estimate which was provision money; under a direct labour system, such monies reverted to the Council for its own use.

In contrast to White, Henry Holloway (not to be confused with the Works Manager), then president of the LMBA, denied the existence of a builders' ring, stating that there were now too many contractors eligible to form such a cabal. The LMBA, he said, had 'no ill feeling' toward the Council and had assisted it. Leading firms did not object to fair wages *per se*, but they did not wish simply to enforce trade union wages. The LMBA wanted its part in the wage bargaining to be officially noted; it wanted the right to set a wage for non-union jobs. His testimony revealed the LMBA's fear that the unions occupied a privileged position in setting wage rates *before* negotiations with the employers occurred. The Works Department was clearly identified with the interests of the unions.[181]

After 1896, it would become increasingly fashionable to claim that the Progressives had ignored London's neediest inhabitants. This argument appeared in Holloway's testimony. The LMBA had a commitment to the perpetually unemployed and the infirm; the payment of low wages ought to be permitted unless 'the works of the Council suffered'. Councillor Fletcher led him through testimony that pointed to the fact that only 2000 of 200,000 London building workers were employed directly by the LCC at a given time. Fletcher himself termed these 'a privileged class of workmen who would work more often for the Council than for anybody else, and who would be in a better position than the 150,000 men outside'.[182] Yet no irreducible condemnation of the department was elicited. The opposition at this point clearly foresaw a scaled-down commitment rather than the abolition of the department. As this account demonstrates, this was in part because some in the private sector did believe in the establishment of public works of civic utility.

Mowlem is still a very large and powerful building concern in London, visible throughout a city where building is a constant noisy presence, a symbol of speculative spending and 'modernisation'. John Mowlem Burt, a forefather of the firm and a grandson of its founder, testified in 1896. The senior partner spoke of his works as less 'ornate', if larger in overall scale, than those of the LCC; Mowlem, Burt and Co. had contracted with the MBW and the LCC. The firm built the northern outfall at Barking. His remarks echoed those of Holloway. Those workers willing or forced to work for lower wages were the object of his shrewdly voiced concerns: 'There are hundreds of men in London who cannot earn the full amount of wages, but by the rules as laid down now they are prevented from finding employment under the County Council because you say we are to pay them certain wages . . . yes, they are very decent men, but they have got beyond their work.'[183] Like Holloway, he asked the LCC to give greater formal recognition to the employers' organisation, though not because it would garner them more money: 'We do say that we ought to be recognised as masters as well as the unions. You may say it is sentimental, but still life is made up of that more or less.'[184]

LABOUR VOICES

Three Labour politicians were called to speak, and their testimony shed light on the ways in which the 'labour question' fitted into pre-existing rhetorics of municipal socialism on the one hand, and trade unionism on the other, rhetorics which did not necessarily overlap. These three were Alderman Taylor, the former secretary of the Bricklayers Union who had represented his union on the Labour Conciliation Board and in the London Chamber of Commerce; Will Steadman, LCC councillor for Stepney (and later MP for Stepney), secretary of the Barge Builders Union, who had been active in the so-called new union movement and was presently vice-chairman of the Works Committee; and, finally, the ubiquitous Burns, himself trained as an engineer.

Taylor still drew a union salary and candidly described himself as 'specially representative of bricklayers as a trade', yet he denied having two masters when Lushington accused him of this. He saw himself, he said, as an agent of the Council and of the citizens who were served by it. When he had helped the LCC to offer painting jobs at Hammersmith Bridge, for example, he had done so 'on account of the deputations and requisitions coming from all sorts of bodies outside this Council when there was a large body of unemployed'.[185]

As a Works Committee member, Taylor was in the habit of

visiting the worksites as many as sixteen times a month. He claimed that the events surrounding the establishment of the department were well known to unionists and that workmen were indeed 'jealous' of the reputation of the work carried out by the Council and its departments.[186] He freely stated that when the department was created, the men had mistakenly believed that they were meant to value quality over speed, a misconception now corrected. Yet Taylor added later that they would refuse to carry out stamped work for the Council or to perform work incorrectly, not out of self-interest, but in order to preserve the best standards. He was questioned about referring to idle men on the jobs and replied that men were no more idle than on other jobs; there were, after all, 'some men who were born a little bit tired'.[187] He opposed strikes on Council works, though admitted that LCC wages could support funds for other unionists who did strike. He did not dispute the notion that a majority of LCC direct labour employees were unionists in disproportion to the 20 per cent of building workers otherwise unionised, but he denied that trade rules were so strict as to forbid the employment of improvers and older workers. He called for greater discipline on the sites.[188]

Steadman recounted the implementation of direct labour policy in his vestry, even before it was enacted by the LCC, a step taken in other lower-tier bodies and by other municipalities throughout the country. He too felt that the Works Department ought to be extended to become the largest London employer. Beachcroft, obviously alarmed, wondered whether the elimination of private contracting would make it impossible to judge the true value of LCC work. Unmoved, Steadman acknowledged that the issue was one of no concern to him. He was very supportive of the workmen on the site, as Taylor before him had been.[189]

John Burns was characteristically less inhibited than the other Labour members, if not necessarily as militant in his speech as Steadman had been. In many respects, his was the key testimony of the investigation. He had expert knowledge of the industry and exuded a sense of confidence in the department and in its rectitude. He explained the origin of the department not simply in terms of the desire to overcome the 'fishy' behaviour of the private contractors with regard to the York Road Sewer but in terms of its overall good for the workmen: better wages and greater safety at work and more jobs through the abolition of overtime.[190] There were also the cost benefits which accrued to the Council and the higher quality of work performed. He spoke of the launching of the department in the same breath as he did of the anti-sweating campaign of those years. He pointed to the use of direct labour by government departments and cited the strides made in public health in Battersea where direct labour departments played a major role in improving public services. Importantly, he flatly *denied* the charge that the Progressives had fought for the Works Department in order eventually to assert control over London labour markets.

Burns did not deny loathing the practices of the private contractors. He pointed to the pressure brought to bear upon them by the failure rate in the industry: 740 failures a year and 2800 in the previous four years with losses amounting to three million pounds. 'As a rule building does not lend itself to the highest form of either personal or civic worth.'[191] No doubt confounding his listeners, Burns simultaneously argued that the very best contractors would agree with his description of the industry, of which he knew a great deal, having been himself employed at Mowlem's for years!

Burns defended the wording of the contract, and its use by the LCC, as essential to the fight to guarantee trade union wages. Without its insistent wording, Burns reckoned that the contractors would rely on the workmen's poverty and lack of organisation to force lower wages. Predictably, he invoked the notions of meritocracy and of exemplary workmanship: when the Council paid the highest wage, it earned the best work partly because the best men sought jobs with the Council, jobs that were attractive because they often led to long-term employment. As compared to conditions in the private sector, there was less incentive for Council workmen to dawdle on the job since another job might quickly follow.

When asked about the potential for strikes on Council works, Burns noted that the Labour members of the Works Committee had thus far failed to capitulate to what he termed the sectional interests of particular trades or the 'labour interest generally', quite an admission.[192] However disingenuous this may have sounded, Burns's experience with 'New Unionism' may well have convinced him of the necessity of standing for a more transcendent populist vision of the future, a stance incompatible with trade union particularism. At the very least, it would have seemed impolitic to him to be particular given the risks the Progressives now faced. When painters at Westminster Bridge demanded that all workers receive a higher wage only reserved for dangerous work, Burns and his allies had refused support. A dispute at Kingsland Fire Station, on the other hand, was an instance in which Burns believed that the NAFL had put a non-unionist up to disrupting the job in its last stages and, not coincidentally, just at the time of the election:

'You do not think that it was a case of seventy wolves complaining that three or four lambs had disturbed their water?'

'No, I think that it was a case of the non-unionist men having the opinion of the Irish juryman, who said as an excuse for his own obstinacy that eleven more obstinate jurymen he had never met in his life.'[193]

Slurs notwithstanding, Burns must have perplexed his questioners. Instead of closing his analysis of strikes by arguing that Council workmen were unlikely to go out in the future, he placed the onus back upon the Council. Workmen might well go out with their fellows in any generalised strike in the industry, but in the case of an employer lockout, why should the LCC necessarily support the actions of private employers? The Council need not follow suit. In this respect at least, LCC employees need not be compelled to participate in all labour action. Here he implied that being the model employer could carry with it more than just the role of setting the pace in the payment of trade union wages. As for having his own relatives in the industry, he had advised them to stay away: 'If Burns had any relations London would have heard of it years ago.'[194] He categorically denied the statement that LCC workers were directly involved in paying his own wages. He was not a union official: 'I was elected by my district for my virtues other than being a labour leader.' Nor had he found a multitude of Battersea workmen employed on the sites. As for related charges – he did not believe that the unionists were prejudiced against older workers and improvers. Most unions allowed the elderly to earn a few shillings less than regular pay even if they were not unionists. The unionised workers looked the other way out of compassion.

Though Burns believed that the department ought to take on sewerage and engineering works 'mainly on the grounds of safety and health', successes such as the pumping stations justified further projects like the building of a town hall or the Blackwall Tunnel.[195] All types of work ought to be done. Waste was a necessary first hazard of opening up any business. How could success be judged narrowly on the basis of 'cost versus estimate'? Here he repeated the argument of his colleagues before him. Fletcher tried to catch Burns in a paradox:

'Is there any class of work that strikes you as work that ought to be put out to contract in order to be better done?'

'No . . .'

'You spoke of the scarcity of good contractors of the type of Mr. Burt. Do you not think that we should be encouraging a race of good contractors if we shared our employment among them?'

'I do not think that you and I could seek re-election on the ground of making the County Council a sort of forcing house or conservatory for good contractors. It is not our business.'[196]

When questioned about his site visits, Burns conveyed an intimate knowledge of the actual works. But, when charged with 'professionalism', he did not take the bait, arguing instead that having 'amateurs' on the committee did no harm. Public-minded men often had clearer heads than the overly technically oriented specialists. The committee ought to continue as presently constituted. He warned that the Moderates were seeking to 'starve out' the department so that its costs would rise proportionate to the fewer numbers of jobs it was allowed to take on. Ostensibly adopting a non-partisan stance, Burns attempted to smoke out his opponents.[197]

A REPRIEVE AND *DÉNOUEMENT*

The March 1897 Commission recommendations to the Council asserted that 'labour policy' had been central to the formation of the Works Department. There was widespread sentiment in favour of maintaining the department and continuing the use of direct labour even in the construction of architectural works.[198] The committee called for a pluralistic approach to the department's future. The manager ought not to be overloaded, and a certain number of contracts should float openly on the market. The 'strong practical demand' for equal recognition of employers' unions was acknowledged.[199] Perhaps the open-book policy should be relaxed. The Works Committee was abolished that year on the recommendation of the inquiry. Instead, the manager began to report to the departments of Council which needed work, to the Architect or the Engineer, and so on. Instead of facing closure, the department was on a better footing, temporarily strengthened by the results of the investigation. But a minority report, written by several Moderate members, cast a cloud over the proceedings. It highlighted the testimony of the labour representatives and called for the abolition of the department, a recommendation that would be affirmed in time.[200]

In October 1897, after the decision to extend the department's life, the London Trades Council (LTC) held a large demonstration in Trafalgar Square which received wide support in the London trade union movement. There was a call for votes to those candidates in the 1898 election who were willing to defend the department's existence.[201] Some candidates adopted a 'fair wages' programme without offering a defence of the department itself. Others, like the intrepid H.H. Marks, opposed the department on the grounds that it had not offered assistance to the unemployed! Though embroiled in controversy, the Progressives managed to secure a substantial victory in this electoral contest. The after-effects of the inquiry were not onerous enough to defeat the party at this juncture.

On the industrial front, there were new developments with the formation of the National Union of Building Trades in 1897 and the LMBA's campaign to increase the number of apprentices in the industry despite trade union practices. Burns claimed that LCC tenders from outside contractors had risen well above the pre-1897 levels: 'The contractors are getting emboldened by the Moderate enmity against direct labour.'[202] The LMBA became further involved with the blackleg NAFL, and in July 1900 the employers sent representatives to testify against direct labour schemes before the Select Committee on Municipal Trading.[203] By 1901, Beatrice Webb could comment that the main purpose of the Works Department had become that of 'keeping the contractors in order'.[204]

In 1902, *The Times* published a diatribe against London municipal socialism and the Progressive LCC. This scathing attack, very likely penned by Emil Garcke, certainly did not spare the Works Department.[205] In the 1903 election, a similarly scurrilous attack was issued by Dixon W. Davies, who called for the defeat of 'communism in London'. An avid opponent of municipalisation, Davies compared the Works Department to the *ateliers-nationaux* of 1848; the LCC now shared in the alien plight of the Continent.[206] *The Times* thereafter issued regular reports on the department, clinically noting each instance in which costs overran estimates. The Progressives were again able to hold their majority, but more and more negative material concerning the department was in circulation.

The ensuing 1906 Liberal victory in the general election meant that for a brief moment it looked as if the parliamentary reins on the LCC might be loosened, prompting swift Conservative reaction. But the 1907 LCC election witnessed the lightning mobilisation of the Conservative electoral machinery throughout London.[207] An unprecedented propaganda war between the parties began in which the Works Department figured prominently. The result was the largest single electoral poll in London municipal history: 55.5 per cent of the eligible electorate voted, hence Charles Masterman's claim for a lower middle class victory, a claim ultimately shared by many others, although the Progressives actually won some new seats and retained many supporters. The vast majority of those voting for the first time apparently voted Conservative.[208] Not coincidentally, 1907 inaugurated both the new Municipal Reform (Conservative) LCC and a new slump in the building industry as a whole, which Avebury, for example, attributed to the rise in the County rate necessitated by the extravagance of the LCC under the Progressives! This slump continued.[209]

The LMBA was greatly enthused over the Municipal Reform victories in both 1907 and 1910, when the Conservatives were again elected as they would be in every election until 1934, and noted with satisfaction that relations with the LCC were very much improved.[210] As an epithet to Progressivism, that indicated the party's diminished support, the LTC *Trades and Labour Gazette* published the following riposte when the electoral results appeared:

> The Progressives have been routed at the County Council elections and they are surprised. Why they should be surprised is hard to imagine, for what, in the name of goodness, have they ever done to stir up the enthusiasm of the worker to whom they look for support?
>
> They are supposed to take up a Collectivist policy and to municipalise all the services, but they have attempted this in such a fainthearted way that they have actually estranged those who gave them a vote thinking that they would pursue a vigorous policy to establish municipalisation.
>
> When he [the voter] turns to the housing policy of the

154

Progressives he finds that they provide him with a rabbit-hutch in a back street at a higher rental than the capitalist.

The Tories know well sooner or later the Liberal Party will be divided into two camps, one favouring individualism and the other collectivism. The Progressives are really between two stools and bound to come to grief. Having had an opportunity to justify their existence and neglected it, we see no reason to pity them.[211]

Edwin Waterhouse dutifully audited the Works Department books as he had for the 1896–97 inquiry. He discovered that just as the Progressives had claimed in recent debate, the department had been given less work in 1905–06 than between 1893 and 1896. Economy of scale had been proven in the negative: the department had in all the years of its existence incurred a 4.4 per cent net excess over estimate and 10.6 per cent of that excess had been incurred over the past four years. Perhaps then it had been 'starved out', just as the Progressives charged.[212] Finally, in 1909, after an appraisal of the department's deteriorating financial state, the Conservative Municipal Reform administration succeeded in promulgating the abolition of the Works Department, the selling off of its properties and the cessation of employment for thousands of building trades workers, at least in their jobs as Works Department employees. From then on, its life would continue only as a symbol of the struggle for municipalisation, as a memory of the vanished era of London Progressivism. The new regime would carry out hiring by the job, usually with contracted labour.

Those Progressives who persisted in the campaigns at the municipal level in London issued a 'Manifesto by Labour Leaders to All Trade Unionists' for the 1910 LCC election. The old cry could still be heard:

> This County Council election is a stern fight between those who believe in the payment of Trade Union Wages and Hours of Labour under the best conditions and the Direct Employment of Labour on the one hand, and those who have destroyed those principles by giving out all the work to contractors ... Workmen, defeat these attacks upon your rights! Whatever may be your views on Politics![213]

Many trade union leaders signed this plea, among them W.C. Steadman, by this time a member of the TUC Parliamentary

155

Committee; W.A. Appleton, Secretary of the General Federation of Trade Unions; Herbert H. Elvin of the NUC; Richard Davies of the Municipal Employees Association; and the omnipresent Sidney Webb.

CONCLUSION

The London labour movement remained profoundly ambivalent about Progressivism right up until the outbreak of the War. Will Steadman's union abandoned him when he refused to sign the London Labour Party constitution. Still other labour representatives, as Paul Thompson has noted, continued to see themselves as Progressives throughout the period, though on the street they might use the language of the class struggle (as the Plasterers' Michael Deller had done in his Progressive Party campaign).[214] Their attraction to Progressivism in part reflected a failure to see any natural, 'organic' relationships between socialist doctrines of the SDF or the ILP and themselves as proletarians. There was equally no failure to see the benefits that conciliation with the employers might bring. On the contrary, both the SDF and the ILP offered a militant-sounding programme without having established an organisational base. In the Progressives, the building trades had advocates with some access to political power; specifically, they had the greatest visionary, Burns, behind them. Yet the militancy of the 1910–11 strike wave in London building provides a great deal of evidence for the view that these workers regarded the LMBA with suspicion. As their economic situation increasingly declined, they were swayed by the need to act outside the existing framework of industrial relations, for temporary gains. Syndicalism was a potent influence amongst London building labour just before and just after the War. The final strike wave in building did not abruptly finish with the guns of August. Given deteriorating conditions in the industry, what is impressive is not so much that many labour supporters ultimately broke away from Progressivism, but the fact that so many had viewed it with hope and faith at the outset. It obviously made sense to them to work for the LCC, to wade through the negotiations that would legitimate the goals which they had already fought for in the private sector and to use the arena of LCC politics to secure better jobs for some. They used the Works Department as a beacon, as a foil, and as a weapon against the contractors for as long as it lasted.

The employers also bought into the deal, however unhappily. The jerrybuilder was squeezed by the presence of the Department more than was a firm like Mowlem. And the jerrybuilder was an impediment to the progress of big profits for big firms as much as he was the enemy of the LCC. Again, for as long as it lasted, the unsteady *rapprochement* between the municipality and some of London's most powerful business leaders (leaving aside cases like that of Lushington, who was both councillor and builder) was possible if not preferable. The LMBA privately plotted to thwart LCC prospects in cahoots with organisations such as the Free Labour Association, but its public strategy was clearly to keep its fingers in the dike so that if Progressivism managed to survive, its members could compete successfully within a pluralist market in building. No one banked on the multiple effects of controversy, now replete in other zones of LCC authority – this multiplicity of tensions gave life to the LCC and willed the downfall of Progressivism.

3

THE APPETITE FOR MANAGING OTHER PEOPLE'S LIVES

In 1908, this letter, written by a resident of Tufnell Park, arrived at County Hall. It concerns the music hall sketch, 'A Bride for Living', then playing at the Islington Hippodrome:

> Stop what I consider the most horrible and offensive scene ever put upon a stage. I am referring to when she hangs her paramour in mistake for her husband, she first covers him in a sheet and commences to hoist him up in full view of the audience, but the effort is too much so she winds the cord thru a wringing machine. The body is then allowed to hang, while the husband returns and she commits suicide, about seven minutes.
>
> My father committed suicide by hanging some years ago, I as a boy discovered him, by that you can tell what a thrill of horror ran through me to witness such a scene again. All the people near me at once said it was disgusting and not fit for any stage. I have never written a letter of complaint but this fills me with disgust to such an extent that I trust you will endeavour to stop it being performed with so much reality.[1]

The campaigns to clean up the music halls were amongst the most notorious of the Progressive era. A scribbled note indicates that in this instance the LCC Theatres and Music Halls Committee (TMHC) took no action. But the author's request for censure was not unprecedented. In the early years of the LCC, a committee might well have attempted to countenance the writer's demand. One person's trauma was another's delight and everyone could not be pleased. The letter reveals the imaginative place occupied by the early LCC, as an arbiter of taste, an agent of consolation and a force for amelioration. This imputation, subtly manifested over time, contributed to the Progressives' downfall. Even their opponents could not shrug off the implications of having crossed, however fancifully, the thresholds of private and perhaps forbidden worlds.

LCC social and cultural policy had its formative years in the Progressive era and was part of the national restructuring of welfare provision. Social purity, National Efficiency, racial purification and maternalism formed the broader context in which specific projects were undertaken by the Council.[2] No national party had a monopoly on passing legislation that affected LCC operations. The Conservatives, the Liberals and the Unionists all had a foot in the bills that mandated the LCC to seek to govern daily life. In 1904, a Municipal Reform leaflet pointed out that major legislation from the Local Government Act of 1888 to housing, public health and education acts had until that moment been largely the legacy of Conservative central government.[3] On the subject of the 'Conservatives and the Non-contentious Work of the Council', they were quick to point out:

> It is a favourite device of the Progressive speakers to expatiate upon the details of the ordinary administrative work of one of the wholly non-political departments of the Council; to dilate upon the importance of this work, and of the careful and conscientious way in which it is executed; and then to take all the credit of it to the progressive party. In effect they say, look how well the County Council Parks are managed; see how our inspectors are checking the use of false weights and measures; observe how many prizes and certificates the Technical Education Board is distributing to your children; therefore vote for the Progressive candidates.

Municipal Reform was eager to proclaim that 'Conservatives wish to see the Council making use of these powers with zeal and vigilance',[4] though a more candid and more politic rendition of their programme may be this line from their 1910 election leaflet: 'Work for Women in Local Government – How they can help the municipal reform movement . . . For good, or ill, many matters of concern to both sexes, including an intimate supervision over the welfare of children, have been brought within the sphere of local government.'[5]

The victory in 1906 of an interventionist Liberal government at the parliamentary level influenced the conception of policy and its

159

implementation. Some of the best-intentioned and most earnest of the LCC staff found their way into the work undertaken in these areas. Some of the staff perceived this early social work as a departure from charity and philanthropy, and employed a rudimentary sociology to describe it even though London's charity organisations continued to function in the same terrain as the Council until the War.[6] It is in the language and the commentary of the Council, in both the illustrative material of parliamentary testimony and the strident confidential memoranda of the committees' 'Presented Papers', that the underbelly of LCC social practice is most plainly visible. Nineteenth-century London remained largely prostrate and impoverished, open to assault and subversion by the new municipal body. In the language that depicts the hundreds of thousands of heads counted, of inspections made, of monies and time disbursed, lie meanings beyond the quantitative treatment (or lack thereof) of social ill and want.[7]

The responsibilities of protecting infant life, of regulating everyday shopping, marketing, school attendance or behaviour in the parks called forth descriptions of their public from those in charge at the LCC. The inspection of places of entertainment, of midwives, of restaurants and of workplaces brought millions of Londoners into view. In these descriptions lie the signs of frustration and of accomplishment, of attempted order and persistent chaos that forged the LCC's reputation and its mission. Faintly audible are the voices of those who sought relief or were more often informed that they needed it. In order to explain the deep ambiguity that surrounded the public response to Progressivism, and in order to assess the early LCC's accomplishments and declining reputation, it is necessary to investigate some of the Council's social and cultural practices. In doing so, close attention is paid to points of fracture and areas of controversy. While this is not an exhaustive survey of all aspects of the Council's work, what follows provides a guide to many LCC practices that touched the greatest number of Londoners and may in turn have raised the gravest doubts about Progressivism's viability and *modus operandi*.

'TOO POOR OR TOO PROFLIGATE': INFANTS, NURSE-MOTHERS, ILLEGITIMACY AND PRIVACY[8]

Isabel Y. Smith was appointed to the Public Control Department in 1894. She and two male colleagues constituted the department inspectorate which their superior called 'a central detective staff for the whole county'.[9] Under the provisions of the Infant Life Protection Acts of 1872 and of 1897, and the Children Act of 1908, Smith's male colleagues were responsible for making sure that the law was made known in 'poor districts'. The LCC was the local enforcing authority for these acts in the County of London.[10] The LCC inspectors watched lying-in houses and searched newspapers for advertisements that might provide clues as to where infants were being 'kept for reward' in the form of payment. In the days of the MBW, the press and public had publicised and condemned 'baby-farming'. In one case, a nurse-mother (the term identified foster mothers as a general category, rather than merely wet-nurses), a Mrs Waters, had been hanged for the fatal poisoning of seven children in her keep, and recorded infanticide in London had diminished from the mid-century onward.[11] The inspectors of the 1890s kept contact with poor law officers, the registrars of births and deaths, and the police, who in turn assisted them by posting notices in police stations and by distributing leaflets addressed to the general public which contained the pertinent details of the Acts.[12]

In its original form, the Infant Life Protection Act required that eligible child-minders deemed 'properly able to maintain infants' be certified by the local authority if they were responsible for more than a single infant, a controversial limit placed on the legislation.[13] These included wet-nurses. Children under a particular age (at first, under twelve months) who were kept with one other child or more for a minimum of twenty-four hours away from home were to be 'registered' with the authorities. Personal details, including the names of the child's parents, were recorded at the time of registration. In 1897, the Act was revised and registration was abolished. Instead, it was made mandatory for those caring for children aged one to five for more than forty-eight hours to notify the LCC of their status. The Act also monitored adoptions of children that were transacted for a fee of less than twenty pounds.

The 1908 Children Act further stipulated that insurance policies that parents had taken out for children in care be voided; significantly, a child's death in care would now bear no monetary reward. The senior inspector had visited 600 houses in which 2400 infants were kept, and over the years 1903–08 two male inspectors had seen 2700 infants 'in single homes'. Half of these children were under one year of age.[14] The Act stipulated that infants be removed from nurse-mothers deemed unacceptable: 'Miss Cooper is a dirty, elderly and apparently unsuitable woman to have care of infants, and the inspector also has some doubts as to the character of Miss Cooper's house', observed an inspector's report.[15] The staff assessed nurse-mothers and children, watching for evidence of insanity, verminousness, illness, poverty, starvation, neglect and intemperance.[16] Cases could be referred to other bodies such as the National Society for the Prevention of Cruelty to Children, an indication of the persistence of charitable venues.[17] Nurse-mothers in violation of the Act could be sent to the work-house. The Department was particularly suspicious of the role of financial incentive: 'infants fall into the hands of dissolute and unworthy persons who measure their profit on the transaction by the length of the infant's life'.[18] The LCC inspectors also acted as go-betweens, fielding complaints from nurse-mothers who had not received payments from the mothers of the children in their care.

As part of her duties in the Public Control Department, and in its reincarnation as the Public Health Department, Isabel Smith visited the houses in which infants were taken in 'for hire'. She inspected thousands of nurse-mothers and judged the conditions in which they were cared for. As a condition of their positions at the Council, Smith and other women inspectors were forbidden from marrying. Only women between the ages of 28 and 40 could apply to join the inspectorate. While an unmarried inspector of children might have seemed a curious irony, even widows with young children were refused appointments.[19] As if to challenge the paradox, applicant Lizzie Middleditch of Stoke Newington, who was a widow without her own children, defended herself as having had 'entire control of children who have resided with my father, as boarders, for a number of years'.[20] Alice Fitzpatrick of East Ham, the widow of an LCC servant and thereby technically eligible for a job as an unmarried woman, admonished, 'I have no encumbrance as my two children have been taken from me by a friend in Essex.' Gerda Banniza Jacobi, whom the Council did decide to hire, presented competitive professional credentials. She had been a hospital registrar and held a Diploma of Sanitary Inspection. Ironically, Alfred Spencer, head of the department, certainly did mean for applicants to possess 'practical experience of management of infants, knowledge of domestic hygiene and experience making investigations and writing reports'.[21]

James Ollis, Spencer's successor, would write with a suggestion of tension of the need for

> qualities of sympathy and tact for dealing with nurse mothers
> . . . [they] not only safeguard infant life from the perils of
> poverty, ignorance and parents or relatives who may require
> the death of an infant. They are a source of protection to nurse
> mothers, who have done their duty by an infant that has from
> some circumstances or other, become the subject of a cor-
> oner's inquest.[22]

The inspectors offered neighbourhood mothers instruction in 'proper maintenance', and Ollis believed that 'to a very large extent, women are more qualified than men to give that advice', echoing the assumptions so prevalent in municipal electoral propaganda which championed women's special talents in 'municipal housekeeping'.[23] Ollis reveals more than he might have. Though legislation sought the protection of young children, in doing so it also invariably challenged nurse-mothers and broached family negotiations over unwanted children. London witnessed persistently high rates of infant mortality throughout the century, and in 1895 over two hundred infant corpses had been discovered in London. These were assumed to be the bodies of babies of 'secretly confined' women, not infants who had died in paid care. Their discovery occurred in the context of a declining birth-rate over time.[24] Five thousand illegitimate children were born in London annually; in any given period there were 15,000 such children aged under 5.[25]

In reporting on parliamentary testimony, the *Daily Telegraph* dramatically surmised from such data that a quarter of the children in the unregistered houses of nurse-mothers might well die.[26] Clearly, the LCC was not equipped to handle these numbers, and indeed, the 1897 Act was described by a veteran inspector (who did not work for the LCC) as an Act that 'scarcely touched the fringe of the cases of children boarded out'.[27] Ollis stated, in regard to the proposal to include infants of under one year in age, that 'the cost and consequences of the proposed remedy have to be considered. If the proposal were adopted, it would be largely disregarded.'[28] The magnitude of the LCC's task is captured by the Council's estimate that 90 per cent of the children whom it inspected were illegitimate.[29] The tensions created by the Council's intrusions were reflected in the revelations of department staff.

163

Perhaps Public Control got more in Isabel Smith than it had bargained for. In 1909, she weighed the results of fourteen years of LCC service while offering testimony to a parliamentary commission: 'Someone should put the matter from the opposite point of view [than that] advanced by the philanthropic ladies.' She had visited six hundred houses in which 2400 infants were cared for:

> Some I have found . . . kept . . . well but by a person who was unsuitable through extreme poverty; for example, by an elderly or old woman no longer able to go out charring, and occupying one small room, who was trying thus to eke out a small allowance from the Poor Law Guardians or from a relative.

Smith believed that these women needed care, instruction and supervision. Most of the infants were illegitimate:

> frequently objects either of secrecy from, or of dissension among the relatives . . . I have many times been told by respectable nurse mothers that the relatives of an infant have implied or have openly told her that they would be glad if she would let it die. It requires no easily detected violence or poison to bring about the death of a young infant. The means successfully employed, either intentionally or otherwise, may be of the most insidious nature; and it is a very difficult matter, especially when there has been no supervision to decide when neglect has been wilful and when not. Efficient supervision and instruction, on the other hand, tended to check neglect from ignorance before it has become serious, and at the same time to detect that which arises from sinister motives.

She observed that mothers often fed infants improperly, leaving the nurse-mothers 'to undo the mischief'. Those nurse-mothers in another camp, who opposed inspection were, to Smith's mind, 'too ignorant to recognise any need for improvement, too self-satisfied and callous to care to be taught better ways'.[30] In defending the need for a new supervisory appointment, which she hoped to get, Smith complained of the drudgery of her work, 'the constant visiting of women who kept infants amidst squalid surroundings, the necessity for giving frequent advice and arguing with ignorant women as to the proper maintenance of infants, and the listening to and sympathizing with such women in their troubles and affairs'.

Her work had doubled in four years, 'so that the former opportunities which she had enjoyed of intellectual stimulus by association with intelligent people interested in rescue work and the welfare of infants disappeared'. Her chairman ventured that Smith took her job too seriously and wrote reports that were too lengthy while her home visits lasted four or five hours at a time.[31] Her frustration is evident in the pronounced ambiguities that she voiced about the policies that she was supposed to carry out. Yet her comments were not lacking in seasoned prejudice against her clients. Smith's maverick behaviour was a source of conflict within the LCC bureaucracy, not of approbation. Her thoroughness was viewed, on occasion, with scepticism by her superiors. In 1897, she asked to appear before the Paddington Board of Guardians to protest against their decision to rescind a relieving order issued in the case of a child; the child was to be returned to her nurse-mother. Department head Spencer cautioned, 'It would be . . . unwise for the Council to assist in any way in relieving persons of the great responsibility they undertake with nurse infants; and still more unwise to actively oppose any other public body who are acting on this view.'[32]

Smith remained implacably critical of the 'unsatisfactory' nurse-mother under her supervision, chastising in 1908:

> The nurse-mothers who object after a fair trial, to the visits of the inspector are invariably the unsatisfactory ones who lack of cleanliness or of proper attention to the infants, whose methods and surroundings generally, have called forth disapproval or a request for alteration.[33]

Under questioning, Smith acknowledged that these cases were a 'small minority'. Those who were 'industrious' and 'willing to profit' stood to gain from inspection and from a link with the department. In times of trouble, they could seek assistance and advice. As other evidence suggests, they could also create a safety net for themselves should they be accused of wrongdoing. There were even mothers who would not put their infants in 'inspected houses'. Smith attributed this to their fear of the publicity that could accompany inspection. Some nurse-mothers disliked being forced by an inspector to replace the food that had been requested by a child's mother only to be deemed unsuitable by an inspector. They too might have preferred an unregulated relationship. This complaint indicates the persistence of ties between nurse-mothers and natural mothers.[34]

But there were other mothers, particularly those who were

unmarried, who contacted the department in order to get listings of inspected houses. Regulation was greeted with ambivalence. Smith attributed the discrepancies in behaviour on the part of nurse-mothers to a set of varying motives for taking in children in the first place. Those who already had their own children sought additional income. Smith assumed that those who were childless were the only ones who would 'take one primarily from abstract maternal love'.[35]

Like many staff members, Smith visited European municipal facilities. Leipzig impressed her. All illegitimate infants in the city were subject to official inspection until they left school. The town council pursued the children's fathers and demanded maintenance benefits from them. The visit whetted Smith's appetite. She found the German system simpler than London's from the point of view of the inspectorate; there was greater assurance of receiving proper payments for infants who were cared for by the authorities. The municipality had inaugurated a medical treatment programme. In the light of such an example, infant life protection in London appeared much more difficult to enforce even if one were convinced of its efficacy.

In 1904, the Council acknowledged that the number of houses of infant care was 'out of all proportion to those under Council supervision'.[36] The Council even contemplated having the boroughs establish crèches, as was the practice in France.[37] Without them, it was felt that a minority 'would always resort to giving infants to neighbours or to voluntary crèches'.[38] In order to limit infringements without putting a nurse-mother entirely out of business, the LCC could resort to limiting the number of children in a particular woman's care to a single infant.[39] There were also special abuses of the adoption system that the Council continued to seek to end. In some instances, a nurse-mother accepted payment from a child's mother and promised that the child would be passed to a rich woman. But as Inspector Browne reported to the Parliamentary Select Committee of 1908, most abuses did not offer grounds for prosecution as they did not constitute acts of desertion of one's own child which were punishable offences under the law. There was some flexibility: one woman was given four months for locking up infants in a dark room.[40] But perhaps a more onerous obstacle to enforcement was the resistance of nurse-mothers to registration in the first place.

Many nurse-mothers opposed inspection and the regulation of

their houses. Since many children stayed temporarily with neighbours, even the LCC staff feared that the order disrupted customary networks of care.[41] Some in the inspectorate contended that
official regulation now inspired three-quarters of the nurse-
mothers to relinquish the infants in their charge. But evidence
about the nurse-mothers' willingness to accept the procedures
was always contradictory. Even Ollis, who insisted that many of
the nurse-mothers did not object to regulation, found himself
explaining:

> English people do not like official inspection, especially in
> matters concerning their private domestic lives. Where cap-
> able, tactful and educated women Inspectors are employed to
> visit the homes; this objection would easily be overcome, and
> the nurse-mothers would welcome the visits as helping them in
> the management of the infants. The difficulty is that the
> Inspector might not have the opportunity of overcoming
> prejudice; that is, supposing the objections to inspection are
> as strong as have been described, and in order to avoid
> inspection, women would have nothing to do with the keep-
> ing of infants.[42]

Their husbands did not want the inspectorate coming in, nor did
their landladies. The stigma of being called a 'baby farmer' was
more than many could take, even though Smith invidiously claimed
that 'desirable nurse-mothers' did not object to inspection.[43] Ollis
ventured that the 'natural criminal instinct' would still prompt
nurse-mothers to evade the law. Ollis also emphasised that the
LCC did not find homes for infants. He explained the difficulties
involved in breaking customary codes as they were 'below a certain
level of society. There would . . . be great advantages from the
opportunities of instilling correct views.' But beyond that level,
Ollis perceived 'valid and natural reasons for maintaining as much
secrecy as possible as to parentage. Unless it can be shown that the
evil is of such a character that it cannot otherwise be met, attempts
to break down the barriers of this secrecy might result in
misfortune'.[44]

The veneer of silence had protected families so that their
unwanted infants could be disposed of without scrutiny. A departure from the norm of discretion would affect 'the child born of
people in a good position of society who never under any circum-
stance come under need of inspection, and where the disclosure of

parentage might result in trouble'.[45] The record of statements about the department's work, from Smith and from her superiors, is often contradictory, revealing the fissures in the conception of inspection and the mixed reactions of the staff to the practice of intruding upon private, familial territory or its equivalent. Ollis typically opposed registering houses where single infants were kept on these grounds: 'where this element of a home atmosphere exists it is of vital importance that nothing should be done by Act of Parliament . . . to chill or impair it'.[46] This is in keeping with the mixed portrayals of the nurse-mothers themselves, who were sometimes described in disparaging terms and in other instances depicted as well-intentioned and moral. Some of the anxiety of description can be attributed to the demands placed upon the department to legitimate its work; some can be attributed to the guiding assumptions of infant care. For example, the notion that 'the aggregation of infants under the same roof is peculiarly fatal to infant life' suggested a reliance upon domestic family care for infants and derived from the wider public discourse surrounding the causes and remedies of high infant mortality rates at the century's close – a debate amongst physicians and policymakers that was never conclusively resolved.[47]

A 'class of lying-in establishments' was perceived as particularly 'evil'.[48] The Council cited instances in which a midwife acted as the conduit for babies whom she had delivered, charging the fleeing mother as much as seventy-five pounds. These midwives cum nurse-mothers were in the practice of handing the infants over to charity institutions and keeping the money, making them the targets of the advocates of more stringent adoption laws, as above. The jurisdictions of voluntary and public agencies overlapped. Indeed, Isabel Smith estimated, in what was yet another attempt at an ordered statistic, that 40 per cent of children in her districts who were in paid care had been placed there by the Rescue Society and other agencies.[49]

The LCC also attempted to supervise midwifery and patrolled a fraction of private dwellings. But it had no jurisdiction over charity institutions and, more importantly, actually strove to limit municipal involvement to some of the most egregious infant cases in order to assure the smooth working of a cottage industry in childcare which did not require even incidental municipally-financed provision. This was the case despite appearances – the lacklustre pursuit of some nurse-mothers will not have deterred others from perceiving the authority as ever-present. The argument in favour of the LCC's dealing ruthlessly with recalcitrant nurse-mothers was easily altered by one that favoured a fictive 'home life' for infants abandoned by their parents or their mothers. It was always acknowledged that many houses would not be discovered or certified, that many infants would die even in certified houses if the legislation were scrupulously applied. Browne testified that some infants were not registered because they were in a delicate position from the moment that they entered care.[50] And there was the factor of resistance on the part of the nurse-mothers to contend with. In 1908, one LCC inspector noted that 'three foster mothers out of every four have intimated their intention of giving up the keeping of an infant, if subject to official inspection . . . they consider that they are doing a kindness-by keeping an infant at 5/- or less per week, and in consequence should not be annoyed'.[51]

As late as 1908, Ollis captured part of the department's dilemma in his summary of the attitudes towards inspection. A large majority of the infants whom they saw were well cared for by women who, as he put it, were 'not partial to inspection'.[52] But as he summarised, 'the untouched evils seem to me to arise from poverty and ignorance, conditions which seriously affect the death rate among the poor generally. I think, also, that more is expected of the law than the law can accomplish.' He insisted that the changes proposed in 1908 would result in frequent prosecutions and an immense supervisory machinery.[53] Ollis was clearly torn between the option of surveillance and that of propriety; this conflict characterises much of his parliamentary testimony. But he did insist upon drawing a graphic class line by maintaining that the 'real good to the community' was in instances in which regulation touched 'mothers too poor or too profligate to maintain their children.'[54]

MIDWIVES

The inspection of midwives occurred in a similar manner. The LCC inspectorate examined their persons, their surroundings, their medical bags and their reputations. The lower fees charged by midwives guaranteed that they delivered more babies in London than doctors did, though a majority of the poor still could not afford their services. The 1902 Midwives Act stipulated the regular inspection and registration of midwives. Failure to register could lead to prosecution but merely attending a woman in childbirth was not a legal offence.[55] After March 1905, no uncertified woman could call herself a midwife, though many still did. Those certified were supposed to be 'trustworthy, sober and of good moral character'. Each woman attending a birth needed a form signed by a Justice of the Peace, a clergyman or someone else acceptable to the Central Midwives Board, which was established in 1903.[56]

By the end of 1904, almost a thousand London midwives were certified and that number had nearly tripled by 1909. Many of those midwives who were solicited by mail did not reply to LCC enquiries including as many as half of those contacted in 1905. In a survey of 120–150 midwives conducted over a four-week period, 2188 births were reported. In eighty-nine of these cases, the infants had died. The LCC claimed that these figures accounted for nearly a quarter of all London births in that short time span and that they represented births 'exclusively among the poorer classes of the population'.[57] The LCC also created twelve annual scholarships in midwifery to be awarded to residents who agreed to practise in London.[58] A typical file on a midwife read as follows: 'She is a middle aged woman, moderately clean in appearance, holds the certificate of the C.O.S. and does a large practice at Battersea. She was trained in the year 1890. She has been inspected and reported upon four times.'[59]

The Act also provided the LCC with a mandate to thwart midwives who assisted in adoptions.[60] Like those who advertised themselves falsely as nurse-mothers and then offered children up to the philanthropic institutions, so the wayward midwife could be found 'diverting people to other charities and getting kickbacks from them'.[61] Indeed, the LCC surmised that in the years after 1902, as the restrictions governing midwifery tightened, adoptions for a 'lump sum' fell off. Under the new rules, children remained with their mothers for a longer interval at the time of birth. It was believed that this fostered more affection for the child on the mother's part and less willingness to relinquish him or her.[62] As was the case with the Infant Life Protection Acts, it was questionable as to whether the law was popularly known and understood: 'Recently at a coroner's inquest . . . a woman denied knowledge of the existence of the act and I am told that this is by no means an isolated case and that many of these women never read the newspapers.'[63] This was a telling remark in that the leading newspapers and medical and nursing journals published the regulations.

The midwives, like nurse-mothers, sometimes protested against inspections. A woman from Hammersmith wrote:

> A Dr. Bennett . . . was admitted to the dining room before I knew who she was . . . her manner was objectionable in the extreme. I might have been guilty of some crime by her tone. I came to the LCC offices today to see you upon the subject and after seeing six or seven officials I am still obliged to write . . . Does she claim to have powers [to] search midwives' premises at her own whim and during what hours?[64]

This letter must be contrasted, however, with another typical complaint received by the LCC, in this instance from a man in Peckham: 'am writing to tell you that there is a woman . . . who is practising as a qualified midwife and knowing she can only manage straightforward cases and is not to be relied upon on account of her drinking. I think it is only right she should be warned.'[65] Despite such private confessions, midwifery, like infant care, was difficult to regulate no matter what the formulae of the law. In 1904, as if to suggest a remedy for both the problem of untrained midwives on the one hand and the high doctors' fees on the other, the BMA unsuccessfully attempted to force the LCC to pay the fees for the majority of husbands who could not do so in emergency cases when the doctors were called in.[66] The absence of municipal facilities for childbirth contributed to the dilemma. Midwives complained that while doctors would not come out when called upon, unless they were assured of payment, the parish doctor would not come out without an order from the relieving officer in charge.[67]

Though the charities attempted to provide care in lying-in houses and a roster of their own midwives, a report from V.E.M. (here termed 'Miss', certainly not 'doctor', as her critic above had assumed) on the inspection of a group of midwives listed with the Royal Maternity Charity stated that:

> in the majority of instances the case books are not properly kept, that apparatus of non-sterilisable material is used, that the instruments are lubricated with non-carbolised vaseline, that in many instances a common tube is used for enema and douche

and that the hands are disinfected with carbolic solution no stronger than one in 10,000 . . . the midwives' equipment do not comply with the rules laid down by the charity.[68]

More grisly cases occurred. Mrs G.E. Price was the object of an intense correspondence. Though she had supporters ('Mrs. Price had certainly nothing to drink when she came here'), she also had detractors who spoke of her ragged fingernail cutting a patient, of her drunkenness, of her use of one of her own hairpins to rupture the membrane, of her failure to use an antiseptic and of her removal of a placenta without washing her hands.[69]

Similar language was used to describe nurse mothers and unacceptable midwives. But when Shirley Murphy, Medical Officer of Health (MOH) for the LCC, came before a parliamentary committee to evaluate the first seven years of work under the 1902 Act, he stressed the poverty of the midwives and the cases in which their fees could not sustain them. He suggested that the charity institutions often took the midwives' money. Rivalry amongst the women had also contributed to their distress: those who lacked certification were often reported upon by those who had earned it.[70] Invoking the standard typology, Murphy observed that the LCC was now able to register 'a better class' of women. But 900 uncertified cases had turned up in a year's time. Predictably, uncertified midwives charged five shillings for a delivery; those with certification charged between seven and ten. Murphy admitted that such a fee was, as he put it, 'above the means of a great many people'.[71]

In the chaos that surrounded LCC policy toward infants in care and midwives, a thread of rationality did prevail. Poverty and its patterning of the lives of Londoners shaped the standards used to judge the efficacy of policy. Unable to control the totality of cases intended for jurisdiction, the LCC retrospectively maintained that it had at least separated out some grossly impoverished offenders amongst its charges. The wink of the bureaucrat assisted the maintenance of customary practices while the open eye was reserved for the unsightly, unseemly inferior whom the Council could afford to address. The fragile routine that was achieved had not been the intention of the law, but it did allow for the LCC to avoid the expense of more comprehensive social legislation. More challenges awaited the Council in the sphere of everyday consumption.

THE RETAIL TRADES AND THE MARKET IN CHILDREN'S LABOUR

Everyday life for Londoners involved a great deal of neighbour-hood shopping. The era of the LCC marked the onset of unprecedented growth in London's retail trades and the assimilation into the city's politics of London's shopkeepers, a sector widely regarded as opponents of the Progressives. Most people shopped in the 130 London retail street markets over which the LCC had authority.[72] The Council's inspectors counted thousands of coster barrows and market stalls. Its committees entertained complaints from grocers who deemed themselves more respectable than the costers and who resented their competitors' shady weighing schemes, though the grocers' practices were often no less corrupt. One inspector cautioned,

> I have to inform you that the shopkeepers whose names are attached are, in my opinion, only one degree removed in class from the hawker. The neighbourhood is a very poor one. All of the grocers in the original complaint had already received cautions; one lodged with another and so on. Their instruments for weighing were approximate to those of the costers of whom they complained.[73]

Under the Bread Act, 'Notices to Bakers and Other Persons Selling Bread' were issued, stating that bread could only be sold by weight. A penalty of two pounds lay in the balance. A refusal to weigh bread on scales and with weights provided by the seller resulted in a five-pound fine.[74]

Many hundreds of thousands of Londoners owned or worked in shops, including juveniles, who were also subject to regulations requiring compulsory schooling. By the late 1890s, almost a third of all of London's shops employed juveniles.[75] Under the Employment of Children Act of 1903, the LCC was saddled with the inspection of these establishments.[76] The United Shop Assistants Union, the National Union of Shop Assistants and the Early Closing Association pressured the LCC to be more active, especially as most inspections in the late 1890s did not result in convictions.[77] There were 220,414 inspections of 73,623 shops conducted during 1899–1900, including inspections of pubs and refreshment houses outside the City.[78] The streets of greatest concern with regard to infringements of shop laws in the late

1890s were Upper Street, Islington, Seven Sisters Road, Deptford Broadway, Brixton Road, Battersea Park Road and Wandsworth High Street. All of these were bustling shopping precincts in central areas of population.[79]

In 1913, over 61,000 cautionary notices were served upon shopowners; many of these were for breaches of the hours provisions covering juveniles. Children's employment had grown suddenly after 1899; the Boer War reservists' places had reportedly been taken by shopboys and children had taken the shopboys' places.[80] In 1906, it was estimated that 55,000 of 750,000 London schoolchildren (that is, 7 per cent) were employed; in poorer schools, these included a full 20 per cent of the children. The principal employers of juvenile labour were butchers, cheesemongers, chemists, dairies, greengrocers, coalsellers, grocers, hairdressers, newsagents and pawnbrokers.[81] Children worked in London for as little as two shillings a week, and in at least half of the children's families their contributions were necessary for survival.[82] Employers were loath to conform to the new restrictions, sometimes arguing that anyone working for less than seventy-four hours a week was of little use to them, and that an 18-year-old was preferable.[83] Child street traders were often in and out of work, depending on illness, unemployment and distress in their families.[84]

The operations of the LCC by-laws governing shops resulted in 1000 prosecutions in 1905.[85] In 1908, there were 70,263 contraventions of the street trading by-laws including 160 prosecutions and 141 convictions.[86] As of 1905, the employment of children under the age of 11 was forbidden; those under 12 could work only for short periods. There were restrictions governing work during school hours. Those who were permitted to work could do so for no more than fifteen hours a week unless they were exempt from school, in which case, they could work no more than a forty-hour week.[87] Only Jews who did not work on Saturdays could carry out Sunday domestic work. The LCC complained about those termed aliens: 'They have to make statutory declarations . . . and they are very tiresome people. There are great numbers of them in Whitechapel.'[88] Children could handle liquor vessels only if they were sealed and they were forbidden to work for laundries, hairdressers or barbers. Children who worked in the music halls had to be at least ten years old. They were to rest for a four-hour period and to leave the halls by 11 p.m. A matron had to attend them; they had to receive dressing gowns and to display licences. They were permitted to perform twice nightly, either in the same hall or in turns in two separate halls.[89]

Of London children under 16, only boys were permitted to be street traders. It was believed that girl traders were morally compromised. Even in cases where relatives acted as 'guardians' of the girl traders, they were regarded as immoral.[90] Shaw himself might have made good use of the statements of a principal in the Education Branch in 1910: 'The importuning in selling flowers is a very bad thing for a girl. When importuning young fellows the language exchanged is often very undesirable. I have myself watched the grave deterioration in such girls.'[91] Mrs Herbert Gladstone inquired of Cyril Jackson, LCC Education Committee head, in the 1910 parliamentary inquiry: 'I suppose the very fact of their being in charge of a barrow puts them at the mercy of anyone who wants to speak to them, or address them, possibly from a bad motive?' Jackson concurred with her sentiments, explaining that the street traders could be differentiated. Those girls who associated with the opposite sex were around men 'many [of whom] are of a very low type of humanity. I think that is quite true of the costermongers as a rule. They are a very low type of people.'[92]

Boy street traders were not immune from charges of sexual impropriety, but, unlike the young women, they were regarded as the initiators of disreputable behaviour:

> The parent of the boy in the street does not know what he earns. That is a very great evil. A boy spends so much of the money as he thinks fit in ways that he likes. He goes to music halls and other places . . . But the street trader goes by himself, or if he can afford it he takes a 'lady friend'. It is a most extraordinary thing, but if you watch these boys after they have had a good day they will often take a 'lady friend'.[93]

As of 1906, almost 14,000 badges had been given to boy street-traders and none to girls. Despite this practice, in 1910 the LCC acknowledged that before November, 1907, the provisions of the Act and its bylaws pertaining to street trading had not been enforced.[94] After the Conservatives came to power, the responsibility of carrying out duties under the by-laws was shifted from the Public Control Department to the Education Branch of the Council. Cyril Jackson, chair of that committee, explained that the work was now in the hands of school attendance officers, 'who already knew a great many of the children and who have street officers already engaged in dealing with children for the purpose of enforcing attendance'. Jackson admitted that Public Control had done little and that they had not had sufficient officers for the work.[95] The work was increased. By 1910, there were more than 3000 boys aged 11–12 licensed for street trading.[96] A quarter of a million leaflets informing parents, employers and street traders were issued (though it concerned Mrs Gladstone that illiterate parents might not be able to obtain the information).[97] The attendance officers began patrolling the streets during the time periods when under-age, unlicensed children might be most likely to be working.[98] The police had to be notified of violations. Though badges were required to be worn from 1907, the boys did not like to display them on their clothing and turned them inside out or put them in their pockets. Jackson surmised that they were 'ashamed' of them.[99]

Within the elaborate structure of the regulations, several ambi-guities in the assumptions that guided policy are apparent, as witnessed in the parliamentary correspondent's report:

> I am aware that most of the schoolmasters that were called stated as their conclusion that child labour should be regulated and not prohibited, but I do not think that the evidence they gave warranted this conclusion, unless they meant by regulated – regulated to vanishing point.[100]

When Dr T.J. Macnamara of the London School Board reported in 1901 to the Home Secretary on the subject of children's employ-ment, the ambivalent operations of yet another piece of LCC regulations were apparent. Macnamara was concerned about the effects of juvenile employment upon education:

> So much difficulty has been found in practice in getting magistrates to convict under the present interpretation, that it would be almost impossible to put now into practice the more restricted views that are set out in my report . . . I think that the public would view with jealousy and suspicion any attempt of the School Board to go beyond the ordinarily recognised powers in any attempt to deal with the children apart from school.[101]

And by the LCC's own admission, the existing structure, based upon the 1903 by-laws, had not necessarily succeeded in rendering unlicensed, under-age street traders things of the past: 'In London the County Council consider that their officers have obtained such a grasp of the situation that no unlicensed trader goes undetected, but the answer given to queries put to small boys in the street does not always tend to confirm this assertion.'[102] And when the powers to inspect were shifted from Public Control to Education, the tendency towards discretion was replete. A 1913 memo frankly noted, 'it is very desirable to avoid as far as possible any unnecessary inspection of shops'.[103]

Amongst the Council's controversial provisions was the requirement that shop assistants restrict their working week to seventy-four hours. Shopowners were required to provide seats for employees under the Seats for Shop Assistants Act of 1899. The legislation governing market weights and prices was especially disputed, including the requirement that the equipment used by hawkers in market stalls be weighed.[104] These sorts of requirements also extended to the measurement of explosives, gas meter testing and the like. Burns wryly noted that the coal merchants had been forced to 'lengthen their sacks',[105] and an 1898 Progressive electoral tract boasted:

> Seventy-seven inspectors have been appointed, with central offices in six of the great divisions of London, from which they swoop down like hawks upon the swindling tradesmen. Of course, these rascals which have had to enlarge their coal sacks are very bitter against the Council, and there can be no doubt that these thieves will vote Moderate to a man.[106]

There were political reasons for lessening the impact of regulatory legislation. The ire of the local merchants was matched by the fury of the publicans who were discovered using private glasses that bore a stamp but actually held less than the required amounts of drink. The seizure of the illegal glasses did not enhance relations with the brewers or the publicans, well-known Tories and vehement opponents of the Progressives.[107] The inspectorate visited 35,000 premises using glass measures during 1894–95; 800,000 glasses were checked.[108] Political considerations aside, it was easier to pursue the visible publican than the unlicensed midwife or the recalcitrant nurse-mother. *De facto*, what the LCC failed to do in the life-sustaining areas of provision it made up for in the more mundane and niggling inspections of daily life. The small proprietor who plied his trade in public space and whose income surely depended on unrestricted use of time and upon cheap labour was a logical target of legislation. He was easier to locate and to prosecute; unfortunately, he was very likely an elector as well. Conflicts of interest plagued policy.

Day-to-day inspection fostered other difficulties. A figure of mockery and of constant annoyance to the LCC was the imposter inspector who learned the tricks of the trade by observing inspections and then impersonating the inspectors! Another more focused force of opposition was formed by the shopkeepers' organisations, which, like the Metropolitan Grocers, Provision Dealers and Oilmen's Association, vigorously protested against the regulatory impulses of the Council, claiming that its enforcement of the Acts involved a large cost to the ratepayers and a financial burden for their members:[109]

> We feel that so far from being guilty of inflicting hardship on these boys the boys are largely taken in the first instance out of kindness to the poorer people . . . the more respectable parents were not so willing to allow their children to come. When I say the poorer classes I do not mean the very bottom.[110]

Geoffrey Crossick has written of the spirit of artisanal radicalism that still influenced shopkeeper rhetoric on the eve of the War. In this instance, the LCC's codes of enforcement pitted it against those who perceived an infringement of their civil liberties and, like their allies in the building industry, invoked the language of 'free trade' in order to challenge state and municipal authority. Even if the sentiment later dissolved, it remained a potent hostile force in the Progressive era. As the LCC encroached on other work and domestic spaces, more feathers were ruffled.[111]

NOXIOUS TRADES, EVERYDAY CONSUMPTION

LCC jurisdiction extended in directions that were neither entirely predictable nor arbitrary. Council powers, as the Progressives always moaned, were far from comprehensive, so the regulatory privileges exercised by the LCC resembled the octopus's tentacles rather than the spider's web. Where lines of authority ran, they ran deeply, but human and fiscal resources were very often limited and this compromised LCC power. Here follow examples of lines of LCC authority that extended beyond the discrete areas addressed by legislation. The LCC's powers intersected significant realms of ordinary life *despite* the gross limitations of the LCC's capacity to change Londoners' material conditions of existence. The appearance of intervention was unavoidable; the presumption of authority on the part of the bureaucrats irresistible. The limits upon power did not prevent the conferring of its illusion upon an individual staff member. But as a part of the white collar workforce already experiencing the indignities described in Chapter 1, the staff of Public Control and related departments also faced daily frustrations as the workload increased.

The private domestic domain and the small workplace came under Council purview. The inspectors observed milk sales and examined cows. Infant mortality in London was largely attributed to diseases that were caused by an infected milk supply. George Newman's survey of London ranked milk-related disease highest on the list of causes of infant death.[112] Shirley Murphy, London's MOH, was well aware of the persistence of high infant death rates in London. The borough of Battersea provided a single exemplary milk station. Most 'regulation' of the milk supply was confined to the inspection of cows kept on private premises, which were, in many instances, made known to the LCC staff by vigilant neighbours.[113] A typical order of the Public Health and Housing Committee read:

> That Mrs. Robbins (Bow) be informed that should she desire to continue to keep the cow in question, she must submit plans and apply for a licence in the usual way and that if she doesn't desire to take this course, it will be necessary for her to dispose of the cow within a period of two months.[114]

A shop could not sell milk for a specified period after a contagious disease had been traced to its door. Under the Public Health (London) Act of 1891, the LCC had responsibility for slaughterhouses, cowhouses and knackers' yards and was supposed to prevent nuisances and to supervise the 'offensive trades'. Dogs, including pets, were not exempt, and after 1896 were slaughtered if they were found in public places unmuzzled and unclaimed for three days. More than 32,000 animals met this fate in the first year of the law.[115] Rabies orders were drawn up. An organised opposition to such measures emerged in the form of the National Canine Defence League. Even smoke pollution was a Council matter. There had been over 9000 infringements of air pollution regulations by 1906 and more than 1000 cases filed against the railway companies alone. Hotels and electric light stations constantly emitted enveloping smoke.[116] But private houses were not regulated under the legislation, and there were one million chimneys fuelling the atmosphere, eerily contributing to a loss of half of London's winter sunshine.[117] The prolific use of gas-lit lamps in private homes often required Council intervention. Witness this report of 1898:

> This accident was caused during a quarrel between the deceased, Mrs. Henegan, and her husband; the woman threw the lighted lamp at her husband. The lamp which was a common tin wall lamp, fell on the floor; the reservoir gave way, and the oil escaped and ignited, and set fire to the deceased's clothes who was severely burned and taken to the hospital where she died.[118]

Not all infringements reported were as significant as those of the railway companies. People living near a bellowing chimney of a pianoforte factory in Wandsworth wrote to say that specks of char emitted were burning holes in the laundry hung out to dry; the rhythm of complaint was entirely explicable.[119] But the enforcement of legislation could be equally mired in loopholes. A smoke abuse violation could be evaded if an employer placed blame upon a stoker. The 'dilatory machinery of fines' could easily allow nuisances to recur again and again, and the time-worn infrastructure posed many impediments to modernity.[120] Restaurants and pubs were now required to observe a higher level of hygiene, a measure ultimately affecting millions of Londoners; a typical citizens' protest letter to the Council pleaded that lavatories and urinals attached to pubs were a 'disgrace to this twentieth century'.[121]

Employers whose workforce included both men and women had to provide separate lavatory accommodation. In 1898, the Public Control Committee received complaints about Benoit's, the Globe and the Pinolis restaurants in Wardour Street and Coventry Street. The inspector found an invisible chimney, in which game entrails and other food garbage were burned, that was spewing noxious vapours.[122] There were threats to food being sold on the markets. Growers at Covent Garden collected manure in the surrounding neighbourhoods in their carts, on top of which they placed empty vegetable containers.[123] Residents of Elm Grove complained that pigs were kept very near houses, in violation of the law.[124] Residents of Islington petitioned the Council to investigate the horse manure at the rear of their houses, an area used as a stable.[125]

Those who dumped filth into sewers were liable for prosecution; the sewer, bridge and street improvement authority was, of course, the LCC. The Council was charged with keeping the water supply constant and making certain that the appropriate fittings were used in plumbing works. The depth of the problem is captured by a note of 1894 declaring that in Islington, dustmen collected refuse only if a card placed in a window of a residence indicated that they should do so and if the owners made specific arrangements. There were dozens of cases of non-collection over four and six-week periods.[126] Watercress and similar foods were found growing in land fed by sewage.[127] In 1898 a survey of Kensington ironically found the dining rooms and coffee houses serving workmen to be generally cleaner than those of high-class restaurants. In eating establishments, water closets opened out into kitchens and dining rooms. Often, the kitchen and w.c. shared a restaurant basement. Diners were at risk 'when a basket of radishes [was] placed on the w.c. floor or when milk-churns [stood] close to the w.c.'. A drain serving an entire house and carrying household sewage was located in a restaurant basement. Not only were sleeping quarters found in such below-ground locations, but in the Strand, a pony was for years stabled in a restaurant kitchen.[128] A common rumour still held that the improvements of upper-class establishments were now 'filtering down' to those underneath. Soho appeared to be cleaner. Sir Thomas Lipton and his cronies in the London Coffee and Eating House Keepers' Association built almshouses with their profits; the spirit of reform and philanthropy had reached the refreshment tycoons before their colleagues saw fit to conform to the new regulatory norms.

SUSPECT WORKPLACES

The Council supervised aspects of metropolitan employment and prohibited underground bakeries and other unsuitable work locations. Hairdressers were notorious for violating the hours restrictions.[129] Unregulated laundries were thought harmful for child labourers 'both as regards health and companionship'.[130] Barbers' and hairdressers' were thought to be unsuitable work locations for children, because they lacked appropriate ventilation and were scenes of betting and 'betting talk'. The bookmakers supposedly made their headquarters there, though the police disputed the notion that the barbers' were uniquely responsible for demoralising the young.[131] A 1910 inquiry revealed that some thought that newsboys suffered the same ill effects: 'When they sell newspapers they always get into the habit of gambling and calling the winners and reading the papers from that point of view.'[132] Though this level of literacy might have been taken as a welcome sign, an LCC official instead cast the perennial eye of the class typologist upon the lads: 'There is not the slightest doubt that the boys who are selling the newspapers are of a distinctly inferior type. Those boys generally come from the poorest and the most neglected class of home.'[133] Children in the trade were routinely picked up for gambling and theft.

Outworkers' premises were inspected under the Factory and Workshops Acts. The boroughs were active in this effort, and in 1904 the greatest numbers of outworkers resided in Finsbury, the City, Stepney and St Marylebone.[134] In 1905, 34,579 names of outworkers were provided to the LCC by local authorities, and women inspectors were increasingly active in many districts in this work.[135] By this time, over 34,000 workshops in London were under some form of local authority supervision.[136] Establishments where men and women employees 'lived in', and massage parlours such as the Savoy Turkish Baths, were required to have separate sleeping areas for men and women.[137] Employment agencies were watched closely; they were thought to be covers for prostitution rings, and the by-laws stated that registrars at such agencies 'shall not enter the name of any person known to be a prostitute or otherwise of ill-repute, or to be connected with a house of ill-fame, and shall not knowingly transact business with such a person'.[138]

Predictably, agencies that housed women seeking employment had to enforce a rule of one person to a bed. Women officers of the LCC were given free access to these premises. In 1904, inspection was limited to firms catering to women and to theatrical agencies. The theatrical and music hall agents formed lobbying groups that acted as watchdogs of the inspections. Finally, a register was established from which these groups were exempt except in cases in which fees were charged. By early 1906, there were more than a thousand entries, including agencies that found work for domestic servants and governesses. Typists, shop assistants and barmaids were the ostensible beneficiaries of this policy, as were young Englishwomen who sought employment overseas. But these steps were not enough for the organisations that saw immorality proliferating in other unregulated areas of life. They instead demanded that agencies for men also be licensed, and a broadly supported petition campaign drew not only the stalwarts of the National Vigilance Society, but the theatre managers and the actors' unions. Groups of shop assistants, hotel and restaurant workers, hairdressers, bakers and confectioners demanded extended licensing provisions. Those seeking work were anxious to avoid fraudulent employers and saw licensing as a check on corrupt practices.[139]

Quite apart from the conflicts over whether particular restrictions ought to exist, there was the acute and perennial problem of enforcement. In 1896, for example, Bethnal Green vestry not surprisingly refused to insist upon the enactment of the provision for separate w.c.s in mixed workplaces.[140] The case involved a folding chair manufacturing establishment in which fourteen persons, including three women and four children, worked and whose employer was 'a poor working man and unable from financial reasons, to build another closet'. Had he been forced to carry out the vestry's wishes, the women would have been fired. The Home Office did not insist.[141] Here again the gap between policies as stated and policies as actuated could not be clearer; exceptions were made according to moral judgements, political lobbying and a fundamental resistance to breaches of custom. But this did not prevent the LCC or other bodies from substituting symbolic actions for coercion. In fact, the failure to patrol London in a comprehensive manner and the knowledge that the capacity to do so was absent may well have created a greater rationale for more conspicuous activity in visible terrain.

PROPRIETY, THE LODGING HOUSES AND CLEANSING: 'PIGS THEMSELVES SOME OF THEM'

The emphasis in regulation upon the separation of men and women and upon sexual propriety extended into many areas of public life. Shirley Murphy testified before the influential parliamentary committee of 1904 on 'Physical Deterioration' which was prompted by the recruitment problems encountered during the Boer War. Murphy had worked amongst the poor of St Giles in the

1860s and reminded his colleagues that starvation was less evident in London in the new century than it had been forty years earlier and that people were better clothed than they had been. But Murphy cautioned that the lodging houses were still places where 'people live[d] perhaps as hard and close as you will find anywhere'. In 1898, approximately 600 houses in which 30,000 people resided were under LCC supervision.[142] At the end of 1904, there were still 451 such structures in London that housed over 28,000 people.[143] By then, larger lodging houses were replacing smaller ones but, as an inspector put it, 'Here we have, then, in the common-lodging houses of London alone, the population of a fair-sized provincial town.'[144]

In addition, perhaps as many as one in a thousand Londoners had neither shelters nor lodging houses in which to sleep. Others were not homeless but were young people of about 20 who left home and who took up with vagrants, in effect becoming vagrants themselves. Still others were casually employed, awaiting call-ups for work. The kitchen of a house near the Thames was filled during daylight hours: 'Let but a runner break in among them with the cry "a ship in!" and there is a general rush for a job.' Newspaper reading, chess games and draughts kept the men busy.[145] Those who frequented the lodging houses travelled around town from place to place stopping wherever food was offered by the charities. Some slept two or three nights out of the houses and then a night in. It was believed that some had enough money to pay more than the house fees but were said to prefer always to pay as little as possible, necessitating their roaming sleeping habits. Though Whitechapel was the site of most of the frequented houses, other districts had visitors of particular tastes. Bermondsey was the 'old haunt of players, musicians and strollers'.[146]

A 1904 street survey indicated that one in every two thousand persons in London was homeless.[147] There were characters who inhabited this world with reputations made and broken; one regular was described by a keeper: 'they used to call him General Blücher, because he was always arguing that Blücher and not Wellington won Waterloo. So the parish buried him as Tom Blucher. Poor old General, he'd been with us this seven year or more.'[148] Death rates amongst the house residents were higher than those of the population at large. Murphy identified the 1901 death rate for 25-year-olds as six in seventy-four in the population at large; in the lodging houses, the death rate for the same age group was fifteen in twenty-four (for age 35, 12/76 and in the lodging houses, 22/62). Rates of phthisis and of alcoholism were similarly skewed. The labour markets of London, still dominated in many sectors by networks of seasonal, casual labour, brought to the lodging houses a population who spent their summers hop-picking in the country. Suburban jerrybuilders who outfitted the new manufacturing population in London's outer fringe and who housed the black-coated proletariat did not seek to accommodate the poor of central London, and few single-room tenements were available in town. In all likelihood, the lodging house had become a regular resting place for those with no ready foothold in the London economy and no access to housing of their own. Murphy's aide claimed:[149] 'We get a great many old soldiers; when they come back from India they cannot find any regular work and they take to the common lodging houses and finally become regular dossers.'[150] Murphy invoked Mayhew's earlier commentary on London vagrancy noting that the LCC had not recorded an increase in drifting lodgers on occasions like the Jubilee celebrations. Mayhew had claimed that the 1848 Chartist activities had drawn itinerants to London.[151] Now, the houses' residents were most often regulars.

In the 1890s, women's accommodation in the lodging houses was inferior to that of men, yet women labourers, hawkers and laundrywomen were charged inflated rates. Often a conversion of a single family house had occurred without additional washing facilities being added; most lacked fixed baths.[152] Once the LCC had become the lodging house authority, a task it inherited from the Metropolitan Police in 1894, it promptly ordered that 90 per cent of bedding in the houses be destroyed and proudly reduced the number of houses available to couples.[153] Parents with children had very rarely been admitted to lodging houses.[154] The inspectors furtively watched for 'immoral use' of those houses that remained mixed. Concerned observers also contacted the LCC, as in the case of an anonymous sailor who wrote in 1905 of a house in Great Pearl Street.[155] In that same year, two LCC inspectors assigned to a house in Stepney reported that at 9:30 p.m., 'they [had] noticed a man and a woman about to go downstairs – they had occupied cubicle no. 37; the bed was warm and the chamber utensil had been used'.[156] The man had paid for an overnight stay. But an interview with a housekeeper revealed that much was left unsaid, despite the new regulations: 'She's feared most o' the women as comes here is unfortunates, and as to the married couples, well, we asks no questions and they tells us no lies, and never produces their marriage certificates.'[157]

There were other common skirting practices: 'The inspectors turn up in the middle of the night, always in twos on such occasions. If there be a back door it must be watched as well, lest the surplus sleepers be hurriedly wakened and expeditiously ejected before the door is open to the inspectors at the front.'[158] These were the same inspectors in many instances who dealt with infant life protection and midwifery, nine of whom served under Murphy in the late 1890s. Their language, and the language of those associated with housing and lodging matters, often deployed an elaborate system of classification of the human subject. Tenants and housekeepers alike were classified: 'the butcher applicant had a large experience of common lodging house work, is temperate and in Mr. Master's opinion is, in every respect, a fit and proper person to be licensed'.[159]

The indefatigable Octavia Hill, housing reformer and high priestess of tenement philanthropy, was interviewed by the LCC. Hill and the borough-level inspectors were asked to provide information that might prove useful in formulating policy. Here, Hill is questioned about residents of 'ten shillings a week' furnished rooms, as distinct from inhabitants of lodging houses:

A.　　They are very much the same character of people as those in common lodging houses.

Q.　　They are of the same class.

A.　　Class is a very difficult word to use in connection with this. But they are people of very much the same character – people of the same kind.

A.　　They are spendthrifts; they are drunkards; they are people with no homes.

A.　　*(York, Hill's co-worker)* Some of them broken-down men.

A.　　Still they have a certain family feeling.

A.　　*(York)* Some of them.[160]

But Mr. Pettit, a Kensington inspector, also reported on a particular street in his district (the 'worst street before the Council took over the houses'), noting that there were a vast variety of occupations represented amongst its tenants, including a clerk, an artist and a grocer, and only four tenants who were possibly immoral women,

> that is to say of the professional immoral class, and this is an accurate return . . . I think we may take it that whenever one finds two women chumming together in a room, they are certain to be prostitutes and there are a certain number of rooms like that in those streets.[161]

He explained further in regard to registered lodging houses:

> I have myself made a night inspection of the registered houses in Finsbury. I have taken two or three streets, put police at each end, and gone right through and counted the people there. The same thing has been done in Kensington.[162]

He affirmed the changes in parts of the district after greater regulation:

> What the Medical Officer of Health says is quite true. Bangor Street is as well-known to the Public Health Department of the LCC as it is to me. There were those classes of people down there . . . in days gone by. Policemen dared not go through those streets singly; they used to go in pairs. Today it is quite different.[163]

These are not LCC personnel speaking, but they are part of the milieu of inspection; they are speaking *with* the LCC, in confidence. A borough committee chair added:

> One of the serious risks of these . . . houses is the women . . . we have down there the dregs of the clearances of Kensington and Marylebone, and the old slums . . . they went down there and kept pigs and the County Council would not allow them to keep pigs, and the pigs were moved out of the County.
> Q. And the survivors?
> A. Became pigs themselves some of them.[164]

H.A. Jury, chief LCC lodging house inspector, testified in 1905 that 10 per cent of LCC common lodging house dwellers were of the 'vagrant class'.[165] Here the interplay of the local and the municipal with the social geography of street migrations suggests a sense of being under siege, of one removal policy simply begetting another. The allegorical pig persisted. And besides the native English poor, inspectors also watched those in lodgings frequented by aliens. They referred to these immigrants as 'greeners'. A typical reference was to a house of nineteen people who came from St Petersburg and who were housed in seven or eight beds.[166]

Inconsistencies in the testimony of matters pertaining to vagrants, amongst other unclean persons, arose. In 1904, Murphy sharply disputed the implication of his questioners in discussing the efficacy of the 'cleansing of persons' legislation, which impelled the sanitary authorities to clean the clothes and persons of those found to be verminous:[167]

> *Q.* I suppose these dirty persons do not see the point of being clean?
>
> *A.* I do not think so altogether, because in Marylebone where provision of this sort has been made, and where there is a large Salvation Army shelter, great numbers of these people have gone there for cleansing operations, so that I am hopeful that people of that class would avail themselves of opportunities if they were really given.[168]

He further explained that a verminous person was certainly regarded as *persona non grata* by other lodging house residents.[169] But he concluded from this and other observations that an enforced cleansing policy 'would have to be done very carefully, because a power of that sort might be used to the annoyance of individuals'.[170] The fear of being overly intrusive is contained in his warning. Similarly, the vaccination work of the Council had provoked conscientious objectors.[171] Was there a way to distinguish amongst those who were given assistance? When appearing before the Committee on Vagrancy in 1905, Murphy spoke of the 'sleepers out', as they were termed: 'My personal view would be that they should be put among the class that it was the business of the state to take care of.' The worst class of person could be effectively segregated away.[172]

Murphy distinguished between the useful and the indigent, however arbitrarily, by employing an explicit distinction embedded in the wider housing policy of the Council. Over 15,000 individuals deemed suitable were living in LCC housing estates by 1904, many self-selected simply on the basis of income.[173] As the Chief Sanitary Inspector of Bethnal Green explained it in 1898: 'The conditions and rents the Council impose, render it simply impossible for poor people to live in their houses.' He claimed that the building of the Boundary Street Estate had resulted in the displacement of thousands of neighbourhood residents; not even 5 per cent of the original inhabitants could afford to return and were now creating overcrowding of lesser, nearby accommodations.[174] After recounting the story of a man who searched for housing, Inspector Foot exclaimed:

> that . . . is how the Act [Public Health of 1875, 1899] works. The poor are hunted from pillar to post, but the housing problem remains unsolved . . . We shift the position of the housing problem, but never solve it . . . See, now, how the County Council's scheme works. A man, with wife and two children and a third expected, have been found occupying a single room in one of the new blocks at Boundary-street. The County Council say: we will turn them out. What a remedy! Does the Council think they occupy one room because they like it? They are living in one room because they cannot for the life of them afford two. If the Council turn them out they will crowd into a worse room in our smaller property and then I shall have to turn them out – when I discover them – and if I succeed in driving them out of the parish, as I do in some instances, God help them; for the same miserable game must be played by other inspectors. But you are never going to tell me that that is solving the housing question.

Foot believed that the Act assumed that affordable and plentiful housing existed for all in need, according to their station. This myth would result in there being 'nothing but streets of workhouses for hundreds of families if the full letter of the law were carried out'.[175] Foot called for more workmen's trains and for amendments to the housing acts such that local authorities would have a greater responsibility to provide housing in keeping with his labour testimony before the 1903 Royal Commission on Housing. Touching on the theme of profitability in enterprise, he concluded that 'only the professional slum owner and the Jew who run these small properties at a decent profit' stood to benefit financially from the system; they charged the maximum in rent and did little by way of maintenance.[176]

Other similar projections of policy showed signs of a persistent spirit of collectivism. A conference of authorities held in 1904, for example, took up the call for the erection of public slaughterhouses and for disinfection crews to be hired 'without the intervention of a contractor', linking the need for public facilities to the call for a publicly employed workforce.[177] But the impulse to expand participation in municipal projects and to provide better services was not endorsed by the LCC in the ways in which such critics saw fit even though it had attempted to pioneer radical design in the construction of public housing both in inner and outer London.[178]

The Cleansing of Persons Act applied to people living in all of London housing, not just in the buildings designated as lodging houses or Council housing. Diseases such as measles were attacked in public notices that described the necessity of cleaning and disinfecting homes. Temporary housing was made available to families under inspection. Those who failed to relinquish the clothing of a victim of disease could be fined. A house in which infection was found had to remain unoccupied. Those infected were not to travel on public vehicles. Bodies were not to be kept in private homes for longer than forty-eight hours.[179] Yet Isabel Smith, in this instance in her guise as enforcer of these rules, asked in 1903 about the problem of an unidentified illness that had not been selected for regulation:

> On whom devolves the duty of acquainting the sanitary authorities of an outbreak of this disease in any particular house, compulsory notification (section 55) being, in this case, not required? I would point out that this disease is very commonly treated, especially among the lower classes, without medical assistance, so that in very many cases the means of acquainting the medical officer would not be available.[180]

Her question is another reminder of the discrepancy between the laws and regulations as stated (along with the ways in which the staff may have assimilated such rules), and the degree to which there was a capacity for their implementation. The perceived limits on policy are very clear in the remarks of the chair of the Kensington Public Health Committee who is referring to lodging house inspection:

> They are inspected eight or nine times a year now. Perhaps it should be done oftener if the tenants are bad enough, but it becomes of course difficult to have an army of inspectors in and out of the place, and there is a point at which the persons inspected become rebels. So really you come back to the moral problem, where everything has been done to control the

people who let these lodgings – whose object, and quite rightly, is that of making money out of them: but the ultimate problem is how are you going to make the people you are acting for act decently. It comes to that.[181]

The motives for placing pressure upon the Council were as varied as the lobbyists themselves. Witness the plea of a licensed Poplar lodging housekeeper: 'I want to call your attention to No. 27 Pennyfield, as they are keeping a Boarding and Lodging House there and are not under your control as my house is, and they are enticing my boarders away from me.'[182] The moralist contended with those who sought economic reward. Differing conceptions of the role and nature of morality increasingly confronted the LCC and made the execution of policies more awkward.[183] The most unambiguous feature of the provision and maintenance of lodging houses remained their inadequacy in the face of London's housing problems. As purveyors of moral rectitude, LCC inspectors certainly did manage in some instances to address problems of disease and overcrowding. But financial and political constraints inhibited a policy of ample provision and contributed to a form of stasis in the levels of vagrancy and unemployment. This pattern was arguably institutionalised in the later history of the 'welfare state'.

PLEASURE AND THE PARKS

The movement to beautify and preserve parklands in metropolitan areas spread through the great European and American cities as the century drew to a close, and the LCC was a leading public authority in this campaign.[184] John Burns took pride in the Council's accomplishments in more than one hundred miles of gardens, parks and open spaces, and his words convey both the spirit of beautification and moral purity that characterised the Progressive endeavour. He praised the park-keepers who had 'enabled the parks of London to be rid of the lecherous loungers who made some of the parks unenjoyable to children, girls and women'. He warned that many such pariahs were 'generally well-dressed and of gentlemanly appearance'.[185] Even though the LCC prided itself on its commitment to the protection of women and children, there were obstacles in its way. Children's testimony, for example, was not accepted as proper evidence against a suspect.[186] In the case of one of its own park employees charged with offences, the Council noted that 'It is a safe rule to believe no one when enquiring into sexual matters.'[187] Yet, in a typical instance of 'acceptable' surveillance, inspectors hiding near a urinal witnessed an alleged homosexual incident for which the perpetrators received three months' imprisonment.[188] In the case of a 17-year-old boy found with a girl aged 7 in Highbury Fields, the boy's stepfather agreed to give him 'a good thrashing, [a] good lecture and [to extract] a promise to behave in the future'.[189] A 12-year-old girl and a 9-year-old boy found together committing an act received no punishment because of their youth. A man who wrote to a girl and arranged to meet her in Highbury Fields and then indecently assaulted her was given six months' hard labour after a third person reported the incident to the authorities. The 'criminal' history of the parks provides a shadowy background to a later history of contestation over parks provision.[190]

The Parks and Open Spaces Committee of the LCC was responsible for opening up much of London for public recreation (see Figure 4). In the summer of 1901 alone, over a thousand performances were staged by the LCC in open spaces and in facilities acquired for the occasions.[191] Hundreds of societies formed in London neighbourhoods for sporting and other purposes. They made frequent use of the only areas of space and sunlight available to most of the population. In 1909, park booking applications were received from organisations as diverse as the London Amateur Wrestling Society, the Clapham Steam and Sailing Club, the Church of England Society for Providing Homes for Waifs and Strays, and the Balham Independent Labour Party. (The latter's request was rejected and its members forced to meet instead on nearby street corners.)[192]

The Council had the responsibility for parks maintenance and the right to take over a public square temporarily in order to improve it and to purchase lands for public walks or for use as pleasure gardens. On a fine, hot Sunday, as many as 25,000 people used the bathing facilities 'carefully screened by shrubs', especially in spaces such as Victoria Park. And in the heavy winter ice of 1894–95, the surfaces of the ponds were broken so bathers could brave the waters.[193] This work did not escape controversy. Sunday games were abolished in 1903, in keeping with the desires of the observant amongst the Progressives. Elaborate rules of public conduct circumscribed everyday use of the parks. Forbidden were:

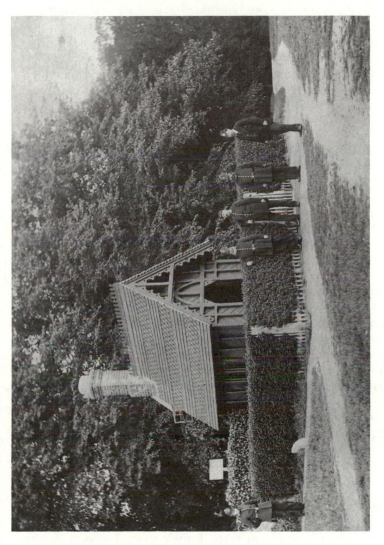

Figure 4 Park keepers, Bostall Woods, *c.* 1895 (Greater London Photograph Library, GLRO)

tents, drying of clothes, beating of carpets, washing of clothes and dogs, sorting of rags, letting of animals without a licence, shooting of game and other animals; use of firearms, acts of indecency or nuisance, distributing bills or selling articles, collecting money, misusing w.c.s or urinals, playing games except where allowed, playing musical instruments, fishing without authority, holding public meetings except on parks set aside for same, within enclosed space where entrance was prohibited, drilling except where authorised, practising gymnastics without proper authority or in any way interfering with the public comfort.[194]

As part of a wider critique of what was derisively termed 'municipal puritanism', Anglican cleric and LCC councillor Stewart Headlam and others polemicised against various LCC measures.[195] The Metropolitan Radical Federation approved a resolution in 1904 in agreement with Headlam. It expressed support for his objection to 'the dangerous and mischievous tendency towards Puritanism of the Progressive members of the LCC . . . we welcome, and will accord our support to any effort to infuse a more liberal spirit into the administration of our music halls, theatres, parks and open spaces'.[196] While Headlam applauded the seizure of 3900 acres of commons land by the LCC, he wanted there to be school parties held in settings such as the terrace of the Marble Hill Estate, now under LCC control. He called for the inauguration of 'music, dancing and drinking on a summer evening', as part of a general plea for the municipalisation of cafes and pubs. As for Sunday restrictions in the parks, he wrote of the denial of 'healthy, manly games in these days of alleged physical degeneracy'. Even the prototypical 'middle-aged ratepayer' was denied the pleasure of playing bowls in the parks. Women could not use the swimming baths on Sunday, and men could use them only between 7 and 9 o'clock in the mornings. Headlam wrote of the 'wastefully long working hours' of young Londoners, and declared:

> all these restrictions tend to prevent many Londoners from using their own common property at all; they handicap the overworked in the interest of their more fortunate fellow citizens . . . the LCC which sets such a bad example in these matters, where it ought to be the model for all employers, might at any rate remove all these Sunday restrictions. If it keeps its clerks working hours of overtime without payment

during the week, it might let them use the Parks for recreation on Sunday.[197]

Here, Headlam draws attention to the alleged hypocrisy of the Council. In its rationalisation of leisure, it censored public taste and sought to impose moral values that were arguably unprofessed and unpopular. Speakers were required to seek permits and were forbidden to use immoral language. The Chief Officer of Parks alone could approve pamphlets and leaflets for sale or distribution in his domain. The London Secularists felt the full force of these rules when some of their literature was banned from sale. The policy continued beyond the Progressive period, and under the Moderate regime the Secularists were frequently denied permission to hold outdoor park meetings.[198] A July 1895 report from a superintendent at Victoria Park attested to the complications of work in the parks. He wrote of a 'most heavy and trying day':

> There were political parties of all grades, religious meetings of numerous denominations, Roman Catholics and anti-Romanists, Atheists, Humorous Sketch Actors, Reciters, a returned convict of fifteen years, (stating his grievances) and numerous other groups studied about; from 10 a.m. till close of [the] Park.

These observations appeared in response to a citizen's complaint that a policeman had jostled him while he listened to a speaker. The superintendent defended the officer in question and added, by way of explanation:

> Itinerant speakers are on the increase, many of them drawing knots or gatherings of people for many to support themselves and family. In fact – their real object is begging under the guise of telling some tale or recitation. I often feel it ought not to be allowed, but under the by-laws I cannot see any regulation to check it, as long as collections are authorised for other objects . . . it is on the increase and bringing disgrace and desecration of the Sabbath into our public parks. Most of them are habitual workers in all the large parks and make their living thereby.[199]

Lewd language, 'with intent to insult any female', was banned in the parks, along with a host of other practices from dancing to brawling to gambling. Physicality was conflated with the spoken word:

> Brawling, fighting, quarrelling, cursing, swearing, or using indecent or improper language or holding or taking part in any running, fighting, boxing, wrestling or walking match; being intoxicated, gambling, playing at any game of chance, betting or playing with cards or dice, begging, telling fortunes, selling or distributing any information book of print, lying on any of the seats, or lying, sleeping, sitting or resting in an indecent posture, or being disorderly or wilfully or designedly doing any act which outrages public decency, or which comes within the meaning of the Vagrant Act, George IV, cap. 83, whether the offence shall have been or be committed with intent to insult any female or not.[200]

Parks employees who identified children with infectious diseases were obliged to report them to the authorities. Urinating in ponds or water or against trees or on seats was forbidden. Only young children could enter lavatories reserved for the opposite sex. There was a five-pound maximum penalty for offences, not to exclude twenty shillings for each day of a continued offence after notice was given. Gypsies, hawkers, beggars, rogues and vagabonds could be excluded or removed from the sites. The unwanted incurred a penalty if they refused to flee. The offences of assault with intent to rob, uttering menacing demands of money, the 'infamous crime', arming oneself with the intent to commit burglary and so on, were forbidden under park regulations.[201] Explicitly prohibited, for example, was 'exposing to view in any public place any obscene print or picture, or [the action of a man] obscenely exposing his person with intent to insult any female'. Wounds and deformities could not be flaunted for the purpose of soliciting alms. Action was taken against a man at Bow Street Police Court in 1909, for example, who was charged with being 'drunk and disorderly' and with assaulting a Council employee. Two residents of Brixton were prosecuted for 'wilfully outraging public decency at Brockwell Park'. An incident of indecency in Victoria Park brought three months' imprisonment.[202] The upstanding were always distinguished from the downtrodden; often the unstated purpose of a rule or an action was to affirm the desire for social separation:

A number of tramps and other apparently homeless persons, are in the habit on certain days of the week of making the Green [Brook Green, Hammersmith] their rendezvous for the day. They arrive early in the morning, and bring parcels of broken food with them, which they got from Nazareth House. They occupy the seats, and lie about the grass all day, and leave their refuse such as paper, boxes and pieces of bread lying about. Some of them are in the most filthy condition and the seats, and Green, are rendered quite unfit for decent people to use after them.[203]

Yet the Council's critics approached what they saw as its puritanism with tactical caution. Headlam did not wish to suggest, for example, that mandatory, conformist sporting activities were desirable, and he warned that the

crude denunciation of Freedom which is popular in some socialist circles may be preparing the way for evils from which England – and the Church – suffered under the Commonwealth . . . the appetite for managing other people's lives in the interests of a supposed morality grows by what it feeds on, and it is not difficult to imagine the advent of a Puritan morality which will for the time make short work of things more important than music halls and public houses and Sunday games.[204]

Even the Earl of Meath, who chaired the Parks and Open Spaces Committee of 1889, advocated the liberation of facilities, especially after observing the use of public spaces in American cities. He wrote in amazement of Jackson Park in Chicago, in which a ballroom large enough to accommodate 2500 people had been erected in a shelter:

I was told that no evils or improprieties had resulted from this liberal course of action, but the privilege was innocently enjoyed and thoroughly appreciated by the citizens. If this can be done in Chicago, a city containing a million of souls composed of all nationalities, why should it not be possible in London? In American parks, even in those where the most stringent police regulations are in force, great facilities are given to the people to enjoy themselves.[205]

A concern not to alienate the public, the commitment to maintaining order and the practical problem of understaffing all deeply influenced parks policy. Despite a public rhetoric of tight regulation, parks constables were issued 'confidential instructions' which indicate that over-zealous duty was a problem:

> One of the frequent remarks of a certain section of the public is that a constable is a servant. This is not so, but on the other hand, a constable is not the master of the public . . . a hard and fast line should not be drawn with regard to the literal meaning of the by-laws. Most of the by-laws are intended to be put into force only when nuisance or damage is arising from the infraction of them.[206]

Constables were not to end meetings abruptly at sunset or to arrest a person who volunteered a name and address. The Council was not to censor the language of speakers unless the speaker actually violated the law, and the hope that 'doctrines and remarks of the speakers are not interfered with' was recorded. Constables were themselves subjected to a strict regimen; they could not, for example, enter a pub in uniform. They could not smoke on duty or read a newspaper lest they appear idle. The serious cases and procedures were reserved for assaults and thefts.[207] But when constables were warned that the mere perception of an individual as an objectionable person was not sufficient justification for turning someone out of a park, members of the public in organised groups often maintained that it was.[208] Those whose appearance was undesirable or whose actions were suggestive were seen as immoral. Here is a complaint signed by a group of Hammersmith ratepayers:

> During the school holidays, they come here in such numbers that the place is like a pandemonium. At nights the seats are occupied by men and women, some of them of the most degraded character and gross acts of indecency are committed . . . they [those complaining] were heavily rated and [wanted] quiet enjoyment of homes secured.[209]

One group of Londoners complained about another, employing the moral categories already familiar to the Council. Instead of uncovering a social hierarchy tightly defined along 'class lines', a councillor of either party was likely to find his constituency composed of tireless bands of citizens protesting against the public behaviour and habits of those around them and not necessarily simply of those thought to be of an inferior social origin, though such sentiment was common and fierce. Even the humble voiced their grievances. In 1893, in response to the regulations imposed upon coster barrows, the North London Male and Female Costermongers Union 'objected to being interfered with by the Council or by vestries and [as they put it, they] desired to be regulated solely by the police regulations'.[210]

In many respects, the LCC met these sentiments halfway. Its parks policy was an extension of the methodology suggested in more general ways by the Council's philosophy of social policy. The heartfelt expectations and hopes of many of its staff were encapsulated in the plea made by Alfred George Chamings to the Parliamentary committee investigating the workings of the 1903 Employment of Children Act. Chamings was asked:

> If the same boy has got nothing to do in future he will belong to the class who will become less intelligent instead of more intelligent?
>
> No; I look at it from a different point of view. If you can once get that smart and quick boy into regular employment he will get on well in life. Once get him into street trading, he gets into a wrong channel. . . . For instance, you well know the good results of training children in industrial schools when they have come from the very worst class; they get into the right channel and you save them for life.[211]

Another kind of judgement against unremunerative 'hand-outs' is discernible in the private deliberations of the Public Health Committee of 1906, which discussed vagrancy and the practices of charity houses. The committee felt that it could 'safely affirm that the weight of evidence given . . . points irresistibly to the conclusion that both free food and free shelters are demoralising to the recipients and a source of danger to the community'. There was even sentiment in favour of closing such shelters in order to force their inhabitants to fend for themselves. Casual wards could be reorganised, those seeking work could be assisted and 'habitual' vagrants could be sent to labour colonies which would 'suffice to secure to the community a more effective and uniform protection than has hitherto existed against tramp-borne disease, and in particular should afford a more satisfactory safeguard against the spread of smallpox'.[212]

The committee concluded that sleeping out should be made a punishable offence because those who did so were 'unclean and verminous and filthy in their habits'. As if to reconcile both kinds of judgements, against charity and in favour of productive labour, the 'bona fide working man' was distinguished from vagrants. The committee called for the children of the 'habitual vagrants' to be 'sent to industrial schools or other places of safety'.[213] Similarly, when the Earl of Meath advocated the extension of the use of London's parks and spaces, he embellished his plea with this observation: 'The experience I have gained as Chairman of the Metropolitan Public Garden Association has shown me that the English working man can always be trusted to protect public property if properly appealed to.'[214] Not only did these intertwined assumptions dictate the approaches discussed within Council circles toward London's working population, but the LCC strove to put the exclusive control of all care facilities into its own hands in order to rationalise municipal philanthropy.

Though the Council was unsuccessful in these efforts to control many of London's social and leisure institutions, as we have seen, there were many exemplary, nominal crusades. For example, when the LCC boasted in 1900 that 'the attempt to reduce the temptation to excessive drinking in our streets, our parks, and our music halls is known of by all men',[215] the Inebriates Acts Committee had only housed thirty women patients in two country mansions. The environmental sentiments that governed their approach to care surely prevented a mass approach: 'Poultry, bees and other details of farm life are not forgotten, and everything is done to take the patients back to simple, natural life such as that typified in the English country homestead.' The few patients did provide something in return:

> Their life histories provide opportunities for reflection alike to the anthropologist and the philanthropist . . . the work is novel, experimental no doubt, but full of hope. It is well that the late century and the Victorian era, with which the progress of the 'new humanity' has been so closely interwoven, did not close without at least inaugurating, under municipal management, a movement for the restoration of our social wrecks, the rehabilitation of the victims of our national curse.[216]

Such hopeful claims, in the face of limited success, were matched by the broadness and earnestness of public grievance. Instead of a movement for social transformation, a cycle of complaint gripped the metropolis. The Registers of 'Insanitary Conditions, Signed

Complaints' contain literally thousands of everyday instances of invective, pique, annoyance, disturbance, accusation and desire for retribution — testaments to this dynamic, popular feature of Londoners' irritations with one another. 'Persons of bad character' were said to be misusing a passage and creating a nuisance in Westminster. Stopped-up drains or defective w.c.s, a result of overcrowding, left filth in their wake. At LCC estates, such as Swan Lake in Bermondsey and the Ann Street Dwellings, tenants crowded into a pub to use the urinal, or 'persons of both sexes' were observed simply using the street. In Lewisham, at the Victoria Villas, a private footpath was used for 'disreputable purposes'. Large numbers of complaints centred upon the issue of offensive odours. In Hackney there was an 'alleged nuisance from the frying of fish in the backyard of no. 34 and the use as a smokehole of an improperly paved stable'. The keeping of cats and pigeons and of fowls and rabbits elicited disgust. Despite the absence of LCC jurisdiction (a constant problem), the Council was informed of a large tree obstructing light and air. A gas company's refuse polluted a river.

In Lambeth, Robert's Restaurant reportedly maintained a forbidden sleeping apartment for waiters. It was rumoured that an 'unsuitable basement kitchen' was used as an unventilated workroom on a dressmaking premises where workers were not permitted time off for dinner. Another workplace persisted in 'dirty and badly ventilated conditions' containing a 'dangerous lift' and an absence of separate w.c.s for men and women. Workmen at Solomon's leather factory were exposed to fumes resulting from the melting of lead and zinc on the premises. And Clegg's of New Bond Street was the scene of the 'alleged overcrowded condition of a workroom occupied by foreign Jews . . . nuisance from the keeping of dogs in one of the rooms . . . [and] an inadequate w.c.'. These are a select few examples from an unending list that proliferated over many years.[217]

The metamorphoses of London's economy and of her habitable environment and the extension of urban life into the bucolic surrounding outer areas provided a measure of social differentiation and another cause for complaint. As a Streatham resident described his predicament:

The inhabitants have not only been disturbed by the noise of the trams and the tremendous increase of people on our common thereby, but apparently are now to have this additional annoyance of socialistic lecturers with their vans. I know perfectly well that these vans have been allowed in the public parks for years past, but we can hardly look upon Streatham, Wandsworth or Clapham in exactly the same way as you can London Parks.[218]

The register allowed Londoners to record their sense of etiquette and propriety as much as their complaints about the work of the Council.

EDUCATION AS AN OPPORTUNITY FOR SOCIAL REGULATION

Here is a description of the procedures of the cleansing operations carried out by the LCC in the schools in 1897:

> The Nurses were allocated to districts, and every third week began a thorough examination of the school; every child was examined and the parents of children with verminous heads were notified by a white card which also gave directions for cleansing. At the end of a week a further examination was made and, if the head was still unclean, the child was made to sit separately in the class and the school attendance officer served an urgent warning (red card) at the home. If at the end of a further week the unclean condition still persisted the parent was prosecuted for not sending the child in a fit state to school. This method was slow but was effective in bringing to the knowledge of a certain number of parents the need for dealing with the trouble.[219]

By 1905, this system involved the inspection of over 119,000 children, fewer than half of whom had clean heads when they were first examined. Over 500 cases were pursued to the point of prosecution.[220] By 1907, seventeen borough councils were participating in this initiative.

Those who believed in the regenerative powers of the Council vested their hopes in massive changes in London education.[221] When the LCC became the schools authority in 1904, it seemed at first as if the many causes of social disorder could be cut off at the root. Yet the addition of the School Board actually put the final touches on the electoral rout of Progressivism. Rates went up, leaving the impression that the LCC was responsible for the rises; many did not realise that the incorporation of the old school board rate into the county rate accounted for a large portion of the rises. Contention over schools policy created further tensions between the Progressives and their supporters.[222] The prior question lingers: how did the schools figure in the overall vision of social amelioration?

No other branch of Council work required more involvement with families and households. The provision of meals, medical and cleansing duties and curricular development in areas such as housewifery were all taken up by this branch. The concern was for the 'children who will be the mothers and housekeepers of the future [for whom] the school dinner may itself be made to serve as a valuable object-lesson and used to re-enforce the practical instruction in hygiene, cookery and domestic economy'.[223] In 1907, perhaps coincident with the greater regulatory powers tested by the Conservatives in the schools, Robert Morant, Chief Education Officer, articulated his guiding premises. These flowed from a sense of the interconnectedness of school endeavours and home life. The invocation of the private was inevitable:

> School hygiene cannot be divorced from home hygiene, and this in turn is intimately bound up with the hygienic conditions of the community. Efficiency and economy require, therefore, an organic relationship between the daily work of the school authority and of the authority responsible for the administration of the wider branches of public health.

Inspection should include, according to Morant, 'the consideration of social factors, such as the occupation of the parents, or the health, habits and physical conditions of the family, all of which have a bearing, direct or indirect, upon the children's health'.[224]

Thousands of voluntary Care Committees in the schools were created to assist the LCC's educational work. They were most often made up of women of 'superior' backgrounds who acted as amateur social workers amongst the schoolchildren and their families. The committees were originally founded in 1907 as canteen committees for 'necessitous schools' under the aegis of the Education (Provision of Meals) Act of 1900.[225] As L.A. Selby-Bigge, a departmental principal, put it in 1909, legislation carried out by the LCC had enabled more public monies to assist in this kind of care, which had previously been handled through the voluntary sector. But now volunteers could lend their assistance to the LCC education work, 'and it is not too much to hope that the workers enlisted in the service of the children may through them obtain influence in the homes, and thus carry on an effective warfare against ignorance' and carelessness.[226] Aspects of this work were candidly termed 'eugenic', and by 1910 the Council understood its purpose in treating unwell children as 'attempting to touch as far as it may, the *cause* of the children's ill-health, malnutrition or neglect. This cause is not in the school, but in the home.'[227]

The Care Committees were admonished to be sure that 'neglectful parents [were] reminded of duties'.[228] The LCC staff may have welcomed the integration of voluntary workers into the department; their mission was now complemented by the work of those who possessed powers of persuasion. As one departmental member put it:

> The municipal officer's outlook and training has fitted him to give orders to subordinates, to demand statistics and to ignore the 'personal operation' in human affairs. In the voluntary system, the officer must learn to suggest rather than to dictate.[229]

Tremendous effort was expended in organising thousands of volunteers. A Miss Morton of the Catholic Women's League lectured on the duties of the Care Committees, instructing their members to inquire about 'wages, who is working [and] outgoings, of families who could not feed their children, and to record their findings in a book to be in turn checked by those who have knowledge of the facts, such as a visitor already in touch with the family, who is able to give a description of the state of the home as to cleanliness'. Free meals were not to be wasted, and the case worker was to record instances in which men drank or were out of work. After all, many children were needy because of their 'parents' character'.[230] Indeed, Morton estimated that 45 per cent of cases could be attributed to intemperance, and these were cases in which the children could be separated from their parents and placed in industrial homes under the Children Act.

During 1907–08, over 2200 children were excluded from school in order for the LCC to prosecute cases drawn from those of the 92,000 children who were inspected. Ultimately, the parents of 255 children were prosecuted.[231] And even in 1911, 15 per cent of all London schoolchildren were deemed 'necessitous', requiring either food, clothing, or boots and shoes at some point during the school year. In some poorer schools, as we have seen above, one-fifth of the children were employed in the hours spent away from school;

in others, as many as half of the children worked and their earnings were needed in order for their families to survive. Even the authorities understood this.[232]

In 1907, when the Conservatives came to power, the duties of the Public Control Committee with regard to infringement of the Shops Acts involving juveniles were transferred to the Education Committee, along with 'many duties not wholly or directly educational but dealing with what may be called the "social welfare" of the child'. (Note the newness of the terminology.)[233] When the teachers were asked to watch out for child labourers, their response was categorical: 'The teachers generally complain of the street-traders being out of control and using bad language, and that kind of thing.'[234] At the same time, those devising new schools policy watched the public's 'jealousy and suspicion' should they step too far into the lives of children outside of school.[235] Others involved in the issues of child labour were critical of parental motives. Public control officials levelled charges of corruption: 'in a great many cases we find it is pure selfishness on the parts of parents. Very often there are quite good wages coming in.'[236] Action and recommendations had to take into account the existence of the dual sectors of care, both voluntary and municipal.

Ironically, the LCC thought that the Care Committee personnel might prefer committee work to inquiry work; actually getting out and investigating the child's home life was perhaps more daunting than voicing the need for this step to be taken. There were discrepancies in provision that resulted from the newly cobbled together system. One child from a family was deemed eligible for care and was fed, another from the same family was not. Families could live adjacent to each other and their children might be fed in one neighbourhood while in another they were not, though the homes the children came from were similarly needy. Blair wanted to record an integrated family history for each child, to take greater pains in cross-referencing reports and in accumulating data on the children.[237] Eventually, under Municipal Reform, the Care Committee work was merged with that of the Juvenile Advisory Committee so that the supervision of a child could occur over the four years after he had left school.[238] In the years just before the War, more recognition was given to the need of the committees to be strengthened and to enlist better-trained members. Cases in which children were molested received a higher order of commitment in departmental policy.[239]

The observed state of children at school led the LCC to homes that needed to be 'cleansed, purified, destroyed or stripped'. In cases where the child was considered habitually dirty, he or she was excluded from school. Verminous clothing was considered a nuisance, and verminous heads deemed a sign of the absence of 'self-respect': 'the revelation of the state of these children often causes astonishment and disgust in the teachers . . . that such conditions are tolerated gives an idea of the conditions of the homes'.[240] The need to enter the homes is repeatedly emphasised in LCC internal memos and correspondence. A letter of 1910 reveals that a head teacher treated the disinfection of a home in which unclean children lived as a customary step, that 'from want of it the children return to school as bad as before the cleansing'.[241] Even though school nurses visited the homes after cleansing the children at school, they were often prevented from completing their inspection: 'She is unable to gain admittance to the house, or to the living rooms'.[242] Children were frequently bathed at school and, at least in St Pancras, they repeatedly took 'joy . . . in hot water immersion'.[243] In verminous cases, children were given haircuts (see Figure 5).[244] In an unusually violent episode during the War, a mother struck a nurse who had cut her daughter's hair. After appearing in court she came to see the nurse and reproached her. The nurse reported that the mother cried,

> 'What do you mean by cutting her hair . . . and why didn't you cut it all off? I know, why you didn't; it's because you are wrong, I know what the Magistrate said last week in the Police Court I know. What do you think we are, Germans that you can do as you like with us, I'll see you don't. I'll have you', and then, shaking her fist at me she said, 'If I thought you were the one who cut the hair I'd do for you.'[245]

As the nurse went to shut the door, the woman's fist came through the glass, and she struck the nurse on the head. Though this might well have been an isolated case, the nurse recounted it as if it were not: 'Men around took no notice. I feel that there is not adequate protection for the nurse working here and surely this is proof; in the cleansing station we are buried away from all hope of police protection and little chance of getting other.'[246] Maud Ould, the mother in question, was fined, though she denied having committed the assault.[247] The Medical Officer's candid report made it clear that there were plenty of complaints

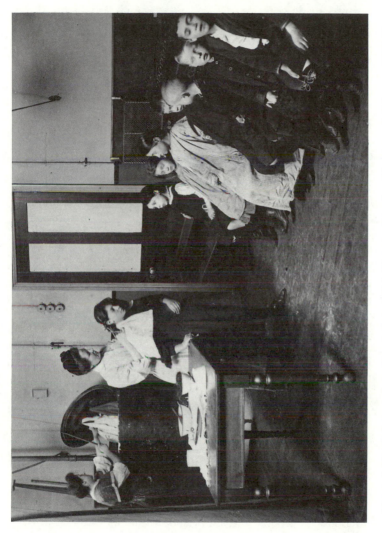

Figure 5 Finch Street cleansing station, 1911 (Greater London Photograph Library, GLRO)

lodged. Medical personnel, both nurses and doctors, attended the police courts that handled the prosecutions of parents of verminous children and cases of child neglect.[248] In 1911, inspection in school was made compulsory, and the Council sought to address the controversial presence of medical personnel in the schools.[249] The medical officer explained: 'It is of great importance to get nurses of the right sort. A kind, tactful, yet firm character in an intelligent and refined nurse manages to conduct a cleansing scheme in even a larger school, with a very few, sometimes no exclusions, for prosecution' (see Figure 6).[250]

In 1913, the Southwark public health officer wrote of the difficulty in a number of cases of children being given voluntary baths without the knowledge or consent of their parents: 'in all cases until that of Evans, I or my officers have succeeded in pacifying the indignant parents'.[251] Professional reports of medical men were solicited in dealing with complaints. A 'Schedule of Medical Inspection' recorded the judgements of the inspecting officers in the schools. They were asked to note instances of 'defects of articulation, lisping, stammers and etc.', and behaviour such as 'attention, response, signs of overstrain'. This reminder was especially revealing: 'the general intelligence may be recorded under the following heads: (a) Bright, fair, dull, backward; (b) mentally defective; (c) imbecile. Omit testing mental capacity of children under six years of age.'[252] The language of such reports can mislead the reader. Parents were reportedly generally compliant in these procedures and in other forms of medical inspection even despite cases of refusal: 'It is usually found that parents will allow their children to be inspected if the benefits of inspection are explained to them . . . the examination is not in any way intended as a reflection upon the care exercised by the parents in respect of the health of their children.'[253] Even when a report such as the one on haircutting, completed in 1914, suggested that children enjoyed being cleansed, there was usually a trace of misgiving, a cautionary plea:

> Doubtless the trouble and annoyance arising out of the visits of the sanitary inspector and the fear of prosecution had some effect in the gradual improvement of the personal habits of such families; but we believe that more could be done by direct education and kindly persuasion and direction towards securing more promptly a better state of affairs in many such cases.[254]

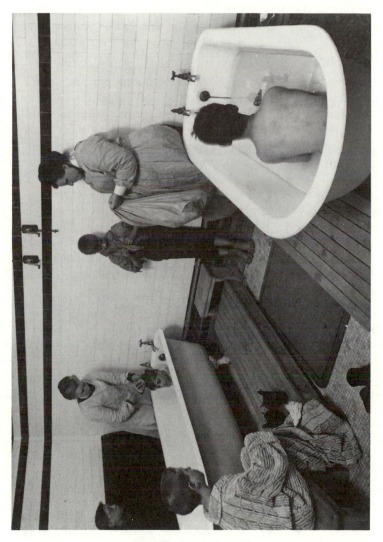

Figure 6 Sun Street cleansing station, 1914 (Greater London Photograph Library, GLRO)

But even the most professional sounding rhetoric could not supplant the tensions of a specific set of social practices so emblematic of the assertion of authority over everyday life. And when a new rhetoric was tried, elaborately formulated notions could at best signal the persistent desire to continue in many of the old ways, despite new appearances. The draft plan for the social welfare branch of the Education Department was written in 1909:

> Experience obtained now of social conditions and first causes should prove of much value, whatever may be the direction of later developments . . . social welfare . . . may prove a useful training ground for a band of officers who, under the direction of the Education Officer, will administer the social enactments of the present and of the future . . . Under the one controlling mind will be required a staff of men and women with a practical knowledge of sociology, with broad sympathies and open minds. Officers who will realise that the state, as a machine, need not necessarily take the form of a steam roller; who will know that the state as a social organiser is on its trial; that humane success in the present sphere of operations may mean within the next generation, the municipalisation of all social operations.[255]

The roads leading from the nineteenth century traditions of philanthropy were many and they were followed by both the Progressives and their successors. They spread across the territories negotiated by the early Council and encountered early professional social work and the architecture of social rationalisation – forces of the inter-war decades, at the crossroads. But in London before the War, curiously, the 'Progressive movement', as distinct from LCC policy, for many was best exemplified by its least sustaining measures, in which physical health, education and the protection of the young were less obviously manifest. On the stages and promenades and in the pubs adjacent, the music hall campaign best expressed, for many, Progressivism's moral essence.

'IT'S NOT WHAT SHE SAYS': MUSIC HALL AND PURITANISM

Who has brought that family public to the music hall? The County Council. What is it that attracted the father, mother, cousin, sister and aunt? It is because we have said that music halls and theatres should be so decently-conducted, and that they should be so proper for the public, profitable for the employer, because we dare to be Daniels, we dare to repress vulgarity – and to check indecency, and will not allow the music hall to resemble the ante-chamber to a brothel or the annex to a vulgar public house.[256]

George Sims praised the early Council and associated himself with its motives and achievements. But as the letter that began this chapter suggests, the imaginative relationships between Londoners and what they heard and saw in the halls and palaces of variety laid bare some of the most pronounced tensions of the early LCC era. Many did not praise Progressivism.

By 1888, the music hall had become London's foremost leisure institution, pubs notwithstanding. There were fourteen million annual visits paid to thirty-five of the halls alone in the early 1890s.[257] By 1904, there was an estimated nightly audience of as many as 59,000 music hall goers as against 47,000 in the theatre. Between 1894 and 1904, the music hall audiences grew by 45 per cent and the four largest halls in the centre of London had audiences on a daily and weekly basis that were as large as those of twelve average-sized proper theatres. In 1904, there were sixty-one London halls that ran full-length variety shows, outdoing in number the fifty-nine 'legitimate' theatres.[258] Four hundred thousand pounds in wages was paid by two hundred halls alone in a given year.[259] Shaw Desmond described London before the War: 'Men and women are sleeping under newspapers in the frozen nights of the Embankment, but just over the water the old Canterbury is gay with gilt and gas from 7:45 to midnight.'[260] Fervent societies like the Midnight Meeting Movement beseeched the Council to refuse music and dancing licences when publicans sought them, especially in London's suburbs, 'which [they said] teem with young people whose moral qualities are of vital worth to the country'.[261]

Under the Municipal Corporations Act of 1835, certain local authorities were vested with the right to provide museums, libraries, open-air bathing and forms of public recreation.[262] These included the right to restrict certain forms of entertainment, so that horse racing, for example, had been banned within ten miles of Charing Cross in 1879. The 1860s witnessed an anti-music hall crusade in which John Hollingshead had to pay a fine of over two hundred pounds for his pantomime ballet production at the Alhambra.[263] As John Palmer described it in 1913, 'The principle of music hall legislation is that any house kept for public dancing and music should either be licensed by some public body or be deemed a disorderly house.'[264] The LCC would come to assume, probably rightly, that the purveyors of the music hall had as their original purpose the hope of making a profit on the sale of drink.[265]

The formidable tasks of licensing were inherited by the LCC from the justices under the Local Government Act, and there was a history of the proprietors confronting the MBW in the late 1880s over attempts to extend the Board's powers.[266] The hall owners had organised themselves into the Entertainments Protection Association in 1880, and they held a major meeting with the Council in 1889 at which their representatives did not raise categorical objections to clauses being placed in draft bills that dealt with what was termed the 'propriety of behaviour'. These issues prompted discussion about the financial structure of the music hall industry. Distinct income groups were visible and halls could now be categorised in part according to the social composition of their audiences.[267] The Progressives clearly expressed a desire to 'purify' and to restrain the tone of performance as well as to govern the establishment of new halls and the repair of the older halls. But many pitfalls awaited the reformers. Sir Algernon West, as chair of the Committee, summarised the position in 1902:

'Faddists, Pharisees and Prowling Prudes' is the charge . . . While on one side we are criticised for doing too much, on the other we are met by a petition presented to the Council a fortnight ago, signed by many hundreds of the clergy, led by the Archbishop of Canterbury, urging us to do more and to prevent Sunday music. Then, again, we appear as the natural enemies of theatre managers and licensees with whom we are anxious as far as possible to live in peace. We have fallen upon a *damnosa hereditas*, which I may freely translate as a damnable inheritance, for we have had to deal with old theatres which existed under conditions which should never have been allowed, and which I am happy to say can never be sanctioned again.[268]

The LCC did not actually close down halls for reasons of indecency. Instead, other modes of control, particularly through the means of self-censorship on the part of the proprietors, were effected, casting further doubt on the will or capacity of the LCC to censor lyrics and to exercise 'social control' over millions in attendance at the halls.[269] Yet the *language* of the time might seduce the unwitting historian. Herbert Samuel inquired during public testimony in 1913: 'I want to know the degree of social control that you think proper over the theatre.' (If Samuel had known the academic ends to which his query could be put, he might have remained silent.)[270] Much of the literature on the halls has sought to measure them as instruments of a purported cultural hegemony. But the historian Peter Bailey offers this careful observation: 'For much of the Victorian period, consumer power in the halls was assertive and effective, and greatly complicated strategies of pro-prietorial control and artistic embourgeoisement.'[271] How was the balance between the drive for purification and the appearance of cooperative order achieved?

While the Lord Chamberlain continued to control most of London's theatres and to act as censor of their plays, the LCC now watched over exhibition halls, sporting facilities, and the mass of buildings used by voluntary and religious societies as well as the music halls. All were issued either annual licences or licences for specific performances.[272] Some few buildings were even licensed by both authorities. Under the Progressives, the LCC unsuccess-fully sought expansion of these powers.[273] From 1882 until 1888, regulation had focused on new additions to old structures. Safety and the well-being of the public were emphasised. But as George Sims claimed, the Progressive LCC vowed to subject the halls to greater moral scrutiny. As the *Financial News* wailed in 1893, 'The austerely-virtuous regard for the public's morals which is the particular characteristic of the LCC is apparently an irrepressible quantity. No rebuff dampens its Pecksniffian ardour; no criticism, however mordant, disturbs its smug equanimity.'[274] The halls thought the Council should be rid of impropriety, the ill effects of readily available alcohol and the pernicious influence of lascivious and vulgar performances.

Amongst the feuding factions paying close attention to LCC manoeuvres were those supporting 'free trade in amusements', who sought the growth of the halls without the obstructive inter-ference of the State. The Nonconformist, 'municipal puritan' reputation of the Council, so derided in the diatribes of Stewart Headlam, strengthened the resolve of the West End playwrights and performers, who preferred the aristocratic indifference of the Lord Chamberlain as a licensing authority. They resisted attempts on the part of the LCC to assert control over their theatrical haunts.[275] This partly had to do with what had become vogue in West End theatre. Sims recalled that 'the taste for domestic scenes with the humour and pathos deftly mingled was common to all classes of playgoers'.[276] On the opposite side of the fence, and indeed on the LCC Theatres and Music Halls Committee (TMHC) itself, sat the supporters and members of groups such as the National Vigilance Society, who fiercely sought to uphold decency and sobriety.[277]

This campaign intersected a campaign against Sunday openings. Organisations such as the Lord's Day Observance Society and the Working Man's Lord's Day Rest Association pressed the Council to abandon its policy of allowing alcohol to be served at events held in music halls on Sunday evenings such as the National Sunday League's 'Sunday Evenings for the People'. This venerable body, founded in 1855, provided music described as being of 'an unobjectionable character', and speakers on a variety of subjects appeared on a programme meant 'generally to promote Intellectual and Elevating Recreation on that Day', typically offering talks such as 'How I Escaped from Siberia to Freedom'. The Lord's Day Act prohibited public amusement or debate on Sunday when a fee was charged but it was no longer enforced unless the music offered at an event was considered suspect.[278]

The National Federation of Sunday Societies, led by Lord Hobhouse, sponsored gatherings that were permitted despite the protests launched against them. The Amalgamated Musicians' Union, the National Union of Theatrical Stage Employees, the Waiters' Society and the London Trades Council were active in the debates over licensing. They demanded that the LCC refuse to license unfair employers, arguing that to do so would constitute a violation of the Council's fair wage clauses.[279] Jesson, secretary of the Amalgamated Musicians' Union, sat on the LCC.[280] The Stage Employees and the Amalgamated Musicians' Union asserted in 1902: 'We recognize that rational Sunday Entertainments are, apparently, inevitable: but, we desire to see them develop on lines that will not injure in any way, those directly concerned.' The Variety Artistes' Federation was convinced that cinema openings on Sunday would lead to the opening of the music halls.[281] The proponents of Sunday observance took stock of the trade union's

position and used it to support their own demands. They appro-
priated the rhetoric of groups such as the Social Democratic
Federation, the Metropolitan Radical Federation (chaired by
James Jeffery, LCC), and the Working Men's Club and Institute
Union.[282]

Ironically, given its role as an organisation that assisted women
searching for employment, the National Union of Women Workers
raised the demand for 'an end to female barmaids', stipulating that
women leaving the trade should receive three years' compensatory
employment. Their moral opposition to this form of women's
labour was in keeping with the spirit of 'municipal puritanism'.
The demand for compensation for publicans and pub employees
suffering the effects of the LCC closures added to the general
clamour. In 1906, the LCC prohibited live background music in
restaurants that were charging high prices for meals in order to
finance the entertainment. The Council maintained that without
such prohibitions, the music halls would lose business.[283] A
People's Concert Society that was founded in the 1870s, to which
Headlam was a contributor, supported Sunday concerts, concerts
attended by those who might have visited the halls. Private supper
clubs were licensed to allow stage plays on Sundays for members
only and this further ignited those lobbying against the LCC.
Neither the puritan interests that sought to censor performances
and to honour the Sabbath nor those who sought to further the
larger music halls' profits could risk support for a competitive,
laissez-faire market in musical events.

In keeping with the Progressive goal of controlling all licensing
of London entertainment, an even wider notion of municipal and
state ownership of opera and theatre and of dance halls and
concert halls had its adherents. The London Trades Council
repeatedly called for the LCC to open a municipal theatre. But
as was the case in other cities, such as Manchester, reactions to
'state control' were divided; it was a slippery concept.[284] Perhaps
the LCC achieved its greatest consensus around the plea for the
dignifying of entertainment, for the prevention of calamity and the
suppression of the rapacious spirit of the propertied in the person
of the hall owners. But the LCC did not possess the political clout
to accomplish these ends and Parliament proved unwilling to
extend LCC powers. The theatrical community perceived the
LCC as intrusive and culturally philistine. As Herbert Tree put it,
'if we have not the advantage of state aid, let us at least be exempt

from state suppression . . . the County Council may have reckoned with its publicans but without its public'.[285]

A long struggle over what constituted a sketch, as distinct from an act that could be performed only in legitimate theatres, fuelled this sentiment. Until 1913, when it became possible for plays to be licensed for performance in premises other than theatres, the Lord Chamberlain had to some extent looked the other way. In fact, the Select Committee of 1892 had managed to persuade music hall and theatre proprietors to draw a line such that a production of a specified length could be performed in the halls.[286] As late as 1911, the Palladium, for example, was fined for allowing performances of *Carmen* and of *Julius Caesar.*[287] When it was proposed that the performer rather than the hall be licensed, Charles Coburn summarily condemned the project as a 'Literary Contagious Diseases Act'.[288]

The very character of theatre itself was at stake in these disputes, in part because of the Lord Chamberlain's own methods of censorship. In 1913, John Palmer suggested that truly critical theatre had finally found a following in England. In a struggle for innovation, a 'radically minded' theatre community would have run smack up against the other bastion of ostensible philistinism: music hall fare itself. Not a shred of radical populism in defence of the integrity of public performance lay behind the 'free trade' voices. Their own right to pursue an entirely different aesthetic uneasily coexisted with the critics of LCC vigilance in the halls:

> No serious form of literature can today escape the impulse towards a criticism of society and its standards. The British theatre before Ibsen was unaffected by the impulse towards critical sociology which began with the later novels of Charles Dickens, simply because it was intellectually and artistically extinguished under the Lord Chamberlain's censorship. As soon as the British theatre began tentatively to come into the mainstream of European thought, what Mr. Bernard Shaw has called the 'conscientiously immoral' play was inevitable, for nine-tenths of the European literature since 1890 which counts is conscientiously immoral.[289]

In 1892, the Parliamentary Select Committee simply found no reason to transfer powers from the Lord Chamberlain. The press scoffed and caricatured the LCC's aspirations: 'The pious linen-drapers and buttermen who aspire to govern Greater London would, no doubt, be in their element in determining whether the skirts of the ballet should reach to the ground, or be permitted to display an inch or so of the ankle.'[290] The subject of the caricature was the committee that sat in judgement, which included members of both parties in Council as did all LCC committees: Sir Thomas George Fardell, MP for South Paddington and LCC councillor, acted as chairman for six years. Fardell was influential in the investigations that led to the downfall of the MBW. The hope that the LCC would foster a new age of municipal respectability would have been uppermost in the mind of a reformer like him, who for good measure also chaired the National Union of Conservative Associations. His party colleague, brewer and MP for Mile End and Tower Hamlets, Spencer Charrington, also served on the committee. A surviving magnate of local politics, Charrington, like his brother Frederick, was an outspoken convert to the movement against vice.[291]

Liberals such as G.W.E. Russell, chairman of the Churchmen's Liberation League, and NVA members such as George Lidgett and John McDougall (Lidgett's son-in-law) also served. McDougall and Lidgett were active along with Mary Bunting, Lidgett's sister, in the 1889 'social purity' campaign, whose historian is Edward Bristow.[292] The upstanding solicitor, Hubert John Greenwood, councillor for St George's Hanover Square, was another typical member. An active Territorial and a patron of St George's Hospital, Greenwood would direct the Government Food Committee for London during the First World War. If there was party-political friction on such a committee, it most often derived from differences over the extent of intervention required rather than over the necessity of it in principle, or even over the goal of 'reforming' the halls. The zeal of a Conservative who had fought local corruption as he saw it was joined with the Nonconformist, teetotal and anti-prostitution sentiments expressed by the NVA stalwarts.

In 1894, the Council struck a blow against alcohol, declaring that licences would now be refused to all new applicants whose halls were opening for the first time under LCC jurisdiction; these halls would have to be dry, a stipulation which the largest proprietors and the grandest halls were best able to accept given their greater financial stability.[293] The audiences creatively adapted as well; Haddon reports that at the Coliseum, for example, over an eight-day period, three thousand people left the house to visit the adjacent pubs.[294] As late as 1901, the Hackney Empire was reportedly served by a supply of 'champagne whiskey' that arrived through a false doorway between the hall and the Ship public house next door. The artistes obtained 'clandestine' drink this way even after closing time.[295] They could offer the most elaborate perform-ances for a fee that compensated for the loss of revenue from sales of alcohol, though Haddon contends that the committee pleaded with the Council to understand the mood of the public in favour of drink; the Council tended to override the committee's attempts at mediation.[296] In an ensuing political debate over the anti-alcohol provisions, Burns declared liquor to be a 'menace to commerce, industry and the State'.[297] He also called for 'Municipalisation of the Liquor Traffic'.[298] At this juncture, most Progressives were testing their desire for rational recreation, abstention and for the municipal control of alcohol sales against the desires of an habituated drinking public.

A kind of *rapprochement* between the Progressives and the largest proprietors was also attempted in a piece of legislation that Asquith had rejected. When an LCC delegation met with the Home Secretary as early as 1894, it was freely acknowledged that after the start of LCC licensing, 'no attempt to stop licences on the grounds of quality of the performances' had occurred.[299] The councillors instead had sought to extend LCC powers so that the groundowners of the lands that the halls occupied would hence-forth be required to pay for certain repairs ordered by Council rather than these costs being passed on to the lessees. This attempt reflected a commitment to the broadly based Liberal–Progressive initiative for the taxation of ground values. But Asquith scoffed at the notion, demanding to know why ground landlords should necessarily take any financial interest in structural costs of this sort. House Liberals clearly resisted the special pleading designed to antagonise the landlords. Perhaps they preferred to save their thunder for causes such as the People's Budget of the subsequent decade.[300] As a result of the meeting with Asquith, the committee decided to abandon the bill.[301] In the face of implacable parlia-mentary opposition from their Liberal allies, the Progressives now faced mutually hostile interest groups at all levels of government. They could not arrive at a coherent strategy to challenge the propertied interests in the capital on the music hall question or on other questions. They stubbornly insisted upon a moral agenda that was already unpopular in many quarters.[302]

The showdowns in the licensing sessions in which witnesses were cross-examined took place before the full Council, which then voted at Spring Gardens on the committee's resolutions.[303] The police described the atmosphere of a hall or reported unlicensed performances, but much depended on the dubious use of a hired inspectorate who at the outset of the period attracted much public attention when a surfeit of zealous applicants attempted to fill the few positions available.[304] The flurry of activity produced results. During 1890–92, over 1200 inspections of London halls had occurred.[305]

The anonymous LCC inspectors inhabited a furtive twilight world. Amidst the gaiety of the halls, they darted from section to section, checking seating provision, watching suspected prostitutes, scribbling remarks about the lyrics and performance styles and even contributing their own makeshift drawings of what they observed to the committee. Despite the claim that structural concerns were uppermost, the subcommittee on inspection resolved that 'the Inspectors . . . should devote their attention chiefly to the nature of the performance, and to the character and conduct of the audience, especially the female portion thereof, rather than to the structural condition and exits of the building'.[306] Those whom they observed might have several roles; the confusion of identification caught the inspectorate in its silent grip. Women were objects of attention both as prostitutes and performers as well as being symbols of the new family-centred style that the Council was promoting at the halls, as suggested by George Sims's commentary above.

The expectations of the committee and of the proprietors gradually converged. The initial cost of repairs caused many small houses to relinquish their licences. Singers were performing on premises unlicensed for singing; dancing was popular in establishments with 'music only' licences; pubs served as music halls. Another cycle of complaint left some halls unregulated once they initially passed muster, while the cases of particularly 'troublesome' or 'popular' halls were invested with more attention by the committee. In 1890, the committee required the continual inspection of the Rose and Crown near the Tower. The bar was near lodging houses that catered to sailors. The entertainment of the evening reportedly consisted of a 'rough and ready band' of street musicians. There were dancing and drinks for an audience of foreign sailors and women of ill repute, all of whom were smoking. The inspector himself was approached by a woman and then overheard an elderly woman reproaching younger women for not advancing toward the bar with the men whom they had solicited. This was a glorified pub, whose licence was revoked. Charrington, president of the Tower Hamlets Federation for the Suppression of the Drink Traffic, lobbied against the licence.[307]

Just as citizens had reported on their fellows in sufficient numbers to fill the registers of the Public Control complaint books, so a network of amateur inspectors' sidekicks, comprising various club members, trade and performers' societies in the industry, and vigilante members of the audiences, competed for the committee's attention. Inspections did not always yield the expected results. Often the inspectors' portraits of the halls revealed an unpredictably nuanced set of circumstances. The inspector reporting on Gatti's in Charing Cross in 1891, for example, eschewed any notion of vice:

> I saw no drunkenness . . . in fact most of the drinking was done at the bars (not at the tables and benches). The audience was respectable – there were 'prostitutes' in the hall, but there were none 'soliciting'. In my opinion, this house is not 'a house of call' or 'place of meeting' for prostitutes and their confederates.

But he added that 'in the event of accident – fire or a panic – this hall would be nothing more or less than a "Death Trap".' The audience could not get out and in my opinion, the consequences would be something appalling.'[308] When the proprietors of the hall were told by the Council of complaints about lyrics made by a member of the audience (who had decoded allusions to sodomy and extra-marital sexual relations), they immediately removed the offending lyrics from the roster. Two waifs as they were described, satirised another sketch in their number, entitled 'Touched':

> Now we want a baby
> You had better go and make one.
> Go and make a kid, go on
> Yes, I'll go and make one out of the old man.
> [roars of laughter][309]

The person filing a complaint about the sketch asked, 'Is this a question, involving as well an impossibility, an act of sodomy? If so, is it not too indecent? Especially amidst hundreds of Youths and Maidens in a Public Hall licensed by the LCC.' A second lyric that had been withdrawn depicted a rich girl who went out in the evening and returned at dawn: 'Flossie sometimes returns and sometimes *not at all*!!!!!'.[310] By 1908, Gatti's had been converted for cinema use, at first by 'Russell's Imperial Bioscope' – a display in which an electric piano accompanied the cinematography. The hall's structural defects resulted from its location under one of the arches of Charing Cross Station and forced the abandonment of live performances.[311]

Sometimes a particular artist was the target of concerted action. In 1907, a controversy arose involving Knowles, 'the Prince of Patter Comedians'. The special complaint against him concerned a line that alluded to the work of Mrs Ormiston Chant, *grande doyenne* of the music hall purification movement: 'Mrs. Chant looked in at Heaven, so at once the order was given – "Angels, go and put on your pyjamas".' Another version ran: 'Dreams of heaven knocked at the door. No woman admitted – that is why it is called heaven – even Mrs. Chant knocked at the door but could not be admitted as she wore pyjamas.'[312]

Other lyrics of Knowles that the Committee found provocative included: 'Marriage is a committee of two with discretionary power to add to their number. Pity is that some people haven't more discretion.' Or, 'kissing is the greatest institution . . . and your hand comes down and makes you feel what you never felt before'. The committee was offered the following explanation of Knowles's *modus operandi*, an exacting account of a method of performance. It suggested the difficulties of censorship:

> The bulk of his part is 'patter' and verse of chorus – namely, the whole of it bearing on women and their tendencies to lead men to think of anything but their strict duty towards their wives – altogether racy and insinuating – without expressing actual facts in plain words – but acting, winking-pointing to leave no doubt to what they mean.[313]

The Council sustained halls that it thought were respectable just as much as it sought to condemn halls in poorer areas or halls frequented by the poorest Londoners. The St James Temperance Music Hall, despite its pretension to good works, was criticised for being the site of 'acts of indecency and immorality . . . because the hall is used by a low class of people'. Boys were seen 'acting indecently to girls with their hands . . . putting hands up girls' clothing', and there was heard 'language . . . something too filthy to come from the mouth of a man, much less to come from the mouth of a woman'.[314]

But the Collins in Islington Green merited praise in 1890: 'With one or two exceptions, this is a place of entertainment that I would not hesitate to take my wife and family to.' The toilets were unfortunately visible and the inspector thought that perhaps women ought to be seated at all times in all the halls, the Collins included. But by 1900, this hall had improved: 'It is frequented by a better class of people than most outlying halls.' The next year the local Trades Council and the ILP asked to use it for a performance of labour hymns to be sung by a fifty-voice Clarion choir. Such cultivation of a neighbourhood constituency leant respectability to a hall and was a common practice, as described by Peter Bailey.[315] If the social composition of a hall elicited an inspector's prejudice, this was routinely reflected in his comments. Witness this 1891 report on the Canterbury:

> The audience seemed to consist principally of mechanics and was generally rather rough and noisy, whistling, shouting, hissing, and joining in the songs. There was, however, no quarrelling or drunkenness. The women were not numerous and were of the same class as the men. I saw none that I should consider to be prostitutes. There were policemen and attendants in every part of the house . . . the audience were principally tradespeople, and their wives, working men, lads and girls, and considering the neighbourhood, well-behaved. I saw no disorder, and I did not observe any persons whose *behaviour* [his emphasis] would mark them as prostitutes, though doubtless among such a large audience, there were many loose characters. I went into the fauteuils, stalls, pit, promenade and balcony.[316]

While the Council did not directly censor lyrics, it did call upon the management to ban certain pieces from the programmes, and increasingly the proprietors claimed to be enforcing the Council's own standards as a matter of course. This was a significant change in procedure and one that would have the greatest impact on the *appearance* of censorship. Some halls deemed 'coarse jests and rough language . . . to be particularly avoided', in this instance by order of English's New Sebright Wholesome Amusement Temple. Others, such as Foresters Hall, insisted that 'Any artists giving expression to any vulgarity, or words having a double meaning, will be subject to instant dismissal, and to the forfeiture of that week's salary.' The Royal Albert, Victoria Dock Road, impossibly forbade direct reference to 'political, religious, or local matters'. Hilariously, many halls refused performers the right to mention officials of the LCC in satirical asides.[317] A lyric that an inspector flagged in 1899 included a reference to one of the County asylums and illustrates the limits some placed upon propriety:

> Doesn't like beer and upon my life
> I've often seen him a-cuddling his wife.
> There's no mistake about poor Jim.
> There's something very wrong with him.
> He doesn't owe the tallyman a cent
> and he thinks its only right to pay the rent.
> Once when the weather happened to be fine, he
> took out his mother-in-law up upon the briny.
> Brought her back safe, well upon my soul,
> I think that proves he's fairly up the pole.
> If I'd have had the chance you bet
> Somebody would have been upset,
> Ah but Jim was always ropey on the thatch.
> They ought to bring him to Colney Hatch.[318]

This lyric also included a reference to a 'lodger as dodger, when Jim's out, he's in . . .'.

The Canterbury drew complaint about songs and acts such as 'The Bewitched Curate', in which a woman passed out on stage after her leg had been stroked by the cleric in question, who had been smitten by the lady and convinced that life on the stage was not as bad as he had once thought it to be. This sketch played continuously throughout London for three years. 'An old frequenter of twenty-five years standing' wrote to object to Peggy Prior's lyrics describing a couple's wedding breakfast; the LCC inspector found these less objectionable than the complainant had.[319] The Canterbury's programme included the typical management inducement to order:

> It is the desire of the management that the entertainments offered at this establishment shall be at all times absolutely free from objectionable features; they invite the cooperation of the public to this end, and will be obliged to anyone who will

inform them of anything offensive upon the stage that may have escaped the notice of the management.[320]

Not all negotiations over lyrics went as smoothly as the statement implies. In one skit, a singer engaged to a man who worked in the Tube was depicted as seeking revenge when he represented himself as more than he was. She replied that he was, after all, only a porter and threatened to tell his pals that 'he ain't got no tube at all'. A committee clerk wrote to the hall that this song would have to be dropped, and the management replied that the song had been performed all over London; this was the first complaint heard against it. Though the records do not show the resolution of this problem, they indicate the ambiguous nature of self-regulation and illustrate the needling style of the Council. The records also note that the Canterbury had been cited previously for an instance of prostitution in a theatre box which had never been proved.

Perhaps the relative obscurity and isolation of the inspectorate determined some of its occasional aesthetic judgements; the suppression of suspect material was not always its first calling. In 1893, a member of the team visited the Palace and noted that the fare was of the 'customary kind, singers, skirt dancers, eccentric comedians, ballet, etc., which involved the usual display of limbs encased in tights'. The acts were described as

skilful and artistic living representations of well-known paintings and sculptures. Some people, however, would simply object to such public and complete display of the female form, by living women . . . It is a matter of difficulty to fix the exact point where propriety ends and impropriety begins. The borderline which divides the legitimate from the objectionable is not well-defined. I have endeavoured to report the facts as impartially as I can, and it is not for me, but for the Committee, to approve or condemn.[321]

Subsequently, there were complaints from the public that posters outside the theatre were 'suggestive . . . demoralizing the crowds of young men and boys who linger about the place', and that young girls who were performing were degraded. Yet an inspector wrote that the 'daring Moorish bath scene still had nothing objectionable about it', and 'it was vigorously applauded'. But when an MP reported complaints from his constituents, and goaded the Council to conciliate public opinion, 'increasingly hostile to these representations', demanding 'prompt action', the manager withdrew the Moorish bath scene on the same day.[322]

It was difficult to draw the lines of both discretion and propriety. In the licensing sessions, the Council members often played the role of intermediaries. In 1896, they reviewed complaints filed about performances at the Oxford. A witness objected to Marie Lloyd's performance of 'I asked Johnny Jones, so I know now', in which Lloyd, dressed as a schoolgirl, precociously inquired of her parents and of a schoolboy, 'what's that for, eh?', with obvious sexual implication. In a second skit, Lady Mansel sang about a dancing girl whose tights burst while on stage, to the rejoinder, 'and what I saw I mustn't tell you now'. These lyrics were considered 'improper for mixed audiences'. But the witness against the licensee was pursued by a committee member: 'Are not such innuendos suggested in the theatres?'[323]

Much of the rest of the Oxford licensing session was devoted to testimony from the social purity wing of the British Women's Temperance Association, well known for its struggle against prostitution. But the councillors again appeared sceptical rather than encouraging of the witnesses. The proprietors' representatives were permitted to engage in hostile questioning. Carina T. Reed, an officer of the Association, described the behaviour of prostitutes whom she had watched in the halls. She was clearly fascinated by them and acknowledged that she had never been in a hall until being asked to visit for the cause: 'They have themselves told me they found the performance intensely dull. They do not care at all for it.' Reed reported that when these women attempted to snare customers, 'sometimes they accosted a man with a look, sometimes by speech . . . [it] usually begins by asking for a drink'. She and her colleagues found the songs and skits especially objectionable: 'The thing that called down the most applause was when Ally Sloper gave an account of his courting a girl at Epping Forest which included the following: "And she said to him, 'now you have brought me out so far, do you mean marriage or what?' and he said 'What'; and from that day he became a what'er".'[324] Reed was not above declaring her own new-found taste; she had come to favour halls like the Metropolitan, Middlesex and the Collins (see Figure 7).[325]

Charles Cory Reed, City buyer by day and temperance campaigner by night, described his attendance at an obscene performance by Madge Ellis, whose refrain was, 'You show me yours and I will show you mine', supposedly referring to the bruises of a

Figure 7 Metropolitan Music Hall, 1892 (Greater London Photograph Library, GLRO)

schoolboy and girl. He also described his encounters with women at the Oxford. He was cross-examined by the applicant's advocate:

> When I say I was accosted – a girl spoke to me in what I may call the usual way, 'Well', and I turned away. Soon after another girl asked me if this was the last item in the programme. It was not what she said but the way in which she said it; and immediately after that another girl came and looked over my programme very closely. I do not say that this is accosting. I tell you what happened.

> Q.   Have you much time to spare?
> A.   No.
> Q.   But you are able to devote a considerable part of your time to looking after the morals of other people.[326]

The committee continued to question Reed, admonishing him that lyrics and story plots were not at issue; tone, innuendo and gesture could convey the immoral. Mrs Chant herself appeared, offering the example of the lyrical dictate: 'meet me in the moonlight alone', and explaining, 'it would depend on how it was sung and who sung it'. In an atmosphere of retrospective interpretation, it was small wonder that the Oxford's representatives bitterly complained that they could not legally pursue those who testified against them: 'Gratifying it must be to these people who live at Crouch End and Hornsey to look at the rest of the world from that point of view.'[327]

The closure of the session illustrates the most common, subtler form of negotiation now occurring between the licensing committee and the more established halls. The Oxford spokesman explained that the hall did not allow soliciting and that the manager approved all of the songs in the programme. Yet the defence reminded the committee: 'it would be absolutely impossible in any form of entertainment – whether it is at a music-hall or at a theatre – to prevent some construction being put upon things that are said'. The licence was granted and the committee advised greater care in the selection of songs.

'WOMEN FOUND NIGHTLY': THE EMPIRE CAMPAIGN

It was easier to spot and to control alcohol than to damn the offensive gesture or the suggestive lyric. Council policy was unified

227

around the opposition to drink. As early as 1892, the Jolly Tanners was allowed to renew its licence only after agreeing that no bar could ever be opened inside it and that no alcohol could be consumed or sold in the auditorium. The hall was at the crossroads of two narrow streets in a heavily populated area, yet no organised opposition had grown up to challenge its licence. Though the hall's opponents said that those in the neighbourhood did object to the hall as it was full of 'working tanners and costermongers', there had been no petition, which was the chief weapon of the vocal factions in the licensing disputes.[328] In a revealing moment, it was asserted that the residents were too poor to mobilise. Those with greater powers of articulation began to be viewed as speaking for London. Never was this more the case than in the disputes surrounding the Empire, which was closed down temporarily by the LCC in 1894 because of 'the character and conduct of the women found nightly on the promenade.'[329]

The opposition to the hall was led by Mrs Ormiston Chant and the temperance advocates, who specifically opposed the presence of prostitutes on the promenades. It was the most celebrated case of the period, and Mrs Chant had already been active in LCC affairs, supporting the ill-fated attempt of Jane Cobden to take a council seat for Bow and Bromley. Now she could seek Council redress in another setting.[330] The LCC's sharp reaction to the Empire's ambience, the surge of defensive public opinion, the advocates of 'free trade in amusements' and the pranks of young aristocratic supporters of the status quo became notorious. Though John Burns himself objected to what he termed the 'superficial palliative which consists only in harrying women – a system which may increase the evil', a writer for the *Liberal* urged that there was 'no place for state regulation of vice'. The municipality should not be in the business of providing 'convenient and luxurious accommodation for male and female loveless love'.[331] *The Times* saluted Council policy: 'it has the effect of raising the whole tone of the performance and leading another class to patronise the music halls'.[332] The legends of the Empire campaign are so well known that they tend to obscure other kinds of expression of popular sentiment that emanated from other distinct and vocal minorities.

The London Patriotic Club of Clerkenwell, established in the auspicious year of 1871, had as its purpose the pursuit of 'the furtherance of Democratic Principles to assist in all Progressive Movements'. It resolved:

1. That the People have a right to be amused in the manner which best suits them, and that they are the proper authorities of the same.
2. That there has been no complaint from the Public against the exhibition shown at the Empire Theatre. We therefore ask the LCC to disregard the recommendations of the Licensing Committee and the action of a narrow-minded and bigoted faction against the well-conducted plan of amusement.[333]

The Cane and Bamboo Workers protested against the Council, albeit in a different way:

That the Union while deploring the existence of prostitution and vice, protest against the ridiculous and Puritanical attitude of the Licensing Committee of the LCC believing that the cause of this vice lies deeper than that Committee seem to comprehend and can only be extinguished by the removal of that cause and not by throwing more women out of work to starvation or the streets.[334]

These dissenting views, the one in favour of popular discretion, the other for social reform, both expressed distaste for Council control. These opinions must also be read juxtaposed with resolutions like the one passed by a large gathering of adherents of the United Methodist Free Church, in favour of removing the lounge at the Empire. It expressed gratitude to the Council for 'endeavouring to purify the public places of amusement'.[335] Petitions flowed in from thousands of Londoners. They were for or against the ban on alcohol, usually referring directly to either the Empire or the Palace. Churches, women's organisations and temperance unions mobilised.[336] The campaigns infected electoral politics: when F.W. Maude presented himself as a candidate in Central Hackney, his support for bars in the auditorium during the Empire case alienated the temperance lobby.[337] Many petitions were simply signed by the 'Inhabitants' of a particular district. A hall might have its own supporters: three thousand staff, tradesmen and ratepayers signed petitions on behalf of the Stanley Hall, Islington, and these were countered by petitions submitted by the Women's Local Government Society and their avid supporter, John Benn.[338] The loosening of restrictions was also supported by petitioners, and, notably, by the committee itself, but was overturned in Council.

Groups calling themselves simply the 'inhabitants of Hackney' or 'of West Newington', 'the ratepayers of South Hackney' and the Clapham Reform Club all supported the imposition of fewer restrictions upon the halls.[339] The astounding outpouring of ordinary voices was the campaign's most intriguing hallmark. Working people were not passive receptacles of social purity interests. The purification of the halls was relentlessly sought not only by 'reactionaries' but by certain Progressives and many of their socialist adherents, who were often the real Calvinists. Various renditions of a *laissez-faire* politic ironically provided a radical edge. The young Winston Churchill was not the only opponent of the restrictions imposed upon the Empire. The 'libertarian' anti-moralist, anti-puritan stance of other groups deserves attention. And neither opponents nor supporters of the Council necessarily represented the members of the massive music hall audience who, in their majority, may well have lacked such motivating political or religious commitment and yet had to pay the price of the ticket.[340] Stewart Headlam criticised leading Liberal John Morley for attacking 'not land monopoly or production for profit or any of the great evils which socialists attack. It was merely upon the barmaid that the stern gaze of the State was to be turned.'[341]

According to Morley, the money lost when publicans surrendered their licences ought to be put back into the community. He again called for parliamentary powers to municipalise the drink trade. Pointing to the fact that the pubs nearest the new LCC housing estates at Millbank and Boundary Street had been forced to relinquish their licences, he spoke of a need for the establishment of municipal restaurants and cafes. Similarly, Mrs Humphrey Ward supported the call for music and dancing at the Passmore Edwards Estate in Tavistock Place.[342] It was felt that pubs ought to have music and dancing licences in order to provide their patrons with more than simply drink. The Conservatives finally took this step in 1911:

> We want fewer privately-managed public houses, more municipal open air cafes and restaurants . . . [and] rational municipal drinking . . . Mr. John Burns frankly said that what was wanted was another Cromwell . . . you find your atheist, sceptic, agnostic as cruel as his religious forefathers condemning not only good wine and Sunday games, but dancing.[343]

As a supporter of the 'Anti-Puritan League in defence of the people's pleasure', Stewart Headlam felt that the public ought to resist the attempt to 'force a narrow and bitter Sabbatarianism upon the democracy' and condemned the LCC's 'coercive Puritanism'.[344] The Progressives imagined that their music hall policy wholly satisfied a primary constituency: those Londoners who were anti-aristocratic, modestly educated, 'lower middle class' and Nonconformist. George Sims could recall a childhood in which he was aware of a 'large body of people opposed to "theatrical" entertainment in any shape or form'.[345] To be sure, the creation of a civic culture, at once rewarding for the deserving and punitive for the dissolute, still seemed a worthy endeavour to many Progressive followers. On the other hand, the 'swell' constituency of the halls, also very possibly 'lower middle class' in origin, was implacably committed to debauchery and unenthused over any incursion upon the outrageous content of skits or their evening interludes in chosen haunts.[346]

The case of the Boer War exhibition at the Olympia Theatre, entitled 'Big Battles: Boers, British and Bantoos', offers a look at the complexities of municipal intervention. Barnum and Bailey brought the show to London. The other offerings included 'freaks' and such regulars as the naked lady, the sword swallower, a 'Troop of Oriental Wonder Workers', 'devout Mohammedans', 'whirling dervishes', and 'wilde men of Borneo'. These were the dominant themes of the Olympia during that year, though the freak show in particular elicited both negative commentary and some challenges to the LCC licensing authorities in the press even before the episode recounted here occurred.[347]

This show opened in 1900 and featured African 'natives' performing in military scenes drawn from the conflict in southern Africa. It was modelled on an earlier re-enactment of the Spanish–American War. The Africans, 150 men and three women, who were identified as 'Kaffir natives', were to be replaced by Sudanese. They were forced to reside in unkempt huts equipped with only minimal hygienic facilities. A basement trough served as a w.c. and was constructed near some urinal stalls. Petwell, Bailey's clerk, had assured the authorities that the facilities used by the performers would be 'entirely cut off from the part used by the public and every care would be taken that nothing to offend anyone's sense of delicacy would be allowed'.[348] The proposals were approved by an official of the Medical Office, who noted that 'natives of this class will not use water closets in the proper way'.[349]

Earls Court was now the scene of a moral panic. Black performers were accused of behaving aggressively toward white women in the vicinity of the hall. They were accused in a ratepayer's letter, for example, of threatening behaviour that posed 'a terror and real danger to all decent women of whatever class'.[350] The LCC, as licensing authority for the Olympia, was besieged with requests for action, much as it was by the music hall vigilantes. One petition carried a hundred signatures. In this instance, however, Progressive moral fervour was not unleashed upon prostitutes, pub owners, or lecherous and 'indecent' music hall performers, but on the Barnum and Bailey London representative, who was summarily accused of inhuman treatment of 'the natives'. One irate petitioner wrote candidly about some of what was at stake: 'Who is to profit by your granting this licence. The Landlords and the English women with their young daughters? Or some unknown Irish-American who no doubt spends money here but who will have gone away in three months?'[351] Though the proprietors claimed that teetotal Senegalese and Sudanese were available as replacements for the original cast, some of whom had reportedly appeared drunk in a police court,[352] the LCC revoked the Olympia's licence and the Africans were shipped back to Africa.[353] Ironically, the licensing session received a favourable inspector's report on the 'Zulu Krall': 'The Zulus all wear long overcoats, they are very orderly and well-behaved, spending their time chiefly in smoking and listening to the Ladies' Orchestra.'[354]

The official show programme read 'Briton, Boer and Black in Savage South Africa' and began with a 'Mimic Stick Fight by [a] Body of Zulus' and a 'Wrestling Competition by Selected Ashantis and Sudanese'. Next came 'Wilson's last stand', in which, it was reported, he, Wilson, was 'annihilated by Blacks'. A Biorama offered war photographs, and the performance of 'Rule Britannia' and 'God Save the Queen'. These were followed by the opening theatrical tableau depicting 'the more salient features of Euro-African life', the centrepiece of which was a 'vividly-coloured intermixture [of] Cape boys and Hottentots, English troopers and Boer horsemen', as well as 'women of different tribes and European ladies'. Before the main event, there was a foot race waged only by Dutch, American, Australian and British competitors. Then came 'Briton, Boer and Black', featuring military scenes in which the Africans were tied to railway tracks, and the Boers were then repulsed by the Brits, who rescued those natives who had survived the onslaught. Those Africans who refused to fight with the Boers were killed by them. The Licensing Committee took corroborative testimony on the krall from a Reverend Johnson, apparently a missionary of forty years' experience in Africa. His views were echoed by the inspector, who nostalgically invoked Stephen Foster:

> The natives are excellent specimens of their tribe – hardy, muscular, brave, picked specimens of the splendid warriors whose pluck has been tested so often by our soldiers and praised so generously by English poets and by those 'contemporary historians', the war correspondents. The Rev. Johnson . . . speaks very highly of their personal and domestic virtues. They are as memorative of the 'auld folks at home' as the best type of Scotch or French emigrants.[355]

Those Londoners who had toured the 'native encampment' and observed the Africans cooking, eating and sleeping in their 'natural environment', or had felt the 'exotic' and 'fearsome' presence of Africans with pay-packets in their pockets drifting through what must have seemed the very foreign soil of Earls Court, also witnessed the spectacle of intervention on behalf of near-slave labourers. Some felt that the Zulus had been insulted by not being trusted to walk about. The darkness that enshrouded the Africans in their off-time when the hall was not lighted for performance was regarded as exploitative. Too little clothing had been given them; one African died. Religious services were held to provide the Africans with moral assistance.[356] When the health inspectors went in, there were other complaints: the food was improperly stored and the performers were not permitted to contact their relatives. The Colonial Office, the Home Office and the police became involved. One 'native' was reportedly suing an overseer for an assault that had occurred in a magistrate's court in Hammersmith.[357] The Olympia management began to feel the losses accruing from negative publicity and nervously speculated that a moment of low morale was surely attributable to the War. Finally, at the end of January 1901, the Africans were shipped out.[358]

The case did not perhaps appear different in kind from those involving the supervision of neighbourhood facilities or the disputes surrounding the music halls where predominantly white performers worked. Many halls did offer minstrel shows as part of their standard fare, and the performers in these shows were very often African-Americans. George Sims reported that the minstrel shows attracted many of the provincials who visited London partly because performers observed their 'proud motto . . . We never perform out of London.'[359] The response of the residents of Earls Court was not an isolated or simply a metropolitan phenomenon. Yet this case surely made the Progressives feel singularly self-righteous. Those who insisted upon charity towards the performers whom they depicted as racial inferiors, the religious lobby advocating the abolition of inhumane conditions, and the panicked residents of Earls Court who wished to repossess their streets, had all been satisfied. In this instance, the convolution of racial fear, moral mandate and state prerogative provided a platform for the Progressive quest. Cases like that of the Olympia fed the fires lit during the music hall controversies.

Victory at the Olympia no doubt confirmed the Progressives' myopia. Such a demonstration of their capacity to regulate 'entertainment' and to satisfy one grumbling group of protesters only served to underline the perceived abuse of Progressive powers in other contexts. Even before the peak of labour troubles in the leisure trades, there were episodic attempts on the part of unions in the industry to obtain higher wages. The unions normally lobbied the LCC. In 1901, for example, the Amalgamated Waiters' Society accosted the Theatres and Music Hall Committee on behalf of unwaged waiters at the Canterbury, who survived solely on tips: 'You are responsible for pauperism. Your workhouses are full, your lunatic asylums are full. Why is this? It is because of the underpaid labour.'[360] The building boom in music halls reached its peak in 1906; in fat years, the Variety Artistes' Federation, amongst other societies formed by those working in the industry, strove to recruit among this very large group of employees. The labour troubles that beset the entertainment industry revealed the failure of LCC policy to alleviate the tensions of the business. If anything, Progressivism fostered a false image of accommodation which encouraged the unions to undertake disillusioning struggles.

During one of the greatest boom years of the music hall – the very year of the defeat of Progressivism – the industry witnessed a protracted strike by performers, musicians, stage hands and the 'respectable' trade unions. Twenty halls were closed down and the strike spread to the provincial towns. Ten thousand artistes attended mass meetings. Lord Askwith finally settled the strike using the means of a music hall Conciliation Board chaired by Henri Gros and including Oswald Stoll, W.C. Steadman of the Bargebuilders, an LCC alderman, and others such as the comedian Arthur Roberts. When the strike was settled, the halls were decked out with flags and buntings to celebrate 'Peace Night'.[361]

In the same year as the strike and in the years to follow, there were some changes in the letter of music hall policy, if not in its overall thrust, after the Conservatives came to power. Progressive leader John Benn warned in 1910 that 'three attempts have been made to break down . . . that temperance licence policy . . . Our present municipal Masters are too much allied with "the trade" to have a free hand in this important matter.'[362] Eventually, promenades returned to the Empire, and liquor licences were sometimes granted despite ardent opposition from Labour councillors such as Harry Gosling. By 1911, it was somewhat more common for licences to be issued for theatrical performances in the halls, a change that dated from 1908, when the Committee began to allow the sale of liquor in such halls, on the grounds that alcohol was permitted in the theatre.[363] But in licensing matters, in which tycoons such as Oswald Stoll, who really stood alone at the top of the ladder of music hall proprietorship by 1910, played greater and greater roles, the Council continued to exhibit a desire to exert certain controls upon the proprietors.[364] Most of these controls were devised to address the problems of safety and defective structures. This purpose was set against that of censorship, and the rationales for it were twisted over time such that it remained a central, realisable policy goal. As John Burns chose to interpret it:

> Much of the outcry against 'moral censorship' which never has met with the approval of the majority of the Council, was raised to hide the real objection that was felt and raised to vested interests being compelled to provide clean, decent, well-built buildings, properly equipped; to provide exit and prevent panic and fire.[365]

But various tensions persisted, even after the defeat of Progressivism. In the years just before the War, Stoll complained of what he described as four points of opposition to his larger, modern halls: the trade opposition including those seeking cinema licences; the clerics who still charged that the halls were demoralising; the educational opponents who saw music hall fare drawing away the constituencies who might have been in, for example, the new LCC evening classes; and finally, the 'poverty opposition', as he called it, which sought to protect, for example, church lands and other buildings near the sites of proposed halls. Still he sought new licences. Stoll insisted that a growing audience, and especially audiences of the new type, could not be housed in the existing stock of halls.[366]

In 1913, Stoll's antagonists, the small proprietors who opposed the large syndicates, complained to the Council of the 'over-production' of halls and of the need to be more 'sensational' in order to attract audiences who had money enough to pay the bills. A leading group of variety theatres experienced a loss in profit for the period, 1908–12.[367] One representative of a small proprietor who opposed Stoll exhorted the committee:

You have forced us to spend thousands of pounds on our undertaking, we have got to comply with your restrictions in every particular, we have sunk our capital in it, and we have endeavoured to comply, not only with the letter but with the spirit of what you wanted us to do. We have brought our entertainment up to the high standard it is, and here you have this mammoth monopolist, Mr. Stoll, to kill us . . . you will put both him and us to the risk, in order to make profits . . . there are a great many things which it is difficult for a Committee or a Council to get hold of – the suggestive attitude for instance. There are songs which to look at in print absolutely mean nothing; but the suggestive attitude, or even the wink or look put into them, can make them most indecent; and I do, therefore, in the interest of the high class of music hall entertainment that you have hitherto insisted on in London, ask you not to put too great a strain on the resources of the people whom I represent.[368]

Stoll was indeed refused a licence in Fulham at this juncture and during the War as well. But he had been granted many London licences. Perhaps in this instance it was felt that he had reached too far. Perhaps the Council was feeling the heat from the trade unions, which were protesting vigorously against Stoll's wages policy. The London Trades Council maintained that smaller proprietors were more willing to pay higher wages and were being squeezed out by the Stoll machine.[369] Here the Council was simply asking him not to step too far outside the accepted norms of conduct. The code of etiquette forged with the proprietors during the Progressive era had proved as durable as the semblance of moral uplift proffered under their regime. After all, in the heat of the original music hall controversies, Burns himself had claimed that a majority of the Council had never embraced moral censorship; instead, clean and decent buildings, safe from fire, had always been the primary goal of licensing.[370] Sims recalled the alternative music hall fare of performers like Harry Clifton, whose songs included 'Work, Boys, Work and Be Contented', 'The Calico Printer's Clerk' and 'Polly Perkins of Paddington Green'.[371]

By the 1920s, neither the syndicates nor the TMHC nor the vigilance and moral purity crusaders had disappeared. The Progressives alone had almost ceased to exist, though individual candidates and a small 'party' formation persisted into the inter-war years. The industry's life, ordered by a set of rules that was deemed acceptable by both Council and owners, was secured at the expense of the smaller, less competitive halls. Because it had placed ill-considered hopes in the eventual extension of LCC powers over entertainment, the Council was left with only the option of rewarding those proprietors who would accept the new constraints imposed on the industry, constraints that did not require parliamentary mandate.[372] It remains to be proved that music hall fare had changed and failed to conform any longer to an inspector's description of the Metropolitan in 1903, as 'not in perfect taste . . . slightly vulgar'. He had recently seen a turn performed by T.E. Dunville:

> The turn is entirely in his usual style. He commences with a dissertation on 'old maids, young maids and married men's wives' followed by a song and two recitations, one dealing with Pierpont Morgan owning the Earth, the Sea, Heaven and Hell. The other on the Seven Ages of Man.[373]

Whatever objections those in the more diverse, latter-day new audiences may have had to the most 'vulgar' aspects of song or programme, the pervasive sexual repartee and the seductive tease that thrived in the halls did seem to renew itself, albeit in a circumscribed way. During the War years, Sims observed, 'Hardly a red nose now remains on the music hall stage, the lodger has gone to fight for his country, and the bibulous bounder who delighted to call himself a rollicking ram has become an anachronism'[374] –

237

though he may have spoken too soon if one takes into account some of the 'excesses' of the 1920s.

There is no proof offered here that moral regulation or super-vision was wholly successful, or that such efforts necessarily guaranteed an increased audience in the halls. The entertainment seems to have appeared to be in many ways what it traditionally had been, if with a greater reliance upon gesture or style of speech, and upon insinuation.[375] Smyth-Piggott, examiner of plays, had provided the Select Committee of 1892 with a shrewd description of the audience of the halls of his day:

> I have always found this, that the equivocal, the risky, the immoral and the indecent plays are intended for West End audiences, certainly not for the East End. The further east you go the more moral your audience is; you may get a gallery full of roughs in which every other boy is a pickpocket, and yet their collective sympathy is in favour of self-sacrifice; collec-tively they have a horror of vice and a ferocious love of virtue.[376]

The letter writer whose words opened this chapter, beleaguered by the spectre of his father's suicide, told us more about the Council's reputation as an arbiter than about its success as a censor. The manager of the Middlesex had tried his best to explain that the domain of language was not easily fenced, no more than the simulation of death could fail to arouse terror: 'We have found cases where boys in the street have altered the texts somewhat. They have applied other words to the same melodies, but you cannot attribute that to the music hall or to the artiste.'[377]

Ada Reeve, music hall performer, who sang 'Trixie of Upper Tooting' for the Prince of Wales at his request, remembered her first success, a song entitled, 'What Do I Care?', each verse of which ended with that question: 'I used to get lots of fun out of seeing how many different shades of meaning I could put into that simple little phrase.'[378] The irreducible desire for fantasy and satire to be played out, to be reworked or altered in public space was as much a part of the performer's trade as it was part of the audience's expectation and protest. Shaw Desmond characterised the repressiveness of his time and, in particular, the reaction of young men to it:

> The theatre of that day was still regarded by the Nonconform-ist Conscience, that is by millions, as a place of damned souls,

and no one at all regarded it as a place of education. It was only 'an entertainment'. The music hall was for millions a place of vice and shame. 'Nice' people took their children to the Moore and Burgess Minstrels, or to the thrills of the Egyptian Hall, or to the waxy horrors of Madame Tussaud's, which, in some way undefined, were supposed to have an 'improving effect' upon the young idea. I can only say that for thousands 'the Chamber of Horrors' was the sole outlet for the suppressed imaginations of twenty-five to thirty years ago, and starved youth thanked its God for Mrs. Maybrick and Jack the Ripper.[379]

Even politics on the stage was partly a matter of the ears of the listener. Palmer's revelations about the state of the legitimate theatre in 1913 point to the permissiveness, as he saw it, of music hall, where 'the utmost freedom of political allusion of every kind' existed 'without creating serious international difficulty'. Indeed, politics might well be abandoned by dramatic authors, said Palmer, 'where they are at present – [as] part of the ordinary stock-in-trade of the gagging music-hall comedian'.[380]

At the same moment, the sting of the censor's whip remained. From the 1890s onwards cinematographers might appear in a music hall programme. In 1912 a deputation from the fledgling film industry visited the Secretary of State to discuss his proposals to establish film censorship; the industry preferred, characteristically, that self-regulation be undertaken instead. In November 1912, the British Board of Censors was established as an industry body: 'nothing would be passed which was calculated to demoralise the public'. Films dealing with religion, politics, the social and the sexual were suspect and 'scenes relating to childbirth, venereal diseases, [and] strained relations between white men and the coloured races in the British Empire' were at issue. One hundred and sixty-six films were removed from a roster of nearly 7000 viewed in 1912. The LCC, charged with administering the Cinematography Act of 1909, decided during the War, through the Theatres and Music Halls Committee, to attach a provision to film house licences that prohibited the screening of films 'likely to be subversive of public morality'.[381]

The music hall controversies offer an elaborate illustration of Progressivism's dilemma. The confusion and fracturing of response replicates a pattern of civic quarrelling that was more hidden in the protracted courses of everyday social policy of the sort undertaken by the Public Control staff in London's neighbour-hoods. The contention over Council housing estates and London's schools is only faintly suggested by the evidence assembled here. If there were fewer spectacular cases like that of the Empire, there were protests, there were consumers, and there were the foibles of the politicians. In tracing a mood and a sensibility, those policies that *are* surveyed here appear in everyday practices as baffled, confounded and proscribed. The Council and its staff, the county's servants, had more power to provoke policy than to provide care in the heady ways in which they might have envis-aged their mission in 1889. In this way, a new structure of municipal endeavour arrived, hesitated, was promulgated and in its wake left a troubled but recognisable inheritance.

CONCLUSION

The Progressives' inspiring initial successes are preserved in a municipal iconography, still visible today, despite the changing London landscape. What was once County Hall on the South Bank stands as a veritable museum to the bygone era of central London government, on the site of the Works Department of the 1890s. Yet the ideas and practices that sustained the vision of the early Council have long lain dormant. This study suggests at least three areas of failure that account for the decline of the vision and for its increasing lack of credibility in its own time: the failure of economy, of the fiscal; the failure in the realm of the political, which was in part a failure to preserve a distinctiveness of doctrine; and a failure in social terms, as captured by the LCC's inability to eradicate London poverty or to relieve much of the distress of its inhabitants. Instead, intrusion and supervision were substituted for grander programmes of social amelioration or cultural enlightenment.

A successful social-reformist regime must possess a committed and resourceful staff. The increasing disaffection of sections of the LCC employees with the Council signalled some of Progressivism's weaknesses. At the same time, what may be termed the 'consciousness' of LCC clerks, their various dispositions and sensibilities, suggest the complexity of the 'identities' of groups of Londoners who defy easy categorisation. Progressivism could not command its own bureaucracy with sufficient aplomb. Municipal employment became a contested terrain of London politics.

The Council's intervention in London's building industry exposed another layer of London's complicated social archaeology to view. 'Direct labour' has now become a byword for union control of municipal work as well as for aesthetic conformity

241

and paybacks. The recent challenges to the survival of direct labour have accompanied moves toward privatisation and toward the private ownership of council housing characteristic of the Thatcher era. The LCC Works Department was a critical, formative experiment, not just rhetorically, but in the built environment created by the first massive direct labour projects, exemplified by Boundary Street and the Blackwall Tunnel. The exchanges between interrogators and witnesses that occurred in the Works Department inquiry contain recognisable versions of the continuing debate about the legitimacy of the welfare state, privatisation schemes and the inefficiency and corruption of the collapsed and collapsing modern socialist and communist regimes. In our time, the demand for local, democratic forms of decision-making and the insistence on the introduction of 'free market' mechanisms are often postulated upon the failure of earlier systems of chicanery and 'pork' that resemble the LCC Works Department as it came to be understood in the popular imagination.

The Works Department scandal was an especially spectacular episode of many in early LCC history, and may have inspired an indifference to or resentment of municipal politics at the popular level. In the story of the Works Department and in this examination of LCC social and cultural policy, there is abundant evidence of the desire to take advantage of what the Council could provide alongside a record of instances in which the hand was bitten. Amelioration was talked about more than it occurred. The sharp contrast between political claims and municipal efficacy is the greatest demonstrable legacy of Progressivism and of the early LCC in social terms. There can be unresolved argument about whether that problem emanated from electoral losses or caused them; there can be argument about considerable well-meaning achievement in the face of opposition. There may even be contention over an 'unhelpful' critique of an institution that in hindsight appears as a constructive attempt at social engineering, especially as compared with the efforts of our time.

Regardless, this work suggests that the ambivalence of responses to the LCC and the elusiveness of opinion from outside the bureaucracy renders the category of 'policy' unstable and inconsistent. It cannot be reduced to a readily quantifiable or estimable whole, an undifferentiated 'achievement'. As Denise Riley observed: 'Social policy may speak with many voices – some of which have a sneaking disrespect for the authority of the others –

or older departmental battles may be fought over again under the guise of a more contemporary rhetoric . . . a policy is also a morass of haste, calculation, and miscalculation, banality, cynicism and of delay.'[1] Moreover, popular memory may have retained a sense of the ambiguity of Londoners' encounters with the early LCC. This may have contributed to a more generalised hesitancy about whether politicians and local government bodies, if not the State writ large, could deliver on their promises. This in turn may have affected political sentiment and the political behaviour of Londoners as they weathered the War years and the inter-war decades.

Organised propertied interest groups in London before 1914 could not swallow a gradualist road to socialism or even a pluralist economic model in which the municipality might become a viable contender for 'profits' as the Works Department sought to do. Confoundingly, the LCC's insistence on the pursuit of a socialised economy and its fiscal position *vis-à-vis* national government left it no choice but to raise the rates – to ask the 'lower middle class' and many members of London's working class to pay the bill for their own redemption and to rescue the fallen in their midst. The hopes of the early years proved too expensive for the political alliance that was Progressivism to sustain.

In historical terms, this was hardly an insignificant result. The events of 1917 bore witness to the argument that gradualism had been superseded by the strategy of a more decisive and immediate seizure of power. The strength of English democracy rendered this option impossible, and, in the wake of war and revolution, a socialist political economy came to mean that of the Soviet Union. 'Property' similarly distanced itself from economic pluralism; in the world of 'business as usual', in the capitalist world of the 1920s, universalist notions of evolutionary socialism seemed tired and naive. Labour now offered itself as the bearer of class interest and sought out those who would ally themselves with that interest. If 'class struggle' rarely occurred, a class language was more audible than was a language of radical civic rejuvenation.[2]

It is tempting to regard Progressivism's decline and its replacement after 1907 on the LCC by a more 'welfare-conscious' Conservatism, simply as part of the general demise of pre-war Liberalism. But the vision described in this book bridged the gaps between New Liberalism, various socialisms and even Unionism on its right flank; little that came after it was as embracing in its conception or its self-confidence. The 1945 government was not simply the ultimate manifestation of municipal socialism in its national English form, though some of the tasks of the early LCC quickly became the province of central government after 1914.[3] This claim for the distinctiveness of the aspiration for a radical metropolitan democracy supports Avner Offer's more general argument that a crucial moment in the possibilities for social transformation in England was lost before the First World War.[4] London's Poplarism, like the provincial Little Moscows of the 1930s, did not command the following that early Progressivism enjoyed.[5] Meanwhile, Conservatism appropriated some of the Progressivist rhetoric and practice, as the evidence on social policy gathered here indicates; it sustained LCC welfare and educational endeavours without broaching propertied interests.[6] Ironically, the Baldwin government, which came to power soon after Labour had wrested control of the LCC in 1934, itself proffered a populism that assigned a special role to those Londoners in the diverse middle classes, as explored by Tom Jeffery.[7]

The ultimate failure of the Progressive vision for London rested in the regime's inability to persuade a majority of the broadly based electorate that their material and cultural interests were necessarily bound up with a single, inclusive political creed. Great numbers of working men and women did not vote at all before the First World War, but many of those men who did were undoubtedly trade unionists. The Women's Local Government Society could describe a piece of proposed legislation as 'drafted so completely from the point of view of the artisan voter that the interest of the voteless Nurse or Midwife has been quite lost sight of'.[8] If in this instance the category of 'artisan' was flatly assumed to be one that did not encompass an understanding of issues of midwifery, certainly the category of 'Progressive voter' was similarly fixed without a recognition that many trade unionists had abandoned Progressivism for independent Labour activity in London before 1907. Experiments such as the Works Department and the building of Council housing increased expectations rather than assuaging them and bred disappointment. Whom might the Progressives have looked toward otherwise? Elusive lower middle class London offered no solution; the middle classes as a whole were divided in their political loyalties as well. Most probably did vote Conservative, and increasingly so, though not because they were frustrated 'nobodies'.

Ironically, London's cosmopolitanism, realised in part in the diversity and complexity of its population, was not matched by a cosmopolitan and libertarian conception of the future that was articulated by the municipal socialists. Instead, family, home and moral purity provided a platform that did not uniquely appeal in the way that the Progressives had hoped, especially when customary platitudes were awkwardly assimilated by a rhetoric of municipal regeneration. What ought to have represented greater personal freedom and opportunity came to be regarded as a vision of a future that did not work. In the heated debates of the inter-war period, 'socialism' for some meant simply the interest of the collectivity pitted against the individual; this part of the pre-war critique of LCC Progressivism survives still and has recently acquired a new lease of life. But some in the metropolis persisted in their commitment to a social mission for London; more LCC staff professed radical politics in 1936 than had in 1890.[9] The LCC had ceased to be a receptacle of socialist hopes, though the fleeting experience of the Livingstone regime of the 1980s provided a quixotic reminder of the pre-war era. Once more was County Hall the scene of a chaotic attempt to address the crises of metropolitan life through radical experimentation and the 'hopeful evolution' of a municipal destiny. By then, a popular memory of the Progressives had all but vanished. Yet Londoners still recall their County Scholarships. The LCC logo unmistakably remains on darkened brick walls throughout the boroughs. It marks the proud material legacy of the early LCC, but where the symbol adorns buildings that are derelict or abandoned, it likewise conveys historical ambiguity.

SOURCES

The Greater London Record Office houses one of the finest municipal archives in the world. The sources for London history contained in its rooms are rich and provocative; this book has drawn on only a fraction of what is there. The research library on London and the Photographic Library in the same building offer an array of resources cared for by an informed staff. But the sheer massiveness of the LCC collections and the gross limitations of finance prohibit comprehensive cataloguing. For this kind of study, it was necessary to plunge into the Presented Papers of the various committees and departments of the Council with some abandon. Agenda papers and minutes of these bodies do provide a kind of index to the monstrous collections of Presented Papers. Yet the length and obsessive detail of these skeletal volumes can isolate the researcher; sometimes it is best to jump into the Presented Papers and to investigate their contents as a starting point or to use the date of a particular event as a guide. Ledgers in the Record Office do map out the broad contents of the volumes; the coding employed in these ledgers is used in the endnotes that appear below (although not in an entirely standardised way), and indicates the location of materials by committee, department and topic.

For records of policy, materials on the activities of the LCC staff and for evidence about the lives of ordinary Londoners, this study relied especially on the archives of the LCC Department of the Clerk, the Public Control Committee and Department, the Public Health Department, the Theatres and Music Halls Committee (including the transcripts of Licensing Committee proceedings), the School Board for London and the Education Officer's Department, the Parks and Open Spaces Committee, and the Works Committee and Department. The LCC Staff Pocket Books contain annual listings of staff members' names, salaries, positions and promotions. The Honour Rolls of those killed in the Great War offer very detailed evidence on the lives of those who served from the ranks of the Council – a sample of all of London's war dead. The researcher will certainly discern that any single aspect of Council work mentioned in this volume might warrant a study in its own right, and the materials are there with which to undertake such work. While LCC housing and education policy have their historians, other facets of Council work remain largely untouched by this author or by others – records of, for example, the Tramways Department or the Asylums Board beckon.

In addition to the materials housed in the GLRO, the Fabian Society membership files in the Library of Nuffield College, Oxford, deserve more scrutiny. They are useful in reconstructing a sense of rank-and-file activity, and the patterning of London lives, often missing in accounts of the Society. The LCC *Staff Gazette* and the *Clerk*, newspaper of the NUC, offer valuable commentary on 'lower middle class' London both before and after the First World War. They are only two of a host of literary and society papers of the time that commanded a similar readership.

Many records of the building industry are listed in the Notes section but I should like to call special attention to the wonderful resource provided by the journal *Building News*. The collections at the British Library of Economic and Political Science at the LSE contain many examples of both Conservative and Progressive propaganda, as well as the microfilm of the London Trades Council minutes, a splendid source for the period which can, for example, be usefully juxtaposed with Beatrice Webb's indispensable diary; an alternative calendar of London life emerges. The Guild-hall Library also contains political propaganda material from the LCC contests (as well as service records from the Boer War). The George Howell Collection at Bishopsgate Library and the Gertrude Tuckwell Collection at the TUC Library, well known to historians of workers' organisations, of the suffrage and of women's work, contain materials in which the LCC figures promi-nently. The Fawcett Library offers records of women's activities in local government, including that of the LCC and its staff. The Parliamentary Papers contain evidence drawn from all sectors of the Council bureaucracy.

No one has yet studied the London press sufficiently to offer an account of Progressivism in microcosm. Many neighbourhood papers carried verbatim accounts of meetings at which councillors spoke and a sense of the rhythm of the very local can be had from these evocative sources. As new histories of cultural sensibilities, industrial relations and public provision are written, all these sources can assist and illuminate. For the social historian, the 'municipal' is at its best an arena in which to pursue the lives and actions of many who are momentarily captured in their fleeting dealings with staff workers and institutions; the stuff of their wider lives leaves traces that allow the architecture of metropolitan existence to become more visible, its vernacular more intelligible.

NOTES

INTRODUCTION (pp. 1–32)

1 For the course of Nonconformist thought in the period, see D.W. Bebbington, *The Nonconformist Conscience*, London, George Allen and Unwin, 1982, esp. Chapter 3. On social purity, see F. Mort, *Dangerous Sexualities*, London, Routledge and Kegan Paul, 1987. For a description of Nonconformity in London, see P. Thompson, *Socialists, Liberals and Labour*, London, Routledge and Kegan Paul, 1967, Chapter 2.

2 M. Wiener, *Between Two Worlds: The Political Thought of Graham Wallas*, Oxford, Clarendon, 1971, p. 10.

3 Cited in A. Gardiner, *John Benn and the Progressive Movement*, London, Ernest Benn, 1925, p. 132.

4 'Mr. John Burns on "Municipal Socialism"', *Battersea Mercury*, 15 November 1902.

5 J. Burns, *The Straight Tip to Workers: Brains Better Than Bets or Beer* (pamphlet), London, Clarion Press, 1902, p. 14.

6 S. Webb, *The London Programme*, London, Swan Sonnenschein, 1891, p. 207, p. v.

7 J. Burns, 'The London County Council. I. Towards a Commune', *Nineteenth Century*, 31, 1892, pp. 496–514. Burns's critic wrote of the LCC, 'its crude betterment schemes, childish petulance at their rejection, and interference with the labour market have not endeared it to landowners, statesmen or employers of labour'; R.E. Prothero, 'London County Council. II. Towards common sense: a reply to Burns', *Nineteenth Century*, 31, 1892, pp. 515–524. Webb added, 'When every parish has its public baths . . . then we shall begin to show the world that we do not, after all, fall behind Imperial Rome in this one item of its splendid magnificence'; S. Webb, op. cit., p. 208.

8 'From Ben Tillett', *Star*, 1 January 1895.

9 From the title of M. Bentley, *Politics without Democracy, 1815–1914*, London, Fontana, 1984. London (including Middlesex) reached 5.6 million by 1901, according to C. Lee, *The British Economy since 1700*, Cambridge, Cambridge University Press, 1986, p. 128.

10 See A. Sutcliffe, *Towards the Planned City*, Oxford, Blackwell, 1981;

Jean-Paul Brunet, *Saint-Denis: La ville rouge*, Paris, Hachette, 1980; B. Stave (ed.), *Socialism and the Cities*, Port Washington, NY, Kennikat, 1975; R.W. Judd, *Socialist Cities*, Albany, State University of New York Press, 1989; B. Ladd, *Urban Planning and Civic Order in Germany, 1860– 1914*, Cambridge, Mass., Harvard University Press, 1990; S. Magri and C. Topalov (eds), *Villes ouvrières*, Paris, L'Harmattan, 1989; J. Scott, 'Social history and the history of socialism: French socialist municipalities of the 1890s', *Le Mouvement Social*, III, April–June, 1980, pp. 145–153; M. Ebner and E. Tobin, (eds), *The Age of Urban Reform: New Perspectives on the Progressive Era*, Port Washington, NY, 1977; D. Hogan, *Class and Reform*, Philadelphia, University of Pennsylvania, 1985.

11 C. Masterman, *The Condition of England*, London, Methuen, 1960, p. 24: 'public penury, private ostentation - that, perhaps, is the heart of the complaint . . . where is the justice of these monstrous inequalities of fortune?'

12 S. Hynes, *The Edwardian Turn of Mind*, Princeton, NJ, Princeton University Press, 1968, p. 54. Hynes continues, 'The question of why the Liberals, possessed of such unusual power, and with such clear occasions for the beneficent use of it, did not act to correct flagrant social wrongs is one of the crucial questions of the Edwardian era.'

13 J. Davis, *Reforming London*, Oxford, Clarendon, 1988, p. 5. This meticulous work on nineteenth century London government offers a distinctive and insightful analysis.

14 P.J. Corfield, *The Impact of English Towns, 1770–1800*, Oxford, Oxford University Press, 1982, p. 147.

15 ibid., p. 167.

16 ibid., p. 147.

17 D. Owen, *The Government of Victorian London, 1855–1889*, Cambridge, Mass., Harvard University Press, 1982, p. 18.

18 See R. Morris, 'Externalities, the market, power structures and the urban agenda', *Urban History Yearbook*, 1991, pp. 99–109; R. Rodger, 'Managing the market – regulating the city', in H. Diedericks, P. Hohenberg and M. Wagenaar (eds), *Economic Policy in Europe since the Middle Ages: The Visible Hand and the Fortune of Cities*, Leicester, Leicester University Press, 1992, pp. 200–219.

19 G. Stedman Jones, *Outcast London*, Harmondsworth, Penguin, 1984 (Oxford, 1971), p. 313. See the equally indispensable work of H. Dyos, including H. Dyos and M. Wolff (eds), *The Victorian City: Images and Realities*, vols. 1, 2, London, Routledge, 1993, *passim*, and H. Dyos, *Victorian Suburb: A Study of the growth of Camberwell*, Leicester, Leicester University Press, 1977, *passim*.

20 D. Owen, op. cit., p. 47.

21 See, e.g., W. Sewell, *Work and Revolution in France*, Cambridge, Cambridge University Press, 1980; S. Lewis, 'Reassessing syndicalism: the *Bourses du Travail* and the origins of French labour politics', CES Working Paper, Cambridge, Mass., Council for European Studies, 1992.

22 See D. Owen, op. cit., Chapter 2; J. Davis, op. cit., Chapters 2–4.
23 D. Reeder, 'Conclusion: perspectives on metropolitan administrative history', in D. Owen, op. cit., p. 353.
24 J. Davis, op. cit., p. 21, fn. 42.
25 Davis uses the term to describe 'Vestrydom'; ibid., p. 23.
26 G. Stedman Jones, op. cit., p. 7.
27 ibid.; see especially the Introduction, pp. 1–16.
28 D. Owen, op. cit., p. 329.
29 J. Davis, op. cit., p. 50.
30 J. Davis, 'Radical clubs and London politics, 1870–1900', in D. Feldman and G. Stedman Jones (eds), *Metropolis: London Histories and Representations since 1800*, London, Routledge, 1989, pp. 103–128; S. Shipley, *Club Life and Socialism in Mid-Victorian London*, History Workshop Pamphlet, Ruskin, Oxford, 1972.
31 D. Reeder, op. cit., p. 358; K. Young and P. Garside, *Metropolitan London*, New York, Holmes and Meier, 1982, p. 19.
32 J. Davis, *Reforming London*, op. cit., pp. 68–70. On New Liberalism and the intellectual and political origins of Progressivism, see A. Gardiner, op. cit.; P. Clarke, 'The Progressive movement in England', *Transactions of the Royal Historical Society*, 5th series, vol. 24, 1974, pp. 159–181; P. Clarke, *Liberals and Social Democrats*, Cambridge, Cambridge University Press, 1978; M. Freedon, *The New Liberalism*, Oxford, 1978, Chapter 2; J. Kellett, 'Municipal socialism, enterprise and trading in the Victorian city', *Urban History Yearbook*, 1978, pp. 36–45. S. Collini, *Liberalism and Sociology*, Cambridge, Cambridge University Press, 1979; M. Bentley, *The Climax of Liberal Politics*, London, Edward Arnold, 1978, Chapter 8; D. Sutton, 'Liberalism, state collectivism and the social relations of citizenship', in M. Langan and B. Schwartz (eds), *Crises in the British State, 1880–1930*, London, Hutchinson, 1985, pp. 63–79; J. Kloppenberg, *Uncertain Victory*, New York, Oxford University Press, 1986, Chapters 6, 9; and especially J. Davis, 'The Progressive Council, 1889–1907', in A. Saint (ed.), *Politics and the People of London*, London, Hambledon, 1989, pp. 27–48.
33 See, e.g., K. Young and P. Garside, op. cit., fn. 32, pp. 46–47, 67.
34 Benn also called for 'the old City to extend the roof of its Guildhall over all its children', *The Times*, 6 April 1909, cited in K. Young and P. Garside, op. cit., p. 119.
35 See P. Clarke, 'The Progressive movement in England', op. cit., *passim*.
36 J. Davis, *Reforming London*, op. cit., p. 119.
37 P. Thompson, op. cit., especially Chapter 8.
38 P. Hollis, *Ladies Elect*, Oxford, Oxford University Press, 1987, especially Chapter 6. On the nature of the franchise, see P. Thompson, op. cit., pp. 70, 80; K. Young, *Local Politics and the Rise of Party*, Leicester, Leicester University Press, 1975, p. 96. Lodgers were briefly included in the electorate during the 1907 contest and helped it swell to its greatest pre-1914 strength.
39 On the general history of the LCC and its powers and accomplishments, see H. Haward, *The London County Council from Within*, London, Chapman and Hall, 1932; G. Gibbon and R.W. Bell, *History of the*

London County Council, London, Macmillan, 1939; K. Young, op. cit.; K. Young and P. Garside, op. cit.; A. Saint (ed.), op. cit.; and J. Davis, *Reforming London*, op. cit.; V. Steffel, 'The Boundary Street estate, an example of urban redevelopment by the London County Council, 1889–1914', *Town Planning Review*, 47, April 1976, pp. 161–173; V. Steffel, 'The slum question: the London County Council and decent dwellings for the working classes, 1880–1914', *Albion*, Winter, 1973, pp. 314–325.

40 J. Davis, in A. Saint (ed.), op. cit., p. 32; Direct Labour Collective, *Building with Direct Labour*, Conference of Socialist Economists, London, 1978, Chapter 1; G. Marks, *Unions in Politics*, Princeton, NJ, Princeton University Press, 1989, pp. 142–144, who relies in part upon J. Zeitlin, 'Craft regulation and the division of labour: engineers and compositors in Britain, 1890–1914', Ph.D. thesis, University of Warwick, 1981.

41 Composite data on staff employment appear in LCC, Staff Pocket Books, 1889–1913. For a national perspective on direct labour struggles, see R. Rodger, 'Control by coercion: employers' associations and the establishment of industrial order in the building industry of England and Wales, 1860–1914', *Business History Review*, 59, 1985, pp. 302–331.

42 For the histories of the LCC manual grades, see B. Dix and S. Williams, *Serving the Public, Building the Union*, London, Lawrence and Wishart, 1987; Industry and Employment Branch, GLC, *In the Service of London: Origins and Development of Council Employment from 1889*, London, Greater London Council, 1985; T. Segars, 'Working for London's fire brigade', in A. Saint (ed.), op. cit., pp. 167–186.

43 H. Haward, op. cit., p. 193.

44 See J. Davis, *Reforming London*, op. cit., Appendix III.

45 H. Haward, op. cit., p. 195.

46 A. Offer, *Property and Politics, 1870–1914*, Cambridge, Cambridge University Press, 1981, p. 224.

47 ibid., Chapter 12.

48 ibid., Part IV, *passim*.

49 ibid., p. 405.

50 ibid., Chapter 18.

51 For aggregate electoral data, see K. Young and P. Garside, op. cit., Appendix I, Table A1.2. In 1889 the Progressives and Liberals won seventy-three seats, the Moderates forty-five. In a 50 per cent poll of the electorate 500,000 people voted. In 1907, Municipal Reform (the former Moderates) won seventy-nine seats, the Progressives thirty-seven (two went to Labour and an Independent). In a 55.5 per cent poll 840,730 voted. John Mason has assisted in establishing an estimate of Progressive gains and losses in 1907, comparing data from *The Times* and the *East End Observer* with categories established by Charles Booth and employed by P. Thompson (see Thompson, op. cit., Appendix A, p. 304). The abstention rate was often 50 per cent; the Municipal Reformers received 240,846 votes in 1907, the

Progressives 195,558 (S. Knott, *The Electoral Crucible: The Politics of London 1900–14*, London, Greene and Co., 1977, p. 97).

52 J. Davis, *Reforming London*, op. cit., p. 256.

53 See D. Bebbington, op. cit., Chapter 7; Parliamentary Papers (hereafter PP) 1903 (270) VII, Municipal Trading, Select Committee Report; PP 1904 XXXII, Report of the Interdepartmental Committee on Physical Deterioration.

54 A. Briggs, 'Excerpt from evidence of the Centre for Environmental Studies', Royal Commission on Local Government in Greater London, 1959, cited in A. Saint (ed.), op. cit., Appendix, p. 268.

55 See B. Donaghue and G.W. Jones, *Herbert Morrison: Portrait of a Politician*, London, Weidenfeld and Nicolson, 1973; M. Clapson, 'Localism, the London Labour Party and the LCC between the wars', in A. Saint (ed.), op. cit., pp. 127–145; T. Jeffery, 'A place in the nation: the lower middle class in England', in R. Koshar (ed.), *Splintered Classes: Politics and the Lower Middle Class in Interwar Europe*, New York, Holmes and Meier, 1990, pp. 70–96; T. Jeffery, 'The suburban nation: politics and class in Lewisham', in D. Feldman and G. Stedman Jones (eds), op. cit., pp. 189–216.

56 A. Offer, op. cit., p. 254.

57 See, for example, ibid., Chapter 18.

58 A. Offer, op. cit., p. 255.

59 ibid., p. 406.

60 W. Sanders, 'London', *Battersea Labour Gazette*, March 1901, p. 2.

61 See K. Young and P. Garside, op. cit., Appendix I, Table A1.1, p. 342.

62 See e.g., A. Saint, Introduction, in A. Saint (ed.), op. cit., pp. ix–xviii; J. Davis, in Saint (ed.), op. cit., p. 48. For a revision of the claim for a distinctive Progressive labour policy, see S. Laurence, 'Moderates, Municipal Reformers and the issue of tariff reform, 1894–1934', in A. Saint (ed.), op. cit., pp. 93–102.

63 See, e.g., S. Collini, op. cit., Chapters 1–3; J. Harris, *Unemployment and Politics*, Oxford, Clarendon, 1972, pp. 366–367.

64 Beatrice Webb wrote in 1903 of the average Progressive as 'either a bounder, a narrow-minded fanatic or a piece of putty'; in July 1905 Sidney Webb lost his seat on the party committee; N. Mackenzie and J. Mackenzie (eds), *The Diary of Beatrice Webb*, vol. 2, *1892–1905*, London, Virago, 1983, 8 July 1903, p. 286 for the quotation; and see also 10 July 1905, p. 349. (In 1904, he lost his seat on the LCC Education Committee.)

65 E.J. Hobsbawm, 'The nineteenth-century London labour market', in *Worlds of Labour*, London, Weidenfeld and Nicolson, 1984, pp. 131–151.

66 J. Davis, in A. Saint (ed.), op. cit., p. 47.

67 See A. Offer, op. cit., Chapter 19; B. Gilbert, *The Evolution of National Insurance in Great Britain*, London, Michael Joseph, 1966, Chapter 5; J. Harris, *Unemployment and Politics*, Oxford, Clarendon, 1972, Chapter 6.

68 See, for example, B. Porter, 'The Edwardians and their empire', in D. Read (ed.), *Edwardian England*, London, Croom Helm, 1982, pp. 128–144; and, e.g., A. Friedberg, *The Weary Titan: Britain and the Experience of*

Relative Decline, 1895–1905, Princeton, NJ, Princeton University Press, 1988, esp. Chapters 1 and 7.

69 See, for example, J. Lewis, 'The working-class wife and mother and state intervention, 1870–1918', in J. Lewis (ed.), *Labour and Love*, Oxford, Basil Blackwell, 1986, pp. 99–120; the classic G. Searle, *The Quest for National Efficiency: A Study in British Politics and Political Thought, 1889–1914*, London, Ashfield, 1989; D. Dwork, *War is Good for Babies and Other Young Children*, London, Tavistock, 1987.

70 A. Wohl, *Public Health in Victorian Britain*, London, Methuen, 1983, p. 318.

71 See P. B. Rich, *Race and Empire in British Politics*, Cambridge, Cambridge University Press, 1990, pp. 57–58.

72 See LCC, Honour Rolls, 1914–1918, *passim*; S. Pennybacker, 'The "labour question" and the London County Council, 1889–1919', Ph.D. thesis, University of Cambridge, 1984, Chapter 4: 'The LCC and the War' and Chapter 5: 'The staff and the War'.

73 See P. Fryer, *Staying Power*, London, Pluto, 1984, Chapter 9.

74 ibid., pp. 262–272.

75 See, for example, S. Pennybacker, 'Racial rhetoric and London radicalism before the Great War', delivered at the American Historical Association, Annual Meeting, 1982, in author's possession; S. Creighton, 'John Archer, a biographical discussion', in author's possession; R. Webb, 'John Archer: Battersea's black activist', *South London Record*, no. 2, 1987, pp. 30–35.

76 See, for example, P. Fryer, op. cit., pp. 177–178; E. August, Introduction, in E. August (ed.), *T. Carlyle, The Nigger Question and J. Mill, The Negro Question*, New York, Appleton, Century Crofts, 1971; C. Hall, *White, Male and Middle Class*, New York, Routledge, 1992, Chapter 10.

77 See D. Feldman, *Englishmen and Jews: Social Relations and Political Culture, 1840–1914*, New Haven, Conn., Yale University Press, 1994, *passim*.

78 A. Wohl, op. cit., pp. 11, 39.

79 See, for example, V. Ware, *Beyond the Pale: White Women, Racism and History*, London, Verso, 1992, Chapters 2–4; J. Winter, *Socialism and the Challenges of War*, Routledge and Kegan Paul, 1974, pp. 42–50.

80 C. Lee, op. cit., p. 274.

81 ibid., p. 139.

82 C. Lee, op. cit., p. 260, citing W.H. Beveridge's *Unemployment: A Problem of Industry*, London, Longmans, 1909, p. 73.

83 W. Rubinstein, *Wealth and Inequality in Britain*, London, Faber, 1986, p. 123, citing B. Webb, *My Apprenticeship*, vol. 2, Harmondsworth, Penguin, 1938, p. 295; see also C. Booth (ed.), *Life and Labour of the People in London*, London, Macmillan, 1892, vol. 2, part 2.

84 G. Routh, *Occupation Pay in Great Britain, 1906–79*, Cambridge, Cambridge University Press, 1980, p. 63. See also W.D. Rubinstein, *Wealth and Inequality in Britain*, op. cit., Chapter 3.

85 For an important comment on the problems of defining 'skill', see R. Harrison and T. Zeitlin (eds), *Divisions of Labour: Skilled Workers and Technological Change in Nineteenth Century England*, Brighton, Harvester, 1985, p. 6 and *passim*.

86 C. Lee, op. cit., p. 41.

87 ibid., p. 46.

88 Sidney Webb believed that only 20,000 of 100,000 women electors actually voted, as cited in P. Hollis, op. cit., p. 38.

89 J. Davis, 'Slums and the vote, 1867–90', *Historical Research*, 64 (155), 1991, pp. 375–388.

90 P. Thompson, op. cit., pp. 286–298.

91 P. Hollis, op. cit., pp. 45–47 and Chapter 1, *passim*.

92 Briggs, for example, stated, 'For the pre-existing "anarchy of London" there was substituted a self-governing community': A. Briggs, in A. Saint (ed.), op. cit., pp. 45–47.

93 D. Tanner, *Political Change and the Labour Party, 1900–18*, Cambridge, Cambridge University Press, 1990, p. 110.

94 K. Young and P. Garside, op. cit., Appendix I, Table A1.2, p. 343.

95 For some relevant arguments, see, for example, P. Clarke, *Lancashire and the New Liberalism*, London, Cambridge University Press, 1971, pp. 397–407; R. McKibbin, *The Ideologies of Class: Social Relations in Britain*, Oxford, Clarendon, 1991; G. Stedman Jones, 'Why is the Labour Party in a mess?', in G. Stedman Jones (ed.), *Languages of Class*, Cambridge, Cambridge University Press, 1983, pp. 239–256; K. Young and P. Garside, op. cit., p. 62; D. Tanner, op. cit., p. 104.

96 See B. Ladd, op. cit.; J. Scott, op. cit.

97 C. Masterman, *The Condition of England*, London, Methuen, 1909, pp. 68–69, 74.

98 The explanation of 1907 as an affirmation of a pre-existing Conservative voting pattern, or even in terms of Unionist fears of official Liberalism, appears as a tautology in the terms of this study. See, for example, K. Young, op. cit., pp. 93–97, who concludes, 'The Municipal Reform victory of 1907 was, then, no aberration; the passage of time which elapsed before it was achieved is more surprising than the eventual result.' As for Labour as a competing force, see Benn's comments as recorded in A. Gardiner, op. cit., p. 344, in which he faults the Independent Labour Party for hindering Progressivism, and p. 361, on the 1907 election: 'the Labour opposition in the Constituencies had lost the Progressives six seats, but even if there had been no split, the Moderates would still have had an overwhelming victory'. Progressive turn-out was lower in certain East End areas in 1907 than it had been in 1904, e.g. Stepney (−25.3 per cent) and Limehouse (−20.2 per cent) (Knott, op. cit., p. 98). Seats were lost in the east by the Progressives in Mile End, Hoxton and St George's. But the great accretion of strength to the Municipal Reformers was in the middle class areas. This conforms to a pattern for the 1910 general election described by Neal Blewett, *The Peers, the Parties and the People*, Toronto, University of Toronto Press, 1972, esp. p. 481, where he corrects Thompson's figures for the percentage of the total electorate voting Liberal in 1910, finding Liberal strength most seriously in decline in the middle class areas. He emphasises throughout the disenchantment with Liberalism, rather than Unionist appeal *per se*, additionally arguing that the Conservatives never

recovered their traditional base (of 1886–1906) in London's working class areas.

99 G. Grossmith, *Diary of a Nobody*, London, Collins, 1894; E.M. Forster, *Howards End*, New York, Knopf, 1921.

100 C. Mills, *White Collar: The American Middle Classes*, London, Oxford University Press, 1951, *passim*; D. Lockwood, *The Blackcoated Worker*, London, Allen and Unwin, 1958, especially pp. 201–213.

101 See R. Price, *Masters, Unions and Men: Work Control in Building and the Rise of Labour, 1830–1914*, Cambridge, Cambridge University Press, 1980, especially Chapters 4 and 5. For the classic study of London's casual labour markets, see G. Stedman Jones, *Outcast London*, op. cit., *passim*.

102 See J. Harris, op. cit., *passim*, for a narrative of the wider context in which these classes were enacted; D. Tanner, op. cit., p. 104.

103 Essays that anticipated or reflected this trend include several in G. Stedman Jones (ed.), *Languages of Class*, op. cit.: 'Class expression versus social control?', pp. 76–89, 'Working-class culture and working-class politics', pp. 179–238, 'Why is the Labour Party in a mess?', pp. 239–256, and R. McKibbin, op. cit., esp. Chapter 1.

104 This study was completed before the publication of E. Ross, *Love and Toil: Motherhood in Outcast London, 1870–1918*, New York, Oxford University Press, 1993, or J. Walkowitz, *City of Dreadful Delight: Narratives of Sexual Danger*, Chicago, University of Chicago Press, 1992. Each offers provocative commentary on some of the wider questions posed in the first and last chapters of this book.

105 B. Gilbert, *The Evolution of National Insurance in Great Britain*, London, Joseph, 1966, p. 143.

106 See S. Pennybacker, 'The "labour question" and the London County Council, 1889–1919', op. cit.

107 See, for example, M. Weir, A. Orloff and T. Skocpol, 'Understanding American social politics', in M. Weir, A. Orloff and T. Skocpol (eds), *The Politics of Social Policy in the United States*, Princeton, NJ, Princeton University Press 1988: 'Modern welfare states, as they have come to be called, had their start between the 1880s and the 1920s in pension and social insurance programs established for industrial workers and needy citizens. Later, from the 1930s through the 1950s, such programmatic beginnings were elaborated into comprehensive systems of income support and social insurance encompassing entire national populations'; p. 5. A more problematised view was encouraged by, for example, P. Thane (ed.), *The Origins of British Social Policy*, London, Croom Helm, 1978, *passim*.

CHAPTER 1: THE WAYS OF LIFE, ASPIRATIONS AND POLITICAL CULTURE OF MEN AND WOMEN 'BLACKCOATED WORKERS' (pp. 33–95)

1 V. Woolf, *The Voyage Out*, London, Grafton, 1978, p. 5.

2 G. Crossick, 'The emergence of the lower middle class in Britain: a

discussion', in G. Crossick (ed.), *The Lower Middle Class in Britain*, London, Croom Helm, p. 19.

3 *The LCC Staff Gazette* (hereafter SG) August 1900, p. 96. Hobson, Jeffries, Omar Khayyam, Whitman, Morris and Meredith were also popular amongst the staff.
4 W.H. Crisp, SG, September 1900, pp. 106–107.
5 LCC, Council's Honour Roll, Vol. 3; SG, February 1909, p. 26; November 1909, p. 145.
6 Fabian Society Membership Cards, The Library, Nuffield College, Oxford; LCC, Council's Honour Roll, op. cit.
7 SG, January 1900, p. 4.
8 LCC, Minutes, 2 April 1889. In 1912, the Council prohibited the use of an 'LCC official position' in relation to campaigning in parliamentary or municipal elections; see LCC, Minutes, 18 June 1912.
9 See 'The latest socialist scheme', *Spectator*, 17 December 1892, p. 880.
10 SG, May 1900, p. 55.
11 ibid., February 1900, pp. 18–19; C.W.N., 'Spring Gardens thirty years ago', May 1900, pp. 57–58.
12 LCC, Minutes, 26 February 1890. Committees increased in number from ten under the MBW to twenty-five under the LCC and sub-committees multiplied at an even faster rate.
13 LCC, Establishment Committee, Presented Papers (hereafter PP), 15 June 1892, letter from H. de la Hooke.
14 LCC, Minutes, 26 October 1899; LCC Establishment Committee, PP, 16 May 1893. Growth figures for the staff are compiled from LCC Staff Pocket Books, 1889–1905.
15 Figures compiled from LCC, Staff Pocket Book, 1905–06; G.L. Gomme, 'The Council's service and the opportunity afforded to boys . . .', LCC, March 1910, p. 8.
16 A. Spoor, *White Collar Union: Sixty Years of NALGO*, London, Heinemann, 1967, p. 4.
17 See G. Clifton, *Professionalism, Patronage and Public Service in Victorian London: The Staff of the Metropolitan Board of Works, 1856–89*, London, Athlone, 1992, *passim.*
18 LCC, Department of the Clerk, Examination Papers, 'Fourth-Class Clerkships and Typists, 1898–1906', 'Particulars as to Clerkships', 1899.
19 J. Roach, *Public Examinations in England, 1850–1900*, Cambridge, Cambridge University Press, 1971, p. 218, concludes, 'the very success of competition weakened the direct connection between government service and the schools and universities of the country which the administrative reformers had been so keen to achieve'.
20 ibid., cited p. 225.
21 LCC Minutes, 16 July 1889. For de la Hooke's remarks, see LCC, Establishment Committee, PP, 21 November 1892.
22 LCC, Department of the Clerk, Examination Papers, 'Clerkships, January, 1905'.
23 ibid., 'Fourth Class Clerkships, March, 1900'.
24 ibid., September 1902.

25 C.D. Andrews and G.C. Burger, *Progress Report*, London, LCC Staff Association, 1959, p. 15.

26 In 1889, eighty pounds was set as a starting salary 'having in view the salaries at which junior clerks begin in most public and commercial institutions'; see LCC Minutes, 16 July 1889. For promotional rules, see LCC, Establishment Committee, PP, 5 May 1896.

27 For wage and salary statistics, see D. Lockwood, *The Blackcoated Worker: A Study in Class Consciousness*, London, Allen and Unwin, 1958, p. 42, and C. Booth, *Life and Labour of the People in London, Second Series: Industry, 3*, London, Macmillan, 1903, pp. 274–277. Booth found that the great mass of clerks were on a level with the great mass of 'artisans' in the income bracket of £75–150 a year; artisans earned between thirty and sixty shillings a week, p. 277.

28 The Fabian Society calculated the average wage per head as £48 a year in 1895; 1.5 million of 16.5 million workers with single incomes earned £150 a year. See Fabian Tract no. 5, 'Facts for socialists from the political economists and statisticians', London, Fabian Society, March 1895, p. 7.

29 For London vestry rates, see Booth, op. cit., *Second Series: Industry, 4*, pp. 21–23. The average wage for all sections of the LCC clerical staff in 1910 was calculated at £200, on the basis of the LCC Staff Pocket Books, 1910.

30 For a description of the actual status of better-paid industrial workers, see A. Reid, 'The division of labour in the British shipbuilding industry', Ph.D. thesis, University of Cambridge, pp. 199–200. 'The severity of industrial fluctuations denied the vast majority of skilled men that economic security which they have been attributed by most historians, especially the proponents of the "labour aristocracy".'

31 See LCC, Minutes, 11 October 1904.

32 There was a separate examination in typing and shorthand. The new lower section had two sections, one for boys over 15 and under 18, the second for those aged 20–30.

33 See LCC, Minutes, 3 December 1912, which state that all Minors who came to work before reaching the age of 23 should be allowed to sit an examination for the second-class clerical division. Even those above the age limit who had been working toward this exam were allowed to take it. See the Minutes for 8 July 1913, which state the Council's bias in favour of Minors replacing classified officers leaving the service, whenever possible.

34 See S. Pennybacker, 'Changing convictions: London County Council blackcoated activism between the wars', in R. Koshar (ed.), *Splintered Classes: Politics and the Lower Middle Classes in Interwar Europe*, New York, Holmes and Meier, 1990, pp. 97–120.

35 LCC Minutes, 6 October 1891, 3 November 1891, 22 January 1895.

36 Spencer wrote an LCC report on irregular boy labour and testified before the 1901 parliamentary committee on the Employment of School Children. For data on school-leavers, see Rev. S. Gibb, 'The irregular employment of boys', London, Christian Social Union, 1903, p. 7. On the LCC resolve to hire its own graduates, see LCC

Establishment Committee, PP, 4 December 1895. The Clerk of the Council, Laurence Gomme, commented, 'I recognize that the Council wishes to act as a model employer and that it may be urged that the Council occupies in relation to boys in its service, a position of responsibility in addition to that of employer', LCC, Establishment Committee, PP, 5 July 1906.

37 LCC, Establishment Committee, PP, 30 October 1906, 27 June 1909, 1 August 1911, 25 February 1913, 6 May 1913. In 1897, eight of the fifteen who sat the higher examination passed it, but not necessarily with a competitive advantage. They were nevertheless appointed.

38 See L. Holcombe, *Victorian Ladies at Work*, Hamden, Conn., Archan, 1973, p. 141; B.V. Humphreys, 'The development of clerical trades unions in the British Civil Service', Ph.D. thesis, University of London, p. 77.

39 LCC, Establishment Committee, PP, 29 September 1898, 'Memo from Stewart'.

40 See Holcombe, op. cit., Chapter 6; 'Problem of the lady clerk', *Daily Telegraph*, 30 July 1907; Barbara Hutchins, 'An enquiry into the salaries and hours of work of typists and shorthand writers', *Nineteenth Century*, pp. 445–449; Gertrude Tuckwell Papers, TUC Library, Box 356, 'Typists' unions', *passim*.

41 LCC, Establishment Committee, PP, op. cit.

42 ibid., 14 July 1898, state that this hiring 'would result in a considerable saving in salaries inasmuch as the pay of lady copyists would, if the scale of government officers is adopted, be from 16 to 25s a week'. An inquiry into London wage rates revealed that 18–20s per week was 'considered reasonable for fairly educated typists'; LCC, Minutes, 26 July 1898. For a similar argument about the creation of a new stratum of clerical work for women, see M. Zimmeck, 'Strategies and stratagems for the employment of women in the British civil service, 1919–1939', *Historical Journal*, 27 (4), 1984, pp. 901–924.

43 LCC, Minutes, 19 July 1898; LCC, Establishment Committee Minutes, August 1898, especially 'letter from George Simkins'.

44 See 'Chit-chat for lady clerks', *Clerk*, 23 July 1890, p. 61; Dolly Lansbury, 'Equal pay for equal work', *Clerk*, February 1912, p. 25.

45 LCC, Minutes, 7 March 1899.

46 Booth states that London commercial typists' wages averaged fifty to sixty pounds a year; very few earned more than a hundred pounds annually; op. cit., *Second Series: Industry*, 3, p. 276. Holcombe summarises 1914 parliamentary data in which women's pay is recorded as ranging from 8s to 78s 6d a week. The average pay of women with less than five years' experience was 26s, and for those with fifteen years' or more, about 45s. The average for all women clerks' salaries was £45 a year. Men earned £143–221 a year; women, £39–65 a year; op. cit., p. 151, citing Royal Commission on the Civil Service, PP 1914, xvi, cd. 7339, Appendix 5, p. 21.

47 See LCC, Minutes, 7 March 1899; LCC, Department of the Clerk, 'Volume on staff and etc., January, 1906–December, 1906', p. 258. Persistence rates are based on calculations made from LCC, Staff

Pocket Books, 1898–1914. Two-thirds of those hired by 1905 were still employed nine years later when the department had grown to include forty women.

48 LCC, Minutes, 11 December 1906, note that a typist left to become a special adviser in the Educational Adviser's Office at her current salary of £100 per year. See LCC Establishment Committee, PP, 8 December 1898, which note that Miss E.M. Harden left the Council to enter business on her own in Sheffield.

49 LCC, CL/ESTAB/1/1, 'General subcommittee of the GPC', 12 November 1906; see also the related report, 'Memo: women doctors in the Public Health Department'.

50 ibid., 'Letter from the deputy chairman of the Council', 24 June 1914.

51 See 'Topics of the day: the employment of married women', *Daily Graphic*, 8 April 1914; 'Is your charwoman married?', *Daily Sketch*, 10 April 1914 in Gertrude Tuckwell Papers, op. cit., Box 614; T. Olcott, 'Dead centre: the women's trade union movement in London, 1874–1914', *London Journal*, 1978, p. 46.

52 L. Gomme, 'Internal memo from Gomme to the GPC', LCC, Department of the Clerk, PP, 6 April 1914.

53 LCC Staff Association, *Progress Report*, op. cit., p. 93; see S. Pennybacker, in R. Koshar (ed.), op. cit., p. 117, fn. 21; M. Zimmeck, 'Strategies and stratagems for the employment of women in the British Civil Service, 1919–1939', *Historical Journal*, 27 (4), 1984, pp. 901–924.

54 L. Bland, 'Marriage laid bare: middle-class women and marital sex *c.* 1880–1914', in J. Lewis (ed.), *Labour and Love: Women's Experience of Home and Family, 1850–1940*, Oxford, Blackwell, 1986, pp. 123–148.

55 'Prospects in the professions: IX. The City', *Cornhill Magazine*, 14, 1902–03, p. 623. No author is given.

56 The same unknown author claimed that it was of greatest importance 'to be a good fellow and able to get on with [one's] fellow creatures . . . good nature and gentility will generally take a man much further than brains. Then he must be quick and "always business" and he must be straight'; ibid., p. 634.

57 E. Hobsbawm, 'The Fabians reconsidered', in *Labouring Men*, London, Weidenfeld and Nicolson, 1976, p. 267.

58 D. Thurtle and E. Thurtle, 'Comradeship for clerks: an appeal for organisation', London, 'The Clerk' Publishing Society, 1913, p. 11.

59 G. Layard, 'Family budgets: II. A lower middle class budget', *Cornhill Magazine*, May 1901, p. 656.

60 C. Booth, op. cit., *Second Series: Industry*, p. 277.

61 L. Holcombe, op. cit., Appendix 6e; D. Lockwood, op. cit., p. 24.

62 On suburbanisation, see H. McLeod, *Class and Religion in the Late Victorian City*, London, Croom Helm, 1974, Chapter 5; P. Thompson, *Socialists, Liberals and Labour*, London, Routledge, 1967, p. 7, and Chapter 1, *passim*.

63 J. Banks and O. Banks, *Feminism and Family Planning in Victorian England*, Liverpool, Liverpool University Press, 1964, p. 85.

64 A. Sherwell, *Life in West London: A Study and a Contrast*, London, Methuen, 1897, pp. 4–5.

65 H. McLeod, op. cit., p. 19, fn. 43, cites C. Booth, op. cit., *Second Series: Industry*, 5, p. 29: in 1891, 50 per cent of household heads were from outside the metropolis. Clerks and those employed in the law were more likely to be in-migrants than were members of the other professions or 'merchants'.

66 R. White, 'Rowton House for clerks', *Nineteenth Century*, 247, 1897, p. 601.

67 *Office Journal*, 1 May 1909, p. 25.

68 G. Crossick, in G. Crossick (ed.), op. cit., p. 39. For further evidence of the status of clerical wages across a wide range of subgroups, see G. Anderson, 'The social economy of late Victorian clerks', in G. Crossick (ed.), op. cit., pp. 113–133.

69 M. Ginsberg, 'The interaction between social classes', *Economic Journal*, 39, 1929, concluded that 'the social ladder so far lifts only relatively small numbers', p. 565.

70 G. Layard, op. cit., p. 658; J. Foster, *The Divorce Court*, 1891, as cited in the influential P. Cominos, 'Late Victorian respectability and the social system', *International Review of Social History*, 8, 1963, p. 233. Cominos employs the distinction between the paradigmatic 'bored husband' and the 'insipid wives', p. 233. 'Mrs Earle, £1800 a year', *Cornhill Magazine*, 11, 1901, p. 59.

71 'Prospects in the professions: IX. The City', op. cit., p. 634.

72 'Prospects in the professions: XI. The home civil service', *Cornhill Magazine*, 15, 1903, p. 126.

73 ibid., p. 130.

74 ibid., p. 127.

75 ibid., p. 130.

76 'Answers', *Clerk*, April 1890, p. 6.

77 E. Cannan, A. Bowley, S. Edgworth, H. Lees-Smith and W. Scott, 'The amount and distribution of income other than wages, below the income tax exemption limit in the UK', *Journal of the Royal Statistical Society*, 74, 1910, pp. 37–66.

78 *Clerk*, January 1912, as cited in G. Anderson, op. cit., in G. Crossick (ed.), op. cit., p. 120.

79 G.L. Gomme, 'The Council's service and the opportunity afforded the boys for obtaining adult employment therein', London, LCC, The County Hall, 1910, p. 8.

80 See LCC, Council Honour Roll, op. cit., *passim*. There were exceptions, including former pupils of St Paul's, King's, Christ's Hospital and University College School amongst the clerks. But more typical were graduates of Bolton High Grade School, Liverpool Institute High School, Bury Grammar or Camberwell Grammar. Toward the bottom of the departmental hierarchy, the prior education or work experiences of recruits diminished in status. As the staff expanded, routine workers were predictably selected from among a less privileged group of applicants.

81 W. Kent, *Testament of a Victorian Youth*, London, Heath Cranton, 1938, p. 71.

82 ibid., p. 153.

83 See LCC, Establishment Committee, Minutes, 5 December 1892, for a report on Clerk's Department employee Estlin, who lost his job at the age of 28 through drink, after salary reductions and broken pledges: 'lately he has taken to drink again and on Thursday morning last he came into the office at half-past nine, signed his name, and immediately passed out by the other entrance without going to his room, since which time he has not appeared at his office'.

84 W. Kent, op. cit., p. 204.

85 ibid., p. 275.

86 T. Crosland, *The Suburbans*, London, John Long, 1905, pp. 76–77.

87 ibid., p. 9.

88 H. Jackson, *The 1890s*, London, Hutchinson, 1913, 1988, p. 26. P. Cominos noted, 'Both Arnold and Allen located the stronghold of the respectable norm in the lower middle class', op. cit., p. 38.

89 G. Layard, 'Family budgets II', op. cit., p. 656. A. Sherwell reported that between 1881 and 1891, the population of Hampstead increased by 69 per cent, which is an index of a certain kind of suburbanisation. Except for the City (25.5 per cent) Soho experienced the greatest decline in population (19.8 per cent) in the same decade, op. cit., pp. 4–5.

90 G. Allen, 'The new hedonism'; *Fortnightly Review*, 60, 1894, p. 378.

91 ibid., p. 381.

92 R. White, op. cit., p. 596.

93 A. Sherwell, op. cit., p. 127.

94 ibid., pp. 127, 137.

95 ibid., p. 147.

96 A. Ransome, *Bohemia in London*, London, Chapman and Hall, 1907, p. 276.

97 ibid., p. 129.

98 ibid., p. 182.

99 ibid., p. 130.

100 'Bohemia in London', SG, December 1912, p. 206.

101 D. Riley, *'Am I That Name?': Feminism and the Category of Women in History*, Minneapolis, University of Minnesota, 1988.

102 C.F.G. Masterman, *Condition of England*, London, Methuen [1909], 1960, p. 65.

103 Cominos, op. cit., p. 218.

104 In a very dense literature, see, e.g., F. Widdowson, *Going Up into the Next Class*, London, Hutchinson, 1983; F. Hunt (ed.), *Lessons for Life: The Schooling of Girls and Women, 1850–1950*, Oxford, Blackwell, 1987; D. Gittins, 'Marital status, work and kinship, 1850–1930', in J. Lewis (ed.), *Labour and Love*, op. cit., pp. 249–267, and, especially, M. Vicinus, *Independent Women*, Chicago, University of Chicago Press, 1985 and G. Anderson (ed.), *The White-Blouse Revolution: Female Office Workers since 1870*, Manchester, Manchester University Press, 1988.

105 'Chitchat from our lady clerks', *Clerk*, 16 June 1890; S. Webb and B. Webb, *Problems of Modern Industry*, London, Longmans, 1898, pp. 68–9.

106 See M. Zimmeck, op. cit., and D. Copelman, 'Women in the classroom struggle: elementary schoolteachers in London, 1870–1914', Ph.D. thesis, Princeton, 1985.

107 D. Thurtle and E. Thurtle, op. cit., pp. 12–14.

108 'Replies to F. Low, "How poor ladies live"', *Nineteenth Century*, 42, 1897, p. 415.

109 See M. Vicinus, op. cit., *passim*.

110 A. Ransome, op. cit., p. 204. At Johnson's and Addison's Artisan's Club, a man who brought his wife paid for her; if she came to fetch him, he spoke with her at the door; and if one called another cuckold, he would be thrown out of the door.

111 See the papers of the Criminal Law Amendment Committee Conference of 3 June 1913, Fawcett Library and especially T. Guggenheim, 'The views of the average young man on solicitation', pp. 52–57: 'For business or social reasons, a young man can't "afford" to be seen in loose company; he does not want to risk catching disease; he may not be able to spend money on these things . . . all celibates are not necessarily moral men', p. 56.

112 J. Banks and O. Banks, op. cit., p. 198.

113 A. Ransome, op. cit., p. 280.

114 Piper, 'Spring Gardens Ballads – no. XXV, "The Aspirant"', SG, December 1912, p. 202.

115 See C. Collett's comment on F. Wood, 'The course of real wages in London, 1900–1912', *Journal of the Royal Statistical Society*, 67, December 1913, p. 59; C. Collett, 'Mrs. Stetson's economic ideal', in *Educated Working Women: Essays on the Economic Position of Women Workers in the Middle Classes*, London, P.S. King, 1902, p. 142.

116 C. Collett, 'Mrs. Stetson's economic ideal', op. cit., p. 127; see D. Copelman, 'Women in the classroom struggle', op. cit., and '"A new comradeship between men and women": family, marriage and London women teachers, 1870–1914', in J. Lewis, (ed.), *Labour and Love*, op. cit., pp. 175–194.

117 S. Webb and B. Webb, *Problems of Modern Industry*, op. cit., p. 69. L. Bland adds that the concept 'probably meant all things to all people', in J. Lewis (ed.), op. cit., p. 133. She also proposes that feminists were likely to abjure from abstinence: 'If feminists were largely in agreement about the dangers and displeasures of marriage, many also agreed over the means for eradicating them and reforming marriage'; p. 138.

118 J. Walkowitz, *Prostitution and Victorian Society: Women, Class and the State*, Cambridge, Cambridge University Press, 1980, p. 256.

119 See M.G. Fawcett Papers, The Fawcett Library, Box 89, Letters, nos. 15, 16, 17; see also the table map of a massive dinner for suffragism at which P. Fawcett is seated, as was L. Gomme, the wife of the LCC Clerk of the Council; Barbican Art Gallery, exhibition entitled 'The Edwardian Era', 12 November 1987–February, 1988.

120 C. Collett, *Educated Working Women*, op. cit., p. 76. She was a high school mistress.

121 See S. Pennybacker, in R. Koshar (ed.), op. cit., *passim*.

122 See A. Ransome, op. cit., p. 230.
123 'It is of course, understood that no officer will come alone, but that he will take this opportunity of bringing his sisters, his cousins and his aunts to a function at which all are welcome'; SG, June 1900, pp. 65–66, with homage to Gilbert and Sullivan.
124 SG, February 1906, p. 16.
125 SG, July 1900, p. 100.
126 SG, November 1907, p. 117.
127 SG, July 1906, p. 112.
128 T. Gourvish describes and estimates a 20 per cent decline in the period, 'The standard of living, 1890–1914', in A. O'Day (ed.), *The Edwardian Age: Conflict and Stability, 1900–1914*, Hamden, Conn., Anchor Books, 1917, p. 23. F. Wood, 'The course of real wages in London, 1900–12', *Journal of the Royal Statistical Society*, 77, 1913, pp. 1–55, *passim*.
129 SG, February 1900, p. 14.
130 Letter to the editor: 'How to overcome the Saturday half-holiday difficulty', SG, November 1901, p. 132.
131 A. Ransome, op. cit., p. 85.
132 SG, July 1910, p. 98.
133 I am grateful to Sue Laurence, Assistant Curator of the Bethnal Green Museum of Childhood, for this reference.
134 SG, May 1900, p. 55.
135 The lodger appeared in lyrical form as well. See G.R. Sims, *My Life*, London, Eveleigh Nash, 1917: 'It was liquor in front of the house and licence on the stage. Lion comiques scored some of their greatest successes in the impersonation of dissipated "swells" who were always on the drunken racket. The red-nosed comedian's favourite topic was drink and the only domestic touch in his songs had reference as a rule to the lodger'; p. 315. See also P. Bailey, 'Ally Sloper's half-holiday: comic art in the 1880's', in *History Workshop Journal*, no. 16, 1983, 4–31.
136 'How to dress on £12 a year', SG, July 1913, p. 131. Food posed similar problems, but could be skimped upon. See, e.g., A. Ransome, *The Souls of the Streets and Other Little Papers*, London, Brown Langham, 1904, p. 30; 'The clerk and his dinner', *Clerk*, December 1908, p. 178, describes vegetarian restaurants serving five hundred at a time in the City between noon and 3 p.m., charging six pence for a three-course dinner. See the wonderfully instructive R. Thorne, 'Places of refreshment in the nineteenth century city', in A. King (ed.), *Buildings and Society*, London, Routledge and Kegan Paul, 1980, pp. 228–253.
137 SG, February 1900, p. 22.
138 See Guildhall Library, City Imperial Volunteers, MS 10, 190, 14th Middlesex, 'History of the I.C.R.V. volunteering in South Africa'. Lionel Curtis of the Clerk's Department was 27 when he enrolled in 1896. He was a good rider and had the rank of captain. The Civil Service Rifles included E.C. Crick, also of the department, who enrolled at the age of 29 in 1893; he had 'six years' efficient riding

and was a first-class shot'. Curtis became the prominent Liberal imperialist.

139 'Volunteers for South Africa', SG, February 1900, p. 16. J.J. Hawes received cheques from his colleagues as a volunteer. See the reports back to the staff, e.g. 'On the way to the front', SG, April 1900, p. 44.

140 'Lionel Curtis', SG, June 1901, p. 71; see also P. Rich, *Race and Empire in British Politics*, Cambridge, Cambridge University Press, 1990, Chapters 2–4, and 7 for a profile of Curtis.

141 SG, July 1900, pp. 77–78.

142 Athletics and sport were not entirely removed from departmental politics. W.A. Jones of the Solicitor's Department was one of many employees reprimanded for his activity in the agitation over staff grievances. He was, however, a 'good sportsman', explaining, 'Some time later in a departmental cricket match against Public Control (at which the Solicitor himself was present), I was lucky enough to score seventy-three runs which rehabilitated me in the Solicitor's good graces', C. Andrews and G. Burger, op. cit., p. 25.

143 'Dulce domum – the influence of men upon women', SG, February 1901, p. 17.

144 J. Ruskin, *The Crown of Wild Olive and Sesame and Lilies*, New York, Lovell, Coryell and Co., n.d., pp. 88–89, 136, 8.

145 C. Collett, *Educated Working Women*, op. cit., p. 62.

146 H. Hadley, 'Place aux dames', SG, March 1901, p. 36.

147 Organised protests of male clerks opposed to women's entry into clerical work were frequent before the War. An oppositional view, and an unpopular one, even amongst many clerical trade unionists, is contained in D. Lansbury, 'Equal pay for equal work', *Clerk*, February 1912, p. 25.

148 'Men's influence over women', SG, May 1901, p. 64.

149 S. Richards, 'The clerks' union', *Clerk*, August 1890, p. 63.

150 SG, February 1909, pp. 26–27.

151 For example, Harry Quelch of the Printers' Warehousemen's Union pressured the London Trades Council to pass a Labour Party proposal to repudiate 'the attack . . . that socialism is antagonistic to the family organisation and declare that disintegration for some time [had been] due to slums, child labour, low wages, sweating and the operation of capitalism'; London Trades Council, *Minutes*, 12 December 1907. For the position of German socialists, see R. Evans, 'Politics and the family' in R. Evans and W. Lee (eds), *The German Family: Essays on the Social History of the Family in Nineteenth and Twentieth Century Germany*, London, Croom Helm, 1981.

152 SG, November 1910, p. 149.

153 ibid.

154 SG, February 1905, p. 24; H.H. Elvin, 'Socialism for Clerks', a Clarion pass-on pamphlet, London, Clarion Press, 1909. Elvin believed that 'the only hope of the clerical worker [was] to be found in socialism', and felt that even if wages went up a bit under free trade, rents would go up and purchasing power would decrease, p. 10.

155 SG, March 1908, p. 32.

156 ibid., p. 32.
157 See, e.g., Municipal Reform Party, 'LCC Election Leaflet, 1910', Guildhall Library Municipal Reform Party Leaflet A1.
158 SG, January 1909, p. 13.
159 See P. Hollis, *Ladies Elect: Women in English Local Government, 1865–1914*, Oxford, Clarendon, 1987, Chapter 8.
160 SG, February 1910, pp. 24–25.
161 SG, February 1909, pp. 26–27. D. Thom, 'The ideology of women's work, 1914–24, with special reference to the NFWU and other trade unions', Ph.D. thesis, Thames Polytechnic, 1982, offers an excellent study of the 'endowment of motherhood' rhetoric as it appeared before, during and after the War.
162 SG, February 1909, pp. 26–27.
163 See S. Pennybacker, in R. Koshar (ed.), op. cit., p. 111.
164 SG, February 1912, p. 30.
165 This survey is based on the membership records of the Fabian Society, held in the Library of Nuffield College, Oxford. Cards for individual members and those donating money and subscribing to Society literature were filed together, alphabetically. The cards were updated periodically, probably annually. This survey represents a full accounting of all those persons, of the several thousand on file, who stated that they were in the employ of the LCC, including councillors and those who served the LCC in advisory capacities. Only those showing affiliation which began before 1919 were counted. The great problem of the survey is that dozens of London teachers did not indicate whether they were LCC teachers or not. The presumption is that most would have been. *Apart* from the teachers, approximately fifty active members or active subscribers declared LCC employment or affiliation before 1919. Some resigned or were struck off during the War. Some of these in turn rejoined later, though less than half of the original group were members in the post-war period. Some indicated London Labour Party membership in addition.
166 See S. Alexander, Introduction to S. Alexander (ed.), *Women's Fabian Tracts*, London, Routledge, 1988, pp. 1–11.
167 LCC, Minutes, 22–23 March 1910. The Council ordered an inquiry into rates of pay. On 23 January 1912, Norman and Karslake moved that the Council policy call for the 'paying of rates of wages and observing conditions of employment recognised by trade unions and associations of employers'; 15 April 1913.
168 LCC, Minutes, 15 December 1908. A barrier at £245 had been erected in 1889 and by 1908, 200 Minor Establishment employees were below that point on the scale. Officers were halted at £150 or £200 until a vacancy occurred in the First Class. This report ends by supporting the notion of two classified clerical sections in which probation would be taken more seriously.
169 Of the twenty-eight junior clerks in the Department of the Clerk in 1900, thirteen had attained first class or better by 1908; LCC Staff Pocket Books, op. cit., 1908.

170 Other types of clerical employment provide comparisons with conditions at the LCC. Ten insurance clerks employed between 1890 and 1914 averaged £423 in earnings by 1914; comparable LCC employees averaged £367. The average increase at the LCC was even higher than at the Royal Exchange, yet those enjoying this benefit were the quarter of the LCC employees who remained until 1914. Gains over time were crucial. See T. Gourvish, in A. O'Day (ed.), op. cit., who cites B. Supple, *The Royal Exchange Assurance,* Cambridge, Cambridge University Press, 1970, p. 380. Even Gourvish's railway clerks experienced salary rises of 3.1 per cent between 1899 and 1913, p. 24.

171 R. Price, 'Society status and jingoism: the social roots of lower middle class patriotism, 1870–1900', in G. Crossick (ed.), op. cit., cites D. Lockwood, op. cit., p. 105.

172 W. Read, 'LCC staff', *Clerk,* January 1909, p. 9.

173 LCC, Minutes, 15 December 1908, 1 February 1910. The new central regulation read: 'Advance from one section of a class to another is made on the authority of the Establishment Committee, to whom is submitted by the head of department concerned, a special certificate that the character of the work of the official recommended for advance, and the manner in which it is performed, justify his advance to the next section.'

174 Advancement to the second class would be handled by committee; advancement to the top of the second class would be therefore infrequent as the analogous move was for men employees.

175 LCC, Minutes, 15 December 1908.

176 SG, January 1909, p. 5.

177 W. Willmot, *The LCC Staff Association, Inception and Progress, 1909–1935,* London, n.d., p. 18. Though Gomme, the Clerk, appeared in order to apologise to the staff and to argue that the scheme would actually allow more officers to reach the first class than ever before, the Moderates claimed in Council that 'classification not finance' was at the bottom of the change; this provoked laughter from the Progressive benches. Progressive representatives obtained permission from the Council to print and to circulate the official record of staff meetings and memoranda, p. 19.

178 LCC, Minutes, 18 March 1912, 11 March 1912; SG, January 1911, p. 8, March 1914, p. 73.

179 W. Willmot, op. cit., p. 15.

180 C. Andrews and G. Burger, *Progress Report,* op. cit., p. 25.

181 SG, December 1911, p. 161; W. Willmot, op. cit., p. 27. As late as 1913, many of the departments in which manual work predominated and a core of white collar staff directed the administrative work, such as asylums, housing, parks and public control, were not represented, possibly because many of the staff were working outside of the County Hall itself.

182 C. Andrews and G. Burger, op. cit., p. 21.

183 LCC, Minutes, 22 March 1910; 23 March 1910.

184 *Clerk,* May 1910, p. 33.

185 See LCC, Minutes, 15 October 1913, for a list of demands.
186 ibid.
187 SG, June 1913, p. 149.
188 SG, March 1914, p. 74.
189 A. Spoor, op. cit., p. 47. Gomme, Chief Clerk of the LCC, was elected president of NALGO in 1906, which was significant in the light of the Staff Association's conflicted position at that earlier moment. Smokers were popular NALGO venues. Spoor recounts that the singing of sentimental, patriotic or religious ballads, dramatic recitations, and 'coon songs' were standard fare. NALGO had a local guild structure.
190 W. Willmot, op. cit., p. 21; LCC, Minutes, 18 November 1913; 19 November 1913.
191 D. Thurtle and E. Thurtle, op. cit., pp. 8–9.
192 SG, January 1914, p. 14.
193 SG, March 1914, p. 71.
194 The *Clerk* reports upon two meetings held in May 1890 in favour of union wage rates. Increased pay, the eight-hour day with one hour for lunch, legal protection from fines and sweating, and an end to overtime were amongst its objectives. This meeting sent memorials to the City, the LCC, the London Chamber of Commerce and the Law Society, in an effort to seek action against unscrupulous employers; 16 June 1890, p. 47.
195 See *Clerk*, November 1908, p. 8, for a report of the NUC Brixton demonstration against women's labour in which the issue of equal pay also arose.
196 *Clerk*, May 1908, p. 67. This letter is from a member of the Association of Shorthand Writers and Typists.
197 W. Read, *The Clerk's Charter*, London, 'The Clerk' Publishing Society, 1909, 1910.
198 SG, March 1914, p. 74.
199 See *Clerk*, 18 June 1910; V.A., 'Women clerks demand the franchise', *Clerk*, July 1910, p. 105.
200 'Vale – atque Salve', SG, July 1914, p. 160.
201 T.W.H. Crosland, *The Suburbans*, London, John Long, 1905, p. 207.
202 C. Masterman, *The Condition of England*, London, Methuen, 1909, p. 83.
203 E.J. Hobsbawm, op. cit., p. 258. I am grateful for Geoffrey Crossick's observation that Hobsbawm appropriated the term from the writings of Leon Gambetta; R.Q. Gray, 'Religion, culture and social class in late nineteenth and early twentieth century Edinburgh', in G. Crossick (ed.), op. cit., p. 151.
204 C. Masterman, op. cit., pp. 68–69, 74.
205 NUC, 'Report of the sixteenth annual conference, London, 1907'; President George Simkins of Brixton: 'clerks . . . work on everything from a [pounds–shillings–pennies] point of view, which was especially in evidence at the recent LCC election', Trades Union Congress, Gertrude Tuckwell Collection, no. 504c.

206 'A fully developed commune', *Outlook*, 12 January 1907, p. 37; 'The limits of municipalism', *Outlook*, 19 January 1907, p. 74.
207 See S. Pennybacker, 'The Millennium by return of post: reconsidering London Progressivism', in D. Feldman and G. Stedman Jones (eds), *Metropolis: London Histories and Representations*, London, Routledge, 1989, pp. 129–162.
208 C. Masterman, op. cit., p. 69.
209 See S. Pennybacker, in R. Koshar (ed.), op. cit., *passim*.
210 C. Andrews and D. Burger, op. cit., p. 22.
211 E. Cannan, A.L. Bowley *et al.* (eds), op. cit., *passim*; Morrison is cited in A. Spoor, *White Collar Union: Sixty Years of NALGO*, London, Heinemann, 1967, p. 62.
212 A. Spoor, ibid., p. 47.
213 *Clerk*, November 1909, p. 170.
214 SG, May 1908, p. 65.
215 J. Lewis, 'Women clerical workers in the late nineteenth and early twentieth centuries', in G. Anderson (ed.), *The White-Bloused Revolution*, Manchester, Manchester University Press, 1989, p. 43.
216 E.J. Hobsbawm, op. cit., p. 257; M. Vicinus, op. cit., *passim*.
217 The NUC described the sentiments of the post office telegraphists who had protested against the classification system at work: 'These deserving officers complained that owing to the smallness of their incomes, they were "unable to perform the duties of manhood" (laughter) – and – were debarred from entering upon the state of matrimony until several years later than a laborious member of the working classes was in a position to do so'; *Clerk*, 15 May 1890, p. 19.
218 See S. Pennybacker, '"It is not what she said but the way in which she said it": the London County Council and the music halls', in P. Bailey (ed.), *Victorian Music Hall*, Vol. 1: *The Business of Pleasure*, Milton Keynes, Open University Press, 1986, pp. 120–140.
219 G. Anderson argues that in overall terms, women actually came onto the clerical labour market at too late a point to affect adversely men's position on the labour market. This notion contradicts Zimmeck's analysis of the Civil Service. See Anderson in G. Crossick (ed.), op. cit., p. 127, and M. Zimmeck, op. cit., pp. 901–905.
220 SG, February 1914, p. 47.
221 'NUC trippers in Germany', *Clerk*, October 1910, p. 156.
222 'The obsession about Socialism: a plea for sweet reasonableness', *Clerk*, January 1911.
223 SG, May 1900, p. 56.
224 See P. Rich, *Race and Empire in British Politics*, Cambridge, Cambridge University Press, 1990, pp. 57–64.
225 For the history of the Clerk's Department and of activism and employment during the First World War, see S. Pennybacker, 'The "labour question" and the London County Council, 1889–1919', op. cit., Chapters 1, 5.

CHAPTER 2: 'THE INDUSTRIAL REORGANISATION OF SOCIETY': THE LCC WORKS DEPARTMENT (pp. 96–157)

1 The title is taken from J. Burns, 'The Unemployed', Fabian Tract no. 47, London, Fabian Society, 1893, p. 5.

2 Rev. H. Latham, 'Nights at play', *Cornhill Magazine*, 12, 1902, pp. 677–685.

3 R. Price, *Masters, Unions and Men: Work Control in Building and the Rise of Labour, 1830–1914*, Cambridge, Cambridge University Press, 1980, pp. 245–246. See also J. Zeitlin, 'Rank and filism in British labour history: a critique', *International Review of Social History*, 34, 1989, pp. 42–61; and R. Price, 'What's in a name? workplace history and rank and filism', *International Review of Social History*, 34, 1989, pp. 62–77.

4 B. Slater, 'Non-elector's Reform Bill', London, *c.* 1870, in the possession of Dorothy Thompson. I am grateful to the late Edward Thompson for calling this tract to my attention.

5 See A. Sutcliffe, *Towards the Planned City: Germany, Britain, the United States and France, 1780–1914*, Oxford, Blackwell, 1981, Chapters 3, 7; A. Sutcliffe (ed.), *The Rise of Modern Urban Planning, 1890–1914*, London, Mansell, 1980, Chapters 1, 5, 6.

6 See the standard work, J. Davis, *Reforming London: The London Government Problem, 1855–1900*, Oxford, 1988; also D. Owen, *The Government of Victorian London*, Cambridge, Mass., Harvard University Press, 1982; K. Young and P. Garside, *Metropolitan London*, New York, Holmes and Meier, 1982; and J. Davis, 'Radical clubs and London politics, 1870–1900', in D. Feldman and G. Stedman Jones (eds), *Metropolis: London Histories and Representations since 1800*, London, Routledge, 1989, pp. 103–128.

7 'Conference of delegates from working men's clubs, political and other associations' held at Lancaster House, Savoy, 16 July 1881, chaired by J.B. Firth and apparently sponsored by the London Municipal Reform League, in possession of Dorothy Thompson. I am grateful to the late Edward Thompson for this reference.

8 S. Webb and B. Webb, *The History of Trade Unionism*, London, Longman, 1920, pp. 390–1.

9 Amalgamated Society of Carpenters and Joiners, Annual Report, 1889, p. 11.

10 B. Webb, *Diary* (manuscript), 26 April 1890.

11 *Building News*, 11 July 1890, 'Notes on Building Prices, III', p. 38.

12 The author added a note of caution, citing the example of the use of certain hydraulic machinery in certain kinds of building work: 'the fewer times the material is handled, the greater the saving. But although the saving of labour in such cases is great, it is not so much as might be supposed, the expense of engines and cranes and their depreciation, and the conveyance to and from the building, the erection and removal of machinery, staging and etc. is a considerable drawback'; ibid., p. 39.

13 Amalgamated Society of Carpenters and Joiners, op. cit., p. 11.
14 See K. Brown, *John Burns*, Royal Historical Studies in History, London, 1977, p. 66, for a discussion of these campaigns.
15 See M. Ward, 'Direct labour', *Battersea and Wandsworth Labour and Social History Group Newsletter*, 5, January 1978, pp. 3–4; 'John Burns and 1892 - a talk by Sean Creighton', 'Wandsworth History Workshop News', September 1992, pp. 2–6; Sean Creighton, 'John Burns' election to the LCC' and 'Battersea's Labour Movement, 1854 to 1914', drafts in possession of their author.
16 Comité Révolutionnaire du Prolétariat, *A la classe ouvrière*, 1874, p. 15, cited in K. Brown, op. cit., p. 9, fn. 1.
17 See S. Pennybacker, 'New unionism and socialism: the practical character of three strikes', University of Pennsylvania, 1977, unpublished manuscript.
18 K. Brown, op. cit., p. 53.
19 S. Webb and B. Webb, op. cit., pp. 408–09, citing a speech delivered by John Burns at the Liverpool Congress, 21 September, 1890.
20 J. Burns, 'The Unemployed', op. cit., pp. 5–13; 15, 17.
21 ibid., p. 7.
22 See S. Pennybacker, 'New unionism and socialism', op. cit.
23 J. Burns, 'The Unemployed', op. cit., p. 18.
24 M. Ward, op. cit., p. 4.
25 H. Haward, *The London County Council from Within*, London, Chapman and Hall, 1932, p. 21.
26 See, e.g., 'Questions for London County Councillors', Fabian Tract no. 26, London, Fabian Society, 1893.
27 N. Mackenzie and J. Mackenzie (eds), op. cit., vol. 1, 29 July 1890, p. 338.
28 ibid., 29 July 1890.
29 H. Muggeridge, 'The anti-municipal conspiracy exposed', pamphlet no. 7, City of London Branch ILP, London, 1903, p. 20.
30 ILP, 'Report of the twentieth annual conference', Merthyr, May 1912, p. 60.
31 ibid., p. 60, comments of W.H. Ayles.
32 ibid., comments of Councillor J.M. McLachlan.
33 See the comments of Tom Mann regarding the exclusion of loafers from the new unions, as recorded in N. Mackenzie and J. Mackenzie (eds), op. cit., vol. 1, 17 November 1889, pp. 304–05.
34 ibid. The London United Committee of Carpenters and Joiners called a conference on the subject which appointed a delegation representing all the trades. This conference inaugurated the work of the London Building Trades Committee.
35 Amalgamated Society of Carpenters and Joiners, Annual Report, Manchester, Cooperative Printing Society, 1889, p. 11.
36 PP 1890, vol. lxxviii, cd. 6176, 445, p. 24, *Reports of Strikes and Lockouts of 1890*.
37 ibid., p. 45.
38 PP 1893–94 lxxxiii Pt. 1, (6890), *Report of Strikes and Lockouts of 1891*.
39 ibid.; see the work of R. Millward and R. Ward on the problem of the

gas enterprises, e.g. 'From private to public ownership of gas under-takings in England and Wales, 1851–1947: chronology, incidence and causes', Working Papers in Economic and Social History, no. 1, University of Manchester, 1990.

40 Amalgamated Society of Carpenters and Joiners, Annual Report, 1891, op. cit., Monthly Report, July 1892; Monthly Report, October 1892, p. 10.

41 ibid.

42 ibid., Annual Report, 1893–94; Monthly Report, December 1894.

43 ibid., Monthly Report: extracts from the reports of the LUBTC; March 1890, identifies the School Board for London as the 'first to adopt the committee's principles'.

44 *The Times*, 14 January 1889, p. 10.

45 *Building News*, 29 June 1894.

46 See Amalgamated Society of Carpenters and Joiners, Monthly Report, March 1893.

47 LCC, WKS/Gen/1/1, 'Report of the special committee on works together with minutes of evidence and appendices, 1896–97', 1898 (hereafter WDI), Appendix B, 'Statement by C.J. Stewart, Clerk; report by J.J. Sexby, Chief officer of parks . . .', 14 January 1897, p. 74. In December 1889, the Architect suggested that all works on the general grounds involving laying out and improvements should be executed by direct labour, including work on Brockwell and Waterlow Parks. Some painting work on the Thames embankments was carried out with direct labour.

48 *Building News and Engineering Journal*, 14 November 1891, p. 702. The delegation included members of the Amalgamated Union of Street Masons, Paviours and Stone-Dressers, and the London Amalgamated Society of Upholsterers.

49 The LCC Committee on Contracts also opposed outwork, asking for lists of those performing it and insisting that a single family be given only 'realistic' amounts of work in a given period of time; *The Times*, 8 April 1891, p. 12.

50 ibid. Others, like Burns, felt that the resolutions were inadequate to deal with the situation of that sector of Council labour.

51 He was 'assisted' by trade unionist Will Steadman of the barge-builders, who defended the motion by arguing that many councillors owed their election to the unions – a dubious choice of argument, given Burns's opponents; *The Times*, 18 May 1892, p. 10f.; 28 May 1892 13f.; TUC, *Gertrude Tuckwell Collection*, Box 9, 'Government clothing regulations and government contracts'.

52 A union of non-classified Council workers had formed in August of 1891, following a Clerkenwell meeting at which councillor Lawrence Stevens presided. Five branches with 500 members were set up within five weeks' time. For the story of LCC manual grades union organisa-tion, see B. Dix and S. Williams, *Serving the Public; Building the Union: The History of NUPE*, Vol. 1, London, Lawrence and Wishart, 1987; and T. Farrer, 'Labour in the parks and labour generally', WKS/GEN/1/16, 1892, which includes an excerpt from the *Pall Mall Gazette*, 18

August 1891, recounting this meeting. The new unions' leaders pointed out that the passage of Burns's motion made it 'difficult to see why the same rule should not also be applied to men employed directly by the Council; why, in short, the labourers of the Council should not form themselves into a trades union, just like other labourers'.

53 'The LCC as their own contractors', *Building News*, 21 October 1892; 'The LCC as builders', 4 November 1892.

54 LCC, Works Department, 'The Works Department from its inception in 1892 to its discontinuance on 31 Dec., 1909', p. 1. Contractors were now forced to sign declarations stating their intentions to guarantee the prescribed wage schedules, under penalty of heavy fines. When the tenders received by the Main Drainage Committee for the York Road Sewer appeared to be far too high (over £11,000 as against an engineer's estimate of £7000; the Council carried it out for about £5000), the Committee and the Chief Engineer decided to build it with direct labour. See WDI, p. vi, 20 March 1897.

55 LCC, Works Department, Special Subcommittee of the General Purposes Committee, 'Report . . . on works', 18 July 1908; 'Report from Blashill to Dickinson', 22 October 1892, p. 6; memo from Blashill, 'The Council's building works', 29 October 1892.

56 ibid., letter from Binnie to Dickinson, p. 3.

57 ibid., p. 4; K. Brown, op. cit., p. 67.

58 ibid.

59 *Building News and Engineering Journal*, 25 January 1889, p. 158.

60 *Building News*, 4 March 1892, 18 March 1892, 25 March 1892, 15 April 1892, 3 June 1892, 25 November 1892.

61 ibid., 25 November 1892.

62 *Building News*, 3 June 1892, p. 756.

63 See the comments of Tom Mann regarding the exclusion of loafers from the new unions, as recorded in N. Mackenzie and J. Mackenzie (eds), op. cit., vol. 1, 22 September 1889.

64 *Building News*, 25 November 1892.

65 Liberty and Property Defence League, *Annual Report*, 1893–94, p. 11.

66 ibid.

67 Liberty and Property Defence League, *Annual Report*, 1892–93, p. 21.

68 'The latest socialist scheme', *Spectator*, 17 December 1892, p. 880.

69 ibid.

70 ibid.

71 ibid.

72 *Star*, 10 January 1889, p. 1.

73 ibid.

74 E. Garcke, 'The limitations of municipal enterprise. A paper read before the National Liberal political and economic circle', 24 October 1900, p. 7. Though E.J. Hobsbawm called Garcke a 'characteristic Fabian' (see E.J. Hobsbawm, *Labouring Men*, London, Weidenfeld and Nicolson, 1976, p. 257), Avner Offer's more extensive treatment identifies Garcke as a 'principal wire-puller', along with Lord Avebury, in the 'anti-municipal crusade' (see A. Offer, *Property and*

Politics, 1870–1914, Cambridge, Cambridge University Press, 1981, pp. 236–237). The paper cited here makes a case that many Liberals would have endorsed.

75 E. Garcke, ibid., p. 9.

76 ibid. I thank David Feldman for suggesting the larger point.

77 See, e.g., London Reform Union, 'A programme for the election of poor law guardians', George Howell Collection, Bishopsgate Library.

78 *The Times*, 26 May 1897, p. 13.

79 LCC, Works Department, Annual Report, 22 November 1892.

80 H. Haward, op. cit., p. 320.

81 In April 1893, for example, the department accepted tenders ranging from £495 to £1250 for a four-wheeled coupled tank locomotive: LCC, Works Department, 'Barking precipitation works; four-wheeled coupled tank locomotive – analysis of tenders received', 13 April 1893.

82 LCC, Staff Pocket Books, 1892–1909. These employees received holidays and sickness benefits, as did the other clerical employees at the central offices, though after May 1895 an employee was required to serve a year before being allowed to contribute to the Superannuation Fund.

83 LCC, Works Committee, PP, 19 June 1893.

84 G. Simkins, 'The NUC: a short history of the movement', *Clerk*, January 1903, p. 5, tells the story of the NUC delegation to the Works Department. For wage data, see LCC, Staff Pocket Books, 1892–1909.

85 SG, March 1903, p. 30.

86 During the week of 7 July 1893, for example, workmen were disbursed from Belvedere Road to the following locations: jobbing works at Chelsea Bridge; Hackney and Holloway sewers; New Cross Fire Station; Plumstead; Barking Outfall; Stratford; Yabsley Street Dwellings, LCC, Works Department, PP, 17 July 1893.

87 LCC, Works Department, 'Orders to foremen', 30 April 1894.

88 LCC, Works Committee, 'Wages and hours of labour subcommittee', Minutes, 11 June 1896.

89 The average per week for the period 1893–99 remained below 1650 workmen; between 1899 and 1904, it hovered between 2000 and 2400, and between 1904 and 1907, it remained over 3000; LCC Works Department, 'The Works Department from its inception . . .', op. cit., p. 13.

90 *Building News*, 15 December 1893, pp. 780–781. The paper was entitled 'The deficiencies of the London workman'. I am grateful to those from the former Greater London Council who planned the summer 1980 RIBA exhibition on LCC housing estates, which featured Fleming and other LCC architects.

91 ibid.

92 ibid.; see comments by Sidney Wells, principal. For a critical study of the TEB and the succeeding LCC practices, see A. Saint, 'Technical education and the early LCC', in A. Saint (ed.), *Politics and the People of London*, London, Hambledown, 1989, pp. 71–91.

93 LTC, Annual Report, 'Report of Delegates to the LCC Technical Education Board', 1901, p. 23.

94 LCC, Works Department, 'The works department from its inception . . .', op. cit., p. 18.

95 J. Williams, *Building and Builders*, London, Longmans, 1968, p. 116.

96 Amalgamated Society of Carpenters and Joiners, Monthly Report, September 1891.

97 When men arrived at work they presented tickets to a timekeeper. He in turn mounted the tickets on a numbered board for the working day. This ticket was used to collect pay at the end of the week. The timekeeper was warned not to use both a new and an old ticket at the same time, indicating that some men were engaged on various projects more than once; LCC, Works Department, 'General orders to foremen', 30 April 1894.

98 J. Williams, op. cit., p. 116; C. Booth, Economic Club of London, 'Family budgets, being the income and expenses of twenty-eight British households, 1891–4', reprinted from *Cornhill Magazine*, 1901, in E. Pike (ed.), *Busy Times: Human Documents of the Age of the Forsytes*, London, Praeger, 1969, 1970, p. 146.

99 Foremen were granted more holidays than their workmen. LCC, Works Committee, 'Wages and Hours of Labour Sub-Committee', Minutes, 21 May 1895. The 1880 Act required proof that the Council or its servants had been negligent; the latter did not require proof and guaranteed half the weekly wage during recuperation if the worker was incapacitated for at least two weeks. The Works Committee granted two weeks from the date of an accident, LCC, 'The works department from its inception . . .', op. cit., p. 13.

100 LCC, Works Department, 'General orders to foremen', 30 April 1894.

101 The Free Labour Association wrote to *The Times*, citing data gathered by the Registrar of Trade Unions reporting that 15 per cent of all building trades workers in the nation were unionised, 4 July 1894, p. 11. Price argues that these agreements were of particular importance because they were first negotiated with the whole body of the unions and marked the unions out as the sole bargaining agent for the rank and file. Nothing more was heard, for example, of seeking non-union representation at the bargaining table; R. Price, op. cit., pp. 225–227.

102 'Piece and day work in the building trades', *Building News and Engineering Journal*, 4 April 1890.

103 See, e.g., Works Department, PP, 31 July 1893, in which a foreman denies such charges, and LCC, Works Committee, Minutes, 17 December 1894, in which a timekeeper is charged with same.

104 *The Times*, 14 June 1894, p. 10; 25 June 1894, p. 6.

105 Archive of the National Federation of Building Trades Employers, GLRO, LMBA Minutes, 27 March 1893, contains evidence of such an alliance; see also 19 June 1893 for communiqués from William Shepherd, secretary of the Cardiff Master Builders' Association and from George Livesey of the South Metropolitan Gas Company, 16 October 1893, for a resolution to create a blacklist in the event of a

strike on members' works. These minutes contain repeated mention of relatively clandestine dealings with the Free Labour Association; see *The Times*, 26 June 1896, p. 13.

106 *The Times*, 28 June 1894, p. 4; 19 July 1894, p. 14.

107 CAMB, Minutes, 9 February 1894, record strikes against non-unionists and some unauthorised employer dismissals of same, undertaken at the bidding of unionists. Those for 4 December 1894 record the commendation of an employer who had used many non-society men in a strike at Vauxhall; those of 8 February 1895 discuss the NAFL list.

108 LCC, WC, Minutes, 17 February 1896; 29 June 1896.

109 See LCC, WC, Minutes, 19 November 1894, 'Letter from the London and Provincial Builders' Foremen's Association', in reference to the discharge of a Council foreman.

110 *Building News and Engineering Journal*, A Builder, 'Builders' workshops and workmen and their management', 12 April 1889, pp. 499, 500.

111 LCC, WC, Minutes, 4 March 1895. See also LCC, Works Department, 'Special subcommittee of the GPC', July 1908, Appendix F, 'Particulars as to strikes of workmen and trade disputes'.

112 LCC, WC, Minutes, 24 June 1895. Other foremen's work is described in comparable terms in J. Melling, 'Non-commissioned officers: British employers and their supervisory workers', *Social History*, 5 (2), May 1980, pp. 183–221.

113 R. Price, op. cit., p. 182.

114 C. Briggs, *A Short History of the Building Crafts*, p. 163. Farriers and lightermen, for example, worked on union-negotiated piece rates. Carpenters and joiners, stonemasons, bricklayers, plumbers and plasterers had banned piecework and subcontracting in 1891. While these bans were difficult to maintain in a locale and in an industry in which a majority of work was still subcontracted, and though the Carpenters and Joiners, for example, later permitted subcontracting under 'fair conditions', the LCC was nevertheless committed to the practices of the unions. (See Amalgamated Society of Carpenters and Joiners, Monthly Report, July 1893). See letter from Will Thorne regarding disputes at the Hackney and Holloway relief sewer; LCC, Works Department, PP, 22 September 1893.

115 LCC, Works Department, PP, 22 September 1893, 16 October 1893.

116 In a long, arduous dispute between bricklayers and navvies at Claybury Asylum, Holloway, the Works Manager, defended the decision to give the drainage work to the bricklayers on grounds of innovation and quality of work. Manholes and inspection chambers were needed in modern times: 'again to make the cement joint it is necessary that a trowel should be used, and this tool has not so far as I know, yet formed part of a navvy's kit. In my opinion the laying of drains is essentially bricklayers' work'; 6 December 1893. The navvies claimed that the bricklayers had simply deemed it so. A laborious process of clarification ensued, in which it was only proved that bricklayers could do the work well, not that the navvies could not have undertaken it; ibid., 18 January 1894.

117 LCC, Works Committee, 19 February 1894; 9 April 1894; R. Price, op. cit., p. 183.
118 LCC, Works Department, PP, 30 August, September, 1893.
119 *The Times*, 17 September 1894, p. 8.
120 A watchman wrote to Councillor McKinnon Wood, who had supposedly replied, 'in all cases of oppression, of withholding what is due, the Council's employees have the right of appeal to the Council's regulations, which . . . guarantees ample protection to its employees'; LCC, Works Committee, PP, 11 September 1893.
121 LCC, Works Department, PP, 13 November 1893.
122 ibid., 22 November 1893.
123 ibid., 3 December 1893.
124 ibid., 15 December 1893.
125 ibid., 7 October 1895.
126 Ben Tillett himself was turned down when he wrote on behalf of two workmen seeking jobs. See LCC, WC, Minutes, 8 October 1894, 23 July 1895. The Exchange subsequently requested that it be sent lists of works being undertaken by the LCC so that men could report to the foremen, but the committee replied that copies of the LCC Minutes went regularly to the vestry and were available for sale in Cockspur Street; 7 October 1895.
127 *The Times*, 1 December 1894, p. 6.
128 ELO, 19 January 1893, p. 5.
129 ibid., 12 January 1895.
130 'The London County Council election', *The Times*, 4 March 1895, p. 7.
131 *The Times*, 5 March 1895, p. 11.
132 'The new members', *The Times*, 4 March 1895, p. 7.
133 ibid. He added that the unskilled electorate had been demoralised by a six-week frost and had become victims of 'suspicion and mistrust'.
134 'The London County Council elections', *The Times*, 5 March 1895, p. 11.
135 *The Times*, Letter to Editor from W. Couison, 5 March 1895. London Reform Union, 'Annual report', 1895.
136 ELO, 19 February 1898, p. 6.
137 White (1847–1914) was later knighted, and served as LCC Vice-chairman under the Moderates between 1909 and 1910, and as chairman, 1911–12.
138 See LCC, Subcommittee, PP, 11 November 1896, 'Works department inquiry reports and evidence received by the special Subcommittee of the Works Committee with regard to transfers . . .'.
139 ibid., p. 3.
140 ibid., pp. 5–6.
141 ibid., pp. 8–9.
142 ibid.
143 ibid., p. 34. Dyson was asked, 'was this matter so common in the office that no particular notice was taken of it?' 'That is so.' 'The whole of your staff were making entries in the books that were not correct, and they knew it?' 'Yes.'; ibid., p. 35.

144 The letter continued: 'So far from the first of May the resolution of the Council in reference to the rate of wages in practice obtained has been grossly violated in the interests of the Master Builders'; John Burns Correspondence, National Association of Operative Plasterers to Burns, British Museum Correspondence no. A6296, vol. xvi, 1896–1897, 3 June 1896.

145 ibid., no known date.

146 *The Times*, 9 May 1895, p. 14.

147 ibid., 15 May 1895, p. 10.

148 GLRO, Progressive Party, Minute Book, 2 March 1896. The speaker was Councillor Thornton.

149 *The Times*, 4 November 1895, p. 12; 18 November, p. 7. Benn accused Moderate councillor Westacott of publishing an inflammatory pamphlet on the department which had ignited the wrongdoers, who in turn feared ill reaction on the part of the ratepayers.

150 Dunraven was the *Daily Telegraph*'s war correspondent in Abyssinia and in the Franco-Prussian war. He was the only person present at both the Kaiser's crowning at Versailles and the signing of the Armistice in 1918. He died in 1926.

151 ELO, 21 November 1896.

152 ibid., 28 November 1896, p. 2.

153 *Star*, 24 November 1896.

154 *Master Builders Association Journal*, 1 December 1896.

155 DNB, 2nd Supplement, Vol. 3, p. 49. William Hillier Onslow, 1853–1911, had represented the Local Government Board under Disraeli, in the Lords. In 1887 he served as under-secretary for the colonies and was made Governor of New Zealand, where he is remembered for giving his son, Huia, a Maori name. He was parliamentary under-secretary for India until 1900 and served on the Board of Agriculture. Crucial to his Moderate stance at the LCC would have been his executive chairmanship of the Central Land Association. He was also president of the Royal Statistical Society during 1905–06. An LCC alderman from 1896 to 1899 and from 1900 to 1903, Onslow led the Moderate Party in Council for a time.

156 *The Times*, 26 November 1896, p. 6. An unnamed 'Firm of Contractors' suggested that a manager ought to be paid more to run 'what indeed is a gigantic contracting business . . . short of that failure is certain'. ELO, 28 November 1896, p. 7.

157 Literary debate ensued. Letters questioned the use of the term 'profit' as it was merely a concept in the architect's head; *The Times*, 26 November 1896, p. 7.

158 Sidney Webb to John Burns, John Burns Correspondence, British Museum, Correspondence no. A6287, vol. vii, 7 December 1896.

159 Arnold served first as alderman from 1889 and as Chairman only during 1895–6. He opposed Campbell-Bannerman on the Boer War.

160 R.M. Beachcroft (1846–1926) was councillor for North Paddington, alderman, deputy chairman in 1896, vice-chair in 1897 and chairman, 1909–1910. He was also the first chairman of the Metropolitan Water Board, 1903–08. He and other Moderates who had laboured

in the vineyards under the Progressive administrations were naturally rewarded once their party came to power.

161 J.S. Fletcher (1841–1924) was chairman of the Hampstead Board of Guardians, 1880–98. Fletcher was deputy chairman of the LCC in 1900.

162 MP for Central Glasgow from 1906, Torrance represented East Islington in Council. He was a National Liberal Club member and died in 1909.

163 Edgar Jones (ed.), *The Memoirs of Edwin Waterhouse*, London, Batsford, 1988, p. 157. I am grateful to Sir Hugo Huntington-Whiteley for bringing this work to my attention.

164 Alexander R. Binnie (1839–1917) was articled as an engineer and became executive engineer for Public Works for the India Department at Nagpur. He established a water supply from Ambajheri and in so doing laid the basis for an important rail line for the Warora colliery. In 1875 he became chief engineer for the Bradford waterworks, and was with the LCC from 1890 to 1901. He was knighted upon the completion of the Blackwall Tunnel in 1897. He directed magnificent projects including the Greenwich Tunnel under the Thames, the Barking Road Bridge over the River Lea, main drainage work, the widening of the Strand and the Aldwych–Kingsway connection with Holborn.

165 WDI, 361.

166 WDI, 354; Moderate member Lushington contended that quality workmanship was not always required in any case!

167 Binnie admitted that he had won each case in which he was at odds with a workman, when it went through the normal appeals channels. But he felt that the absence of absolute authority at the works lessened incentives.

168 WDI, 43.

169 WDI, 84.

170 WDI, 373, 371, 20, 361.

171 WDI, 1107. Blashill noted that 12 per cent of the architectural works had resulted in 'losses', while the engineering works had resulted in 'profits' in 9 per cent of cases. He spoke of the 'somewhat bigoted adherence to what are said to be trade rules . . .', alluding to the costliness of strict conformity; WDI 1424. He noted that some of the expense in the cases of fire stations or artisans' dwellings projects were due to the LCC's investment in extra features of a high quality. But he also suggested that the committee had occasionally sanctioned a job at a high estimate, so that when it was completed for less, the result would appear impressive.

172 Lushington died in 1907. He was permanent under-secretary at the Home Office between 1885 and 1895.

173 WDI, 2185.

174 WDI, 2408.

175 WDI, 2579.

176 WDI, 2720.

177 WDI, 2721.

178 WDI, 3883, 3875.
179 WDI, 3883.
180 WDI, 3344.
181 WDI, 4651, 4428. The contractors objected to open books, to open price lists, and to deferred arbitration clauses. They opposed the RIBA–Institute of Builders stipulation that the architect on a job be the arbiter of a dispute. They felt that this encouraged the arrogance of the architect and made squabbles more difficult to settle on architectural building works where there were more disagreements about specifications than there were on engineering works.
182 WDI, 4400, 4532.
183 WDI, 4667.
184 WDI, 4749.
185 WDI, 5258.
186 WDI, 5141, 5142.
187 WDI, 5156.
188 Taylor also did not dispute the charge that members of his family were employed by the LCC; one of three brothers who were bricklayers had worked for the Council.
189 Steadman felt that workers ought to be able to ask each other whether they were unionists and ought not to be fired for urging others to join a union. He pointed to the existence of some closed shops in the industry.
190 WDI, 5258.
191 WDI, 5303.
192 WDI, 5417.
193 WDI, 5421.
194 WDI, 5285.
195 WDI, 5378.
196 WDI, 5433–34.
197 WDI, 5331, 5405.
198 LCC, Works Department, 'Report of the special committee on the Works Department', 29 March 1897, p. 1, points 4–5.
199 ibid., point 24.
200 ibid., 'Minority report: Statement prepared by R.M. Beachcroft, J.S. Fletcher, G.B. Longstaff and Sir Godfrey Lushington'.
201 LTC, Annual Report, 1898, p. 6.
202 Direct Labour Collective, *Building with Direct Labour*, Birmingham, Housing Workshop of the Conference of Socialist Economists, 1978, p. 8.
203 LMBA, *Minute Books*, 16 August 1897, 16 January 1899, 9 July 1900.
204 N. Mackenzie and J. Mackenzie (eds), op. cit., vol. 2, p. 281, 15 June 1903.
205 *The Times*, August–November 1902.
206 D.W. Davies, 'The cost of municipal trading', London, Society of Arts, 1903, pp. 8–9.
207 See A. Offer, op. cit., Chapter 18; P. Garside and K. Young, *Metropolitan London*, New York, Holmes and Meier, 1982, Chapter 5.
208 See, e.g., P. Thompson, *Socialists, Liberals and Labour*, London,

Routledge, 1967, Chapters 4, 11; K. Young, *Local Politics and the Rise of Party*, Leicester, Leicester University Press, 1975, Chapter 3; A. Offer, op. cit., Chapter 18; S. Pennybacker, 'The Millennium by return of post: reconsidering London Progressivism', in D. Feldman and G. Stedman Jones (eds), *Metropolis: London Histories and Representations*, London, Routledge, 1989, pp. 129–162.

209 See the remarks of Leonard Horner of Ashby and Horner, president of the LMBA, who stated in its Annual Report for 1910–11 that the 'general state of trade continues to be very much depressed'. He wrote of the continuing 'abnormally low prices in tendering for work, which have prevailed over the last five years'.

210 LMBA, Minutes, 4 July 1910, report of 27 February 1911.

211 *Trades and Labour Gazette*, March 1907, 'Reflections on the LCC election', p. 1.

212 In condemning what it saw as the 'determination' of the LCC to close down the department, the LTC referred to the policy of 'starving the department', a charge also made by the opposition in Council, LTC, Minutes, 13 August 1908.

213 Progressive Party Leaflet no. 18A, 'LCC election, 1910'.

214 P. Thompson, op. cit., pp. 270–271.

CHAPTER 3: THE APPETITE FOR MANAGING OTHER PEOPLE'S LIVES (pp. 158–240)

1 LCC, TMHC, PP, 1889–1909, Collins Music Hall, Islington Green, 27 December 1908.

2 E. Bristow, *Vice and Vigilance: Purity Movements in Britain since 1800*, Dublin, Gill and Macmillan, 1977; F. Mort, *Dangerous Sexualities: Medico-moral Politics in England since 1830*, London, Routledge, 1987; J. Lewis, *The Politics of Motherhood: Child and Maternal Welfare in England, 1900–1939*, London, Croom Helm, 1980; and S. Koven and S. Michel, Introduction to S. Koven and S. Michel (eds), *Mothers of a New World: Maternalist Politics and the Origins of Welfare States*, New York, Routledge, 1993, are representative of a wide literature on the period.

3 Municipal Reform, 'LCC election 1904, facts and arguments', cites the 1888 Act; the Public Health Acts of 1891 and 1896; the Education Acts of 1891 and 1903; the Technical Instruction Acts of 1889 and 1891; the Sale of Food and Drugs Act of 1899; the Weights and Measures Act of 1889; the Housing of the Working Classes Acts of 1890–1903; and factory, workshop and shop hours legislation; p. 239.

4 ibid., p. 253.

5 Municipal Reform, Leaflet no. A14, claims that there were over 119,349 women on the county voting register in 1907 and 17,739 teachers in the county in 1909. At least five of twelve persons coopted to the LCC Education Committee were women. Women were able economisers in the departments: 'In this good work women are called upon to play their part, and as they have a keener

eye for minor extravagances than men, their cooperation should be invaluable'; pp. 2–3.

6 See S. Koven, 'Borderlands: women, voluntary action, and child welfare in Britain, 1890 to 1914', in S. Koven and S. Michel (eds), op. cit., pp. 94–135.

7 For accounts of London's nineteenth century poverty, see A. Wohl, *Endangered Lives: Public Health in Victorian Britain*, London, Methuen, 1983; P. Mandler (ed.), *The Uses of Charity: The Poor on Relief in the Nineteenth Century Metropolis*, Chapters 1, 3, 6.

8 PP 1908 (99) ix 147, 'Report of Select Committee on Infant Life Protection', testimony of James Ollis, Chief Officer, LCC Public Control Department, refers to women who could not 'maintain their children' (1276).

9 LCC, 'Miscellaneous reports to Joint Committee of Parliament and the Public Control Committee on Infant Life Protection', 9 November 1908, p. 9, J. Ollis.

10 For general histories of such legislation and related issues, see L. Rose, *The Massacre of Innocents*, London, Routledge and Kegan Paul, 1986; *The Erosion of Childhood*, London, Routledge, 1991.

11 G. Gibbon and R. Bell, *History of the London County Council*, London, Macmillan, 1939, p. 295.

12 See PP 1908 (99) ix 147, op. cit., Ollis (1260); PH/GEN/1/1, Spencer to Bathurst, New Scotland Yard, 9 December 1897, 15 December 1897.

13 PC/GEN/1/4, 1893–94.

14 PP 1908 (99) ix l47, op. cit., Ollis (1260).

15 LCC/MINS/9583, 2 March 1898.

16 PP 1908 (99) ix 147, op. cit., Appendix 6, 'LCC, Infant Life Protection, 1897'.

17 ibid., Ollis (1260).

18 LCC, 'Miscellaneous reports . . . on Infant Life Protection', op. cit., 9 November 1908, p. 9, Ollis.

19 LCC/PC/PP, 1898: 'Candidates must be single (or, if widows must be without young children). Marriage will disqualify any person from continuing to hold the appointment.'

20 LCC/PC/PP, 1898; Middleditch held diplomas in physiology and physical training.

21 LCC/MINS/9583, 8 February 1892; PC/GEN/2/18, 1897–98; LCC, PC, PP, January–June 1898. Jacobi was born on 11 October 1867. She earned LRCP and LRCS credentials in 1893 and possessed a certificate from the Royal College of Physicians and Surgeons. In 1895 she earned the Diploma of the Sanitary Institute. She was registrar of the Royal Hospital for Children and Women from 1895 to 1897. She was clinical assistant in the Children's Hospital, Shadwell, from 1894 to 1897. She presented references from three doctors and from the editor of the *British Medical Journal*. The other candidates were Bird, 31, who held a Sanitary Institute certificate; Elcum, 33, who also held the certificate and had been a lecturer on nursing hygiene and first aid and had been at St Bartholomew's for three

years; Hammond, a governess and Secretary to the Feeble-Minded Association; Hobson, 31, a former nurse with the Sanitary Institute who held its certificate and that of the National Health Society; and Maclaran, an employee of the St Pancras Workhouse Infirmary.

22 LCC, 'Miscellaneous reports . . . on Infant Life Protection', op. cit., p. 8.

23 PP 1908 (99) ix 147, op. cit., Ollis (1342).

24 ibid. (1270); Appendix 6 records the LCC death rate in London of notified infants for 1906–07 of 56.5 per thousand above the age of 1 year and 126.7 per thousand under the age of 1 year; see also G. Newman, *Infant Mortality, A Social Problem*, New York, Dutton, 1907, Chapters 1, 2; D. Dwork, *War is Good for Babies and Other Young Children*, London, Tavistock, 1987, *passim*.

25 PP 1908 (99) ix 147, op. cit. (1276).

26 *Daily Telegraph*, 13 September 1896, refers to the testimony of the coroner, Wynne Baxter.

27 Women's Local Government Society, London, n.d., 'Speeches at the local government section of the women's congress at the Japan–Britain Exhibition, 6–7 June, 1910', speech by Miss Zanetti, Infant Life Protection inspector, p. 29.

28 PP 1908 (99), ix, 147, op. cit. (1276); As stated, Ollis reports that five thousand illegitimate children were born annually in London.

29 PH/GEN/1/2, 9 November 1908.

30 ibid., 25 February 1908, letter to Parker with testimony, pp. 1, 7.

31 LCC, 'Miscellaneous reports . . . on Infant Life Protection', op. cit., 12 February 1909, pp. 1–3.

32 PH/GEN/1/1, 10 October 1897.

33 PH/GEN/1/2, Smith's précis of evidence, p. 6.

34 PH/GEN/1/2, memo on evidence, 25 February 1908.

35 ibid.

36 PC/GEN/2/18, 29 April 1904; PC/GEN/1/2; PP 1908 (99) ix 147. Appendix 6, op. cit., states that approximately 200 houses were on the rolls during the year and the department made 3759 visits. Thirty-three nurse-mothers under inspection moved out of the County and six were removed to workhouses.

37 See, e.g., J. Jenson, 'Representations of gender: policies to "protect" women workers and infants in France and the United States before 1914', in L. Gordon (ed.), *Women, the State and Welfare*, Madison, University of Wisconsin Press, 1990, esp. pp. 153–159.

38 LCC, PC, PP, 1904–05, 'Report on Creches' by the Chief Officer, delivered before the County Hall Conference of Sanitary Authorities of 1903', July 1904. PP 1904, xxxii, 'Reports from Commissions, Inspections and Others, Physical Deterioration Committee,' 2 February 1904–15 August 1904, testimony of Dr Eustace Smith, London Children's Hospital, states that existing crèches can only take a limited number of children (8444). Smith called for municipal crèches under medical supervision (8447). See also LCC, Public Control, PP, 'Report on Creches', Chief Officer of Public Control, 8 July 1904. Here Shirley Murphy, MOH, reports on the resolutions of the Committee on Physical Deterioration. The report describes crèche care as 'an evil

in that it discourages breastfeeding and spreads disease but could be properly managed'.

39 As stated, the 1897 revision of the Infant Life Protection Act also covered adoptions in which a child was purchased for twenty pounds or less. See PH/GEN/1/2, on Ollis's testimony before the Select Committee on Infant Life Protection, 10 March 1908.

40 PH/GEN/1/2, testimony of E.C. Browne, p. 61.

41 PC/GEN/2/18, 1896–97.

42 PP 1908 (99) ix 147, op. cit. (1261).

43 PH/GEN/1/2, cites E.C. Browne's testimony before the Select Committee; see also Smith's testimony, p. 61.

44 PP 1908 (99) ix 147, op. cit. (1272, 1276).

45 ibid.

46 LCC, 'Miscellaneous reports to Joint Committee of Parliament', op. cit., J. Ollis, p. 9.

47 PC/GEN/1/4, 1892–93. See, e.g., D. Dwork, op. cit., Chapter 1 and Conclusion.

48 PC/GEN/1/4, 1892–93.

49 PH/GEN/1/2; 25 February 1908, Smith to Parker.

50 ibid.

51 ibid.

52 PP, 1908 (99) ix 147, op. cit. (1260, 1276).

53 ibid., (1276).

54 ibid. (1276), Ollis refers to women who could not 'maintain their children'.

55 LCC/MIN/8670; see decision of S. Berry, solicitor, 17 November 1905.

56 PH/PHS/2/1, 'Notice to Midwives', 13 April 1904.

57 LCC/MIN/8670, report by the Medical Officer, 17 November 1905; PP 1909 xxiii, cd. 4823, 'Report of Departmental Committee on the Working of the Midwives Act of 1902', testimony of S. Murphy (4198).

58 LCC/MIN/8670, 20 October 1905. Those eligible had to pass a qualifying examination in which they showed that they could write from dictation and perform elementary arithmetic, more than many practising London midwives could do.

59 LCC, PH, PP, 9 March 1906.

60 On the Midwives Act and its wider implications, see J. Lewis, op. cit., Chapter 5.

61 LCC, Midwives Act, Special Committee Papers, October 1904–05.

62 PP 1908 (99) ix 147, op. cit., Ollis (1287).

63 LCC, Midwives Act, Special Committee Papers, 7 February 1905.

64 ibid.

65 LCC/MIN/8670, letter of Mr Tagg, 10 October 1905.

66 LCC, Midwives Act, Special Committee Papers, 1904–05, 17 October 1904.

67 LCC/MIN/8670, 1 December 1905.

68 LCC, Midwives Act, Special Committee Papers, 1904–05, 10 February 1905; Bennett had earned an MBBS at London University.

69 ibid.; see, e.g., letter from J.J. Bayley; letter from Mrs Wilkinson and copy of transcript of 'enquiry re. J.E. Price'; letter of R.M. Beaton, 24 March 1905.

70 PP, 'Report of the Departmental Committee on the Working of the Midwives Act', op. cit. (4211).

71 ibid. (4213, 4217, 4222).

72 See, e.g., PC/SHO/3/6, 'Regarding the reorganisation and redistribution of London's markets, 1891–1927'. During 1893–94, Sir Samuel Montague tried to get the LCC to take over the markets. This was the beginning of a long struggle over authority in which high food prices were a perennial complaint. Progressives did not wish for the LCC to become the chief market authority.

73 LCC/PC/PP. The original complaint read: 'We the undersigned greengrocers and fruiterers most respectfully petition you to report to the proper quarters that the very numerous class of costermongers are carrying on their trades – very detrimental to us – by their sharp practice of false weights and measures. This is a great hardship to us who have to help bear the pressure of the Rates'; 29 April 1898; 5 May 1898.

74 PC/WM/3/15.

75 PC/GEN/2/18, 1898–99, p. 13.

76 This Act was amended by the Shops Act of 1912, the Education Act of 1918 and the Employment of Women, Young Persons and Children Act of 1920.

77 PC/SHO/3/7, report by A. Spencer, 6 May 1898.

78 PC/SHO/3/7, Shops Act, Miscellaneous Printed Reports, 1892–1948, 'Shop Hours Act, 1892–95, report by the Chief Officer, 6 May, 1898'. In 1896, four inquiries per day constituted the desired goal of the department.

79 PC/SHO/3/9 contains, for example, a large poster issued on 25 April 1912 directed at shopkeepers and listing hours of employment, mealtimes of assistants, hours of employment of young persons under the age of 18, the provision of seats requirements for shop assistants, the closing rules applied to weekly half-holidays, and the evening closing rules. Heavy penalties are listed for those who fail to comply; PC/SHO/317, 6 May 1898.

80 LCC, T. Macnamara, 'Report of the Interdepartmental Committee on the Employment of Schoolchildren to the Home Secretary'; 1901 (4164, 4170).

81 ibid., Return A (4102). Hairdressers kept children for the longest hours, as many as forty to fifty hours a week (4104, 4118). Children worked in railway termini (4155) and as boot cleaners and steps cleaners (4161), two jobs that paid as little as a penny a step or a shilling a week.

82 PP 1906, Cd. 2809 xc 1, 'Report on the Byelaws made by the LCC under the Employment of Children Act, 1903, By Chester Jones. of the Middle Temple, Barrister-at-Law'. This inquiry included the testimony of fifty-two witnesses, amongst them schoolmasters, attendance officers, police inspectors, barbers and barbers' boys,

and newsagents. It investigated the application of the Employment of Children Act 1903. See, e.g., the testimony of C. Guy of Poplar, who was ten years old and one of a family of ten. His father was a dock labourer; his income went 'to keep the family in boots and clothes'. He had only one school absence during that year (no. 33), p. 269.

83 LCC/PC/PP, 28 January 1898. See the case of James Nash of Peckham, a dealer in the second-hand furniture trade, who was accused of employing William Jeary for seventy-eight and a half hours per week, including mealtimes. He had previously been fined for an eighty-three-hour week violation. He replied that he had given the boy Christmas and Boxing Day off and that those days spread out over time shortened the ostensible working hours endured; he had no use for someone who would work less than seventy-four hours a week.

84 See PP 1910, Cd. 5229 xxviii 1 and 1910 Cd. 5230 xxviii 25, 'Report of the Departmental Committee on the Employment of Children Act, 1903, and Evidence'; L. Rose, *The Erosion of Childhood*, London, Routledge, 1991, *passim*.

85 PC/SHO/1/31. A Lewisham Borough Council representative testified that Londoners were more accepting of the LCC's everyday presence in the courts than they were of the more antagonistic borough councils; PC/SHO/3/7, 'Conference on the Administration of the Shops Act of 1912', p. 5. In 1905, 34,579 names of outworkers were provided by local authorities to the LCC; LCC/PC/PP, 1904–05.

86 See also, 'Report of the Departmental Committee on the Employment of Children Act, 1903', op. cit., Appendix XVI.

87 ibid.; Alfred G. Chamings, principal assistant to the Education Officer, noted that of 200,000 boys and girls on the register aged 11–14, 13,873 were children exempt from school (9010–9012).

88 ibid., C. Jackson, LCC Education Committee chair (8890).

89 See PC/GEN/2/18, 1901–02. The National Vigilance Association pursued employment agencies that were accused of 'procuring girls for immoral purposes'. Theatrical agencies were similarly suspect.

90 See 'Report of the Departmental Committee on the Employment of Children Act, 1903', op. cit. Jackson commented on a brother and sister: 'and he stood in a public house round the corner, and when any person came up he was produced from the public house to act as her guardian'. An officer seized a girl street trader: 'The child was taken away by our superintendent, who took a personal interest in the case, because the mother seemed to be a respectable woman. He managed to get her a little situation as a nurse girl, or something like that, in Walthamstow.' Agencies such as the Skilled Employment Committees and the Associations for Befriending Young Servants existed with the purpose of engaging in this sort of rescue work. The School Care Committees found jobs for girls, with the aid of five thousand volunteers throughout the London schools (8774, 8781, 8804, 8807).

91 ibid.; Chamings also suspected that sister and brother 'guardians' of flower sellers were actually unrelated (8780, 9058, 9062).

92 ibid. (8787, 8791).

93 ibid., A. Chamings (9172, 9174).
94 'Report of the Departmental Commission on the Employment of Children Act, 1903, and Evidence', op. cit., Appendix XVI.
95 ibid. (8734).
96 ibid., Appendix I, D.
97 ibid. (8816–17, 8739).
98 ibid. (8745).
99 ibid., Appendix I (8751, 8753).
100 'Report of the Byelaws made by the LCC under the Employment of Children Act, 1903 by Chester Jones', op. cit., p. 8.
101 LCC, T. Macnamara, 'Report of the Interdepartmental Committee on the Employment of Schoolchildren', op. cit. (4176, 4199). Macnamara referred to the appeal rights of parents with regard to the refusal of a labour certificate, mentioning the 'jealousy which does exist in connection with interference as to the children' (4204).
102 'Report of the Departmental Commission on the Employment of Children Act, 1903, pp. 1910, cd. 5229, xxviii, 1, p. 9.
103 PC/SHO/1/31, 'Children's and young persons' legislation including correspondence with the Education Officer's department': 'Memo for the Public Control Committee from the Education Committee', 9 July 1913, p. 1. R. Blair, LCC Education Chief Officer, reported that during the preceding years, when the educational authorities carried out such inspections, the work was done 'without friction or serious complaint from employers, employed or magistrates'.
104 PC/GEN/2/18, for example, 1893–94.
105 J. Burns, 'The London County Council. I. Towards a Commune', *Nineteenth Century*, 31, 1892, p. 512.
106 'The fight for the County Council: an elector's catechism or 101 reasons why every loyal Londoner should vote Progressive', *Westminster Gazette*, popular no. 15, February 1898; 'Bread and fuel: the County Council sees that buyers get good weight', *London*, 8 September 1898, describes the second economy in coal: 'small quantities of coal are taken from the various sacks until sufficient has been pilfered to make up a separate sackful. These frauds are very difficult to detect, and a carman must be caught in the act if proceedings are to be successful.' Carmen also engaged in fraud: 'In these cases the carmen have been prosecuted by the sellers, and sentenced to imprisonment with hard labour.' For a splendid account of related issues, see J. Davis, 'Lawbreaking and law enforcement: the creation of a criminal class in mid-Victorian London', Ph.D. thesis, Boston College, 1985.
107 PC/GEN/2/18, p. 7; PC/WM/3/4, 'Weights and Measures Act, 1878', 1889.
108 PC/GEN/2/18, Annual Report 1894–95, p. 11.
109 LCC, T. Macnamara, 'Report of the Interdepartmental Committee on the Employment of Schoolchildren', op. cit., A.J. Giles, secretary of the Association, was asked whether the group's 'votes would succeed in keeping them [the LCC] within the bounds of proper action?' He replied, 'If they did it now our votes would not

cooperate for another two years. It is not an unknown thing for local authorities to make bye-laws exceedingly harsh which cost both time and money to set aside' (4968).
110 ibid. (4974, 5012).
111 See G. Crossick and H. Haupt, 'Shopkeepers, master artisans and the historian', in G. Crossick and H. Haupt (eds), *Shopkeepers and Master Artisans in Nineteenth-Century Europe*, London, Methuen, 1984, pp. 3–34.
112 G. Newman, op. cit., pp. 318–19; John Burns gave the inaugural address at the National Conference on Infant Mortality, *Local Government Officer*, 3 November 1906, cited in PH/GEN/1/2.
113 See D. Dwork, op. cit., Chapter 4; PP, 1904, XXXII, 'Royal Commission on Physical Deterioration' (9442); PH/GEN/1/2 cites *The Municipal Journal*, 5 January 1906.
114 LCC/MIN/9944, 'Public health and housing committee', Minutes, 2 February 1894. The Acts in question were the 1894 Diseases of Animals Act and the Muzzling of Dogs Temporary Order of 1897.
115 PC/GEN/2/18, 1896–97, p. 23.
116 LCC/PC/PP, 6 May 1898. The supply of steam coal in 1898 practically ceased owing to the Welsh miners' strike. Bituminous coal, the replacement fuel, burned poorly. For records of the cases pending against the railway companies, see LCC/MIN/9592, 12 May 1911, involving, amongst others, the Great Eastern, the Southeastern and Chatham and the Great Northern.
117 PC/GEN/2/18, 1901–02, Report on the Coal Abatement Society, 571,768 inhabited houses with over a million chimneys.
118 LCC/PC/PP, 28 January 1898.
119 LCC/PC/PP, 2 February 1898.
120 PC/GEN/1/34, 'Law relating to smoke abatement'.
121 LCC, PC, PP, 1904–05, 4 November 1905, letter from G.W. Byrne of Battersea to the Clerk.
122 LCC, PC, PP, 28 January 1898.
123 LCC/MIN/10025, 'Report from the Board of Works for the Strand', 14 May 1896; letter from Andrews to Stewart.
124 ibid., 12 May 1896.
125 LCC/MIN/9994, op. cit., 19 January 1893.
126 ibid., 15 November 1894.
127 LCC, PC, PP, 12 October 1905.
128 PN/GEN/2/19, 'Factories and Workshops Acts, miscellaneous reports on health provisions', 26 March 1902; Dr Hamer, 'Report', 1898.
129 LCC, PC Committee, Annual Report, 1892–93. John Lubbock, LCC councillor, was head of the Early Closing Association.
130 PP 1906, Cd. 2809 xc 1, op. cit., p. 11.
131 ibid.
132 Report of the Departmental Committee on the Employment of Children Act, 1903, 1910. Jackson, op. cit., (8845).
133 ibid., Chamings (9126).

134 PH/GEN/2/19, 23 February 1904, L. Gomme, 'Registration and periodical inspection of places of employment of outworkers by the boroughs'.

135 LCC, PC, PP, 1904–05. LCC/MIN/10025, 14 May 1896.

136 LCC, PP, PC, 1904–05, Annual Report, discusses the 1901 Factory and Workshop Act.

137 PC/MASS/2/1, LCC, 'Massage establishments, Savoy Turkish Baths, Ltd.'.

138 See, e.g., PC/EMP/3/1, PC/EMP/3/1, 'Employment – miscellaneous printed reports, copies of byelaws and regulations, etc., 1905–47', regulation no. 9.

139 PC/EMP/3/1. The House of Commons Police and Sanitary Regulations Committee encountered considerable opposition from theatrical and music hall agents.

140 LCC/MIN/10025, 16 April 1896, 'Letter to LCC Public Health Committee from Gould, the Home Office'. The letter enquires about the refusal of occupiers of factories and workshops to provide separate w.c.s, specifically mentioning a case in Bethnal Green.

141 ibid., 16 April 1896, 'Letter from John Foot of the Sanitary Department of Bethnal Green to C.J. Stewart, Clerk, LCC'; 'Letter from the Home Office', 8 April 1896.

142 'A day with County Council lodging house inspectors', *London*, 20 October 1898, p. 671. The Rowton's and Salvation Army inspectorate thought that the lodging houses ought to be under their jurisdiction, illustrating the tensions between the charities and the municipality. See S. Koven, 'Borderlands', op. cit.. 'Report by the Committee on Physical Deterioration', op. cit., (9485).

143 PH/GEN/2/21; For a typical instance of the inspection and registration of a house, see LCC/MIN/10025, 19 March 1896. Murphy's MOH report for Battersea stated: 'The house is a small tenement containing two small rooms on the second floor used by lodgers. In the back room there is one single bed and in the front room there are three single beds making a total of four. The lodgers consist of a journeyman butcher, two painters and a bricklayer who pay 3/6 per week in advance for their lodgings but who do not cook their own food or wash their own clothes.' Murphy directed the sanitary authorities to register the house under their by-laws. When the LCC took over the lodging house inspection, there were 654 houses with 29,827 people registered. By 1904 the count stood at 28,896 registered, of whom 2450 were women, including 422 couples.

144 'A day with County Council lodging house inspectors', op. cit.

145 ibid.

146 ibid.

147 PH/GEN/2/21, 'Report of the Departmental Committee on Vagrancy, evidence of the LCC', Appendix A. In February 1905, there were more than five thousand homeless women. Some were turned out of the lodging houses because they had no money. By 1903, the greatest number of homeless were to be found in Stepney and Westminster.

148 'A day with County Council lodging house inspectors', op. cit.
149 'Report by the Committee on Physical Deterioration', op. cit., Murphy (9380, 9485–86).
150 'Report of the Departmental Committee on Vagrancy', pp. 1906, cd. 2891, ciii, 131 (5860).
151 PH/GEN/2/21. Murphy testified: 'Mayhew notes that at the period of social commotion, they are drawn towards the scene of excitement in large numbers, and he instances the Chartist Riots of 1848 . . . in June, 1897 . . . no special increases in the number of lodgers was noted.'
152 PH/REG/1/24.
153 See PP Cd. 2892 ciii 639, 'Report of the Departmental Committee on Vagrancy, Vol. 3, Appendix XXXV', for the relevant by-laws. Table 3, p. 4, states that between 1902 and 1904 houses with men, women and married couples were abolished. The numbers housing men and married couples declined from 15 to 2; women and married couples from 27 to 1 and men and women from 3 to 1. In 1897 there were 73 houses with 732 doubles; and in 1905, 17 houses with 310 doubles. The greatest number were in Stepney; LCC, PC, PP, 16 November 1905.
154 PH/REG/1/24.
155 LCC, PC, PP, 16 November 1905.
156 LCC, PC, PP, 1904–05, 30 November 1905; PH/REG/1/24. The old police regulations of the 1880s, as part of the regulations governing common lodging houses, had called for the separation of the sexes through the means of a partition that had to be high enough to 'secure the privacy of each married couple'.
157 'A day with County Council lodging house inspectors', op. cit. This was a keeper of a house of 1400 lodgers in the West End, which the inspector thought was cleaner than houses in poorer areas.
158 ibid.
159 LCC, PC, PP, 16 October 1905, application of Edward Austin to operate a licensed lodging house.
160 PH/REG/1/33, 'Furnished rooms'.
161 ibid. Here the inspector is speaking of Notting Dale, Kensington. For an earlier portrait of the area and the discourse around housing, see J. Davis, 'Jennings' buildings and the Royal Borough: the construction of the underclass in mid-Victorian England', in D. Feldman and G. Stedman Jones (eds), *Metropolis: London Histories and Representations since 1800*, London, Routledge, 1989, pp. 11–39.
162 PH/REG/1/33.
163 ibid.
164 ibid., testimony of William F. Craines, Chair of the Public Health Committee of the Borough of Kensington, p. 30. Craines added, in describing the inhabitants of furnished rooms, that 'a certain number of them as I have said come there because their womenkind will not keep a proper home for them'. And finally, with regard to ultimate solutions: 'It is no good going to the landlord: you must go to the keeper himself. On the other hand, if you put the standard up too

high they will drop this business; and where are the people going. That is the question – the old question. In my more desperate moments I have suggested we keep special chambers, but that is only an extreme way of putting it. There are some who ought to be put under control and cleaned by force. I would believe you would get them clean in time'; p. 35.

165 PP 1906, Cd. 2891 ciii 131, vol. 2, 'Report of the Departmental Committee on Vagrancy', op. cit., (5645).

166 LCC, PC; 16 November 1905, 'Report on houses used for the accommodation of aliens'.

167 PH/GEN/2/21. In St Marylebone, St Pancras and Hackney, cleansing was carried out in the casual wards or in the disinfecting station.

168 'Interdepartmental Committee on Physical Deterioration', op. cit., Murphy (9470).

169 LCC/MIN/10025, 16 April 1896. Even the lodging house keepers could come under fire: 'female deputy keeper was considerably the worse for liquor, was using very dirty language, and . . . the whole kitchen was in an uproar. The inspector further stated that the neighbours and other common lodging house keepers complained of the premises.'

170 'Interdepartmental Committee on Physical Deterioration', op. cit., Murphy (9471).

171 LCC, PC, PP, 6 November 1905, 'Letter from the Shoreditch Guardians'. Here they complain of government works being closed to conscientious objectors and LCC scholarships not going to those who had refused vaccination.

172 PP 1906, 'Report of the Departmental Committee on Vagrancy', vol. II, op. cit., Murphy (5750, 5759).

173 See LCC, PC, PP, 'Annual Report of the MOH for 1904.' There were 15,667 persons living in LCC buildings.

174 'Lessons from the Bethnal Green Calamity', *London*, 6 January 1898, p. 5.

175 ibid., p. 5.

176 ibid.

177 LCC/PC/PP, 1904–05, op. cit., July 1904.

178 See, e.g., R. Thorne, 'The White Hart Lane Estate: an LCC venture in suburban development', *London Journal*, 12 (1), 1986, pp. 80–88.

179 PH/GEN/1/1, 'Measles Notice', 16 March 1903. For a typical report on a violation of such rules, see LCC/MIN/10025, 'Public Health Committee papers', 19 March 1896, report of December 1895 which refers to a 'temporary shelter or house accommodation . . . in which dangerous, infectious disease has appeared'.

180 PH/GEN/1/1, 16 March 1903, 'Special report from Isabel Y. Smith'.

181 PH/REG/1. See also LCC/MIN/10025, in which MOH Shirley Murphy gives evidence on the neglect of public health inspection, 14 May 1896. There was no general practice of house-to-house inspection with regard to underground rooms and disinfection work: 'No doubt it might be possible to raise questions as to the

right of entry of the officer of the sanitary authority into a house concerning which there is no prima facie reason for supposing that an insanitary condition exists within it . . . In practice the right to enter is hardly ever questioned by the householder and therefore no practical difficulty exists if the sanitary authority are desirous of adopting a system of house to house inspection. With regard to houses occupied by some of the poorest people nothing but a periodical house to house inspection, perhaps repeated two or three times a year, will suffice to maintain them in proper condition.'

182 LCC, PC, PP, 11 November 1905.

183 LCC, 'Letitia Fairfield Papers', 'Public assistance in relation to venereal diseases', 5 March 1936: 'In London we have for many years worked in close cooperation with the LCC when they were surveying common lodging houses. A great deal of trouble was taken to persuade the proprietress to insist that any girl in a common lodging house, and most of the professional prostitutes do live in common lodging houses, should go into hospital, if there was any suspicion of V.D.'. Fairfield felt that the prostitutes should be in-patients. In describing the patients of the 1930s she assisted, Fairfield commented: 'they also include some of the most degraded; girls who are irresponsible and girls who have a grudge against the community, and the worst types of population.' For the earlier history of responses to prostitution, see J. Walkowitz, *Prostitution and Victorian Society*, Cambridge, Cambridge University Press, 1980, *passim.*

184 For an overview of socialist attitudes toward recreation, see C. Waters, *British Socialists and the Politics of Popular Culture, 1884–1914*, Stanford, Calif., Stanford University Press, 1990. See, e.g., 'The fight for the County Council – an elector's catechism or 101 reasons why every loyal Londoner should vote Progressive', *Popular*, 15, 1898, p. 12; *Standard and St. James' Gazette*, 5 February 1913, Gertrude Tuckwell Collection, Trades Union Congress, Box 340.

185 J. Burns, op. cit., p. 53.

186 LCC/MIN/8892, 8 October 1909. The case of a 33-year-old man accused of assaulting a little girl was dismissed on grounds of hers being the sole testimony. For an exposition of the American situation, see L. Gordon, *Heroes of Their Own Lives*, New York, Viking, 1988, Chapters 1–3.

187 LCC/MIN/8892, 23 July 1909. See 'Council vs. Alfred Beauchamp of Bethnal Green, charged with indecent assault of Mabel Hughes on children's testimony', a case declared of insufficient evidence, 16 July 1909. (Citation appears 23 July 1909).

188 The urinals and lavatories were strictly governed. Attendants cleaned toilet seats before and after use, and the public were asked to report any uncleanliness. A comb and brush were supplied to all persons paying for the use of a washing basin (here the hygienic component of policy seems obscured . . .), though basins were not supplied everywhere. See LCC/MIN/8892, 15 October 1909, for the case of Edward Humphries, aged 21. A keeper saw him and a 16-year-old

going into a lavatory and followed them. Humphries was arrested. A criminal court trial was held at Old Street police court. The accused pleaded guilty. As it was his first offence, he was given a five-pound fine. The Salvation Army offered a good character reference on him. In a second incident, two keepers saw Frederick Harrison, aged 60, with a man aged 25. They committed a 'gross indecency' together in a public lavatory and in the Central Criminal Court got fifteen and twelve months respectively. (See J. Weeks, *Sex, Politics and Society: The Regulation of Sexuality since 1800*, London, Longman, 1981, and F. Mort, op. cit.). Of related interest: J. Davis, 'A poor man's system of justice: the London police courts in the second half of the nineteenth century', *Historical Journal*, 27, June 1984, pp. 309–335.

189 LCC/MIN/8892, 23 July 1909, 15 October 1909.

190 LCC/MIN/8892, 15 October 1909; see, e.g., P. Bailey, *Leisure and Class in Victorian England: Rational Recreation and the Contest for Control, 1830–1885*, London, Routledge and Kegan Paul, 1978.

191 LCC, POS, Vol. 1, 'Notebook on the parks, gardens, recreation grounds and open spaces of London', pp. 32–33 (entry for 1896).

192 LCC/MIN/8892, 12 July 1909.

193 Notebook, 1899.

194 ibid. In 1895, there were over 40,000 games of lawn tennis played. Players were required to wear tennis shoes and were advised that they 'must also only engage boys to scout for them whose conduct has been satisfactory, and is evidenced by their being granted a badge by the park superintendent or other officer in charge'.

195 For a full discussion of these and related issues, see C. Waters, op. cit., esp. Chapter 5.

196 S. Headlam, 'On the dangers of municipal puritanism', London, Frederick Verinder, Guild of St Matthew, 1904. On Headlam, see also F. Bettany, *Stewart Headlam, a Biography*, London, J. Murray, 1926.

197 ibid., p. 13. Headlam was quick to point out that the LCC allowed Sunday work on the trams by its employees, even though it pretended that Sunday was a day of rest.

198 See E. Royle, *Radicals, Secularists and Republicans*, Manchester, Rowman and Littlefield, 1980, pp. 51, 285, 288.

199 LCC/MIN/8823, POS, PP, 19 July 1895.

200 LCC, POS, vol. 1, 'Notebook on the parks, gardens, recreation grounds and open spaces of London', op. cit. (entry for 1903).

201 ibid.

202 LCC/MIN/8892, 23 July 1909.

203 LCC/MIN/8892, 25 July 1909.

204 S. Headlam, op. cit., p. 13.

205 LCC, POS, Vol. 2, Meath, 'Report on the public parks of America', 1889.

206 LCC, POS, Vol. 1, 'Parks staff regulations', 1903, p. 76.

207 LCC, POS, 'Staff book, including byelaws', 23 July 1915. Though the LCC took a 'hard and fast line', the note that 'most bye-laws are intended to be put in force only when nuisance or damage is arising'

also appears, p. 29. Parks staff were watched by their superiors as this note in regard to an underkeeper suggests: 'It is a safe rule to believe no one when enquiring into sexual matters, but this man has, by his own admission to me, engaged in a line of conversation with strangers which at anytime would be reprehensible, but which in his official capacity is inexcusable. There is no doubt that ConCannon is simple-minded, weak, facile and garrulous'; LCC/MIN/8892, 23 July 1909.

208 LCC, POS, Vol. 1, 'Notebook on the parks . . .', op. cit. (entry for 1903): 'It cannot be too strongly urged upon constables that they do not have the power to turn people out of a park or garden or off an open space simply because such people are known to be objectionable characters. They must have committed an offence under the bye-laws before this action can be taken.'

209 LCC/MIN/8892, 25 July 1909.

210 PC/GEN/2/18, 14 April 1893.

211 'Report of the Departmental Committee on the Employment of Children', op. cit. (9189).

212 PH/GEN/2/21, 'Departmental Committee on Vagrancy: LCC evidence' (citing 'Report of the Departmental Committee on Vagrancy', vol. III, op. cit.).

213 PH/GEN/2/21, 'Adjourned report of the Public Health Committee', 24 May 1906.

214 LCC, POS, Vol. 2, Meath, op. cit.

215 PC/GEN/1/4, Annual Report, 1900.

216 ibid. The report adds that most of the inmates identified themselves as laundresses, because they preferred the work of prison laundries. 'Predisposing' was believed to be the central cause of their disorders. They suffered from a hereditary taint, insanity or neurotic disease. Four of the thirty-one patients were illiterate and seventeen of the thirty-one were married.

217 PH/REG/5/2, 'Insanitary conditions, signed complaints', register no. 1, items 2, 3, 22, 28, 29, 34, 44, 48, 49, 53, 64, 104.

218 ibid., PH/REG/5/2.

219 PH/GEN/2/15, 'Cleansing of Persons Act, 1897, miscellaneous reports.'

220 PH/GEN/2/15. During twelve months of 1904–05, 119,762 children were examined, of whom 67,387 were clean, while 44,010 were deemed verminous. Of those, 16,174 received white cards, 4989 received red cards, and 1347 were proposed for exclusion. Of these, a final 515 were excluded for prosecution; 31 March 1905.

221 In a very wide literature, see, e.g., G. Sutherland, *Policy-making in Elementary Education, 1870–1895*, Oxford, Oxford University Press, 1973, Chapter 4; W. Marsden, *Unequal Educational Provision*, London, Woburn, 1987, *passim*; P. Hollis, *Ladies Elect*, Oxford, Oxford University Press, 1987, Chapter 2; B. Bebbington, *The Nonconformist Conscience*, London, Allen and Unwin, 1982, Chapter 7.

222 ibid.; G. Gibbon and R. Bell, *History of the London County Council, 1889–1939*, London, Macmillan, 1939, Chapters 10 and 11.

223 BOE, PP, 'Report on the workings of the Education (Provision of Meals) Act, 1906, up to 31 March, 1909', L.A. Selby-Bigge, Principal Assistant Secretary, LCC Elementary Education Branch, p. 6.

224 PH/SHS/1/14, 'Memo on medical inspection of children in public elementary schools', Board of Education Circular 576, 22 November 1907. Morant specifically mentioned water and milk supplies, food, housing, sanitation, infant mortality, bacteriological investigation, hospital accommodation, disinfection and cleansing of verminous persons, and disease notification . . . as related phenomena, a propos of the relationship between social and home hygiene.

225 EO/WEL/1/1, 'Report as to increased duties of Care Committees and the pressure of work on the organized staff', 8 October 1911.

226 'Report on the working of the Education (Provision of Meals) Act, 1906, up to 31 March, 1909', op. cit., p. 5.

227 EO/WEL/1/1, Turner to Blair, 16 November 1909: 'I feel that the work under the Provision of Meals Act falls in very appropriately and organically with the work of the Education Branch; much more so than with Special and Industrial Schools. [They were considering how to allocate specific programmes in the transition of the Education Department.] The work in question is eugenic work, that is, work for the healthy development of the mass of normal children; the special and industrial schools branch on the other hand, works for the defective child as such, that is, it makes the best of what is recognised as human debris of no eugenic value. A different and opposed set of ideals should, it seems to me, govern the two administrative processes.' See also 'Memo', 11 January 1910.

228 ibid., EO/WEL/1/1.

229 EO/WEL/1/1, 18 February 1911, 'Report from Chief Inspector's Branch to Mr. Blair.'

230 EO/WEL/5/6, p. 2. Miss Morton described the duties of the committees: 'school meals and general relief, medical treatment and health work, employment of boys and girls leaving school . . . recreation, country holidays . . . and general cultivation of the imagination, including thrift work'.

231 LCC, BOE, PP, 'Annual Report for 1908', the Chief Medical Officer, 1910, p. 49. This was viewed as an improvement as compared with four or five years earlier.

232 EO/WEL/1/1, op. cit., 'Report as to increased duties . . . ', 4 May 1912.

233 EO/WEL/1/1, 'Children's Care Organization, 1909–14', 'Need for a social welfare branch in the Education Department', July 1914. The memo specifically mentions the Education (Provision of Meals) Act 1906; the Education (Administrative Provision) Act 1907, which provided for vaccination in the schools and medical inspection and provision; and the Children Act 1908, which, as they termed it at the time, 'places in the hands of the Council a powerful weapon with which it can fight for the bodily and mental well being of children of

School Age'. It was also anticipated here that the revision of the poor law would heap more 'social work' upon the LCC.

234 'Report of the Departmental Committee on the Employment of Children Act, 1903', op. cit. (8999).

235 LCC, T. Macnamara, 'Report of the Interdepartmental Committee on the Employment of Schoolchildren to the Home Secretary', op. cit. A. Spencer, Chief Officer of Public Control at the LCC, told Macnamara: 'I think that the public would view with jealousy and suspicion any attempt of the School Board to go beyond the ordinarily recognised powers, any attempt to deal with the children apart from school' (4199).

236 'Report of the Departmental Committee on the Employment of Children Act, 1903', op. cit. (8981).

237 EO/WEL/1/1, 'Organisation of Care Committees'.

238 EO/WEL/1/1, 'Report on increased duties of Care Committees', 18 October 1911.

239 EO/WEL/1/1, 'Duties of organising staff', to Blair from the Education Officer's Department, 13 September 1913. In this era, future LCC councillor Nettie Adler, for example, sat on the Hackney Juvenile Advisory Committee.

240 LCC, BOE, PP, 'Annual Report for 1908', 1910, op. cit., p. 51.

241 PH/SHS/3/6, 'Cleansing of verminous children', inquiry by C. Jackson, LCC Education Officer's Department, Children's Care Bureau, 'Letter to the Education Officer', 25 November 1910.

242 ibid., Broad Street School, 10 January 1911.

243 LCC, BOE, PP, 'Annual Report for 1908', op. cit., pp. 46–47. The report from the borough adds that there is a 'great need we have for stronger measures in dealing with the homes'.

244 EO/WEL/1/1, 18 October 1911, 'Report as to the increased duties of Care Committees and the pressure of work on the organising staff'; PH/GEN/2/15, 'Cleansing of Persons Act, report by the MOH, 1920. The LCC General Powers Act of 1904 and that of 1907 both stipulated such prerogatives. See also 'Report of the Interdepartmental Committee on Physical Deterioration', op. cit. S. Murphy testified that he had seen weekly showers given in the schools on the Continent and wanted weekly washing in English schools. In Europe, they had first been seen as an intrusion and then grew in popularity (9478).

245 PH/SHS/3/10, 'Cutting of hair', 19 March 1915. No action was taken. The same file reveals that in January 1919 the Solicitor feared that assault charges might be filed.

246 LCC, PH, PP, 22 February 1915. See PH/SHS/1/14, Children's Care Branch, 'General inquiries, medical treatment', 17 February 1910, Letter from Mrs A. Knight. She asked 'by what authority' the Council would pursue parents about inspection. She had a private doctor, and added, 'I may add that the children have been warned about it, July a fortnight before, keeping them in a nervous state all that time.' The Council replied categorically, expressing 'hope that you will be able to see your way to cooperate with the Council in the

fulfilment of its statutory obligation and allow your daughter to be examined. The examination is undertaken solely in the interests of the children and enables the parents to obtain useful information as to the state of their children's health.'

247 PH/SHS/3/10, 'Cutting of hair', cites the *Times* of 12 March 1915 on the case, which occurred at Camberwell. The Education Officer is quoted as having said that a given case was 'only one complaint amongst thousands of cases'; 6 January 1914.

248 PH/SHS/3/10. The LCC solicitor, Edward Tanner, informed the LCC Education Committee that LCC powers were wide enough to cut hair even over the objections of parents, but, his notes stated, 'great care [was] needed, especially in case of female children, and as it might become necessary to prove to the satisfaction of a court that the child could not be properly cleansed without resource to the cutting of hair, it would be desirable that in all such cases the evidence of some responsible person, such a [sic] medical man, should be forthcoming . . . only course to adopt'; 19 March 1915.

249 PH/SHS/1/14, 'Education Officers Branch', 1 September 1910. In 1911 the House of Commons debated the issue of whether the Education (Administrative Provision) Act of 1907 was compulsory or not. See letter from Runciman of 20 February 1911. An overview of policy stated that 'One of the main difficulties in connection with the Council's cleansing scheme has been the opposition of parents of those children whose head contained mites only, to the necessary cleansing being carried out at the stations where bad cases were dealt with.' At this writing, it had become possible to remove the nits without hair cutting and there were by then shampoo centres and ordinary cleansing centres, PH/GEN/2/15, which appeared to have been written at the end of the War.

250 LCC, PP, BOE, 1907-08, 'Report of Medical Officer, George Newman', p. 49.

251 LCC, PH, PP, 24 October 1913.

252 LCC, PP, Board of Education, 1907–08, Appendix C, 'Schedule of medical inspection, notes for inspecting officer', p. 154.

253 PH/SHS/1/14, op. cit., Deputy Education Officer to Jephson, 17 May 1911, 'Letter to Robbshow', 16 May 1991.

254 PH/SHS/3/10, 'Cutting of hair', 4 December 1914.

255 EO/WEL/1/1, 'Need for a social welfare branch in the Education Department, 7 July 1909', signature unclear.

256 LCC, TMHC, Palace Theatre of Varieties, 1888–1903, as attached to the report of the licensing discussion, 28 November 1902.

257 PP 1892 (240) xviii, 1 'Select Committee on Theatres and Places of Entertainment', (3004–3006). This figure was based on the assumption that 45,000 nightly visits took place at thirty-five halls equalling 270,000 weekly visits between the 1890s and the 1920s; A. Haddon, *The Story of the Music Hall*, London, Fleetway, 1935, p. 133.

258 A. Haddon, op. cit., p. 133.

259 ibid.

260 S. Desmond, *London Nights of Long Ago*, Duckworth, London, 1927, p. 17.
261 LCC, TMHC, Minutes, 'Letter to Hoare, LCC, who planned to attend the committee with a deputation from this movement', 27 September 1898.
262 See S. Ruck, *Municipal Entertainment and the Arts*, London, Allen and Unwin, 1965. Acts of 1845, 1846 and 1847 extended these powers. Legislation passed during the tenure of the Progressive LCC, included the London Government Act of 1899 and the Municipal Corporations Act of 1894 which were 'aimed at the improvement of the moral, mental and physical conditions of the masses'; p. 19.
263 A. Haddon, op. cit., p. 133.
264 J. Palmer, *The Censor and the Theatres*, New York, Mitchell Kennerley, 1913, p. 52.
265 PC/ENT/2/17, Richard Roberts, Chairman, THMC, Report, 30 May 1894: 'As far as can be ascertained, it seems an indisputable fact that the profit on the sale of refreshments was, in the first instance, the primary object in the establishment of music-halls.'
266 LCC, TMHC, 'Proposed legislation, 1887–1905', cited the *Standard*, 10 December 1887.
267 See LCC, TMHC, 'Places of public entertainment; miscellaneous printed reports (general), 1889–1939'; the Conference included the Theatres and Music Halls Committee of the LCC and a deputation of managers of theatres and music halls. For a more detailed description of the meetings of 1889, ibid., 1889.
268 PC/ENT/2/17, 29 October 1902; LCC, TMHC, PP, 'Sunday entertainment, 1893–1909', 'Report by the Clerk', 28 January 1903, alluded to a petition submitted by Lt. Rotton, 375 clergymen and others including the late Archbishop of Canterbury against Sunday openings, dated 21 October 1902. This is probably what West is referring to. In 1902 both the Shakespeare and the Empire Sun were denied Sunday licenses.
269 For several points of view in this debate, see E. Bristow, op. cit., esp. Chapter 9; P. Summerfield, 'The Effingham Arms and the Empire: deliberate selection in the evolution of Music Hall in London', in E. Yeo and S. Yeo (eds), *Popular Culture and Class Conflict, 1590–1914*, Brighton, Harvester, 1981, pp. 209–240; G. Stedman Jones, 'Working-class culture and working-class politics in London, 1870–1900', in *Languages of Class*, Cambridge, Cambridge University Press, 1983, pp. 179–238.
270 J. Palmer, op. cit., p. 271.
271 P. Bailey, 'Custom, capital and culture', in R. Storch (ed.), *Popular Culture and Custom in Nineteenth-Century England*, London, Croom Helm, 1982, p. 204.
272 The Lord Chamberlain upheld the following rules for the London theatre: 'No profanity or impropriety of language to be permitted on the stage. No indecency of dress, dance or gesture to be permitted on the stage. No offensive personalities or presentations of living persons to be permitted on the stage, nor anything calculated to

produce riot or breach of the peace. No exhibition of wild beasts or dangerous performances'; LCC, TMHC, PP, 'Lord Chamberlain's case, 1888–1907', 1889, 'Rules with regulations with regard to theatres in the jurisdiction of the Lord Chamberlain'.

273 J. Palmer, op. cit., pp. 52–66; A. Haddon, op. cit., pp. 136–137; LCC, 'Annual Report', 1889–90; LCC, TMHC, 'Proposed Legislation 1887–1905'; D. Howard, *London Theatres and Music Halls, 1850–1950*, London, Library Association, 1970, pp. xi, 269.

274 LCC, TMHC, 'Proposed legislation, 1887–1905', cites *Financial News*, 21 November 1893.

275 See, e.g., a summary of letters of opinion received on these questions, *Daily Telegraph*, 12 March 1891. Ibid., 1894, including 'Letter from the General Body of Protestant Dissenting Ministers of the three Denominations (Presbyterians, Independents and Baptists)', which congratulated the LCC for its determination to secure legislation.

276 G. Sims, *My Life*, London, Eveleigh Nash, 1917, p. 292.

277 See E. Bristow, op. cit., pp. 209–211.

278 LCC, TMHC, PP, 25 January 1893. The London Trades Council launched a Sunday campaign in protest against the continued restrictions upon the Sunday use of schools under the Conservatives. An LTC resolution read: 'That this Council representing 60,000 organised workers protests against the reactionary conduct of the LCC in refusing to allow the schools to be used for socialist Sunday schools'; LTC, Minutes, 13 June 1907. The *Free Sunday Advocate* reported such events in other town halls, including presentations entitled 'The British Navy of Today', 'Thunder Storms', 'Houses of Lords and Commons' and 'Londoners and Parisians', TMHC, PP, 22 June 1896.

279 The Select Committee ruled against repeal of the Sunday clauses. Five hundred thousand employees in the industry did not want to be undercut by Sunday labour. See, e.g., LCC, TMHC, PP, 1893–1903, 11 February 1903. For names and addresses of those who opposed Sunday labour, see LCC, TMHC, 'Sunday entertainments, 1893–1909'.

280 LTC, *Minutes*, 12 July 1900. The AMU also protested against the LTC endorsement of candidates who did not conform to the Union's views.

281 LCC, TMHC, PP, 'Sunday entertainments, 1893–1909', 27 November 1902. 'Letter from Monte Bayly to the Clerk', which discussed animated pictures, 1906.

282 LCC, TMHC, PP, 1893–1909, 24 January 1899; LCC, TMHC, 'Sunday entertainment, 1893–1909'. A letter from the SDF called for 'The Socialisation of the Means of Production, Distribution and Exchange, to be controlled by a Democratic State in the interests of the entire community, and the complete Emancipation of Labour from the Domination of Capitalism and Landlordism, with the establishment of Social and Economic Equality Between the Sexes', 1898.

283 LCC, TMHC, PP, 1893–1909, cited the *Daily Chronicle*, 25 September 1906.

284 See S. Headlam, 'On the dangers of municipal puritanism', op. cit.; 'Subsidized Shakespeare: a municipal innovation by the LCC', *Municipal Journal*, 30 May 1919; 'Municipal amusements: a renewed crusade for rate-aided opera', *Municipal Journal*, 8 August 1919. The LTC asked that a deputation be received to discuss the creation of a municipal theatre like those on the Continent; LTC, Minutes, 10 October 1901.

285 'Select Committee on Theatres and Places of Entertainment', *Daily Telegraph*, 27 February 1891.

286 J. Palmer, op. cit., p. 56. After 1913, the Lord Chamberlain consented to license plays in theatres of variety, proffering a new venue in the industry.

287 A. Haddon, op. cit., p. 134.

288 'Select Committee on Theatres and Places of Entertainment', *Daily Telegraph*, 2 March 1891.

289 J. Palmer, op. cit., p. 206. Palmer added: 'the distinction between immorality and indecency dogs the discussion of censorship at every step'. Between 1895 and 1909, 30 of 700 plays before the Lord Chamberlain were censored and some censoring occurred spontaneously, on a weekly basis; PP/ENT/2/17.

290 LCC, TMHC, 'Proposed legislation', op. cit., citing *Financial News*, 21 November 1893.

291 See P. Thompson, *Socialists, Liberals and Labour*, London, Routledge and Kegan Paul, 1967, pp. 73–4.

292 See E. Bristow, op. cit., pp. 209–211.

293 See A. Haddon, op. cit., p. 136. Twenty halls were not given permission to offer refreshment facilities of the sort available in legitimate theatres, cabarets and other halls, p. 136.

294 ibid.

295 LCC, TMHC, Hackney Empire, 13 December 1901.

296 A. Haddon, op. cit., p. 136. In October 1893, the LCC Licensing Committee also reviewed the case of the Lord Raglan. A new licence to reopen was denied on the grounds that the hall was essentially a cover for a pub next door, whose sales would peak even if the hall itself remained dry.

297 'John Burns on London', *Daily News*, 31 August 1904.

298 J. Burns, *Battersea Labour Gazette*, 19 January 1901.

299 LCC, TMHC, 'Proposed legislation, 1887–1905', transcript, 17 April 1894 (Russell), p. 12.

300 ibid., p. 12. See especially comments by Russell to McDougall, which suggest that the anti-landlord scheme was a larger priority than censorship: 'But I mean that you have not relied upon questions of decency or quality of performance such as the Lord Chamberlain might take into account.' A terminable annuity system was proposed in which landlords would have to repay proprietors for repairs undertaken at the behest of the LCC.

301 LCC, TMHC Minutes, 'Inspection subcommittee', 1890–95, 27 April 1894. The Home Secretary invoked the Select Committee of 1892, which had concluded that there was no point in transferring

licensing duties from the Lord Chamberlain to the LCC. The Home Secretary thought it urgent that the Committee pursue structural reforms and shorter-term licenses, and pursue prosecutions against unlicensed facilities.

302 In the early 1890s, the LCC also sought the control of fairs and shows. Thomas Fardell offered an example from Whitechapel: 'There was a considerable crowd in the pavement, and an organ was being played inside. A black man, said to be a Zulu, was dancing at the door at intervals, and had bells on him, so that he drew a big crowd when he danced.' This had been seen as a nuisance by the Whitechapel District Board. The setting was described as a place of thieves and the noise was said to disturb patients at nearby London Hospital. As if to underline the urgency of government support, and its absence, H.L. Cripps wrote to the TMHC in January 1894: 'There is not in my opinion the smallest prospect of the Council being able to pass next session a Public Bill into an Act – dealing with the London theatres otherwise than with, not only the acquiescence but the support of the Government', LCC, TMHC, 'Proposed legislation, 1887–1905', op. cit., 10 January 1894.

303 LCC, TMHC, 'Register of inspections, 1905–09'; LCC, TMHC, Minutes, 11 January 1893, see record of a visit to the Oxford; LCC, TMHC, 'Printed papers of Sessions', 1909–11; 'Report', 12 November 1909.

304 LCC, TMHC, 22 October 1890. Those chosen were occupationally diverse: a travelling engineer, a draughtsman from the Architect's Department, a stationer's manager, several clerks. Some had military or public service backgrounds.

305 'Select Committee on Theatres and Places of Entertainment', op. cit., Appendix F, p. 389.

306 LCC, TMHC, Minutes, 31 July 1890.

307 LCC, TMHC, PP, Rose and Crown, 1889–96, 30 December 1890.

308 ibid., Charing Cross Hall, 1889–1908, 20 August 1890.

309 LCC, TMHC, PP, Charing Cross Music Hall, 1889–1908, 'Letter from Chigwell, Lavender Hill, Enfield, Middlesex', 18 October 1896.

310 ibid., 'Letter of William Henry Butt'. These letters went to J.B. Maple of Bow, MP and a member of the LCC Licensing Committee, and to H.H. Marks. See the evidence indicating that the hall withdrew both numbers following receipt of a letter from the LCC, 26 October 1896.

311 ibid., 22 July 1908.

312 ibid., 26 October 1897.

313 ibid.

314 LCC, 'Proceedings before the licensing committee', St James Temperance Music Hall, Stoke Newington, pp. 5, 7, 10, October, 1892. Lady Brassey served as a shareholder and the licensing session heard conflicting evidence concerning the hall's atmosphere and purpose. The COS had investigated it and published a pamphlet about it.

315 TMHC, PP, Collins Music Hall, Islington Green, 1889–1909, 25

August 1890, 9 August 1900 and 3 October 1907. See P. Bailey, op. cit., Chapter 2.

316 LCC, TMHC, Canterbury Music Hall, 1888–1904, 23 February 1891, 9 August 1891.

317 'Select Committee on Theatres and Places of Entertainment', op. cit., pp. 440–442.

318 LCC, TMHC, PP, 1888–1904, 18 January 1899.

319 ibid., 'Canterbury Music Hall, 1888–1904', letter of 27 August 1897: 'I attended your hall last night and with several friends in stalls was simply disgusted at the *saying of Peggy Pryde*, in her description of a Wedding; to say the least of it the remarks of not washing hands and faces or *anything else* and the *smell of fish*, is beyond all decency and have communicated with the Inspector County Council and ask him to attend *tonight*. I have also written the Artiste in question about such vulgarity' (his emphasis).

320 ibid., August 1897.

321 ibid., Palace Theatre of Varieties, 1888–1904, 28 August 1897. An inspector questioned the appropriateness of the tableaux at the Metropolitan for a young audience. The 'Grand Final Tableau' was 'Lord Kitchener, the hero of Omdurman and Khartoum', LCC, TMHC, PP, Metropolitan, 24 November 1898.

322 LCC, TMHC, PP, Palace Theatre, 28 August 1897.

323 LCC, 'Proceedings before the Licensing Committee', Oxford Music Hall, October 1896, pp. 2, 3.

324 ibid., October 1893, p. 13.

325 ibid., October 1896, pp. 11, 13.

326 ibid., p. 17.

327 ibid., p. 17, 35.

328 ibid., Jolly Tanners Music Hall, 5 October 1892.

329 *London*, 18 October 1894, p. 659.

330 ibid.

331 J. Burns, in *London*, 1 November 1894, p. 691; *The Liberal*, 17 November 1894, cited in *London*, 17 November 1894.

332 *The Times*, 29 September 1898.

333 LCC, TMHC, PP, Empire Music Hall, 10 October 1894.

334 ibid., 25 October 1894.

335 ibid.

336 LCC, TMHC, 'Minutes of the inspection subcommittee', 23 October 1895. Those with the greatest numbers of signatures attached were: inhabitants of Holloway (243); worshippers at Fulham Congregational Church, Queens Road, Battersea (150); the Gospel Temperance Society (170); the East London Women's Christian Temperance Union for Poplar and Limehouse (131); the Gresham Baptist Church (137) and inhabitants of Plumstead (261). In favour of the lifting of restrictions were many groups of inhabitants from various neighbourhoods, and groups such as the Ratepayers of South Hackney and the Clapham Reform Club.

337 *Star*, 17 January 1895. The temperance candidate, Tom Smith, was also found lacking by the local Liberal Association. The London

Compositors, when questioned on Smith's rectitude, had reported that the name of his printing house was absent from a list of fair houses.

338 *London*, 25 October 1894.
339 LCC, TMHC, 'Inspection subcommittee', Minutes, 23 October 1895.
340 For a useful perspective on social purity movements and their relationship to a wider set of problems in working class life, see J. Walkowitz, 'Male vice and feminist virtue: feminism and the politics of prostitution in 19th century Britain', *History Workshop*, no. 13, Spring 1982, pp. 79–93. For Churchill's account, see W. Churchill, *My Early Life: A Roving Commission*, London, Mandarin, 1930, p. 74.
341 S. Headlam, 'On the danger of municipal puritanism', op. cit., p. 3.
342 *London*, 1897, p. 746.
343 S. Headlam, 'On the danger of municipal puritanism', op. cit., p. 9.
344 S. Headlam, 'The Anti-Puritan League . . .', op. cit..
345 G. Sims, *My Life*, op. cit., pp. 98–99.
346 Sims recalled this set of ' "sports" young and old, betting men and members of the flash fraternity' who indulged in 'liquor in front of the house and licence on the stage. Lion comiques scored some of their greatest successes in the impersonation of dissipated "swells" who were always on the drunken racket. The red-nosed comedian's favourite topic was drink, and the only domestic touch in his songs had reference as a rule to the lodger'; ibid., p. 315.
347 LCC, TMHC, PP, Olympia, 1896–1905, December 1898.
348 ibid., October 1899, 'Letter from Petwell to the Clerk', 3 November 1899.
349 ibid., 7 November 1899.
350 ibid., 17 November 1899.
351 ibid., 15 November 1899.
352 ibid., 'Licensing session', 17 November 1899.
353 ibid.; For a related case, see B. Shepard, 'Showbiz imperialism: the case of Peter Lobengula', in J. Mackenzie (ed.), *Imperialism and Popular Culture*, Manchester, Manchester University Press, 1986, pp. 24–112.
354 LCC, TMHC, PP, 'Olympia', op. cit., 3 December 1889.
355 ibid., 3 December 1899.
356 ibid., 13 December 1899.
357 ibid., 30 December 1899. 'Letter of Lord Selbourne's private secretary to Sir Algernon West'; 'Letter of Robert Coleman', 12 January 1900.
358 ibid., 25 January 1901, 'Metropolitan Police report on *Conjolwana* v. *McDonald*'.
359 G. Sims, op. cit., p. 311.
360 LCC, TMHC, PP, 'Canterbury', op. cit., 1901, 'Letter from P. Vogel', appeared in the *Globe*, 8 November 1901. Vogel was the secretary of the Amalgamated Waiters' Society.
361 See A. Haddon, op. cit., p. 131.
362 J. Benn, 'Progressive–Socialist Manifesto', *London Municipal Notes*, July 1909, p. 124. I would like to thank Beatrix Walsh for assistance with these points.

363 PC/ENT/2/17; See reports taken from *Reynolds* and from the *Era* of 1908 and 1911. The decision to allow double licenses was termed a victory for 'free trade in amusements'. And a report of 1917 shows that the LCC still attempted to restrict the sale of intoxicants to the bar.

364 A. Haddon, op. cit., p. 130. The Moss Empires organisation outdid its competitors.

365 J. Burns, 'The LCC: Towards a Commune', op. cit., p. 511.

366 LCC, 'Proceedings before the Licensing Committee', Fulham Empire, 14 and 15 November 1912, p. 25.

367 ibid., 'Fulham Empire', 1913, pp. 74, 75, 79. This testimony included the presentation of a record of receipts of theatres owned by Variety Theatres Consolidated, one of the industry's largest conglomerates, showing a decline in net profits over the period 1908–12, based on information collected by the owners of the Chelsea, Euston, South London and Walthamstow Palace Theatres.

368 ibid., p. 79.

369 LTC, Minutes, 9 November 1916.

370 J. Burns, 'The LCC: Towards a Commune', op. cit., p. 511.

371 G. Sims, op. cit., p. 317.

372 'Select Committee on Theatres and Places of Entertainment', op. cit., p. 3 (24). T. Fardell categorically stated that the 1890 LCC bill, an attempt to extend its powers, had failed to win over the owners, who foresaw the eternal and relentless inspection of their structures.

373 LCC, TMHC, PP, 1888–1904, 'Edgware Road', 27 February 1903.

374 G. Sims, op. cit., p. 319.

375 P. Summerfield suggests this when she observes: 'Vulgarity increasingly became an aspect of the style of performance rather than the content of the song', 'Effingham Arms . . .', op. cit., p. 234. She links this observation to a wider analysis of lyrical content.

376 'Select Committee on Theatres and Places of Entertainment', op. cit. (5197).

377 'Select Committee on Theatres', op. cit. (2944).

378 A. Reeve, *Take It for a Fact*, Heinemann, London, 1954, p. 40. 'Trixie . . .' went as follows: 'Trixie is a terror, Trixie is a Turk, Trixie sets the neighbourhood a-hooting; And since she came to stay, All the curates moved away, For Trixie is the talk of Upper Tooting'; p. 93.

379 S. Desmond, op. cit., pp. 157–158. Desmond notes on p. 166 that the Old St James Hall was the home of black face, successor of the Old Christy Minstrels.

380 J. Palmer, op. cit., p. 266.

381 PC/ENT/2/17, 18 April 1916.

CONCLUSION (pp. 241–245)

1 D. Riley, 'Some peculiarities of social policy concerning women in wartime and postwar Britain', in M. Higonnet, J. Jenson, S. Michel

and M. Weitz (eds), *Behind the Lines: Gender and the Two World Wars*, New Haven, Conn., Yale University Press, 1987, p. 270.

2 Other vantage points are offered in R. McKibbin, *The Evolution of the Labour Party, 1910–24*, Oxford, Oxford University Press, 1974, Conclusion. R. McKibbin, *The Ideologies of Class: Social Relations in Britain*, Oxford, Clarendon, 1991, Chapters 1, 9; H. Pelling, *Popular Politics and Society in Late Victorian Britain*, Macmillan, 1979, Chapter 1; D. Tanner, *Political Change and the Labour Party*, Cambridge, Cambridge University Press, 1990, Conclusion; S. Macintyre, *A Proletarian Science: Marxism in Britain, 1917–33*, London, Lawrence and Wishart, 1986, Conclusion.

3 See, e.g., D. Dwork, *War is Good for Babies and Other Young Children*, London, Tavistock, 1987, Conclusion; J. Lewis, *The Politics of Motherhood*, London, Croom Helm, 1980, *passim*; J. Harris, *Unemployment and Politics*, Oxford, Clarendon, 1984, Chapter 7.

4 A. Offer, *Property and Politics, 1870–1914*, Cambridge, Cambridge University Press, 1981, Chapter 23.

5 See J. Gillespie, 'Poplarism and proletarianism: unemployment and Labour politics in London, 1918–1934', in D. Feldman and G. Stedman Jones (eds), *Metropolis: London Histories and Representations since 1800*, London, Routledge, 1989, pp. 163–188; S. MacIntyre, *Little Moscows*, London, Croom Helm, 1980; J. Gillespie, 'Municipalism, monopoly and management: the demise of "Socialism in one county", 1918–1933', in A. Saint (ed.), *Politics and the People of London*, London, Hambledon, 1989, pp. 103–125.

6 See, especially, essays by A. Saint, S. Lawrence, J. Gillespie, M. Richardson and J. Sheldrake, in A. Saint (ed.), op. cit., Chapters 4–6, 8, 10.

7 T. Jeffery, 'The suburban nation: politics and class in Lewisham', in D. Feldman and G. Stedman Jones (eds), op. cit., pp. 163–188; 'A place in the nation: the lower middle class in England', in R. Koshar (ed.), *Splintered Classes: Politics and the Lower Middle Classes in Interwar Europe*, New York, Holmes and Meier, 1990, pp. 70–96.

8 National Union of Women's Suffrage Societies, 'A word to midwives and trained nurses on pending legislation', 1911, p. 5.

9 See S. Pennybacker, 'Changing convictions: London County Council blackcoated activism between the wars', in R. Koshar (ed.), op. cit., pp. 97–120.

INDEX

INDEX

Shakespeare, William 55
Shaw, George Bernard 54, 80, 175
Sherwell, Arthur 56
Shop Hours Act 42, 177–8
shopping and shops 173–8, 181–3;
see also Seats for Shop Assistants
Act; Shop Hours Act
Shoreditch 23, 96, 123
Simon, Sir John 7
Sims, George 211, 213, 219, 231,
234, 237
Slater, B. 99–100
slavery 21
Sloper, Ally 225
Smith, Aeneas 111
Smith, Frank 81, 84
Smith, Isabel Y. 160, 164–8, 190
Social Democratic Federation
(SDF) 111–12, 134, 156, 215
social purity 3, 159, 230
Socialists, Liberals and Labour 11
Soho 57
Southwark 208
Soviet Union 243
Spectator 116
Spencer, Alfred 42, 162, 165
Spencer, Herbert 35, 76
Spoor, Alec 91
Spring Gardens Club 36, 71,
74–80, 95
Staff Association 71, 81, 83–8, 90
Staff Gazette 58, 70, 91, 247
Stalinism 145
Star 117, 139
Steadman, Will 113, 134, 140,
148–9, 155, 156, 235
Stepney 70, 134, 135, 148, 182, 185
Stewart, C.J. 142
Stoke Newington 39, 162
Stoll, Oswald 235–6
Streatham 201
syndicalism 156

Taylor, H.R. 110, 113, 126, 148–9
taxation 7, 13
Tennyson, Alfred Lord 77
Territorials 95
Testament of a Victorian Youth 53
Thatcher, Margaret 5, 242

Theatres and Music Halls
Committee, LCC 36, 51, 158,
210–40; see also music halls
Thompson, Paul 11, 26, 156
Thorne, Will 127, 131
Thurtle, Dorothy Lansbury see
Lansbury, Dolly
Thurtle, Ernest 60
Tillett, Ben 4, 18, 25, 131
Times, The 134, 135, 153, 228
Torrance, A. 141
Tottenham 96–7
Tower Hamlets 217
Trades and Labour Gazette 154
Trades Union Act 128
Trades Union Congress (TUC)
101, 104, 107, 155
traffic 220
transport 7
Tree, Herbert 215–16
Tubbs, Maggie 79–80
Tuckwell, Gertrude 43
typists 43–5, 59–65, 71–4, 88, 92,
182

Unionists 5, 18, 27, 159, 243
United Methodist Free Church 229
United Shop Assistants Union 173
Upper Kennington 53
Upper Tooting 36

vagrancy 187–202
Variety Artistes' Federation 214,
234
Vicinus, Martha 92

Waiters' Society 214
Wales, Prince of 238
Walkowitz, Judith 64
Wandsworth 111, 174, 180
Wapping 111
Ward, Henry 137, 139, 145–7
Ward, Mrs Humphrey 230
Waterhouse, Edwin 142, 155; see
also Price, Waterhouse
Webb, Beatrice 17, 63, 101, 105–6,
153
Webb, Sidney 4, 10, 17, 25, 51, 63,
80, 130, 141, 156